INSTITUTE OF MODERN LANGUAGES RESEARCH
UNIVERSITY OF LONDON

BITHELL SERIES OF DISSERTATIONS
VOLUME 45

MIT WORTEN LÛTER UNDE GLANZ: METAPOETICS IN KONRAD VON WÜRZBURG'S *TROJANERKRIEG*

INSTITUTE OF MODERN LANGUAGES RESEARCH

BITHELL SERIES OF DISSERTATIONS

Launched in 1978 by the then Institute of Germanic Studies, the Bithell Series of Dissertations is designed to help young scholars publish recent work of high quality which has been accepted for the award of a research degree by a University in the United Kingdom or the Republic of Ireland. Volumes 14 to 41 were published in conjunction with the Modern Humanities Research Association. From 2015 onwards, publication has been resumed by the Institute of Modern Languages Research (IMLR). For a list of previous volumes in the series, see http://modernlanguages.sas.ac.uk/publications/bithell-series-dissertations/.

Theses for possible inclusion in the series are considered by the Bithell Editorial Board twice annually, in May and November. Recommendations for theses to be considered should be made by the supervisor and/or examiner(s), should be accompanied by a copy of the Examiners' Report and Abstract, and sent to Dr Godela Weiss-Sussex at the Institute of Modern Languages Research, University of London, Senate House, Malet Street, London WC1E 7HU (email: godela.weiss-sussex@sas.ac.uk).

MIT WORTEN LÛTER UNDE GLANZ:
METAPOETICS IN KONRAD VON WÜRZBURG'S *TROJANERKRIEG*

by
ESTHER LAUFER

Institute of Modern Languages Research
2016

Published by the

Institute of Modern Languages Research
School of Advanced Study, University of London
Senate House, Malet Street, London WC1E 7HU
http://modernlanguages.sas.ac.uk

Cover image: Paris presents Venus with the Apple of Discord. Illustration in a manuscript of Konrad von Würzburg's *Trojanerkrieg* from the workshop of Diebold Lauber (Hagenau, 1445), Ms. germ. fol. 1, Staatsbibliothek zu Berlin – PK, 25r, resolver.staatsbibliothek-berlin.de/SBB0000EB8400000000

First published 2016

ISBN 978 0 85457 253 3

ISSN 0266-7932

CONTENTS

ACKNOWLEDGEMENTS

First and foremost, I would like to thank my supervisor Mark Chinca for always understanding what I was trying to say (even if I did not) and for his brilliant guidance and support all along. Many thanks also to Manfred Eikelmann, who has been a great mentor from my undergraduate to my postdoctoral studies and to Bernd Bastert, who has supported me for many years. They are a big part of the reason why coming back to Bochum felt like coming home. I am furthermore grateful to Dorothee Lindemann, without whom I might never have become a medievalist in the first place. I am also indebted to Chris Young, Almut Suerbaum and Sebastian Coxon, whose constructive questions have undoubtedly made this a better book. I am very grateful for the financial support from St John's College and the AHRC without which this research would not have been possible. I also want to thank the editors of the Bithell series for accepting this work for publication and Anne Simon for being the most thorough and supportive editor anyone could ever wish for. Furthermore I would like to thank Sarah Bowden for being a lovely *Doktorschwester* and friend, as well as my EAP-girls Annela, Bianca and Padmakshi, whose friendship since the very first day has meant everything to me. Many heartfelt thanks to my Merry Boys Huw and Cameron, who made the final year of my PhD one of the best years of my life – despite the torments of writing up – and to Alban for his love and support for many years. I also want to thank my Bochum colleagues Rabea, Nadine, Silvia, Arne, Fabian, Sibylle, Lina, Bianca, Holger and Philipp for many academic discussions and even more non-academic fun and my childhood friends Ina and Kati for always being there for me even when we were apart. Finally, I would like to thank my family, especially Matthes, who has made our family complete and whom we have always been able to count on.

This work is dedicated to Dagmar and Marie, whom I love more than I ever tell them.

NOTE ON REFERENCING

The following abbreviations are used in the text:

Journals

DVjs	*Deutsche Vierteljahrsschrift für Literaturwissenschaft und Geistesgeschichte*
GRM	*Germanisch-Romanische Monatsschrift*
JOWG	*Jahrbuch der Oswald von Wolkenstein-Gesellschaft*
PBB	*Beiträge zur Geschichte der deutschen Sprache und Literatur*
ZfdA	*Zeitschrift für deutsches Altertum und deutsche Literatur*
ZfdPh	*Zeitschrift für deutsche Philologie*

Editions

MF	*Des Minnesangs Frühling*, ed. by Karl Lachmann and others, 38th rev. edn by Hugo Moser and Helmut Tervooren (Stuttgart: Hirzel, 1988)

INTRODUCTION

Scholarship has long considered Konrad von Würzburg (d. 1287) a virtuoso of rhetorical pomp who was no match for the inner gravity of the *Blütezeit* masters.[1] In particular his late work, the monumental fragment of the *Trojanerkrieg* (after 1281), was thought to suffer from the vice of superficiality. Thus Kurt Herbert Halbach emphasizes the smoothness and clarity of Konrad's style but criticizes its monotony and redundant verbosity: 'Alles wird ins Breite gewalzt'.[2] Comparing Konrad to Gottfried von Straßburg, he describes the contrast as one between 'Extensität' versus 'Intensität'.[3] In the same vein, Dennis Green diagnoses a poor integration of the individual descriptions into the narration and a general dissociation of style from content, a 'Liebe zum Wortrausch um seiner selbst willen und die Überwucherung des Inhalts durch die losgelöste, eigengesetzlich gewordene Form'.[4] Helmut de Boor describes the *Trojanerkrieg* as Konrad's 'zugleich glänzendstes und am wenigsten geglücktes Werk'. While he appreciates some of its 'genrehaften Einzelbilder', he finds fault with its relentless 'Redseligkeit, die sich an der eigenen Virtuosität des Wortes berauscht'.[5] Even Wolfgang Monecke, who delivers a very perceptive description of the peculiarities of the text's poetics and interprets them as the manifestation of the specific

1 A detailed account of research on Konrad von Würzburg up to 1984 is provided by Rüdiger Brandt, *Konrad von Würzburg*, Erträge der Forschung, 249 (Darmstadt: Wissenschaftliche Buchgesellschaft, 1987); see also Elisabeth Lienert, *Geschichte und Erzählen: Studien zu Konrads von Würzburg 'Trojanerkrieg'*, Wissensliteratur im Mittelalter, 22 (Wiesbaden: Reichert, 1996), pp. 3–10.

2 Kurt Herbert Halbach, *Gottfried von Strassburg und Konrad von Würzburg: 'Klassik' und 'Barock' im 13. Jahrhundert: Stilgeschichtliche Studie*, Tübinger Germanistische Arbeiten, 12 (Stuttgart: Kohlhammer, 1930), p. 53. Similarly, Hermann Dunger, who praises the 'staunenswerthe Gewandtheit im Versbau, glänzende Diction, unerschöpfliche[n] Reichthum an dichterischen Gedanken und Bildern' but concedes: 'Freilich darf man auch gegen die Fehler Konrad's nicht blind sein; er ist oft ermüdend breit in Schilderungen, [...] auch in Ausführung von Reden lässt er sich oft sehr gehen; es verletzen uns wohl zuweilen störende Uebertreibungen oder eine gekünstelte Sprache' (Hermann Dunger, *Die Sage vom trojanischen Krieg in den Bearbeitungen des Mittelalters und ihren antiken Quellen* (Leipzig: Vogel, 1869), p. 44).

3 Halbach, *Gottfried von Strassburg und Konrad von Würzburg*, p. 66.

4 Dennis Howard Green, *Konrads 'Trojanerkrieg' und Gottfrieds 'Tristan': Vorstudien zum gotischen Stil in der Dichtung* (Waldkirch: Waldkircher Verlagsgesellschaft, 1949), p. 50.

5 Helmut de Boor, *Die Deutsche Literatur im späten Mittelalter: Zerfall und Neubeginn*, Geschichte der deutschen Literatur von den Anfängen bis zur Gegenwart, III, i (Munich: Beck, 1962), p. 37.

stylistic principle of *wildekeit*, or *stilus alienus*, rather than as mere epigonal ineptness, nevertheless questions the accomplished coherence of the *Trojanerkrieg*. He speaks of an 'Einbuße des Ganzen an Bedeutung und Verbindlichkeit', so that the text remains a 'Stück selbstgenügsamen Kunstfleißes'.[6]

The dominant view of the *Trojanerkrieg* as a rhetorically accomplished but incoherent assemblage of all available sources was refuted in the late seventies by Christoph Cormeau. He argues that it is, in fact, a carefully composed entity united by a coherent perspective, a position which has since become the general consensus even though the specifics of this unity are still debated.[7] From the late eighties Konrad has come thoroughly back into fashion. The results of a conference in honour of the 700th anniversary of the poet's death were published in the *Jahrbuch der Oswald von Wolkenstein-Gesellschaft* for 1988/1989. In the introduction Horst Brunner, who also gives a sovereign overview of Konrad's works in the *Verfasserlexikon*,[8] emphatically rejects the traditional depreciation of Konrad as an epigone and virtuoso without substance by emphasizing his many innovations and the breadth of his oeuvre. He declares Konrad to have been one of the 'interessantesten und glänzendsten Erscheinungen des deutschen Mittelalters'.[9] This surge in interest was fittingly accompanied and furthered by Rüdiger Brandt's summary of research on Konrad and his works that appeared in the series 'Erträge der Forschung'.[10] A first monographic treatment of Konrad's works was presented in 1989 by Hartmut Kokott.[11] Research into the *Trojanerkrieg* specifically has been advanced by several studies published between 1987 and 1996 by Elisabeth Lienert. She not only illuminates the long and varied transmission of the *Trojanerkrieg* but also gives a detailed and systematic account of the vast number of Latin and vernacular sources that Konrad used to compose his monumental work. She describes the intricate composition and coordination between the different narrative strands and discusses some central aspects of

6 Wolfgang Monecke, *Studien zur epischen Technik Konrads von Würzburg: Das Erzählprinzip der 'wildekeit'*, Germanistische Abhandlungen, 24 (Stuttgart: Metzler, 1968), pp. 82–83.

7 Christoph Cormeau, 'Quellenkompendium oder Erzählkonzept? Eine Skizze zu Konrads von Würzburg *Trojanerkrieg*', in *Befund und Deutung: Zum Verhältnis von Empirie und Interpretation in Sprach- und Literaturwissenschaft: Festschrift für Hans Fromm*, ed. by Klaus Grubmüller and others (Tübingen: Niemeyer, 1979), pp. 304–07.

8 Horst Brunner, 'Konrad von Würzburg', in *Die deutsche Literatur des Mittelalters: Verfasserlexikon*, 2nd rev. edn (Berlin: de Gruyter, 1978–2008), V (1985), cols 272–304.

9 Horst Brunner, 'Zugang zu Konrad von Würzburg', *JOWG*, 5 (1988/1989), 15–21 (p. 20).

10 Brandt, *Konrad von Würzburg*.

11 Hartmut Kokott, *Konrad von Würzburg: Ein Autor zwischen Auftrag und Autonomie* (Stuttgart: Hirzel, 1989).

the work's poetics.[12] That the *Trojanerkrieg* continues to be very much at the centre of scholarly debate is illustrated by a number of important articles by well established researchers like Franz Josef Worstbrock, Burkhard Hasebrink, Jan-Dirk Müller, Beate Kellner and Hartmut Bleumer as well as by the recent doctoral dissertations by Olga Seus and Bent Gebert.[13]

One aspect of Konrad's work that has long been recognized as a key feature is its self-conscious poetics. In a way, this observation is already implicit in negative assessments of Konrad's writing as too 'gekünstelt', too calculated

12 Elisabeth Lienert, 'Helena – thematisches Zentrum von Konrads von Würzburg *Trojanerkrieg*', *JOWG*, 5 (1988/1989), 409–20; 'Die Überlieferung von Konrads von Würzburg *Trojanerkrieg*', in *Die deutsche Trojaliteratur: Materialien und Untersuchungen*, ed. by Horst Brunner, Wissensliteratur im Mittelalter, 3 (Wiesbaden: Reichert, 1990), pp. 325–405; 'Der Trojanische Krieg in Basel: Interesse an Geschichte und Autonomie des Erzählens bei Konrad von Würzburg', in *Literarische Interessenbildung im Mittelalter: DFG-Symposion 1991*, ed. by Joachim Heinzle, Germanistische Symposien Berichtsbände, 14 (Stuttgart: Metzler, 1993), pp. 266–79; *Geschichte und Erzählen.*

13 Franz Josef Worstbrock, 'Der Tod des Hercules: Eine Problemskizze zur Poetik des Zerfalls in Konrads von Würzburg *Trojanerkrieg*', in *Erzählungen in Erzählungen: Phänomene der Narration in Mittelalter und früher Neuzeit*, ed. by Harald Haferland and Michael Mecklenburg, Forschungen zur Geschichte der älteren deutschen Literatur, 19 (Munich: Fink, 1996), pp. 273–84; Burkhard Hasebrink, 'Rache als Geste: Medea im *Trojanerkrieg* Konrads von Würzburg', in *Literarische Leben*: *Rollenentwürfe in der Literatur des Hoch- und Spätmittelalters: Festschrift für Volker Mertens zum 65. Geburtstag*, ed. by Matthias Meyer and Hans-Jochen Schiewer (Tübingen: Niemeyer, 2002), pp. 209–30; Jan-Dirk Müller, '*schîn* und Verwandtes: Zum Problem der "Ästhetisierung" in Konrads von Würzburg *Trojanerkrieg* (Mit einem Nachwort zu Terminologie-Problemen der Mediävistik)', in *Im Wortfeld des Textes: Worthistorische Beiträge zur Bezeichnung von Rede und Schrift im Mittelalter*, ed. by Gerd Dicke, Manfred Eikelmann and Burkhard Hasebrink, Trends in Medieval Philology, 10 (Berlin: de Gruyter, 2006), pp. 287–307; Jan-Dirk Müller, 'Blinding Sight: Some Observations on German Epics of the Thirteenth Century', in *Rethinking the Medieval Senses: Heritage/ Fascinations/ Frames*, ed. by Stephen G. Nichols, Andreas Kablitz and Alison Calhoun (Baltimore: Johns Hopkins University Press, 2008), pp. 206–17; Beate Kellner, '*daz alte buoch von Troye* [...] *daz ich ez welle erniuwen*: Poetologie im Spannungsfeld von "wiederholen" und "erneuern" in den Trojaromanen Herborts von Fritzlar und Konrads von Würzburg', in *Im Wortfeld des Textes*, ed. by Dicke, Eikelmann and Hasebrink, pp. 231–62; Beate Kellner, 'Meisterschaft: Konrad von Würzburg – Heinrich von Mügeln', in *Interartifizialität: Die Diskussion der Künste in der mittelalterlichen Literatur*, ed. by Susanne Bürkle and Ursula Peters (= *ZfdPh*, 128 (2009)), pp. 137–62; Beate Kellner, 'Konrads von Würzburg *Trojanerkrieg*: Kontinuität und Diskontinuität zwischen Antike und Mittelalter', *Poetica*, 42 (2010), 81–116; Hartmut Bleumer, 'Zwischen Wort und Bild: Narrativität und Visualität im *Trojanischen Krieg* Konrads von Würzburg (Mit einer kritischen Revision der Sichtbarkeitsdebatte)', in *Zwischen Wort und Bild: Wahrnehmungen und Deutungen im Mittelalter*, ed. by Hartmut Bleumer and others (Cologne: Böhlau, 2010), pp. 109–56; Olga Seus, *Heilsgeschichten vor dem Heil? Studien zu mittelhochdeutschen Trojaverserzählungen* (Stuttgart: Hirzel, 2011); Bent Gebert, *Mythos als Wissensform: Epistemik und Poetik des 'Trojanerkriegs' Konrads von Würzburg*, spectrum Literaturwissenschaft, 35 (Berlin: de Gruyter, 2013).

and showy instead of heartfelt and immediate – literary self-awareness has often been seen as the mark that set the epigones apart from the *Blütezeit* poets.[14] Konrad's obvious interest in the issue of poetry, which he discusses in his prologues and some of his lyric poems, has also not gone unnoticed: 'Konrad von Würzburg hat über sein poetisches Geschäft mehr nachgedacht und sich öfter dazu geäußert als die meisten vor und nach ihm, Gottfried von Straßburg und Rudolf von Ems ausgenommen'.[15] His striking reflections on poetry have always received a great deal of attention and have often been discussed separately, for example in literary histories. Especially overviews of the 'Kunstauffassung' of Middle High German poets have found a rich vein of material to tap in Konrad's works.[16] Interest in the prologue of the *Trojanerkrieg* has never really waned since it was first discussed by Georg Gottfried Gervinus in 1835,[17] but in recent years there has also been greater concentration on the way in which the main text raises awareness of its own poeticity. In her 'Vorüberlegungen zu einer Ästhetik des *Trojanerkriegs*' Lienert argues that Konrad's eccentric imagery and his preference for the unrealistic and artificial direct attention away from the narrated world towards the process of narration itself and create 'eine Wirklichkeit, die nur in seinen Worten existiert. Dargestellt ist letztlich eine Kunstwelt, und Konrad ist ihr

14 Karl Viëtor, 'Die Kunstanschauung der höfischen Epigonen', *PBB*, 46 (1922), 85–124 (p. 85); Bruno Boesch, *Die Kunstanschauung in der mittelhochdeutschen Dichtung von der Blütezeit bis zum Meistersang* (Bern: Haupt, 1936; repr. Hildesheim: Olms, 1976), pp. 6–7; Konrad Burdach, *Reinmar und Walther von der Vogelweide: Ein Beitrag zur Geschichte des Minnesangs* (Leipzig: Hirzel, 1880). On this opinion, which is based on Romantic aesthetics, see also Sabine Obermaier, *Von Nachtigallen und Handwerkern: 'Dichtung über Dichtung' in Minnesang und Sangspruchdichtung*, Hermea, 75 (Tübingen: Niemeyer, 1995), pp. 9–12.

15 Werner Schröder, *Text und Interpretation III: Zur Kunstanschauung Gottfrieds von Straßburg und Konrads von Würzburg nach dem Zeugnis ihrer Prologe*, Sitzungsberichte der Wissenschaftlichen Gesellschaft an der Johann-Wolfgang-Goethe-Universität Frankfurt am Main, 26,5 (Stuttgart: Steiner, 1990), p. 175.

16 Boesch, *Die Kunstanschauung*; Viëtor, 'Die Kunstanschauung'; Hennig Brinkmann, *Zu Wesen und Form mittelalterlicher Dichtung* (Halle a.S.: Niemeyer, 1928; repr. Darmstadt: Wissenschaftliche Buchgesellschaft, 1979), pp. 10–29; Walter Haug, *Literaturtheorie im deutschen Mittelalter: Von den Anfängen bis zum Ende des 13. Jahrhunderts*, 2nd rev. edn (Darmstadt: Wissenschaftliche Buchgesellschaft, 1992), pp. 344–63. See also Obermaier, who analyses the portrayal of poetry in Konrad's lyric poetry (*Von Nachtigallen und Handwerkern*, pp. 218–36).

17 Georg Gottfried Gervinus, *Geschichte der poetischen National-Literatur der Deutschen*, 5 vols (Leipzig: Engelmann, 1835–42), I (1835): *Von den ersten Spuren der deutschen Dichtung bis gegen das Ende des 13. Jahrhunderts*, pp. 472–74. See also the more recent contributions by Kellner, 'Poetologie'; and Stefanie Schmitt, 'Autorisierung des Erzählens in Romanen mit historischen Stoffen? Überlegungen zu Rudolfs von Ems *Alexander* und Konrads von Würzburg *Trojanerkrieg*', in *Geltung der Literatur: Formen ihrer Autorisierung und Legitimierung im Mittelalter*, ed. by Beate Kellner, Peter Strohschneider and Franziska Wenzel, Philologische Studien und Quellen, 190 (Berlin: Schmidt, 2005), pp. 187–201.

Schöpfer'.[18] She furthermore states with regard to the frequent ineffability and modesty topoi: 'Indem Konrad die Nicht- oder Kaum-Erzählbarkeit seiner Geschichte der Superlative thematisiert und zugleich derart das Erzählen des Erzählens inszeniert, erscheint der Trojanische Krieg weniger als (historisches) Ereignis, mehr als Erzählproblem und Erzählerfolg'.[19] Müller, who discusses the imagery of the *Goldene Schmiede* and the *Trojanerkrieg*, points out that the pervasive motif of radiance connects 'objektsprachliche und metasprachlich-poetologische Aspekte [...]: *schîn* ist das, was den Gegenstand der Erzählung auszeichnet, und *schîn* ist das, was der Erzähler seiner Erzählung verleiht'.[20] The self-reflexive quality of Konrad's poetics of detail, light, colour and iridescence that Müller investigates is, in fact, already addressed in the studies by Green and Monecke.[21] Focusing on the same characteristics, this trend in interpretation is maintained right up to the present day by Bleumer, who asserts: 'Man sieht bei der Lektüre des *Trojanischen Krieges* nicht einfach das Erzählte, man sieht auch und zuerst das Erzählen'; and by Christina Lechtermann, who speaks of an 'immer gleichzeitiges Zum-Erscheinen-Kommen des Erzählten *und* seiner sprachlichen Verfasstheit'.[22] A different route of interpretation is taken by Hasebrink and Hans Jürgen Scheuer, who both argue that Medea's magic rejuvenation (*erniuwen*) of Jason's father mirrors the activity of the poet, which is also described as an act of renewing (*erniuwen*) the old book of Troy in the prologue.[23] Most recently, Gebert's treatment of the *Trojanerkrieg* as mythography discusses several ways in which the text draws attention to its own discourse. He emphasizes, however, that its poetics are not completely homogeneous and that there are also passages in the text which render the discourse transparent by creating the illusion of an unmediated immersion in the narrated world, so that 'selbst noch der

18 Lienert, *Geschichte und Erzählen*, pp. 285–88 (p. 288); similarly Kellner, 'Kontinutät und Diskontinuität', 113.

19 Lienert, *Geschichte und Erzählen*, p. 260.

20 Müller, '*schîn* und Verwandtes', p. 297; Köbele makes a similar observation with regard to the words *wilde* and *wildekeit* in the *Goldene Schmiede*. See Susanne Köbele, 'Zwischen Klang und Sinn: Das Gottfried-Idiom in Konrads von Würzburg *Goldener Schmiede* (mit einer Anmerkung zur paradoxen Dynamik von Alteritätsschüben)', in *Alterität als Leitkonzept für historisches Interpretieren*, ed. by Anja Becker and Jan Mohr, Studien und Quellen, 8 (Berlin: Akademie, 2012), pp. 303–33.

21 Green, *Vorstudien zum gotischen Stil*; Monecke, *Das Erzählprinzip der 'wildekeit'*.

22 Bleumer, 'Zwischen Wort und Bild', p. 112. See also Christina Lechtermann, 'Figuren der Abhebung: Schillerndes Erzählen im *Trojanischen Krieg*', in *Deixis und Evidenz*, ed. by Horst Wenzel and Ludwig Jäger, Scenae, 8 (Freiburg: Rombach, 2008), pp. 43–64 (p. 60).

23 Hasebrink, 'Rache als Geste', pp. 223–27; Hans Jürgen Scheuer, '*wîsheit*: Grabungen in einem Wortfeld zwischen Poesie und Wissen', in *Im Wortfeld des Textes*, ed. by Dicke, Eikelmann and Hasebrink, pp. 83–106 (pp. 103–05).

Kommunikationsakt dem Blick entzogen wird'.[24] These 'Präsenzeffekte', which can be found particularly in the battle scenes of the second half of the text, are, for example, created by the descriptions of weaponry which stimulate the imagination with light and colour effects while undermining the semiotic aspect of heraldry through generic recurrence; or by a trans-personal mode of focalization that shifts from minute detail to panoramic overview and cannot be attributed to any consistent centre of perception; or again by the frequent recurrence of formulaic expressions which counteracts the emphasized artistry and artificiality of other passages and associates the text with the simple and transparent style of historiography.[25] Gebert's highly learned and stimulating discussion provides a very comprehensive treatment of the text's poetics. However, he also interprets some passages – such as the description of Helen – as examples of a poetic strategy of rendering invisible the inevitable tension between the represented object and the act of representation ('Was *im* Erzählen *präsent* wird, ist *durch* Erzählen präsent *gemacht*'),[26] whereas I, on the contrary, will read these passages as an exhibition of this very same tension.

My approach takes these observations of the self-reflexive quality of the *Trojanerkrieg* as a starting point for providing the first monographic treatment of its metapoetics.[27] As a general qualification a metapoetic text is a text that includes within itself reflections on its own poetic identity;[28] put even more

24 Gebert, *Mythos als Wissensform*, p. 318.

25 Gebert, *Mythos als Wissensform*, pp. 22–320. He argues that these and other poetic strategies lead to an 'Emergenz des Wissens' that is unusual in medieval mythography, which normally presents myths as referring to something other than themselves, for example in the sense of *integumentum* (p. 318). Drawing on Luhmann's concept, Gebert describes knowledge as 'Paradoxieabsorption' (p. 59), which means that the distinction that must be made in order to observe something has to obscure what it excludes in order to gain validity: 'Wissen lässt sich als Invisibilisierung von Beobachtungsparadoxien beschreiben, die selbstreferentielle Anschlussmöglichkeiten wahrscheinlich, fremdreferentielle Anschlussmöglichkeiten in der Kommunikation unwahrscheinlich machen und verdecken' (p. 62).

26 Gebert, *Mythos als Wissensform*, pp. 473–74.

27 A meta-legendary quality has been attributed to Konrad's legends by Peter Strohschneider, 'Weltabschied, Christusnachfolge und die Kraft der Legende', *GRM*, 60 (2010), 143–63; Hartmut Bleumer, '"Historische Narratologie"? Metalegendarisches Erzählen im *Silvester* Konrads von Würzburg', in *Historische Narratologie: Mediävistische Perspektiven*, ed. by Harald Haferland and Matthias Meyer, Trends in Medieval Philology, 19 (Berlin: de Gruyter, 2010), pp. 231–61. Köbele expresses some reservations about the interpretations of Konrad's legends as metatexts (Susanne Köbele, 'Die Illusion der "einfachen Form": Über das ästhetische und religiöse Risiko der Legende', *PBB*, 134 (2012), 365–404 (pp. 380–92).

28 This definition is a reformulation of the definition of metafiction proposed by Linda Hutcheon, *Narcissistic Narrative: The Metafictional Paradox* (New York: Methuen, 1980), p. 1. In German scholarship the term 'Poetologie' is also common to denote the self-reflexive aspects of a text. It is thus distinguished from 'Poetik' as a term denoting the sum of the

simply: it is poetry about poetry.[29] Individual passages of such a text can be described as metapoetic if they refer to the subject of poetry in a broad sense. In a narrative work like the *Trojanerkrieg* this means that these self-reflexive elements refer to the discourse instead of the story;[30] rather than

---

peculiar poetic characteristics of a text, text group or author (the poetic practice often described as 'immanente Poetik') or a discursive treatise on the production of poetry (usually referred to as 'exogene Poetik'). The term 'Poetologie' was coined by Alfred Weber as a thematic qualification for poetry: '"Poetologische Lyrik" meint [...] nicht nur Gedichte vom Typ einer *ars poetica*, die ein in sich geschlossenes System der Poetik enthalten, sondern auch solche, die nur einen Aspekt oder ein besonderes Problem der Dichtungstheorie zum Thema haben, ganz gleich, ob sie überwiegend vom *poeta*, von der *poesis* oder vom *poema* handeln' (Alfred Weber, 'Kann die Harfe durch ihre Propeller schießen? Poetologische Lyrik in Amerika', in *Amerikanische Literatur im 20. Jahrhundert*, ed. by Alfred Weber and Dietmar Haack (Göttingen: Vandenhoeck & Ruprecht, 1971), pp. 175–91 (p. 181)). Weber rejects the equivalent terms 'Verspoetik' and 'werkimmanente Poetik' for the self-reflexive poem, because they place too much emphasis on 'Poetik': 'Die "poetologischen Gedichte" sollen nicht nur als Dokument der Poetik, sondern vor allem auch als Dichtung gesehen und untersucht werden' (p. 190, fn. 9). See also Armin P. Frank, 'Theorie im Gedicht und Theorie als Gedicht', in Armin P. Frank, *Literaturwissenschaft zwischen Extremen: Aufsätze und Ansätze zu aktuellen Fragen einer unsicher gemachten Disziplin* (Berlin: de Gruyter, 1977), pp. 131–69, pp. 188–93. He discusses the differences between versified normative and discursive poetics and poetological poems whose poetic form mimics their content, while conceding that even the former contain more poetic forms of expression, namely the illustrative examples, and that his differentiation depends on a modern concept of poetry. Sometimes, however, 'Poetologie' is also used similarly to 'Poetik' as a term referring to the poetic characteristics of a text or text group without an emphasis on self-reflexivity. Thus, Anna Kathrin Bleuler merely chooses the terms 'Poetologie' and the corresponding adjective 'poetologisch' over 'Poetik' and 'poetisch' to avoid associations with the second meaning of 'Poetik' (a discursive treatise on the production of poetry): 'Um nicht den Eindruck zu erwecken, man habe es beim vorliegenden Corpus mit Texten zu tun, die von einem Autor nach den Regeln einer normativen Poetik verfasst worden sind, wird in der vorliegenden Arbeit nicht von "poetischer Konzeption" gesprochen, sondern von "poetologischer Konzeption" im Sinne von "die die Poetik des Textes betreffende Konzeption"' (Anna Kathrin Bleuler, *Überlieferungskritik und Poetologie: Strukturierung und Beurteilung der Sommerliedüberlieferung Neidharts auf der Basis des poetologischen Musters*, Münchener Texte und Untersuchungen zur deutschen Literatur des Mittelalters, 136 (Tübingen: Niemeyer, 2008), p. 5, fn. 22).

29 This definition refers to the title of Obermaier's study of Middle High German metapoetic poems *Von Nachtigallen und Handwerkern: 'Dichtung über Dichtung' in Minnesang und Sangspruchdichtung*. The only reservation about this definition for the purposes of this study is the possible suggestion that poetry has to be the explicit and primary subject of a metapoetic text. In fact there is often a considerable tension between elements of self-reflexivity and non-reflexive narration in the *Trojanerkrieg*. In many cases the metapoetic significance of a passage is only a further dimension of meaning in addition to its primary textual function of representing events or elements within the narrated world.

30 Following the distinction between *histoire* and *discours* established by Todorov, I shall differentiate between the narrated world in which the action takes place (story) and its narrative communication (discourse) (see Tzvetan Todorov, 'Les catégories du récit littéraire',

drawing attention to the events that are narrated, they draw attention to the act of narration itself. However, I choose the term 'metapoetics' instead of 'metanarration' to include also passages of the text that are not strictly narrative in the sense that they represent a series of connected events, but are, instead, either discursive, like the reflections on poetry in the prologue, or descriptive of objects and persons within the narrated world.[31]

Metapoetic significance can be created through diverse textual devices which can be classed into different types. First, it is important to distinguish between explicit and implicit metapoetics. Metapoetic expressions can either occur in the form of explicit statements about poetry or induce the reader to reflect upon issues pertaining to the subject of poetry in a less overt way. Second, metapoetic elements can be located on the level of either the discourse or the story. In the discourse they can take on the form of explicit utterances by the narrator or consist of poetic devices such as certain metaphors or descriptive vocabulary that draw attention to the discourse. On the level of the story characters can make explicit statements about poetry; or metapoetic issues can be highlighted by aspects of the narrative action that involve the topics of poetry or language, for instance. The third aspect concerns the quantitative and qualitative relationship of individual metapoetic passages to the text as a whole. They can be short or extensive; located at marginal or central positions in the text; they can be relatively isolated with little or no relevance beyond the point of their occurrence or be connected to other passages of metapoetic significance and reflect on the interpretation of the text as a whole.[32] Fourth, their reference can be restricted either to the text in

Communications, 8 (1966), 125–51). Following the terminology of Genette, I shall further describe actions or elements within the narrated world as 'intradiegetic' and statements and positions outside the story as 'extradiegetic' (see Gérard Genette, *Narrative Discourse: An Essay in Method* (Ithaca, NY: Cornell, 1972).

31 This term also avoids confusion with Genette's concept of 'metanarrative' as a narrative within a narrative. Genette uses the term polysemously to refer also to the directing function of the voice referring to the structure of the discourse in our sense of the word (Genette, *Narrative Discourse*, p. 228, p. 255). For a definition of 'metanarration' as a term 'designating self-reflexive utterances, i.e. comments referring to the discourse rather than to the story' and a brief history of research on the subject, see Birgit Neumann and Ansgar Nünning, 'Metanarration and Metafiction', in *Handbook of Narratology: 2nd edition, fully revised and expanded*, ed. by Peter Hühn and others, 2 vols (Berlin: de Gruyter, 2014), I, pp. 344–52 (p. 343). Narration and description are, of course, not always strictly distinguishable, as Wolf Schmid points out (Wolf Schmid, *Elemente der Narratologie*, 2nd rev. edn (Berlin: de Gruyter, 2008), pp. 1–9). The general term metapoetics allows the inclusion of different functions of poetic utterances while obviating the need to draw strict lines.

32 This model is loosely based on the typology developed by Werner Wolf ('Metatext und Metatextualität', in *Metzler Lexikon Literatur- und Kulturtheorie: Ansätze – Personen – Grundbegriffe*, ed. by Ansgar Nünning, 5th rev. edn (Stuttgart: Metzler, 2013), pp. 520–21); and its elaboration as a typology of metanarration by Neumann and Nünning

which they occur, or to other texts by different authors, or it can extend to the topic of poetry in general.

Apart from 'Illusionsdurchbrechung', metapoetic reflections generally serve the same functions that Werner Wolf attributes to metafiction: 'Schaffen poetologischer Reflexionsräume; ästhetische Selbst- und Fremdkommentierung und Bereitstellung von Verstehenshilfen [...]; Feier des Erzählten oder des Erzählers; spielerisches Ausloten der Möglichkeiten des Mediums'.[33] Whether further, possibly historically specific functions can be added to this list will be investigated in this study. What makes the *Trojanerkrieg* particularly suited to the discussion of the different forms and functions of metapoetics is the fact that its unusually extensive explicit metapoetic reflections are intricately linked to a multitude of implicit metapoetic allusions which permeate the entire text on the level of the story as well as the discourse.

Explicit statements concerning the nature, function and challenges of poetry, its relationship to the audience and the role of the poet can be found in the prologue as well as in narratorial remarks such as the topoi of modesty, ineffability and superiority which occur throughout the text. While the prologue with its striking imagery has been discussed many times before, the narratorial remarks are usually disregarded because they are considered merely topical.[34] In order to appreciate the complexity of Konrad's metapoetic statements and images it is essential to trace their origins and contextualize them in the field

('Metanarration and Metafiction', p. 349). A further differentiation that is related to, but not identical with, the distinction between metapoetics on the level of the story and metapoetics on the level of the discourse is proposed by Hutcheon, who also distinguishes between overt and covert forms of self-reflection: 'There are texts which are [...] diegetically self-aware, that is, conscious of their own narrative process. Others are linguistically self-reflective, demonstrating their awareness of both the limits and the powers of their own language. In the first case, the text presents itself as diegesis, as narrative; in the second, it is unobfuscated text, language' (Hutcheon, *Narcissistic Narrative*, pp. 22–23). One differentiation concerns the space of metapoetic reflection, while the other focuses on the object of this reflection. In practice, a single text can, of course, exhibit all these forms of metapoeticity in various combinations.

33 Werner Wolf, 'Metafiktion', in *Grundbegriffe der Literaturtheorie*, ed. by Ansgar Nünning, Sammlung Metzler, 347 (Stuttgart: Metzler, 2004), 172–74 (p. 173). On self-referentiality as an essential characteristic of literary or poetic texts in deconstructivist theory see Winko: 'Selbstreferentialität als "Normalfall" der Sprache [...] wird in wissenschaftlichen und Alltagsdiskursen vermieden, in Literatur aber zugelassen; die rhetorische Verfasstheit von Sprache wird erst im literarischen Sprechen bewusst' (Simone Winko, 'Auf der Suche nach der Weltformel: Literarizität und Poetizität in der neueren literaturtheoretischen Diskussion', in *Grenzen der Literatur: Zu Begriff und Phänomen des Literarischen*, ed. by Simone Winko, Fotis Jannidis and Gerhard Lauer, Revisionen: Grundbegriffe der Literaturtheorie, 2 (Berlin: de Gruyter, 2009), pp. 374–96 (p. 385).

34 On the ancient tradition of these topoi see Ernst Robert Curtius, *Europäische Literatur und lateinisches Mittelalter*, 2nd rev. edn (Berlin: Francke, 1954), pp. 93–95, pp. 168–69, pp. 171–74.

of the Latin as well as the vernacular tradition.[35] However, the analysis cannot stop at establishing these sources but must also show how Konrad employs and merges different traditions to suit his very own poetic purposes.

In addition to Konrad's explicit metapoetic utterances this study also discusses the *Trojanerkrieg*'s implicit metapoetics. Descriptions have long been recognized as spaces for the self-conscious exhibition of poetic mastery and intertextual as well as interartificial competition.[36] However, since the study of implicit metapoetics always carries the risk of over-interpretation, it is imperative to demonstrate that Konrad does, in fact, exploit the inherent metapoetic potential of description consciously. For the same reason, the fact that certain words which Konrad associates with poetry – for example, *blüemen*, *schîn*, *kunst*, *meisterschaft*, *wîsheit* – are also used to describe elements of the narrated world cannot justify a metapoetic reading of every passage in which they occur unless such a reading is supported by further indicators.

While previous research on metapoetics in the *Trojanerkrieg* has focused mainly on the traditional spaces of explicit and implicit literary self-reflection – the prologue and the descriptions – this study also analyses the metapoetic significance of certain aspects of the story. Although Konrad does not invent any of the events he narrates, his presentation, selection and combination of source material are so sovereign that he can easily create story-level structures which mirror the issues he explores on the discourse level. This coordination of discourse and story is also achieved through the employment of certain keywords such as *prîs*, although these terminological links have to be treated with caution for the reason discussed above.

35 The necessity to interpret metaphors in Middle High German poetry which usually rely on and vary basic metaphorical topoi on the basis of culture-historically specific contextual knowledge is emphasized by Udo Friedrich: 'Metaphern habe eine Geschichte, und ihre Konnotationen sind von epochenspezifischen Wissensbeständen abhängig' (Udo Friedrich, 'Historische Metaphorologie', in *Literatur- und Kulturtheorien in der Germanistischen Mediävistik: Ein Handbuch*, ed. by Christiane Ackermann and Michael Egerding (Berlin: de Gruyter, 2015), pp. 169–211 (p. 177)). On rhetoric and poetics in the Latin Middle Ages, see *Les arts poétiques du XIIe et du XIIIe siècle*, ed. by Edmond Faral (Paris: Librairie Ancienne Honoré Champion, 1924); Charles Sears Baldwin, *Medieval Rhetoric and Poetic: Interpreted from Representative Works* (New York: Macmillan, 1928; repr. Gloucester, MA: Smith, 1959); Richard McKeon, 'Poetry and Philosophy in the Twelfth Century: The Renaissance of Rhetoric', in *Critics and Criticism: Ancient and Modern*, ed. by R. S. Crane (Chicago: University of Chicago Press, 1952), pp. 297–318 (first publ. in *Modern Philology*, 43 (1946), 217–34); Brinkmann, *Wesen und Form*, pp. 29–81; *Medieval Literary Theory and Criticism c. 1100 – c. 1375: The Commentary Tradition*, ed. by Alastair J. Minnis and Alexander Brian Scott, 2nd rev. edn (Oxford: Clarendon, 1991); Curtius, *Europäische Literatur*.

36 Franz Josef Worstbrock, '*Dilatatio materiae*: Zur Poetik des *Erec* Hartmanns von Aue', *Frühmittelalterliche Studien*, 19 (1985), 1–30; see also *Interartifizialität*, ed. by Bürkle and Peters.

It is important to clarify that this study of different aspects of metapoetics in the *Trojanerkrieg* does not aim at reconstructing Konrad's 'Literaturtheorie' or 'Kunstauffassung'. That the application of these terms to Middle High German literature is generally problematic is pointed out by Brandt:

> Einzelne Äußerungen über Funktion und Beschaffenheit von Literatur, Kunst, Künstlertum und Künstlern können nur unter strengsten Vorbehalten zu einer 'Theorie' zusammengestellt werden. Diese Möglichkeit wird außerdem eingeschränkt durch die Tatsache, daß solche Äußerungen untrennbar mit dem jeweiligen Kunstwerk selbst verbunden sind und sich abstrakter Auslegung entziehen (literarische Traditionen, Topoi usw.). Butzmann weist zu Recht auf das 'Unsichere, Schimmernde, Glatte' der Begrifflichkeit innerhalb entsprechender Passagen hin. [...] Mir persönlich scheint es sogar fraglich, ob man auch nur die verschiedenen Äußerungen eines einzelnen Autors zur Kunstthematik zu einem solchen System zusammenschließen darf, wenn nicht neben den reinen Äußerungen noch weitere Indikatoren zur Verfügung stehen.[37]

Christian Kiening exercises similar caution when he explains that he applies the term 'Literaturtheorie' to twelfth-century German literature not in the sense of a 'systematische Diskursform' but only 'im Sinne unsystematischer poetologischer Aussageformen im Medium der Dichtung selbst'. He defines this understanding furthermore as a form of *theoria* which lacks logical coherence and a firm terminological basis, which remains restricted to the individual text and cannot be generalized. It exhibits 'mehr den Ausdruckswillen als die Präzision eines theoretischen Programmes'. He also warns against forcing these metapoetic utterances into the system of contemporary Latin poetics or classical rhetoric.[38] The difference between vernacular metapoetics and Latin poetics is also addressed by Sabine Obermaier: 'Poetologische Gedichte lassen sich im Vergleich zu Poetik und Verspoetik eher negativ als positiv bestimmen: Sie sind weniger systematisch, weniger vollständig, weniger eindeutig, weniger begrifflich präzise'. She emphasizes, however, that this vagueness can be an advantage for metapoetic poetry, which can also work more freely with metaphors and similes.[39]

37 Brandt, *Konrad von Würzburg*, p. 196.

38 Christian Kiening, 'Freiräume literarischer Theoriebildung: Dimensionen und Grenzen programmatischer Aussagen in der deutschen Literatur des 12. Jahrhunderts', *DVjs*, 66 (1992), 405–49 (pp. 406–07). See also Brandt, who explains that it is difficult to establish a link between Latin literary and aesthetic theory and Middle High German practice. He adds: 'Es ist immer damit zu rechnen, daß mittelalterliche Literatur*praxis* die Literatur*theorie* überholt' (Brandt, *Konrad von Würzburg*, p. 196).

39 Obermaier, *Von Nachtigallen und Handwerkern*, p. 15; similarly in 'Möglichkeiten und Grenzen der Interpretation', in *Mittelalterliche Lyrik: Probleme der Poetik*, ed. by Thomas Cramer and Ingrid Kasten (Berlin: Erich Schmidt, 1999), pp. 11–32.

The term 'theory' certainly implies a manner of formalization, generalization and coherence that does not apply to the notoriously vague vocabulary and frequently ad hoc argumentation that characterizes even the most discursive metapoetic passages of the *Trojanerkrieg*. It would furthermore mean disregarding one of the most intriguing qualities of poetry on poetry to reduce its evocative and multifaceted metaphors to mere illustrations of a clear-cut theoretical position. I would therefore even go one step further than Brandt and question whether the statements of *one* author within *one* work can be described as a 'Literaturtheorie'. That these statements also do not necessarily reflect the author's actual position is rightly stressed by Obermaier: 'In Gedichten über das Dichten ist [...] zunächst nur die dargestellte Dichtungsauffassung oder das dargestellte Selbstverständnis eines Dichters greifbar, was der tatsächlichen Dichtungsauffassung und dem tatsächlichen Selbstverständnis des Autors entsprechen kann, aber nicht *a priori* entsprechen muß'.[40] This does not mean that trying to relate these statements to the author's actual circumstances is necessarily futile – this has, for example, been attempted for Konrad's complaint about his unappreciative audience in the prologue – but this study will focus primarily on the rhetorical and text-immanent functions of these utterances.

Although Konrad picks up and elaborates certain key images and highlights similar metapoetic issues throughout the *Trojanerkrieg*, he exhibits various, frequently paradoxical aspects of poetry rather than presenting a definitive concept of literature which could be generalized as the basis of the entire work. Nevertheless, the striking cohesion that characterizes his reflections means that each of the individual passages of metapoetic relevance can only be fully appreciated if these connections are understood, so that it is crucial to discuss them in a comprehensive manner. Contrary to what has been said about the *Trojanerkrieg* in older scholarship, poetic form and content are in fact intricately linked – although this connection is frequently one of diametrical opposition. A study of the text's poetic self-awareness is, therefore, not just a study of its stylistic surface but will inevitably have to address central questions about its overall interpretation as well.

The point at which the significance of poetic self-reflection for the overall interpretation of the *Trojanerkrieg* becomes most evident is the fact that Konrad's metapoetic vocabulary regularly draws on imagery of religious origin. The combination of this imagery with the subject matter of the Trojan War, however, appears highly uneasy. Unlike Alexander the Great, who appears in the Bible and was interpreted by Jerome as the representative of the third world empire announced in Daniel's prophecies, the Trojan War was

40 Obermaier, *Von Nachtigallen und Handwerkern*, p. 22.

not an integral part of salvation history. Troy was only indirectly connected to Christian eschatology as the origin of Aeneas, the founder of the fourth world empire, Rome. As the cradle of knighthood and courtly love as well as the alleged origin of numerous dynasties, people and cities, Troy served as a primarily secular identification model.[41] This explains why Green, who notices several religious allusions in the *Trojanerkrieg*, such as the fact that Hector is stylized as an 'Erlöserfigur' when the Trojans praise him ('in sîn eines hende | stêt unser heil und unser trôst. | er hât ûz sorgen uns erlôst'),[42] interprets these as merely superficial additions: '[D]ie Verweltlichung der religiösen Begriffe [ist] auch mit einer Preisgabe des religiösen Gefühls verbunden [...]. Konrads religiöser Wortschatz dient also nur noch der Idealisierung seiner Gestalten.'[43] Likewise, Müller draws a strict separation between texts that criticize courtly splendour from a religious point of view – including Konrad's own *Der Welt Lohn* – and the *Trojanerkrieg*: 'Konrad depicts a pagan society where conversion is not an option [...] and where courtly order cannot be replaced by a celestial one. In Troy, the cradle of knighthood, worldly beauty can be praised without any religious remorse.'[44] In contrast to this, Kellner interprets *Der Welt Lohn* as a condensed version of the issues expounded in the *Trojanerkrieg* and proposes a decidedly eschatological reading of the latter, according to which certain analogies such as that between the Apple of Discord and the Apple of Paradise exhibit the sinfulness of the lavish heathen world.[45] Most recently, the *Gretchenfrage* of whether Konrad, who never explicitly condemns but exuberantly praises the magnificence of the narrated world, really celebrates pagan courtliness as some kind of 'innerweltlicher Heilsersatz' or, on the contrary, assumes a disapproving Christian perspective towards it has also been addressed by Seus.[46] She concludes that the fall of Troy is ensured by divine intervention at crucial points of the story, when the catastrophe could have been averted, and is therefore presented as God's 'Heilsplan' in which Aeneas has to found the Roman Empire.[47] She furthermore interprets descriptions in which the characters of the text are associated with the radiance of angels

41 Elisabeth Lienert, *Deutsche Antikenromane des Mittelalters*, Grundlagen der Germanistik, 39 (Berlin: Schmidt, 2001), p. 103.

42 Konrad von Würzburg, *Trojanerkrieg und die anonym überlieferte Fortsetzung*, ed. by Heinz Thoelen and Bianca Häberlein (Wiesbaden: Reichert, 2015), ll. 37644–46.

43 Green, *Vorstudien zum gotischen Stil*, pp. 76–83 (p. 78). See also Gerhard P. Knapp, *Hector und Achill: Die Rezeption des Trojastoffes im deutschen Mittelalter: Personenbild und struktureller Wandel*, Utah Studies in Literature and Linguistics, 1 (Bern: Lang, 1974), p. 73. He attributes the role of a secularized saviour to Achilles.

44 Müller, 'Blinding Sight', p. 215.

45 Kellner, 'Kontinuität und Diskontinuität', 116.

46 Seus, *Heilsgeschichten vor dem Heil?*, p. 118.

47 Seus, *Heilsgeschichten vor dem Heil?*, pp. 140–47.

or with Mariological symbols as a secular 'Scheintranszendenz' that serves to highlight what the pagan world lacks: divine grace that would provide respite from the unchained mechanisms of love and war leading to destruction.[48] While Seus focuses mainly on explicit religious references, she does not usually recognize or discuss the religious origin of Konrad's metapoetic vocabulary. A study evaluating how the *Trojanerkrieg* conceptualizes the status and function of poetry in general and how it envisages its own reception can therefore contribute to the controversial discussion of its possibly religious interpretation.

In addition to the relevance for the interpretation of the *Trojanerkrieg* an analysis of its metapoetics also provides an insight into the cultural-historical specificity of self-reflexivity in Middle High German literature. It thus addresses itself to the lacuna identified by Neumann and Nünning: 'Desiderata for narratological research still include differentiated investigations of the forms, functions, and diachronic development of [...] metanarration. One relatively unexplored issue is the development of [...] metanarration across different periods of literary history in different literary genres'.[49] While this monograph can only provide the synchronic snapshot of a case study, Konrad's metapoetic style provides an instructive example of the peculiarities of self-reflexive writing in Middle High German literature because it clearly refers to prominent metapoetic passages by seminal poets like Gottfried von Straßburg and Hartmann von Aue on the one hand and exploits the potential of poetic self-reflexion in a unique way on the other. An interpretation of Konrad's metapoetics thus maps out the space of possible conceptualizations of textuality, language and poetry in its culturally specific context.[50] The extraordinary variety of metapoetic expression in the *Trojanerkrieg* furthermore helps to identify typical modes of self-reflexivity in Middle High German literature such as *descriptio*, interartificial discourses,

48 Seus, *Heilsgeschichten vor dem Heil?*, pp. 177–78.

49 Neumann and Nünning, 'Metanarration and Metafiction', p. 350. Weber describes 'Poetologie' as an international and trans-temporal as well as a cultural-historically specific phenomenon, claiming that while all literatures know forms of self-reflexive poetry they reflect very different concerns and concepts of poetry: 'So wie sich im Laufe der Jahrhunderte das Verhältnis der Menschen zur Dichtung, das Dichtungsideal und das Selbstverständnis des Dichters änderten und auch die poetische Technik anders wurde, so änderte sich auch die poetische Lyrik in ihren Intentionen, in ihren dominanten Themen und in ihren Strukturen' (Weber, 'Kann die Harfe durch ihre Propeller schießen?', p. 186).

50 On the scope of medieval conceptualizations of textuality, see Peter Strohschneider, *Höfische Textgeschichten: Über Selbstentwürfe vormoderner Literatur* (Heidelberg: Winter, 2014); on the informative value of metapoetic reflection for a reconstruction of a Middle High German poetics see Obermaier: 'Selbst eine – wenn auch nur dargestellte, funktionalisierte – Dichtungstheorie dürfte das enthalten, was im Vorstellungsbereich eines mittelalterlichen Autors zu einer Dichtungstheorie gehört' ('Möglichkeiten und Grenzen', p. 18).

or the creative exploitation of traditional metapoetic topoi. While the latter are often passed over in analyses because of their conventional status, Haug correctly emphasizes that the study of metapoetic utterances in Middle High German literature has to acknowledge their traditionalism while at the same time also exploring how conventional elements are selected, arranged and varied to express more specific positions, both with regard to the individual work and to its time and cultural context. Thus Haug argues that classical modesty and ineffability topoi can take on a novel seriousness in the context of a Christian literature that believes in the categorical distinction between the divine and the mundane:

> Diese Bescheidenheitstopik, die nicht selten die Einleitungsfloskeln zu Werken lieferte, die diese Klischees dann durch umso brilliantere Stilkunst Lügen straften, mußte nun einen neuen Ernst gewinnen. Denn wenn man sich unter christlichem Aspekt zu einem schlichten Stil bekennt, dann braucht dies nicht Unfähigkeit vorzutäuschen, es kann dies vielmehr echter Humilitas entspringen. Ebenso wird die topische Behauptung, daß man mit seiner Kunst der Größe und Bedeutung des Gegenstandes nicht gerecht zu werden vermöge, unter christlichen Prämissen zutiefst wahr.[51]

This statement rings particularly true in view of the religious traditions on which Konrad draws to articulate the challenges of his literary project. His allusion to religious imagery – most importantly the motif of depth and light – is only one of his strategies for making his modesty and ineffability topoi into something more than mere commonplaces. His effort to restore a degree of authenticity to the expression of traditional metapoetic concerns as well as their implications for the interpretation of the text as a whole make a careful examination of their articulation in the *Trojanerkrieg* worthwhile. Last, but not least, the present study also discusses ways in which typical pitfalls of metapoetic interpretation of Middle High German texts – for example harmonization and disambiguation of equivocal or inconsistent expressions; generic attribution of metapoetic significance to masterfully executed descriptions – can be avoided.

The study is divided into four chapters. The first and longest chapter focuses on the prologue, which, as one might expect, contains the majority of Konrad's explicit statements on poetry and whose imagery provides an essential basis for the interpretation of the main text. Although the prologue has a long research tradition, some of its most prominent images have never been discussed in depth while others have been unduly reduced to mere illustrations of very definitive compositional principles. The description of the Apple of Discord,

51 Haug, *Literaturtheorie*, p. 22. On this issue see also Kiening, 'Freiräume literarischer Theoriebildung', 407–11.

whose curious optics and wondrous inscription have been at the centre of recent metapoetic interpretations of the *Trojanerkrieg*, will be treated in the second chapter. The Apple will be interpreted as the culmination point of a number of epic realizations of metaphors for poetry. In addition to this a new eschatological interpretation of the Apple's inscription will be proposed which has far-reaching consequences for the assessment of the attitude evinced in the text towards courtly splendour. The third chapter concentrates on verbal praise, which is characterized in the text as the preeminent poetic challenge that faces the narrator and also plays a significant role in the story. Following a semantic analysis of the key terms *lop* and *prîs* which highlights their potential for articulating concerns related to the medium of language, the intradiegetic reception of the story of Hercules' death is read as a cautionary tale which hints at the intended reception of the *Trojanerkrieg* itself. The second half of the chapter focuses on the intricate connection between praise and love. Paris's *Fernminne* for Helen and his reflections on the relationship between Helen and her praise are interpreted as the story-level equivalent to the narrator's reflections on Helen's ineffability and the power of her literary praise. Picking up the thread from the third chapter, the final chapter analyses the famous eulogy of Helen, which has frequently been discussed as the poetic core of the *Trojanerkrieg*. Paying special attention to the interlacing of the narrator's statements with Paris's praise of Helen and his assessment of her verbal and visual inaccessibility, it examines the complex relationship between Helen as an ineffable beauty and Helen as a powerful verbal and literary phenomenon. Finally, the investigation of the text's poetics of detail, light, colour and iridescence, which could be described as an excess of visuality, opens up the discussion to current discourses in the study of German medieval literature by challenging the characterization of courtly literature as a 'poetics of visualization'.

CHAPTER 1

The Prologue

It is a curious fact that the prologue of the *Trojanerkrieg*, which has received much attention from modern scholars, apparently did not hold a great deal of interest for its medieval audience. This is at least what its transmission suggests: only two of the six complete manuscripts contain the prologue. Although this may be accidental in some cases, the manuscripts from the Lauber workshop omit it intentionally.[1] This phenomenon certainly provides important clues to the reception of the text. Sebastian Coxon, for example, interprets it as a reflection of the lack of interest in Konrad's authorship and a 'preoccupation with the material itself', which is also demonstrated by the seamless transition from Konrad's work into that of the anonymous continuator.[2] Even though the prologue's sketchy transmission intimates that Konrad's keen interest in the poetics of his text may not have been shared by some of its readers, it is still the obvious place to begin an investigation of metapoetics in the *Trojanerkrieg*. Its reflections are echoed throughout the remainder of the text, so that its unconventional arguments and imagery not only warrant analysis in their own right, but also provide an indispensable basis for any comprehensive treatment of the *Trojanerkrieg*'s metapoetics. While prologues are generally privileged spaces for reflections on the nature and function of poetry, Konrad's introduction to his monumental work is particularly rich – not only with regard to its metapoetic content, but also with regard to its mode of discourse, which ranges from explicit theoretical argumentation to obscure metaphors. The prologue explores the frequently paradoxical peculiarities of poetry from the angles of production, product and reception. Since previous research has often focused on individual aspects such as the famous nightingale simile or the concept of retextualization, it will be important to treat the prologue

1 The two manuscripts in question are St. Gallen, Stiftsbibliothek, Cod. 617 (the beginning of the prologue is missing) and Strasbourg, Johanniter-Bibliothek, A. 90 (burned in 1870); on the transmission of the prologue, see Lienert, 'Die Überlieferung', pp. 389–90. Parts of the prologue are transmitted in a fragment described by Hartmut Beckers, 'Brüsseler Bruchstücke', *ZfdA*, 124 (1995), 319–27.

2 Sebastian Coxon, *The Presentation of Authorship in Medieval German Narrative Literature: 1220–1290* (Oxford: Clarendon, 2001), pp. 122–23.

as a whole to uncover its tightly knit coherences as well as its apparent inconsistencies. In addition to this, special attention will be devoted to the evaluation and contextualization of the prologue's core images, such as the bad audience as bats or the poet's tongue as an anchor, which have never been discussed in any detail.

Before Konrad turns his attention to the topic of the *Trojanerkrieg* in particular, describing the exceptional demands of his literary project, naming its subject matter and his patron, he devotes a considerable portion of the prologue to the discussion of the status of literature in society.[3] Since the rich and explicit metapoetic material of the prologue presents the basis for analysis in the following chapters and because it is necessary to explore the broad tradition of its partly uncharted imagery as well as to represent the extensive and controversial scholarly debate, this chapter will be the longest in the study. It is therefore divided into three focal sections. The first section treats the representation of the relationship between the poet and the audience, which has at times been read as a revolutionary concept of artistic autonomy. The second section evaluates Konrad's theoretical argument about the superior status of literature among other arts. The third section deals with the concept of literary renewal that has lately received considerable scholarly attention. This division does not aim at considering these subjects in isolation but follows the general thread of Konrad's argumentative structure.

The Poet and His Audience

Opening with the question 'Waz sol nû sprechen unde sanc?' (*Trojanerkrieg*, l. 1), Konrad paints a rather bleak picture of the conditions of his own poetic enterprise. Despite the fact that there are only a very few masters, 'die wol gebluomter rede pflegent, | diu schoene ist unde waehe' (*Trojanerkrieg*, ll.

3 This division of the prologue into a first part establishing contact with the audience and a second part introducing the specific work corresponds to the definitions of *prologus praeter rem* and *prologus ante rem* by Hennig Brinkmann, 'Der Prolog im Mittelalter als literarische Erscheinung: Bau und Aussage', *Wirkendes Wort*, 14 (1964), 79–105. However, his influential categorization and terminology have since been criticized for misrepresenting their medieval sources Conrad of Hirsau and John of Garland, who refer to different kinds of prologue rather than to different parts of a prologue. This issue is discussed by Samuel Jaffe, 'Gottfried von Straßburg and the rhetoric of history', in *Medieval Eloquence: Studies in the Theory and Practice of Medieval Rhetoric*, ed. by James J. Murphy (Berkeley: University of California Press, 1978), pp. 288–318; Haug, *Literaturtheorie*, pp. 12–15; and Eckart Conrad Lutz, *Rhetorica Divina: Mittelhochdeutsche Prologgebete und die rhetorische Kultur des Mittelalters*, Quellen und Forschungen zur Sprach- und Kulturgeschichte der germanischen Völker, 82 (Berlin: de Gruyter, 1984), pp. 10–11, pp. 50–64. Lutz proposes alternative origins for the two-part scheme of medieval prologues.

12–13), they are no longer appreciated. Instead, society perversely celebrates artless words and disregards good literature.[4] Konrad manages to put his own spin on what might otherwise be considered a generic *Zeitklage* by illustrating the unfavourable situation with a number of memorable similes. Although they might appear unconnected at first, they are held together by the fact that they cast the elements of the uneasy relationship between poetry, poet and audience in images of winged creatures: the phoenix, the bat and the nightingale.[5] The following discussion will focus on each of them in order of appearance.

The Phoenix of Poetry

Konrad emphasizes the absurdity of contemporary literary tastes by contrasting them to a basic economic principle of everyday experience: rare things are usually valued higher than those that are available in abundance (*Trojanerkrieg*, ll. 14–19). He applies this mercantile rule to literature in his *Partonopier* prologue as well, where it is expressed *ex negativo* as a process of inflation: things that are very common are not valued; poetry has become so common and is practised by so many unskilled poets, who are likened to larks, that the voice of the true poet is silenced by their clamour and goes unappreciated.[6] Although both prologues raise similar concerns, the reproach in the *Partonopier* prologue is primarily targeted at unskilled rivals, whereas criticism in the *Trojanerkrieg* prologue focuses more on the unappreciative audience. The first example that Konrad adduces in the *Trojanerkrieg* in order to illustrate the principle of valuation by availability is the orphan gemstone in the imperial crown. It is held in high esteem precisely because of the uniqueness to which it owes its name (*Trojanerkrieg*, ll. 20–23). The orphan gemstone as an image for accomplished poetry also appears in the prologue of Heinrich von dem Türlin's *Die Krone*: just as the orphan gemstone is surrounded by lesser gems that are improved by this vicinity, so can the perfect wisdom and skill of the masters of poetry cast some of their splendour onto lesser poets like

4 The complaint resembles Gottfried's criticism of the lack of judgement in his times: 'Ir ist sô vil, die des nu pflegent, | daz si daz guote z'übele wegent, | daz übel wider ze guote wegent: | die pflegent niht, si widerpflegent' (Gottfried von Straßburg, *Tristan*, ed. by Walter Haug and Manfred Günter Scholz, trans. by Walter Haug, Bibliothek des Mittelalters, 10 (Berlin: Deutscher Klassiker Verlag, 2011), ll. 29–32).

5 This connection is pointed out by Seus, *Heilsgeschichten vor dem Heil?*, p. 119.

6 Konrad von Würzburg, *Partonopier und Meliur – Turnei von Nantheiz – Sant Nicolaus – Lieder und Sprüche*, ed. by Karl Bartsch (Wien: Braunmüller, 1871), ll. 68–103. A detailed analysis of the *Partonopier* prologue is provided by Haug, *Literaturtheorie*, pp. 351–61; Trude Ehlert, 'Zu Konrads von Würzburg Auffassung vom Wert der Kunst und von der Rolle des Künstlers', *JOWG*, 5 (1988/1989), 79–94 (pp. 81–89).

Heinrich himself.[7] Even though the thrust of the argument is quite different, the qualities of the stone highlighted in Heinrich's simile are also implicit in Konrad's comparison. Based on its position in the imperial crown and on its metonymic representation of the Empire, the orphan gemstone emphasizes not only the rarity but also the supreme status of artful literature, which, like the endogenous stone, can act like a beacon to society and, in Heinrich's case, to other poets.[8]

The second example Konrad presents to support his point that the few true masters of literature ought to be celebrated by their audience is the phoenix, which would surely be valued higher than an ordinary sparrowhawk because there is always only one specimen of the bird in existence: 'jô lebt er alterseine | und wart nie sîn genôz erkant' (*Trojanerkrieg*, ll. 38–39).[9] The connotations of the simile, however, transgress this explicit point of comparison. The introductory images of the orphan gemstone and the phoenix not only serve to underline the precious rarity of poetry, but also anchor the complaint firmly in the courtly realm. While the orphan gemstone is *per se* a symbol of aristocratic hierarchy, the phoenix is imagined as the ultimate courtly accessory, a hunting bird distinguishing its aristocratic owner through its exotic uniqueness:

7 Heinrich von dem Türlin, *Die Krone*, ed. by Fritz Peter Knapp and others, 2 vols, Altdeutsche Textbibliothek, 112, 118 (Tübingen: Niemeyer, 2000–05), ll. 40–72.

8 Walther von der Vogelweide also emphasizes the guiding function of the orphan gemstone and the office it represents by describing it as 'aller fürste leitsterne' (Walther von der Vogelweide, *Spruchlyrik*, ed. and trans. by Günther Schweikle (Stuttgart: Reclam, 1994), L 18,29). The symbolic meaning of the orphan gemstone is discussed by Ulrich Engelen, *Die Edelsteine in der deutschen Dichtung des 12. und 13. Jahrhunderts*, Münstersche Mittelalter-Schriften, 27 (Munich: Fink, 1978), pp. 381–83.

9 The uniqueness of the phoenix is mentioned, for example, by Clement I in *The Apostolic Fathers*, trans. by Kirsopp Lake, 2 vols (Cambridge, MA: Harvard University Press, 1912–13; repr. 1965), II, pp. 1–121 (XXV, 2); and in some Middle High German Alexander romances: Straßburger Alexander: 'nist wen der eine' (Pfaffe Lambrecht: *Alexanderroman*, ed. and trans. by Elisabeth Lienert (Leipzig: Reclam, 2007), l. 5155); 'Ir wirt nymmer erkant | In der werlt dan ainer allain' (*Der Grosse Alexander aus der Wernigeroder Handschrift*, ed. by Gustav Guth, Deutsche Texte des Mittelalters, 13 (Berlin: Weidmann, 1908), ll. 4762–63). The tradition of the phoenix myth is treated by Heimo Reinitzer, 'Vom Vogel Phoenix: Über Naturbetrachtung und Naturdeutung', in *Natura loquax: Naturkunde und allegorische Deutung vom Mittelalter bis zur frühen Neuzeit*, ed. by Wolfgang Harms and Heimo Reinitzer, Mikrokosmos: Beiträge zur Literaturwissenschaft und Bedeutungsforschung, 7 (Frankfurt a.M.: Lang, 1981), pp. 17–72; J. Gruber and J. Engemann, 'Phoenix', in *Lexikon des Mittelalters*, ed. by Robert-Henri Bautier and others, 10 vols (Munich: Artemis & Winkler, 1980–99), VI (1993), cols 2106–07; Lutz Käppel, 'Phoenix [5]', in *Der neue Pauly: Enzyklopädie der Antike*, ed. by Hubert Cancik and Helmuth Schneider, 16 vols (Stuttgart: Metzler, 1996–2003), IX (2000), cols 937–38. The role of the phoenix in Alexander romances is discussed by Christoph Gerhardt, 'Der Phönix auf dem dürren Baum ('Historia de preliis', cap. 106)', in *Natura loquax*, ed. by Harms and Reinitzer, pp. 73–108.

flüg er ûf eines herren hant,
mich diuhte wol gefüege,
daz er in gerner trüege
denn einen sperwaere,
der niht sô fremde waere
noch alsô tiure worden. (*Trojanerkrieg*, ll. 40–45)

Valuing or even supporting skilful poetry as a patron thus appears as the most effective instrument of courtly representation. Although Konrad proclaims at one point that good literature ought to be appreciated at court and elsewhere (*Trojanerkrieg*, l. 139), yet is disregarded by rich and poor alike (*Trojanerkrieg*, l. 9), his reproach is targeted quite specifically at the German nobility (*Trojanerkrieg*, l. 48). The basic paradox he bewails and underlines by his choice of words is that noble literature ('sprechen höfelich' (*Trojanerkrieg*, l. 59); 'edele sprüche' (*Trojanerkrieg*, l. 151)) is not valued by noblemen and at court ('liuten adelbaere' (*Trojanerkrieg*, l. 55); 'ze hofe' (*Trojanerkrieg*, l. 162)).[10]

In addition to this, Konrad refers to another prominent feature of the wondrous bird, the fact that it is reborn from its own ashes: 'ze pulver sich der brennet, | dar ûz er lebende wider wirt' (*Trojanerkrieg*, ll. 34–35). Based on this trait, Kern reads the phoenix example as an expression of Konrad's ambition to revive the art of poetry:

> Der Niedergang der Kunstdisziplin verspricht – im Bild des Phönix gedacht – eine im vorliegenden Roman vollzogene Wiedergeburt, die auf das Alte rekurriert und es zugleich einzustellen weiß. Ein neuer poetischer Phönix wird sich aus der Asche der Meister erheben und ist sich dessen, was er hinter sich lässt, mindestens ebenso bewusst wie dessen, was er dem alten Phönix schuldet.[11]

While Kern describes the relationship between the old and the new phoenix as one not only of *imitatio* but also of *aemulatio* and distinction, Konrad places a curious emphasis on the identity of the old and the renewed bird: 'sô daz kein ander vogel birt | sîn fleisch und sîn gebeine' (*Trojanerkrieg*, ll. 36–37). It was, in fact, a matter of learned debate as to whether another phoenix or the very same bird is born from the ashes of the old. Thus Clement I defends the belief in resurrection by citing the example of the phoenix: after the bird has ended its lifespan of five hundred years, a worm is nurtured from its decaying

10 He voices a similar complaint in one of his didactic poems, where he accuses noblemen of ignoring good poets while rewarding the unskilled imposters (*Lieder und Sprüche*, 32, 166–95).

11 Manfred Kern, *Weltflucht: Poesie und Poetik der Vergänglichkeit in der weltlichen Dichtung des 12. bis 15. Jahrhunderts*, Quellen und Forschungen zur Literatur- und Kulturgeschichte, 54 (Berlin: de Gruyter, 2009), p. 434.

remains which then grows wings and becomes a new phoenix that carries the bones of its predecessor from Arabia to Egypt. This description, as Reinitzer points out, relies on the specific concept of resurrection influenced by the teachings of Paul the Apostle, 'daß zwischen Erdenleib und Auferstehungsleib zwar Kontinuität, nicht aber Identität bestünde, der neue Leib ein aufgrund göttlicher Gnade erweckter und verwandelter sei'. Other authors, however, such as Cyril of Jerusalem, who bases his argument on Clement, stress that it is in fact the very same bird which is reborn, thereby propagating the idea of 'Auferweckung des gestorbenen Leibes in materieller Identität' that remained dominant throughout the following millenium.[12] In Konrad's time this position was again revised by Thomas Aquinas's teachings, which proposed a complicated relationship between the old and the resurrected body. According to this model the resurrected body is formed from the same material as the mortal body; but without the form of the soul this material resembles the *materia prima* so that the border between re-creation and new creation is blurred.[13] Reinitzer demonstrates that this learned discussion permeated vernacular literature with reference to a poem by der Marner, who still claims the identity of the old and the new bird – 'der fênix der verbrennet sich und lebet nâch dem viure wider'[14] – and der Meißner, who rejects this opinion polemically and insists on distinction: 'der verbrennet sich unt wirt, so sagent die pfaffen, | ûz der aschen ein ander'.[15] In the spectrum of this contemporary debate, Konrad clearly represents the more traditional notion that it is the very same bird which is reborn from its own ashes.[16] Apart from the *Trojanerkrieg* prologue this can also be observed in the *Goldene Schmiede*, where he likens the incarnation of God that overcomes original sin to the phoenix which rejuvenates itself in the fire.[17] Since the religious symbolism of the phoenix is never made explicit in the *Trojanerkrieg*, it remains purely speculative as to whether Konrad's insistence on the identity of the bird indicates a commitment to a more orthodox concept of resurrection. In any case, the vital importance of literary renewal is suggested by the choice of an image that is traditionally associated with some of the core mysteries of Christian belief. The choice between two rival accounts of the bird's renewal

12 Reinitzer, 'Vom Vogel Phoenix', p. 23.

13 Reinitzer, 'Vom Vogel Phoenix', p. 24.

14 *Der Marner*, ed. by Philipp Strauch (Berlin: de Gruyter, 1965), XV,15, l. 294.

15 Der Meißner, 'Zurechtweisung', in *Mittelalter: Texte und Zeugnisse*, ed. by Helmut de Boor, 2 vols (Munich: Beck, 1965), I, pp. 899–901, II, 24–25.

16 In contrast to this see *Der Große Alexander*: 'Da wechset dan ain würmlein, | Daz wirt zu ainem fogellein, | Dar aüz ein ander fenix wirt | Der nymmer ander vogel pirt' (ll. 4773–76).

17 Konrad von Würzburg, *Die Goldene Schmiede*, ed. by Edward Schröder (Göttingen: Vandenhoeck & Ruprecht, 1926), ll. 364–89.

has consequences for the proposed concept of literary renewal. It presents the opportunity to position it on the scale between the old and the new. By siding with the more traditional theory Konrad highlights the aspects of continuity and identity, instead of emphasizing the aspects of novelty and difference as Kern suggests.[18] In addition to underlining the rare and supreme status of artful poetry, locating it in the realm of courtly values and representation, and announcing the ambition to revive a lost cultural tradition, the phoenix simile thus also foregrounds the issue of retextualization that is encapsulated in the term *erniuwen*.

The Bad/Bat Audience

The hostile audience are characterized as courtiers who are blind or dark with regard to courtly virtues such as 'êre' (*Trojanerkrieg*, l. 10), 'bescheidenheit' (*Trojanerkrieg*, l. 143) and 'wîsliche huote' (*Trojanerkrieg*, l. 164) and therefore stand in stark opposition to the moral and courtly attributes associated with good literature ('guot' (*Trojanerkrieg*, l. 29); 'edel' and 'tugentsam' (*Trojanerkrieg*, l. 151)). Konrad thus contrasts a concept of nobility by birth with that of a more exclusive, inner nobility, which is above all manifested in literary taste. This operation resembles Gottfried's setting up of his ideal audience of the 'edele herzen' (*Tristan*, ll. 45–124), a concept that has obviously resonated with Konrad as he adopts the term to address the benevolent audience in the *Partonopier* prologue (*Partonopier*, l. 226). Starting out with a general criticism of the literary audience of his time, Konrad eventually narrows his reproach down to a specific group of courtiers, the 'wilden junges muotes' (*Trojanerkrieg*, l. 142), who are blind and deaf with regard to 'bescheidenheit'. Like the quality of nobility, which is presented as a state of mind rather than a birthright, the group of those whose minds are young and unruly is not characterized by biological age, but by an inner, moral immaturity, because soon afterwards Konrad declares that he can expect appreciation from neither young nor old (*Trojanerkrieg*, l. 179).[19] These philistines, who mistake base and rotten things for the radiant gem of good poetry, act like a bat, which flies at night and mistakes the gleaming of a rotting piece of wood for true light:

18 The phoenix simile is discussed briefly by Seus, who points out that the phoenix can be a symbol of the Resurrection and deduces that Konrad's simile might therefore point to the divine inspiration of poetry. She furthermore makes a connection between the phoenix burning to ashes and Jason and Hercules burning to death in the story: the fact that, unlike these heroes, poetry can overcome this irreversible destruction makes it unique (*Heilsgeschichten vor dem Heil?*, pp. 119–20).

19 That bescheidenheit is not the exclusive property of old age is also shown in the *Partonopier* prologue (ll. 1–5), where a 'jungelinc' qualifies as 'bescheiden' because he likes to listen to poetry.

si tuont der fledermiuse
gelîch, diu nahtes fliuget,
daz si der glanz betriuget
an einem fûlen spâne,
daz si lebt in dem wâne,
daz von dem holze fiuhte
ein wârez lieht dâ liuhte
und ein gar endelicher schîn.
sus kan ze hofe manger sîn
sô finster an dem muote
und an wîslicher huote
sô gar unmâzen tunkel,
daz als ein lieht karfunkel
ein fûler und ein boeser funt
in sînes trüeben herzen grunt
vür edele sprüche schînet. (*Trojanerkrieg*, ll. 154–69)

First of all, the carbuncle, which was often identified with the ruby, recalls the orphan gemstone and lends some coherence to an apparently eclectic mix of similes. Both stones represent accomplished poetry and were thought to radiate light endogenously to illuminate the darkness. Based on this quality, they can be likened to the Virgin guiding man out of the darkness of sin or defeating darkness altogether.[20] In this religious context the carbuncle also appears in an elaborate simile in Konrad's *Goldene Schmiede*, where it is also contrasted to the dim gleaming of rotten wood, which, unlike the stone, appears radiant only in the darkness. Just as the light of day outshines the weak shimmer of decaying wood, so the dawn of the Virgin and the sun of Christ outshine the deceptive splendour of heathendom:

ein holz erworden liuhtet
die naht als ein karfunkel,
und wirt dann aber tunkel,
so der tac uf dringet hie:
frouwe, sich, also zergie
von dinem claren schine ganz
des valschen ungelouben glanz,

20 See Engelen, *Die Edelsteine*, pp. 324–27, 381–83. Der Stricker also mentions the phenomenon of shimmering rotting wood, but rather than contrasting it to endogenous gemstones like Konrad, he emphasizes this similarity as a case in point for his argument that gemstones do not possess magic powers and are quite overrated: 'Sô hât der edel rubîn | von sîner art solhen schîn, | daz man in wol siht in der naht. | ein fûlez holz hât ouch die maht, | daz man ez nahtes wol siht | unt enahtet dar ûf niemen niht' (*Kleinere Gedichte von dem Stricker*, ed. by Karl August Hahn, Bibliothek der gesammten deutschen National-Literatur von der ältesten bis auf die neuere Zeit, 18 (Quedlinburg: Basse, 1839), X, 193–98).

der, als ein holz erfulet gar,
in tumber liute sinne dar
sin trügelichez schinen bot,
e du, vil liehtez morgenrot,
uf gegangen wærest
und Jesum Crist gebærest,
den eweclichen sunnenschin. (*Goldene Schmiede*, ll. 672–85)[21]

The unusual motif of the bat that is erroneously attracted to a light source plays no role in the *Goldene Schmiede*, but can instead be found in two of Konrad's didactic poems, where it exemplifies human vices and poor moral judgement. In one case, the presumptuous man who wants to decorate himself with a radiant prestige he does not merit is compared to a bat that is attracted to the glint of a sword on which it cuts itself to death (*Lieder und Sprüche*, 24, 18–34). In the other case, the bat that mistakes the deceptive gleaming of a rotten piece of wood for real light serves as a simile for the stingy rich man without virtue who mistakenly assumes that his shining garb is sufficient to provide him with radiant nobility (*Lieder und Sprüche*, 25, 61–80).

As a nocturnal animal the bat was considered to be a rather sinister creature throughout the Middle Ages. The Bible counts bats among the impure animals.[22] In superstition they are often associated with demonic powers, witches or the devil and are thought to herald death or bad luck.[23] Apart from some Alexander romances in which Alexander and his men are attacked by large bats during their Oriental expedition,[24] bats rarely play a role in Middle High German narrative texts. In didactic texts, however, they exemplify human vices such as opportunism, envy or pretentiousness because they were believed to occupy a hybrid status between birds and mice.[25] While

21 For similes contrasting the full brightness of the divine light to a weaker light, for example comparing the sun of Christ to the stars and the moon representing the prophets of the Old Testament, see Gudrun Schleusener-Eichholz, *Das Auge im Mittelalter*, 2 vols, Münstersche Mittelalter-Schriften, 35 (Munich: Fink, 1985), I, pp. 154–55.

22 Deuteronomy 14.18; Leviticus 11.19; Isaiah 2.20.

23 Richard Riegler, 'Fledermaus', in *Handwörterbuch des deutschen Aberglaubens*, ed. by Hanns Bächtold-Stäubli, 10 vols (Berlin: de Gruyter, 1927–42), II (1929–30), cols 1579–98; Dietrich Schmidtke, 'Fledermaus', in *Enzyklopädie des Märchens: Handwörterbuch zur historischen und vergleichenden Erzählforschung*, ed. by Kurt Ranke and others, 13 vols (de Gruyter: Berlin, 1977–2009), IV (1984), cols 1248–56; Christian Hünemörder, 'Fledermaus', in *Lexikon des Mittelalters*, ed. by Bautier and others, IV (1989), cols 540–41.

24 Ulrich von Etzenbach, *Alexander*, ed. by Wendelin Toischer (Tübingen: Litterarischer Verein Stuttgart, 1888), ll. 25631–44, ll. 25775–88; *Der Große Alexander*, ll. 3693–708; *Seifrits Alexander*, ed. by Paul Gereke, Deutsche Texte des Mittelalters, 36 (Berlin: Weidmann, 1932), ll. 5609–25.

25 Schmidtke, 'Fledermaus', cols 1250–52; Hans-Ulrich Seifert, 'Fledermaus', in *Thesaurus proverbiorum medii aevi: Lexikon der Sprichwörter des romanisch-germanischen Mittelalters*,

this generally negative connotation has probably influenced Konrad's simile, he seems predominantly to have been inspired by the learned tradition of the bat as an image for the limitations of human cognition. Although there was some controversy about the question as to whether the bat has very good eyes because it can navigate in the dark, or is instead blind,[26] the comparisons in question are based on the opinion that the bat, as a nocturnal animal, either cannot bear the light of the sun or does not even see it at all. Since light is a pervasive metaphor for the divine[27] – a tradition which has clearly influenced Konrad, as the quotation from the *Goldene Schmiede* above exemplifies – the bat, as well as other nocturnal or supposedly blind animals like the owl or the mole, is used to illustrate either the inability of the human soul to recognize God or, in a more negative sense, the unwillingness to turn to God.[28] Thus in his *Itinerarium Mentis in Deum* Bonaventure quotes and expands on a bat-simile by Aristotle[29] to explain why the human soul cannot behold the divine light:

> Mira igitur est caecitas intellectus, qui non considerat illud quod prius videt et sine quo nihil potest *cognoscere*. Sed sicut oculus intentus in varias colorum differentias lucem, per quam videt cetera, non videt, et si videt, non advertit; sic oculus mentis nostrae, intentus in entia *particularia* et *universalia*, ipsum esse *extra omne genus*, licet primo occurrat menti, et per ipsum alia, tamen non advertit. Unde verissime apparet, quod 'sicut oculus vespertilionis se habet ad lucem, ita se habet oculus mentis nostrae ad manifestissima naturae;' quia assuefactus ad tenebras entium et phantasmata sensibilium, cum ipsam lucem summi esse intuetur, videtur sibi nihil videre; non intelligens, quod ipsa caligo summa est mentis nostrae illuminatio, sicut, quando videt oculus puram lucem, videtur sibi nihil videre.

> [How remarkable, then, is the blindness of the intellect which does not take note of that which it sees first, and without which it can know nothing. But just as the eye, when it is concerned with the variety of colors, does not see the light through

ed. by Kuratorium Singer, 13 vols (Berlin: de Gruyter, 1995–2002), III (1996), pp. 282–83; Riegler, 'Fledermaus', cols 1579–82.

26 For the learned debate on this question see Riegler, 'Fledermaus', cols 1582–84; Hünemörder, 'Fledermaus', cols 540–41.

27 Hans Blumenberg, 'Licht als Metapher der Wahrheit: Im Vorfeld der philosophischen Begriffsbildung', *Studium Generale*, 10 (1957), 432–47.

28 Seifert, 'Fledermaus', pp. 282–83; Schleusener-Eichholz, *Das Auge im Mittelalter*, pp. 180–87. Heinrich der Teichner, for example, compares Jews, heathens and heretics, who do not want to be saved by the Virgin, to owls, bats and moles, which flee the sun (Heinrich der Teichner, *Gedichte*, ed. by Heinrich Niewöhner, 3 vols, Deutsche Texte des Mittelalters, 44, 46, 48 (Berlin: Akademie, 1953–1956), II (1954), 465).

29 Aristotle, *The Metaphysics*, trans. by Hugh Tredennick, Loeb Classical Library, 271 (Cambridge, MA: Harvard University Press, 1933; repr. 1968), II.

which it sees other things, or if it sees it, pays no attention to it, so the eye of our mind, intent as it is on particular and universal beings, pays no attention to that being which is beyond every genus even though it is that which first comes to the mind, and it is through this that all other things are known. Therefore it seems to be very true that 'as the eye of a bat is related to light, so the eye of our mind is related to the most evident things of nature.' Accustomed as it is to the darkness of things and to the phantasms of sensible objects, when the mind looks upon the light of the highest being, it seems to see nothing. And it does not understand that this darkness itself is the highest illumination of our mind, just as when the eye sees pure light it seems to it that it sees nothing.][30]

Even though the simile of the bat's eyes as an image of man's limited capacity for recognizing the divine is not attested in Middle High German before the *Trojanerkrieg*,[31] it seems very likely that Konrad was aware of this tradition. He and his clerical patron Dietrich were undoubtedly familiar with the learned discourse on sight and cognition that informs it. The bat-like, limited human mind in Bonaventure does not turn to complete darkness, but towards the lesser, deceptive light of the Creation, which is merely a reflection of the divine light. Just like the human mind, which cannot perceive the ultimate light of God, the bad courtiers in the *Trojanerkrieg* are unable to appreciate the real light and true gem of good poetry and are attracted instead to the lesser light of artless literature. While we have seen that in his didactic poems Konrad does not use the motif of the misguided bat to teach a particularly religious lesson, the term 'wârez lieht' attributed to good literature in the *Trojanerkrieg* clearly resonates with the concept of divine truth.[32] The idea of the divine

30 Bonaventure, *Itinerarium Mentis in Deum*, ed. by Quaracchi, trans. by Philotheus Boehner (Mansfield, OH: The Franciscan Institute, 2002), V, 4, pp. 114–15. On the notion that the divine light blinds the deficient human soul and appears dark as a consequence, see Schleusener-Eichholz, *Das Auge im Mittelalter*, p. 150; Blumenberg, 'Licht als Metapher der Wahrheit', 435, 441.

31 Heinrich Seuse's discussion of the nature of God in his Vita is basically a translation of Bonaventure and in the Grosses Briefbuch Seuse warns that many people are so blind that they turn their love towards visible things because they cannot see the eternal light itself. They are like somebody turning away from the sun towards the bottom of a cauldron, like the bat fleeing the day and seeking the night (Heinrich Seuse, *Deutsche Schriften*, ed. by Karl Bihlmeyer (Stuttgart: Minerva, 1907; repr. 1961), *Vita*, LI, *Grosses Briefbuch*, VII); similarly Heinzelein von Konstanz: 'Menschlicher sîn die wîsheit dîn | begrîfen mac mit nihte. | uns seit die schrift, daz unser sin | gein gotes kunst sich rihte | sam gegen des liehten sunnen schîn | der fledermiuse gesihte' (Heinzelein von Konstanz, *Von den zwein Sanct Johansen*, ed. by Franz Pfeiffer (Leipzig: Weigel, 1852), 75, 1–6).

32 On light as a metapoetic metaphor in twelfth-century German literature, see Schneider, who points out the close association of light and language in Genesis and shows how the poetic work can be presented as a reflection of divine light (Almut Schneider, 'Licht-Bilder: Zur Metaphorik poetischer Sprechweisen in frühmittelhochdeutschen Texten', in *Im Wortfeld des Textes*, ed. by Dicke, Eikelmann and Hasebrink, pp. 189–209).

darkness that is really misunderstood brightness furthermore offers a model for understanding why the human bats should not only mistake weak literature for good literature, but also consider good literature weak or dark. Finally, the reason why the bad courtiers do not recognize true light – a lack of virtue causes darkness of their minds – accords with the reason given by theologians for the inability of the human soul to recognize God: the darkness of the soul. According to the Platonic principle that like can only be known by like, the eye can recognize light only because it resembles it. Whatever is brighter than the eye, such as the light of the sun, cannot be seen directly. By analogy, the eye of the human soul that is darkened by original sin or individual vices cannot perceive the divine light directly unless it is enlightened by divine grace.[33] Likewise, in Konrad's prologue a dull heart cannot recognize the splendour of good poetry, a mind lacking 'wîsliche huote' cannot possibly appreciate 'edele sprüche tugentsam'. This principle of cognition can also be found in the *Goldene Schmiede*, in which Konrad likens the Virgin, who is so utterly free from doubt that she is the only human whose heart can behold the divine light fully, to an eagle, which is the only creature that can bear to gaze directly into the sun:

> kein dinc mag an der sunnen schin
> geblicken, sunder lougen,
> so vaste mit den ougen
> so der selbe vogel tuot:
> davon zel ich in, frouwe guot,
> bezeichenlichen wol ze dir.
> nie mensche mit des herzen gir
> noch mit dem gelouben sin
> möht an der gotheite schin
> geblicken also vaste nie
> sam dines herzen ougen ie
> taten und ouch iemer tuont. (*Goldene Schmiede*, ll. 1110–21)[34]

33 Schleusener-Eichholz, *Das Auge im Mittelalter*, pp. 137, 143–45, 152–54, 158–59, 160–64. See also Artur Schneider, 'Der Gedanke der Erkenntnis des Gleichen durch Gleiches in antiker und patristischer Zeit', in *Abhandlungen zur Geschichte der Philosophie des Mittelalters: Festgabe Clemens Baeumker zum 70. Geburtstag*, ed. by Franz Ehrle and others, Beiträge zur Geschichte der Philosophie des Mittelalters, 2 (Münster: Aschendorff, 1923), pp. 65–77.

34 For the tradition of and variations on this motif see Florence McCulloch, *Medieval Latin and French Bestiaries*, University of North Carolina Studies in the Romance Languages and Literatures, 33 (Chapel Hill: University of North Carolina Press, 1960), pp. 113–15; Vroni Mumprecht, 'Adler', in *Thesaurus proverbiorum medii aevi*, ed. by Kuratorium Singer, I, pp. 40–43; Schleusener-Eichholz, *Das Auge im Mittelalter*, p. 153. The belief that only the eagle's eyes are bright enough to behold the sun is also implicit in the *Trojanerkrieg*: in his fight against Hector, Peleus wears the wings and the head of an eagle whose eyes burn like two gemstones and thus indicate this special capacity (*Trojanerkrieg*, ll. 3836–47). This detail is

Drawing on the learned and religious discourse of cognition, the bat simile in the *Trojanerkrieg* proposes a paradoxical model for the reception of the work. On the one hand, the text composed of 'worten lûter unde glanz' (*Trojanerkrieg*, l. 275) can be identified with the true light of valuable literature. On the other hand, the audience who are most sorely in need of its light, which provides 'ein bilde ûf tugentrîchez leben | und ûf bescheidenliche tât' (*Trojanerkrieg*, ll. 264–65) as well as 'saelic bilde und edel bîschaft' (*Trojanerkrieg*, ll. 284–85), are the bat-like courtiers whose minds are so darkened by vices that they are effectively prevented from being enlightened by literature. Most importantly, they lack 'bescheidenheit', which is required not only to distinguish good from bad literature, but also to draw the right moral lessons from the text, which presents good as well as bad examples: 'man hoeret übel unde wol | gedenken hie der liute' (*Trojanerkrieg*, ll. 286–87).[35] In the *Engelhard* prologue Konrad articulates his doubts about the power of poetry to educate the wicked more explicitly. At first he declares himself hopeful that the listener who already possesses the quality of 'triuwe' will be encouraged to stick to this value by listening to his story about loyal friendship while the misguided listener might realize his error and become 'triuwe' as well.[36] Then, however, he changes his opinion: wicked people are so stubborn in their wickedness that somebody disloyal will hardly want to listen to a story about loyalty. The precondition for any educative effect is thus already missing:

> wan der ungetriuwe zage
> ungerne dâ belîbet
> dâ man gerne trîbet
> von triuwen guoter mære vil.
> dâ von sô muoz ich unde wil
> komen ûz der zuoversiht
> daz ein triuwelôser wiht
> von disem mære ûf triuwe kome. (*Engelhard*, ll. 182–89)

In the *Trojanerkrieg*, though, Konrad carries on exploring the implications of the seemingly hopeless case of an unappreciative and incorrigible court

---

discussed by Bleumer, 'Zwischen Wort und Bild', p. 130. Achilles' tutor, the Centaur Chiron, also has such bright eyes that he can gaze directly into the sun: 'dâ stuonden ougen under, | diu faster denne ein zunder | ûz sîme kopfe brunnen, | er mohte durch die sunnen | geblicket hân mit der gesiht' (*Trojanerkrieg*, ll. 5929–33).

35 On Middle High German *bescheidenheit* (Lat. *discretio*) as an ethical term which designates the ability to distinguish right from wrong and act accordingly, see Jost Trier, *Der deutsche Wortschatz im Sinnbezirk des Verstandes: Die Geschichte eines sprachlichen Feldes: Von den Anfängen bis zum Beginn des 13. Jahrhunderts* (Heidelberg: Winter, 1931), pp. 308–10.

36 Konrad von Würzburg, *Engelhard*, ed. by Paul Gereke, 3rd rev. edn by Ingo Reiffenstein (Tübingen: Niemeyer, 1982), ll. 152–72.

audience further and proposes a model of self-sufficient poetry that has been the subject of much scholarly debate.

The Poet as a Nightingale

Having established the notion that artful poetry no longer finds a receptive audience, Konrad refuses to give up singing just because nobody values his art. He thereby suggests retrospectively that he in fact counts himself among the few true poets whose lack of appreciation he has just criticized. Even if he wanted to give up his singing, he continues, he could not stop, because the divine gift of composing poetry is an intrinsic part of his existence:

> doch mac ich mîner zungen
> ir ambet niht verbieten,
> ich wil und muoz mich nieten
> getihtes, al die wîle ich lebe. (*Trojanerkrieg*, ll. 180–83)

His calling, however, is not only a burden but also a blessing because he enjoys his own art so much that he will practise it purely for his own pleasure. In the absence of an audience who reward him, the poet becomes his own audience and finds his reward in listening to his own singing: 'ze lône und z'einer hôhen gebe | mir selben üeben mîne kunst' (*Trojanerkrieg*, ll. 184–85). Konrad famously likens his determination to keep on singing, even though it might only be for his own enjoyment, to the behaviour of the nightingale:

> ich taete alsam diu nahtegal,
> diu mit ir sanges dône
> ir selben dicke schône
> die langen stunde kürzet:
> swenn über si gestürzet
> wirt ein gezelt von loube,
> sô wirt von ir daz toube
> gefilde lûte erschellet.
> ir dôn ir wol gefellet,
> durch daz er trûren stoeret,
> ob si dâ nieman hoeret,
> daz ist ir alsô maere,
> als ob ieman dâ waere,
> der si vernemen künde wol. (*Trojanerkrieg*, ll. 192–205)

While the didactic purpose of poetry in general and the *Trojanerkrieg* in particular is reaffirmed at the end of the prologue, the idea of a poet singing only for himself disqualifies this function momentarily. In this passage the end of poetry is presented as purely aesthetic. The motif appears in even more drastic form in the prologue of *Partonopier* (ll. 128–34), where the nightingale sings itself to death, thus emphasizing the existential compulsion of the poet to sing.[37]

Some interpreters have taken the independence from his audience that Konrad proclaims in the *Partonopier* and *Trojanerkrieg* prologues very literally. Burdach contrasts it to the concept of poetry in the *Blütezeit* which, according to him, was still characterized by a natural harmony between life and art, poet and audience. Unlike his predecessors Konrad attempts to remove poetry from ordinary life and even from its audience, an 'Irrtum' he shares with the over-artificial and learned weekend poets of late *Meistersang* and with the *Geniezeit*, beginning with Klopstock, 'wo das Genie aus sich heraus eine neue Welt, eine neue Literatur gebären will, also der Gegensatz zwischen dem Einzel-Ich des Dichters und der übrigen Welt bis zum Widersinn gesteigert ist'.[38] Viëtor also sees Konrad's autonomous stance as a departure from the attitude of the *Blütezeit* poets, who have only 'ein sociales selbstgefühl', but does not pass as damning a judgement when stating that Konrad's poetry has instead 'rechtfertigung und sinn in ihm selbst'.[39] Likewise, Gervinus voices only slight reservations about Konrad's apparent self-sufficiency:

> Eine solche Bescheidenheit und Genügsamkeit möchte vielleicht den Philosophen und überhaupt jeden Mann zieren, der sich vor allem über sich und die Welt aufklären will, wer aber irgend wie mit Kräften seines Geistes wuchern, wer producierend wirken, wer dichtend auftreten will, der drängt sich doch besser [...] in den Kreis der siegreichen Könige und sucht seine Weisheit in der Welt leuchten zu lassen.[40]

Commenting on the nightingale similes and on the *artes* discussion, Gustav Roethe even distinguishes Konrad positively from his contemporaries:

> Was Sunburg, den Meissner und seines Gleichen mit grenzenloser Verachtung herabsehen lässt auf den Pöbel der *künstelôsen*, das ist eben nicht der berechtigte Stolz des gottbegnadeten Dichters, nein, es ist der pure bare Gelehrtenhochmut:

37 Ehlert discusses the nightingale motif in the Middle High German tradition and demonstrates that the direct model for the simile in the *Partonopier* prologue is probably Thomas of Cantimpré's natural history (Ehlert, 'Wert der Kunst', 86–87). Unlike Pliny and Albertus Magnus, who relate that the nightingale sings itself to death in competition with its peers, Thomas says that the nightingale sings itself to death because it loves its own song so much (Thomas of Cantimpré, *Liber de natura rerum*, ed. by H. Boese (Berlin: de Gruyter, 1973), I, 5, 108, 6–8). On possible Medieval Latin models for the *Trojanerkrieg* version of the simile, see Wiebke Freytag, 'Zur Logik *wilder aventiure* in Konrads von Würzburg Paris-Urteil', *JOWG*, 5 (1988/1989), 373–94 (p. 392).

38 Burdach, *Reinmar und Walther*, pp. 29–33 (p. 31).

39 Viëtor, 'Kunstanschauung', 113–15.

40 Gervinus, *Geschichte der poetischen National-Literatur*, p. 473.

> *kunst* ist Studium, Wissenschaft, der Inbegriff der sieben Künste, unter denen die Musik nicht zu vergessen ist: von jener Kunst vor den Künsten, die nicht gelernt werden kann, die durch Gottes Kunst aus dem Herzen spriesst und um ihrer selbst willen da ist, unbekümmert, wie sie Andern gefalle, von dieser *kunst* Konrads von Würzburg wissen die andern Meister Nichts.[41]

Almost a century later, Wolfgang Obst still takes the nightingale at face value and describes Konrad's concept of poetry in the terms of a French artistic movement of the 1830s that is, of course, an expression of very specific socio-cultural circumstances: 'Dichtung braucht nach Konrads Auffassung kein Publikum. Er betreibt *l'art pour l'art*. Er dichtet zur eigenen Freude und Kurzweil'.[42]

While the critics cited above stress the unusual, even revolutionary nature of Konrad's stance, Monecke demonstrates that it is not quite as extraordinary, with reference to Heinrich von Morungen's song 'Ez ist site der nahtegal'.[43] In this song the singer contrasts the nightingale that falls silent once it has finished its song to the swallow that keeps on singing no matter whether it is happy or sad. Morungen then identifies his own need to continue singing, even though people do not appreciate it, with the habit of the latter bird. His stubborn commitment to his art makes Konrad's position appear much less special:

> ôwê,
> daz in ie sô wol gelanc,
> und ich lie dur si mînen sanc!
> ich wil singen aber als ê.[44]

Arguing against the tradition of literal interpretation, Brinkmann cautions that the similes in both the *Partonopier* and *Trojanerkrieg* prologues have to

41 Reinmar von Zweter, *Gedichte*, ed. by Gustav Roethe (Leipzig: Hirzel, 1887; repr. Amsterdam: Rodopi, 1967), p. 187; similarly Essen: 'Die Kunst um der Kunst willen. Der Dichter dichtet um seiner selbst willen' (Erika Essen, *Die Lyrik Konrads von Würzburg* (Marburg: Bauer, 1938), p. 32). Compare also Carl Leo Cholevius, *Geschichte der deutschen Poesie nach ihren antiken Elementen*, 2 vols (Leipzig: Brockhaus, 1854–56), I (1854): *Von der christlich-römischen Cultur des Mittelalters bis zu Wieland's französischer Gräzität*, p. 131.

42 Wolfgang Obst, 'Der Partonopier-Roman Konrads von Würzburg und seine französische Vorlage' (unpublished doctoral thesis, University of Würzburg, 1976), p. 124. On the position of the *l'art pour l'art* movement in the spectrum of the highly diverse concepts of artistic autonomy in modern art discourse see Wolfgang Ullrich, 'Kunst/ Künste/ System der Künste', in *Ästhetische Grundbegriffe: Historisches Wörterbuch*, ed. by Karlheinz Barck, Martin Fontius and Dieter Schlenstedt, 7 vols (Stuttgart: Metzler, 2000–2005), III (2001), pp. 556–616 (pp. 593–605).

43 Monecke, *Das Erzählprinzip der 'wildekeit'*, p. 25.

44 *Des Minnesangs Frühling*, ed. by Karl Lachmann and others, 38th rev. edn by Hugo Moser and Helmut Tervooren (Stuttgart: Hirzel, 1988), 128, 11–14.

be understood in the context of the argument that good literature deserves appreciation and do not mean that Konrad denies the social determination of poetry.[45] Boesch then identifies the similes as serving the traditional exordial strategy of *captatio benevolentiae*, an interpretation which still represents the general consensus today:

> So wenig wie jeder andere mittelhochdeutsche Dichter vermöchte er ohne Anerkennung und Gunst der Welt zu leben. Sein 'Dichterstolz', den man besser vielleicht 'Dichtertrotz' nennen würde, ist durchaus kein absonderliches Sichabwenden, sondern nur eine andere Form seiner werbenden Haltung, der Protest gegen das interesselose Publikum, auf dessen Entgegenkommen, williges Herz und Ohr, es ihm letztlich ankommt.[46]

The projection of a proto-modern concept of autonomy onto the late thirteenth-century text has also been criticized as anachronistic. Kokott assumes that, owning his own house, Konrad had reached a certain amount of financial independence and that his patron Dietrich would not have been so dependent on raising his profile through representation at the end of his career: 'Das ästhetische Interesse könnte so bei beiden die erste Stelle eingenommen haben'.[47] He is, however, careful to distinguish the 'relative künstlerische Freiheit' of the non-aristocratic professional poet from absolute autonomy.[48] Brandt argues similarly that real artistic autonomy, which starts emerging only in the eighteenth century and requires not only a new artistic self-image but also a new type of audience and patronage, should not be confused with the 'eher platte Tatsache, daß sich ein arrivierter Künstler mehr "erlauben" kann als ein weniger erfolgreicher'.[49] The issue of autonomy is also discussed by Lienert, who demonstrates that the *Trojanerkrieg* cannot easily be explained in terms of extra-literary interests. She argues that while social prestige might always be one aspect motivating patronage of an aesthetically pleasing text, and despite the fact that there is some circumstantial evidence suggesting that Dietrich in fact liked rhetorically ornate poetry, this does not explain the choice of subject

45 Brinkmann, *Wesen und Form*, pp. 25–26.

46 Boesch, *Kunstanschauung*, pp. 152–57 (p. 152). Similarly Hans Butzmann, *Studien zum Sprachstil Konrads von Würzburg* (Würzburg: Werkbund, 1930), pp. 18–19; Monecke, *Das Erzählprinzip der 'wildekeit'*, p. 27; Green, *Vorstudien zum gotischen Stil*, p. 49; Brandt, *Konrad von Würzburg*, p. 197, pp. 203–05; Ehlert, 'Wert der Kunst'; Lienert, 'Der Trojanische Krieg in Basel', p. 266 and *Geschichte und Erzählen*, pp. 19–20; Coxon, *Authorship*, pp. 112–16; Müller, '*schîn* und Verwandtes', p. 296; Ursula Schulze, 'Stationen der *ars poetica* auf dem Weg zu ihrer relativen Autonomie', in *Interartifizialität*, ed. by Bürkle and Peters, pp. 93–111 (p. 100); Kellner, 'Poetologie', pp. 252–61.

47 Kokott, *Auftrag und Autonomie*, p. 292.

48 Kokott, *Auftrag und Autonomie*, p. 293.

49 Brandt, *Konrad von Würzburg*, p. 205.

matter or the monumental proportions of the text. There are a multitude of possible interests, including clerical historiographical concerns, Troy as an example of knighthood, courtliness and possibly urban aristocracy, but at the same time no single one of these aspects becomes particularly evident; and it is telling that Konrad makes no attempt at exploiting the ideological potential of the subject for genealogical purposes or to project the events of the Trojan War onto present times. Lienert concludes that the peculiarities of the *Trojanerkrieg*, which uses history as a licence for aesthetic play and aesthetics as the 'einzig denkbare Form der Bewältigung von Leid', cannot be taken to represent Dietrich's interests but reflect Konrad's artistic autonomy.[50] In qualification of Lienert's argument, however, it could be pointed out that the idea of absolute artistic independence evoked by the nightingale simile is most certainly challenged by the praise of Konrad's patron, the cantor Dietrich von Basel an dem Orte,[51] who is presented as the opposite of the 'wilden junges muotes':

> daz ich ez hebe mit willen an,
> dar ûf hât wol gestiuret mich
> der werde singer DIETRICH
> VON BASEL AN DEM ORTE,
> der als ein êren borte
> mit zühten ist gesteinet.
> vor schanden ist gereinet
> sîn herze alsam ein lûter golt.
> durch sîner miltekeite solt,
> den ich hân dicke enpfangen,
> ist von mir an gefangen
> vil snellecliche ein ursuoch,
> der zieren künne wol diz buoch
> mit rede in allen enden. (*Trojanerkrieg*, ll. 244–57)

While the hostile audience lacks all courtly virtues, Dietrich is embellished with noble qualities. Where the bat-like courtier has a dark heart that cannot

50 Lienert, 'Der Trojanische Krieg in Basel', p. 278.

51 On the patronage of Dietrich an dem Orte (also called 'de Fine'), who is documented as the cantor of the Basel Domstift from 1281, see Edward Schröder, 'Studien zu Konrad von Würzburg IV', *Nachrichten von der königlichen Gesellschaft der Wissenschaft zu Göttingen* (1917), 96–116; Inge Leipold, *Die Auftraggeber und Gönner Konrads von Würzburg: Versuch einer Theorie der 'Literatur als soziales Handeln'* (Göppingen: Kümmerle, 1976), pp. 119–27; Kokott, *Auftrag und Autonomie*, p. 263, pp. 283–86; Joachim Bumke, *Mäzene im Mittelalter: Die Gönner und Auftraggeber der höfischen Literatur in Deutschland: 1150–1300* (Munich: Beck, 1979), pp. 262–64; Brandt, *Konrad von Würzburg*, pp. 71–72; Lienert, 'Der Trojanische Krieg in Basel'. For a discussion of the representation of patronage and other forms of support in Konrad's narrative works see Coxon, *Authorship*, pp. 95–141.

recognize valuable literature, Dietrich has a heart like shining gold that is most certainly prepared to see poetry's true light. Most importantly, Konrad cannot expect any 'lôn' for his art from the majority, whereas Dietrich supports him generously. Kellner therefore comments that the independence declared in the nightingale simile refers only to the reception of poetry while the production of poetry is still shown to rely on a patron, a source and divine inspiration, so that the concept of autonomy is very distinct from modern understandings.[52] However, even the gloomy picture of the absence of an appreciative audience other than the poet himself and his benefactor is soon revealed to be hyperbole. In the *Partonopier* prologue Konrad concedes that, despite a general disregard for good poetry, there is still an exclusive group of noble people who will heed his art (*Partonopier*, ll. 158–67). Likewise, in the *Trojanerkrieg* prologue Konrad addresses his work to those who, unlike the bats, heed the courtly values of *zuht* and *êre* that distinguish Dietrich and are willing to open their ears and hearts to his poetry (*Trojanerkrieg*, ll. 288–89). Before the sympathetic audience gain shape in this target group and its representative, Dietrich, they are already present in the guise of the poet's implied interlocutors, who grant Konrad permission to expand on the topic of the value of good literature (*Trojanerkrieg*, ll. 68–69) and serve as the addressees of his explanations (*Trojanerkrieg*, l. 92, l. 206).[53] Through the direct personal address 'ir', they are clearly distinguished from the group of the bad courtiers, who are referred to only in the third person. Konrad's actual audience do not have to feel criticized but are given the opportunity to prove themselves part of a small aesthetic and moral elite by appreciating his poetry. This strategy for gaining favour with the audience resembles Gottfried's elite of the 'edele herzen', a concept which invites, rather than excludes, the identification of the audience while creating an aura of exclusivity, as Günter Eifler explains:

> Gottfried [legt] grundsätzlich j e d e m m ö g l i c h e n Hörer und Leser die positive Aufnahme seines Werkes nahe [...]. Es gibt keinen Hinweis für eine willentliche Begrenzung des Adressatenkreises auf eine kleine elitäre Lesergemeinde. [...] Auch die durch diesen Namen ['edele herzen'] bezeichnete Rezipientenrolle mit den ihr beigelegten besonderen Eigenschaften [könnte] ein werbendes Identifikationsmuster [...] sein und [muß] nicht unbedingt selektiv abweisend verstanden werden.[54]

52 Kellner, 'Meisterschaft', p. 146.

53 See Ehlert, 'Wert der Kunst', 92.

54 Günter Eifler, 'Publikumsbeeinflussung im strophischen Prolog zum *Tristan* Gottfrieds von Strassburg', in *Festschrift für Karl Bischof zum 70. Geburtstag*, ed. by Günter Bellman, Günter Eifler and Wolfgang Kleiber (Cologne: Böhlau, 1975), pp. 357–89 (p. 388). On the similarity of Gottfried's and Konrad's prologues see Lienert, *Geschichte und Erzählen*, pp. 19–20, pp. 22–23.

The bat and the nightingale similes thus work together to serve the rhetorical function of *captatio benevolentiae*. However, the fact that this rhetorical strategy ultimately aims at the unity of poet and audience does not mean that the artistic autonomy it declares is undermined completely, as Brinkmann rightly stresses: 'Immerhin, auch dann spricht sich sein stolzes Dichterbewußtsein in einer überraschend pointierten Form aus'.[55] No matter how much or how little Konrad's artistic freedom at the end of his career would actually have been restricted by his patron and certain extra-literary interests, the fact remains that he presents himself as a very self-confident artist: although Dietrich's support is appreciated and enables Konrad to pursue his poetic duty, composing poetry is a divine calling and an existential necessity, not primarily a patron's commission. This conclusion is also drawn by Coxon, who describes the *Trojanerkrieg* prologue as the 'most articulate expression of artistic self-assurance' in Konrad's body of literary work, because his reliance on God and his patron are acknowledged only after an extensive discussion of the status of literature and after a special, existential relationship between the author and his subject matter has been established.[56] Konrad cannot and will not give up his high literary standards even if nobody were to appreciate his art – which, luckily, is not the case. Instead, the audience have to prove themselves worthy of his poetry. The bat and the nightingale similes thus express a particularly strong poetic conviction and a complex moral interdependence of poetry and its audience.

'Waz sol nû sprechen unde sanc?'

The function of *captatio benevolentiae* that has been established for the bat and nightingale similes raises the question as to whether the elaborate *Zeitklage* of which they are part can offer any hints about the actual relationship between Konrad and his social and cultural environment or is merely rhetorical. The argumentative logic of the *Zeitklage* topos is captured concisely by Albrecht Juergens: '[J]e drastischer die Klage über Kunst und Publikum, desto eindrücklicher die Widerlegung durch das jeweilige Werk und seine aktuelle Rezeption; die Esoterik des der düsteren Normalität fernen Verfassens und die des Hörens potenzieren sich wechselseitig'.[57] He argues that although it would be problematic to take Konrad's complaints as the authentic expression of his situation, the fact that such complaints are topical does not mean that they cannot also be authentic either. Likewise, Brandt attributes the function

55 Brinkmann, *Wesen und Form*, p. 26.

56 Coxon, *Authorship*, p. 123.

57 Albrecht Juergens, 'Über den Umgang mit Geschichte in Konrads von Würzburg *Trojanerkrieg*-Fragment', *JOWG*, 5 (1988/1989), 431–42 (p. 432).

of *captatio benevolentiae* to this topos, but points out that the *laudatio temporis acti* becomes more common from the second half of the thirteenth century onwards, which might suggest that the complaints were not just rhetorical.[58] While several scholars hold the opinion that Konrad's *Zeitklage* in the *Trojanerkrieg* does indeed reflect a change from the literary situation of the *Blütezeit* to the situation of an urban poet in the late thirteenth century, the specifics of this assumed change vary. Wilhelm Scherer saw Konrad's *Trojanerkrieg* and *Partonopier* prologues as well as the poem *Klage der Kunst* as a sign 'daß die Zeit der Poesie wenig günstig war, daß die Protection abnahm'.[59] Dieter Seitz instead interprets both Konrad's autonomous stance and the emphasis on the practical purpose of literature as a reaction to the utilitarian attitude of the urban audience.[60] Haug, who also assumes a 'Veränderung des Rezeptionsprozesses' in Konrad's time, supports this thesis by contrasting Gottfried's *Tristan* to Konrad's *Engelhard*.[61] As we have already seen above, in the prologue to this work Konrad gives up on the incorrigible audience that does not heed the value of *triuwe* he sets out to propagate. Instead, he has to content himself with encouraging the already loyal:

> ich wil daz den getriuwen frome
> dis âventiure aleine,
> sô daz ir triuwe reine
> dâ von gesterket werden.
> swer nû wil ûf erden
> vernemen ganzer triuwen hort,

58 Brandt, *Konrad von Würzburg*, pp. 198–99.

59 Wilhelm Scherer, *Geschichte der deutschen Litteratur* (Berlin: Weidmann, 1883), p. 190. Similarly Viëtor, 'Kunstanschauung', 118–20; Gustav Ehrismann, *Geschichte der deutschen Literatur bis zum Ausgang des Mittelalters*, 2 vols (Munich: Beck, 1918–35), II, 2, p. 37; Hans Joachim Gernentz, 'Konrad von Würzburg: Charakter und Bedeutung seiner Dichtung', *Weimarer Beträge*, 7 (1961), 27–45 (pp. 33–35); Gerhard P. Knapp, 'Die bedingte Metapher: Ein Beitrag zum frühneuhochdeutschen Roman', in *Kommunikative Metaphorik: die Funktion des literarischen Bildes in der deutschen Literatur von ihren Anfängen bis zur Gegenwart*, ed. by Holger A. Pausch, Studien zur Germanistik, Anglistik und Komparatistik, 20 (Bonn: Bouvier, 1976), pp. 61–80 (pp. 61–62); Barbara Könneker, 'Erzähltypus und epische Struktur des Engelhard: Ein Beitrag zur literaturhistorischen Stellung Konrads von Würzburg', *Euphorion*, 62 (1968), 239–77 (p. 242).

60 Dieter Seitz, 'Konrad von Würzburg', in *Einführung in die deutsche Literatur des 12. bis 16. Jahrhunderts*, ed. by Winfried Frey, Walter Raitz and Dieter Seitz (Opladen: Westdeutscher Verlag, 1982), II, *Patriziat und Landesherrschaft, 13. bis 15. Jahrhundert*, pp. 135–54 (pp. 135–37).

61 Haug, *Literaturtheorie*, p. 360. He also points out another difference between Gottfried's and Konrad's prologues: 'Singen, auch wenn niemand zuhört: diese Forderung steht diametral Gottfrieds Auffassung gegenüber, nach der Kunst ihren Sinn verliert, wenn sie keine Anerkennung findet' (p. 361) (compare Tristan, ll. 21–28). Similarly Kellner, 'Poetologie', pp. 256–57; 'Meisterschaft', pp. 147–48.

der ruoche hœren disiu wort
und neige herze und ôren her. (*Engelhard*, ll. 190–97)[62]

Haug argues that Konrad's position in this passage superficially resembles that of Gottfried, who addresses his work to the small group of noble hearts who are already morally predisposed to relate to it in the right way, but that it is actually quite different. Gottfried composed for a relatively homogeneous aristocratic group at court, which meant that he 'sein Publikum noch fordernd auf sein Thema verpflichten [konnte]'. In contrast to this, Haug goes on, the professional poet Konrad was confronted with a socially heterogeneous urban audience that had in common only a 'Katalog von relativ abstrakten und damit nicht mehr an eine enge Gruppe gebundenen ethischen Werten', so that addressing his work on 'triuwe' to the small group of 'getriuwen' reflects the realities of the necessarily limited effect of his works.[63] Since Konrad proposes the same model of reception in the *Trojanerkrieg* prologue – he disregards the bat-like audience that might benefit most from the moral guidance of his work but is morally indisposed to receive its lessons and turns towards those who heed courtly values instead – Haug's argument can also be applied to this text. Lienert, who points out that the address to an ideal audience reveals the proclaimed didactic function of the *Trojanerkrieg* to be merely topical, while Konrad is in fact interested only in the aesthetic quality of his work, supports Haug's thesis:

> Wenn Konrad nur noch für sich und die wenigen Kenner dichten und höfisches Verhalten nur noch denen vor Augen führen will, die ohnehin bereits höfische Qualitäten besitzen, so deutet dies darauf, daß Kunst zur Sache eines esoterischen Zirkels, einer exklusiven Elite geworden ist, auch wenn Konrad paradoxerweise in den sich durch das Werk ziehenden Publikumsanreden immer wieder ein ganz allgemeines Publikum (*swer*) anspricht. [64]

The strategy of addressing only the benevolent or at least basically good audience and articulating the hopelessness of the bad audience is not uncommon among Middle High German poets.[65] Thomasin, for example,

62 The thought is expressed more aggressively in Konrad's gnomic poems: 'wê daz ein îderslange mac dur herten cokodrillen, | und daz niht gebillen | mîn zunge in arge sinne mac! | swaz ich singe ald ich gesage der valschen rîchen edelen schar, | des nimt si ze kleine war; | ir muot alsô vereinet | an triuwen unde an êren ist, daz si niht tugende meinet [...] Des argen ôre müeze sîn verwâzen und vertüemet, | daz niht wil hœren dâ man tugende rîche liute rüemet' (*Lieder und Sprüche*, 32, 231–42). For a discussion of these statements see Brandt, *Konrad von Würzburg*, p. 204.

63 Haug, *Literaturtheorie*, p. 363.

64 Lienert, 'Der Trojanische Krieg in Basel', pp. 267–72 (p. 267).

65 Boesch provides a list of references (*Kunstanschauung*, pp. 99–106). However, the situation for the bat-like courtiers in the *Trojanerkrieg* does not seem entirely hopeless. After all, they

declares that he does not want his didactic work *Der Welsche Gast* wasted on incorrigible people:

> dehein lêre hât die kraft
> daz si mache tugenthaft
> den an dem tugent niht enist.
> [...]
> ist in einem manne sin,
> swie træge er sî an guoten dingen,
> man mag in doch mit lêre bringen
> ze tugende unde vrümekeit.
> [...]
> alsam macht die lêre wachen
> den sin und kans doch machen niht.
> dâ von ist lêre den tôrn enwiht.[66]

Considering the topical nature of such statements, the interpretations of Haug and Lienert cannot rely on any textual difference between Konrad's address to an exclusive audience and those of earlier poets which would indicate that the former is meant in earnest while the latter is purely rhetorical. They are instead based on assumptions about aspects of reception that would have to be supported by further evidence. I shall therefore provide a brief overview of research on the question of whether Konrad's work reflects socio-cultural circumstances that are markedly distinct from those of courtly authors.

Already Scherer describes Konrad's writing as 'handwerksmäßig' in contrast to his courtly predecessors.[67] Green then argues that, although fascinated by courtly splendour, Konrad did not really understand the knightly ethos any more: despite their uniformly courtly epithets the behaviour of his protagonists is decidedly uncourtly, just like the sexualized concept of love that characterizes the *Trojanerkrieg*.[68] De Boor calls Konrad an 'im Kern nüchterner Bürger einer zum Rationalismus neigenden Zeit',[69] who, as a townsman, cannot describe battles as well as knightly poets like Wolfram von Eschenbach.[70] Konrad's *Heinrich von Kempten* is used as evidence for his post-

are described as having young or inexperienced minds, which suggests that there is still a slim chance for growth if they are exposed, even against their wish, to good literature. Likewise in *Engelhard* Konrad's resignation is not the last word, because in the epilogue he articulates his hope that a disloyal person will feel ashamed of himself if he hears the story of the two loyal friends (*Engelhard*, ll. 6500–04).

66 Thomasin von Zirclaria, *Der Wälsche Gast*, ed. by Heinrich Rückert (Berlin: de Gruyter, 1965), ll. 14641–60.

67 Scherer, *Geschichte der deutschen Litteratur*, p. 190.

68 Green, *Vorstudien zum gotischen Stil*, pp. 45, 51–52, 59–62.

69 De Boor, *Deutsche Literatur im späten Mittelalter*, p. 34.

70 De Boor, *Deutsche Literatur im späten Mittelalter*, p. 39.

courtly perspective by several scholars, albeit with mutually contradictory arguments: Gernentz describes Konrad as a 'frühbürgerlicher Dichter'[71] who readjusts aristocratic values to suit a newly emerging bourgeois ideology and has a 'gesteigerten Realitätssinn mit Ansätzen zu einer Gesellschaftskritik'.[72] He emphasizes the fact that the Emperor is presented negatively in *Heinrich von Kempten*. Hubertus Fischer and Paul-Gerhard Völker, on the other hand, interpret the text as a propagandistic work advocating the already crumbling values of feudal loyalty and aristocratic solidarity in times of violent conflict between the noble clergy and the citizens of Strasbourg. In contrast to Gernentz they highlight the negative description of the citizens plotting an ambush on the Emperor.[73] More recently Lienert has attempted to identify possible reflections of Konrad's urban environment in the *Trojanerkrieg*. She argues that the superlative description of Troy and its noble inhabitants may have presented an aspirational model of identification for the aristocratic citizens of Basel, but also points out that, apart from this, specifically urban topics do not play a role in the text. She concludes that references to contemporary times are extremely rare and that although a few elements such as the remarks about the negative impact of internal strife could be understood to reflect certain political events in Basel, this interpretation is by no means inevitable.[74] Similarly, Bumke emphasizes that the literary tastes of Konrad's patrons from Basel did not differ from those of the courtly patrons of the *Blütezeit* and were, if anything, more conservative than those of contemporary courtly patrons: 'Einem Werk wie dem *Trojanerkrieg* von Konrad von Würzburg ist nicht anzusehen, daß es für ein städtisches Publikum (und im Auftrag eines geistlichen Herrn) gedichtet wurde'.[75] In her study on urban literature in the thirteenth and fourteenth centuries Ursula Peters furthermore demonstrates convincingly that cities like Basel and Strasbourg in fact presented a literary environment very similar to that of the feudal courts, namely:

71 Gernentz, 'Charakter und Bedeutung', 32.

72 Gernentz, 'Charakter und Bedeutung', 43.

73 Hubertus Fischer and Paul-Gerhard Völker, 'Konrad von Würzburg: *Heinrich von Kempten*: Individuum und feudale Anarchie', in *Literaturwissenschaft und Sozialwissenschaften 5: Literatur im Feudalismus*, ed. by Dieter Richter (Stuttgart: Metzler, 1975), pp. 83–130. See also Seitz, who discusses *Engelhard* and *Partonopier* with a similar thesis to Fischer and Völker ('Konrad von Würzburg', pp. 135–54).

74 Lienert, 'Der Trojanische Krieg in Basel'.

75 Bumke, *Mäzene*, pp. 287–90 (p. 293). A similar position is already taken by Ehrismann, *Geschichte der deutschen Literatur*, pp. 35–37; also Joachim Heinzle, *Geschichte der deutschen Literatur von den Anfängen bis zum Beginn der Neuzeit*, 3 vols (Königstein i.T.: Athenäum, 1984–2004), II (1984): *Vom hohen bis zum späten Mittelalter: Wandlungen und Neuansätze im 13. Jahrhundert (1220/30 - 1280/90)*, pp. 50–60; Hartmut Kokott, 'Ein Autor zwischen Auftrag und Autonomie: Konturen eines neuen Konrad von Würzburg-Bildes', *JOWG*, 5 (1988/1989), 69–77 (pp. 69–70).

> eine wohlhabende, aristokratisch lebende Führungsschicht mit einem gemeinsamen Standes- und Elitebewußtsein. Und wie sich das Publikum der Fürstenhöfe und des Landadels aus verschiedenen sozialen Gruppierungen – Angehörigen gräflicher Familien, geistlichen Herren, Freiherren und Ministrialen – zusammensetzt, die als Literaturrezipienten eine homogene höfische Gesellschaft darstellen, so bildet auch in Basel die Gruppe der geistlichen Herren, der *milites* und *cives* trotz möglicher Unterschiede in ihrer wirtschaftlichen, sozialen und politischen Position als aristokratische Elite und Publikum volkssprachiger wie lateinischer Autoren eine Kommunikationsgemeinschaft höfischer Literaturkenner.[76]

Looking at the *Trojanerkrieg* prologue itself there is certainly nothing that sets it apart from courtly literature. It has been shown that Konrad directs his reproach at a noble audience. The orphan gemstone and the phoenix similes as well as adjectives like 'hövelich' and 'edel' present poetry as a particularly aristocratic discipline. The virtues of *zuht* and *êre*, or – in the case of *Engelhard* – *triuwe* which Konrad attributes to his ideal audience would have been neither out of place in courtly texts around 1200 nor controversial among the urban audience of Konrad's time, as Haug suggests. Of course, the concept of *êre* becomes highly problematic in the story of the *Trojanerkrieg*, just as the value of *triuwe* becomes ambivalent in the course of the *Engelhard*.[77] Gernentz argues that *triuwe* is one of the courtly ideals that Konrad 'im bürgerlichen Sinne umformt' so that it no longer designates 'in erster Linie das aus der Feudalität erwachsene Verhältnis zwischen dem Herrn und dem Vasallen, sondern die gesinnungsmäßige Bindung zweier Menschen'.[78] However, this conflict of loyalty certainly does not set the later text apart from its literary model *Tristan* and its concept of *triuwe*.[79] In the absence of any indication to the contrary, I see no compelling reason why Konrad's *Zeitklage* and address to a moral elite in *Engelhard* and the *Trojanerkrieg* should be considered any less rhetorical than that of Gottfried or other *Blütezeit* authors.[80] After

76 Ursula Peters, *Literatur in der Stadt: Studien zu den sozialen Voraussetzungen und kulturellen Organisationsformen städtischer Literatur im 13. und 14. Jahrhundert*, Studien und Texte zur Sozialgeschichte der Literatur, 7 (Tübingen: Niemeyer, 1983), p. 127.

77 See Brandt, *Konrad von Würzburg*, pp. 142–43.

78 Gernentz, 'Charakter und Bedeutung', 38.

79 Kokott argues that the ambivalence of the hero and values like *triuwe*, *minne* and trust in God betray Konrad's sensitivity towards the 'Aporien der von ihm dargestellten Handlung im Rahmen einer höfischen bzw. feudal-adligen Gesellschaft, wie sie dem Roman zugrundeliegt' (Kokott, 'Auftrag und Autonomie', 72–73).

80 Gebert also arrives at the conclusion that Konrad's complaint does not reflect actual historical circumstances but is a strategy to create an aura of exclusivity and intimacy: 'Die Kommunikationsbeziehung als solche wird exklusiv, auch wenn diese Position prinzipiell von jedem Rezipienten eingenommen werden kann' (Gebert, *Mythos als Wissensform*, p. 137, pp. 332–33 (especially p. 332)).

all, Gottfried's very particular definition of his ideal audience as those noble hearts who are willing to tolerate pain for the sake of pleasure probably does not reflect any pre-existing group identity at court but only creates it through this description. In comparison, Konrad's ideal audience in the *Trojanerkrieg* is characterized by rather generic courtly values (*zuht*, *êre*, *bescheidenheit*) whose continuing relevance for the urban elite can safely be assumed.

'zwîvalt êre': The Status of Poetry Among Other Arts

In line with his argument that accomplished poetry and its creators deserve particular appreciation because of their rarity, Konrad continues to argue the case for the nobility of poetry by emphasizing its unique status. He explains that God has endowed the poet with two blessings that make his art fundamentally different from all other arts. The first point of difference is the fact that the art of poetry cannot be learned like other arts:

> sîn herze sunderlîchen treit
> ob allen künsten die vernunst,
> daz sîne fuoge und sîne kunst
> nâch vollecIichen êren
> mac nieman in gelêren
> wan gotes gunst aleine.
> kein mensche lebt sô reine,
> dem got der saelden günde,
> daz er gelernen künde
> wort unde wîse tihten.
> swaz künste man verrihten
> hie kan ûf al der erden,
> diu mac gelernet werden
> von liuten – wan der eine list,
> der tihten wol geheizen ist
> und iemer ist alsô genant.
> diz ist ein êre wîte erkant
> und rîlîche ein wirdikeit,
> die got besunder hât geleit
> ûf einen tihter ûzerwelt. (*Trojanerkrieg*, ll. 72–91)

The second aspect that sets poetry apart from and above all other arts is the fact that it does not rely on any instruments other than the intellect and the mouth or tongue of the poet to proceed from the conceptual stage to its expression:

sîn ander lop wirt iu gezelt,
dâ mite in hât getiuret got:
im gap sîn götelich gebot
als edelliche zuoversiht,
daz er bedürfe râtes niht,
noch helfe zuo der künste sin,
wan daz im unser trehtin
sinn unde mundes günne,
dâ mite er schône künne
gedenken unde reden wol.
swer ander kunst bewaeren sol
den jungen und den alten,
der muoz geziuges walten
und helferîcher stiure,
mit der sîn kunst gehiure
müg an daz lieht gefliezen.
und sol ein schütze schiezen,
er muoz hân bogen unde bolz.
kein snîder lebt sô rehte stolz,
der sîne kunst bewaere,
gebristet im der schaere,
dâ mite er schrôte ein edel tuoch.
ein kurdiwaener waehen schuoch
nâch lobelichen sachen
mac niemer wol gemachen,
hât er niht alen unde burst.
nieman des wilden waldes hurst
ân akes mac gehouwen.
swer durch die werden frouwen
rîlîche sol turnieren,
den müezen schône zieren
ros unde wâpenkleider:
jô darf er wol ir beider,
sol im sîn frouwe nîgen.
tambûren, harpfen gîgen
bedürfen ouch geziuges wol. (*Trojanerkrieg*, ll. 92–127)

Like the nightingale simile, this passage has often been read as the expression of a proto-modern concept of poetry that distinguishes itself from normativity as well as from craft. The following section will engage with this line of interpretation and evaluate the novelty value of Konrad's original arguments for the supremacy of poetry by contextualizing them within the framework of the contemporary discourse on *ars*.

Learnability

It has frequently been pointed out that the terms *ars* and *technē* in pre-modern times, as well as the synonymous Middle High German terms *kunst* and *list*,[81] encompass a very broad semantic scope, including science and crafts as well as the disciplines that make up the modern system of the *beaux arts* – usually painting, sculpture, architecture, music and poetry.[82] The common trait of these diverse 'arts', which include the comparatively stable canon of the *artes liberales* – the language-based Trivium (grammar, rhetoric, dialectic) and the mathematical Quadrivium (arithmetic, geometry, astronomy, music) – as well as various less systematized skills and crafts, is their reliance on rule-based knowledge. They can be learned and taught. Their intellectual nature is underlined by the association with terms like *wîsheit*, *witze*, *rât*, *vernunst* and *sin*.[83] This concept is also reflected in Hugh of St. Victor's influential *Didascalicon*, in which the origin of art is described as the regularization of practice:

> omnes enim scientiae prius erant in usu quam in arte. sed considerantes deinde homines usum in artem posse converti et quod vagum fuerat et licentiosum prius certis regulis et praeceptis posse restringi, coeperunt, ut dictum est, consuetudinem quae partim casu, partim natura exorta fuerat, ad artem reducere, id quod pravum usus habebat emendantes, quod minus habebat supplentes, quod superfluum habebat resecantes, et de cetero singulis certas regulas et praecepta praescribentes.[84]
>
> [All sciences, indeed, were matters of use before they became matters of art. But when men subsequently considered that use can be transformed into art, and what was previously vague and subject to caprice can be brought into order by definite rules and precepts, they began, we are told, to reduce to art the habits

81 See Scheidweiler, who refutes Trier's thesis that the younger term *kunst* has nobler, more courtly and ethical connotations than the older *list* and shows the words to be mainly synonymous (Felix Scheidweiler, '*kunst* und *list*', *ZfdA*, 78 (1941), 62–87).

82 On the formation of the system of *beaux arts* and the pre-modern concept of *ars*, see Paul Oskar Kristeller, *Humanismus und Renaissance*, ed. by Eckhard Keßler, trans. by Renate Schweyen-Ott, 2 vols (Munich: Fink, 1974–1976), II (1976): *Philosophie, Bildung und Kunst*, pp. 164–206, pp. 287–312; Ullrich describes the pre-modern concept of art similarly ('Kunst', p. 571), but criticizes Kristeller's thesis that the system of the five main *beaux arts* assumed its ultimate form in the eighteenth century: 'Bis in die Gegenwart ist ein definitives System der Künste [...] nicht vorhanden' ('Kunst', p. 581).

83 On the semantics of Middle High German *kunst* see Viëtor, 'Kunstanschauung', 88–89; Trier, *Sinnbezirk des Verstandes*, pp. 310–22 and passim; Boesch, *Kunstanschauung*, pp. 11–26.

84 Hugh of St Victor, *Didascalicon*, ed. by C. H. Buttimer, Catholic University of America Studies in Medieval & Renaissance Latin, 10 (Washington, DC: The Catholic University Press, 1939), I, 11.

> which had arisen partly by chance, partly by nature – correcting what was bad in use, supplying what was missing, eliminating what was superfluous, and furthermore prescribing definite rules and precepts for each usage.][85]

In addition to the fact that 'art' in pre-modern culture is not restricted to the aesthetic disciplines and that the thirteenth century did not have a formalized aesthetic theory about art,[86] this normativity has often been considered another key marker of alterity compared with a modern, especially Romantic, understanding of art as something based on innate talent and intuitive creation. This strict opposition is, of course, a very rough generalization. In reality the modern concept of art has been neither static nor uncontroversial.[87] At the same time, the medieval concept of art cannot be reduced to normativity, although the aspect of learnability is usually implicit, as Kellner states with reference to poetry: '[D]ie Kunst des Dichtens [ist] auch im Mittelalter mehr als eine bloße Fertigkeit [...]. Mehr oder weniger explizit wird in der literarischen Kommunikation des Mittelalters der semantische und spezifisch ästhetische Überschuss der Dichtkunst betont'.[88]

Nevertheless, the notion of rule-based knowledge and learnability remains central to the medieval concept of art. Considering this tradition, Konrad's argument for the uniqueness of poetry is particularly interesting. For him, poetry is the noblest of all arts precisely because it cannot be learned like the others. However, crucially, the customary definition of *kunst* as a learnable

85 Hugh of St Victor, *Didascalicon*, trans. by Jerome Taylor (New York: Columbia University Press, 1961), p. 59. In the introduction to this translation Taylor describes the considerable influence of Hugh's treatise, which survived in nearly one hundred manuscripts dating from the twelfth to fifteenth centuries in libraries all across Europe and influenced not only his successors to the Victorine chair but also writers such as John of Salisbury, William of Conches, Peter Comestor, Thomas Aquinas, Bonaventure and Vincent of Beauvais (pp. 4–5).

86 See Kristeller, who argues that Thomas Aquinas and other medieval philosophers did not discuss the concept of beauty (*pulchrum*) with reference to art but only with reference to God and His creation, but concedes that this does not mean that art was never perceived in aesthetic terms (Kristeller, *Philosophie, Bildung und Kunst*, pp. 174–75); similarly Andreas Speer, who further points out that dispersed reflections on beauty, such as those of Aquinas, do not form a coherent aesthetic theory and are often generalized and interpreted out of context (Andreas Speer, 'Vom Verstehen mittelalterlicher Kunst', in *Mittelalterliches Kunsterleben nach Quellen des 11. bis 13. Jahrhunderts*, ed. by Günther Binding and Andreas Speer (Stuttgart: Frommann, 1994), pp. 13–52). See also the contributions in *Das fremde Schöne: Dimensionen des Ästhetischen in der Literatur des Mittelalters*, ed. by Manuel Braun and Christopher Young, Trends in Medieval Philology, 12 (Berlin: de Gruyter, 2007).

87 For details see Ullrich, 'Kunst'.

88 Kellner, 'Meisterschaft', p. 138. See also Bürkle, who rejects a generalized definition of the medieval concept of art on the basis of normativity, because this categorically excludes an aesthetic concept of art and, moreover, makes the Hegelian identification of art with aesthetics the measure of all things (Susanne Bürkle, 'Einleitung', in *Interartifizialität*, ed. by Bürkle and Peters, pp. 1–16 (p. 3)).

skill is not discounted altogether. Although Konrad claims that nobody can ever be virtuous enough to earn the divine privilege of being able to learn how to compose poetry, poetry is said to be acquired through the *teaching* of God's grace (*Trojanerkrieg*, ll. 69–71, ll. 74–77). Conventional human teaching ('von liuten') is thus contrasted with divine teaching rather than with a complete lack of instruction.[89] Although Konrad sets poetry apart from all other arts, he does not claim a categorical difference by redefining the term *kunst*. He draws up a hierarchy of arts with poetry at the apex of the system. Poetry is the least typical discipline but is still counted among the *künste* – nor is this status denied to the disciplines that can be learned conventionally.[90] It would therefore go too far to describe Konrad's definition of poetry as a proto-modern concept of art that relies on natural talent rather than on cultural rules. Brandt points out that the concept of poetry as a divine gift does not preclude the notion of learnability and distinguishes the medieval concept of innate talent from the modern concept of the poetic genius:

> Entsprechend nicht nur theologischen Theorien über die Tätigkeit des Dichters, sondern auch dem grundsätzlich religiös gebundenen Weltbild kann *kunst* nur von Gott herrühren. Gerade *weil* dies dem MA so selbstverständlich ist, hat man darin aber kein Pendant zu späteren irrationalen Grundlegungen der Kunst zu sehen. [...] Mag auch die Lernfähigkeit wie alles andere von Gott stammen: Lernen gehört als Voraussetzung unabdingbar zur künstlerischen Produktion dazu, und das bringt immer eine stark rationale Tendenz mit sich.[91]

That the idea of poetry as a divine gift, which appears frequently in Middle High German literature, does not categorically exclude the necessity of training and education is expressed in several Latin poetics, for example in Matthew of Vendôme's *ars versificatoria*: 'Quamvis enim natura fundat ingenium, provehit tamen usus, sive exercitium confirmat, perseverantia coronat'[92] [Although

89 In contrast to this Kellner: 'Hier wird deutlich, dass mittelalterliche Dichtung gerade jenseits von Lehr- und Lernbarkeit situiert wird' (Kellner, 'Meisterschaft', p. 148, also p. 149); similarly Roethe, *Reinmar von Zweter*, pp. 31–32; Ehlert, 'Wert der Kunst', 91; Lienert, 'Der Trojanische Krieg in Basel', p. 267 and *Geschichte und Erzählen*, p. 18; Müller, '*schîn* und Verwandtes', p. 295; W. Schröder, '*Kunstanschauung*', p. 91.

90 See Brinkmann: 'Die Dichtung ist also *ars* wie die übrigen Künste, nur nimmt sie unter ihnen eine bevorzugte Stellung ein' (Brinkmann, *Wesen und Form*, p. 13); similarly Boesch, *Kunstanschauung*, p. 24; Obermaier, *Von Nachtigallen und Handwerkern*, p. 220; Gernentz, 'Charakter und Bedeutung', 33. For a different opinion see, for example, Rupp, who claims that Konrad declares 'Dichtkunst sei keine *ars*' (Heinz Rupp, 'Rudolf von Ems und Konrad von Würzburg. Das Problem des Epigonentums', *Der Deutschunterricht*, 17 (1965), 5–17 (p. 33)).

91 Brandt, *Konrad von Würzburg*, pp. 197–98.

92 Matthew of Vendôme, *Ars versificatoria*, in *Les arts poétiques du XIIe et du XIIIe siècle*, ed. by Edmond Faral (Paris: Librairie Ancienne Honoré Champion, 1924), pp. 106–93, IV, 36.

nature is the foundation of talent, usage develops it, and practice strengthens it, and perseverance crowns it].[93] However, the concept of poetry Konrad presents in the *Trojanerkrieg* prologue is often interpreted as a rejection of this traditional notion of *ars*. Thus, on the basis of the nightingale simile Müller argues that the product of the poet is not presented as the result of 'eingeübter, "zünftisch" kontrollierter Praxis' and as an 'Akt bemühter Arbeit'.[94] This interpretation certainly captures the notion of the instinctive compulsion to sing suggested by the simile and can be supported by the fact that Konrad does not highlight his undoubtedly considerable education. At the same time, there are other statements in the prologue that do not fit the concept of literature presented by Müller. Konrad also associates poetry with terms indicating its rational foundation as well as aspects of effort and training, which suggests that divine grace alone does not suffice to create good poety: good poets are called 'wîse' (*Trojanerkrieg*, l. 57) and 'meister' (*Trojanerkrieg*, l. 6, l. 52), while the blessing that makes the poet's heart independent of conventional teaching is called 'vernunst' (*Trojanerkrieg*, l. 73).[95] Konrad refers to his long experience as a writer and describes the effort of composition as 'kumber' (*Trojanerkrieg*, l. 215) and 'flîz' (*Trojanerkrieg*, l. 217, l. 261). It can, of course, be argued that divine teaching must be understood as something fundamentally different from human teaching, a metaphorical expression for a divine gift that defies human attempts at regularization and thus approaches a modern notion of artistic talent. However, the fact that Konrad does not group the different skills into *kunst* and non-*kunst*, as well as the fact that even a concept of innate talent is still cast in the terms of learnability and does not preclude the necessity of further training, testify to the power of the traditional, normative concept of art that still governs his argument. This reliance on traditional notions of art can even be observed in Wolfram's more radical rejection of bookish learning, which still describes divine inspiration as some kind of learning, albeit in a possibly ironic sense:

> swaz an den buochen stât geschriben,
> des bin ich künstelôs beliben.
> niht anders ich gelêret bin:
> wan hân ich kunst, die gît mir sin.[96]

93 Matthew of Vendôme, *Ars versificatoria (The Art of the Versemaker)*, trans. by Roger P. Parr (Milwaukee: Marquette University Press, 1981), p. 102. See Boesch, *Kunstanschauung*, p. 13, and Brinkmann, *Wesen und Form*, pp. 12–13.

94 Müller, '*schîn* und Verwandtes', pp. 296–97.

95 On this point see also Freytag, 'Zur Logik *wilder aventiure*', 393–94.

96 Wolfram von Eschenbach, *Willehalm*, ed. and trans. by Joachim Heinzle, Bibliothek des Mittelalters, 9 (Frankfurt a.M.: Deutscher Klassiker Verlag, 1991), 2, 19–22. Similarities and differences between Konrad's and Wolfram's prologues are discussed by Lienert, *Geschichte und Erzählen*, pp. 18–19, fn. 11; Kern, *Weltflucht*, pp. 434–35, fn. 38.

The conservative aspects that remain in this passage from the *Trojanerkrieg* prologue become more visible if it is contrasted with a didactic song by Konrad that expresses a more drastic version of the thought:

> Vür alle fuoge ist edel sanc getiuret und gehêret,
> dar umbe daz er sich von nihte breitet unde mêret.
> elliu kunst gelêret
> mac werden schône mit vernunst,
> wan daz nieman gelernen kan red und gedœne singen;
> diu beide müezent von in selben wahsen unde entspringen:
> ûz dem herzen klingen
> muoz ir begin von gotes gunst.
> ander fuoge durfen alle râtes und geziuges wol.
> swer si trîben rehte sol,
> der muoz hân daz gerüste,
> dâ mite er si volende nâch der liute muotgelüste;
> son darf der sanc niht helfe, wan der zungen und der brüste:
> sunder valsche âküste
> gêt er dâ von vür alle kunst. (*Lieder und Sprüche*, 32, ll. 301–15)[97]

The fact that the claim is not supported with examples of other teachable arts gives this strophe a more apodictic tone than the argument in the *Trojanerkrieg* prologue.[98] The metaphor of natural growth from within furthermore counterposes the innate skill of poetic composition to the acquired cultural skills that rely on outside teaching and instruments. While *vernunst* is the blessing of the poet's heart in the *Trojanerkrieg*, here it is presented as the rational foundation of the other arts only. The most radical aspect of the strophe, however, is the notion that the poet creates 'von nihte', suggesting an idea of original creation *ex nihilo* which is due only to God Himself, as Hugh of St. Victor states in no uncertain terms: 'opus Dei est, quod non erat creare [...]. opus naturae, quod latuit ad actum producere [...]. opus artificis est disgregata coniungere vel coniuncta segregare' (*Didascalicon*, I, 9) [The work of God is to create that which was not [...]; the work of nature is to bring forth into actuality that which lay hidden [...]; the work of the artificer is to put together things disjoined or to disjoin those put together (*Didascalicon*, p. 55)].[99] While poetic talent is immediately identified as a divine gift in the

97 A translation and an interpretation of the poem in the context of the *Trojanerkrieg* are given by Schröder, *Kunstanschauung*, p. 147, p. 159.

98 See Obermaier, *Von Nachtigallen und Handwerkern*, p. 222.

99 On the difference between divine, natural and human creation see also Thomas Aquinas, *The Summa Theologica*, ed. by Daniel J. Sullivan, trans. by Fathers of the English Dominican Province (Chicago: Encyclopaedia Britannica, 1952), I q 45 a 2 c; and the discussion of Thomas's and Hugh's concepts of *ars* by Speer, 'Vom Verstehen mittelalterlicher Kunst', pp.

Trojanerkrieg prologue, the mention of God as the ultimate source of poetic creation only occurs in the middle of the strophe, so that the more radical and even blasphemous thought of poetry as original creation is allowed to linger for a moment before it is reined in to a more conventional definition. The *Trojanerkrieg* prologue is clearly less daring than the didactic strophe that seems at least to anticipate many aspects that characterize a modern concept of poetry.

Poetry and 'Handwerk'

In order to illustrate his second point – that poetry is unlike other arts because it does not require any equipment – Konrad lists six skills: archery, tailoring, shoemaking, forestry, competing in knightly tournaments and instrumental music. Despite their reliance on instruments – Konrad names the equipment needed to practise each one – they appear to have very little in common, at least from a modern perspective.[100] Some, such as shoemaking and tailoring, produce material artefacts, while instrumental music is an ephemeral performance art like jousting, which is presented as a way to impress women. Some of these skills produce artefacts or performances that lend themselves to aesthetic appreciation – music is the most obvious but not the only example. The tailor works with 'edel tuoch' and making a good impression at a tournament is dependent on one's armour and horse, which are not described in functional terms but as decorating their owner beautifully ('schône zieren' (*Trojanerkrieg*. l. 122)). Although Konrad does not distinguish according to a hierarchy, some of the arts he lists would traditionally be accorded a higher social status than others. The aristocratic pastime of jousting, for example, should rank higher than the hard physical labour of forestry. Müller's statement that '[s]ein *ambet* [...] den Dichter aus den sozialen Abhängigkeiten der übrigen Künste [löst]', does not, therefore, take the noble activity of jousting into account.[101] Brandt, on the other hand, comments more convincingly that Konrad is obviously not interested in a 'sozialständische Abgrenzung' from professional craftsmen, for 'dazu ist der Vergleich mit den Rittern zu hoch und der mit den Schützen und Holzfällern zu niedrig angesetzt'.[102] Some arts

13–52, pp. 23–30. The relevance of this position for the concept of authorship is discussed by Thomas Cramer, '*Solus creator est deus*: Der Autor auf dem Weg zum Schöpfertum', *Daphnis*, 15 (1986), 261–76.

100 Braun points out that arts in Middle High German literature are often grouped together in very heterogeneous collections (Manuel Braun, 'Zwischen *ars* und "Kunst": Zum Verhältnis der "Künste" in der Sangspruchdichtung und im Meistergesang', in *Interartifizialität*, ed. by Bürkle and Peters, pp. 69–91 (pp. 69–70)).

101 Müller, '*schîn* und Verwandtes', p. 296.

102 Brandt, *Konrad von Würzburg*, p. 200.

seem better suited to be contrasted to literature than others. For instance, the association between instrumental music and poetry, which is also presented as a musical art ('sanc') in the prologue, is very old. Already Plato and Aristotle treated music as a subcategory of poetry, especially of lyric poetry and drama.[103] The superiority of singing over instrumental music is sometimes discussed in the genre of *Sangspruchdichtung*: the common argument is that while both arts give the audience pleasure, only the verbal art can also be didactic and is therefore the nobler one.[104] A comparison of these arts thus provides an opportunity to elaborate on the supremacy of the verbal-musical discipline over the purely musical that Konrad does not exploit. Tailoring is also an activity that is traditionally associated with poetry and could be cited to reject the common comparison between the work of a poet and that of a tailor. Although the term *Text* is not adopted until the fourteenth century,[105] textile metaphors are ubiquitous in earlier German poetry and can serve to highlight various aspects of poetry. Relevant examples for the *Trojanerkrieg* prologue can be found in Gottfried's praise of Bligger von Steinach (*Tristan*, ll. 4691–713) or in Konrad's *Goldene Schmiede*, where the poet announces his intention to spin an *erenkleit* for the Virgin from his verses (*Goldene Schmiede*, ll. 884–93).[106] In this tradition even shoemaking, which, like tailoring, involves

103 Kristeller, *Philosophie, Bildung und Kunst*, p. 169.

104 See Braun, 'Zwischen *ars* und "Kunst"', pp. 69–91. Other arguments put forward in *Sangspruchdichtung* are that singing, as a verbal art, participates in the dignity of the divine word and is thus associated with life, while instrumental music is associated with death (the living voice can also be contrasted to the dead instruments); and that a song can be written down and thus transcends the ephemeral quality of music. On the comparison of sung poetry with the less prestigious instrumental music see also Obermaier, *Von Nachtigallen und Handwerkern*, pp. 188–91, p. 220.

105 Meinolf Schumacher, '*… der kann den texst und och die gloß*: Zum Wortgebrauch von "Text" und "Glosse" in deutschen Dichtungen des Spätmittelalters', in '*Textus' im Mittelalter: Komponenten und Situationen des Wortgebrauchs im schriftsemantischen Feld*, ed. by Ludolf Kuchenbuch and Uta Kleine, Veröffentlichungen des Max-Planck-Instituts für Geschichte, 216 (Göttingen: Vandenhoek & Ruprecht, 2006) pp. 207–27.

106 On the metapoetic *textus*-metaphor in general see Erika Greber, *Textile Texte: Poetologische Metaphorik und Literaturtheorie: Studien zur Tradition des Wortflechtens und der Kombinatorik*, Pictura et poesis, 9 (Cologne: Böhlau, 2002); Hans Günter Bickert, 'Der Dichter als Handwerker: Zu Herkunft und Bedeutung einiger Begriffe der Dichtungstheorie', in *Sprache in Vergangenheit und Gegenwart: Beiträge aus dem Institut für Germanistische Sprachwissenschaft der Philipps-Universität Marburg*, ed. by Wolfgang Brandt and Rudolf Freudenberg, Marburger Studien zur Germanistik, 9 (Marburg: Hitzeroth, 1988), pp. 1–14; Beate Wagner-Hasel, '*Textus* und texere, *hýphos* und *hyphaínein*: Zur metaphorischen Bedeutung des Webens in der griechisch-römischen Antike', in '*Textus' im Mittelalter*, ed. by Kuchenbuch and Kleine, pp. 15–42. See also Hedwig Röckelein, who demonstrates that weaving metaphors in Latin hagiography can, for example, be employed to highlight aspects of *dispositio*, *compilatio* and *elocutio* (Hedwig Röckelein, 'Vom webenden Hagiographen zum hagiographischen Text', in '*Textus' im Mittelalter*, ed. by Kuchenbuch and Kleine,

the activity of sewing, can be used as a metaphor for composing poetry.[107] Compared to this rich tradition the employment of the motif of archery as a metapoetic metaphor is less conventional, but still finds a prominent model in *Parzival*, in which Wolfram likens his straightforward way of narration to the straight sinew and a complicated narrative organization to the curve of the bow.[108] It might also refer to Konrad's following description of his poetic effort as a straining of his mind: 'mîn sin der spannet unde dont' (*Trojanerkrieg*, l. 216).[109] Other skills, however, have to be pressed quite hard to find a possible relationship with poetry. The activity of cultivating a 'wilden waldes hurst' (*Trojanerkrieg*, l. 118) could be transposed into a metaphor for imposing order on the 'âventiuren wilde' (*Trojanerkrieg*, l. 283), but there is nothing to suggest that Konrad intended this metaphorical extension. Fighting in a tournament shares an aesthetic appeal and ephemeral quality with poetry and perhaps also the potential to woo women, but Konrad does not exploit the possibility of linking knighthood as expressed in the prologue closely to the actual content of the *Trojanerkrieg* – the self-indulgent tournament is, rather, the antithesis of the deadly serious warfare represented in the text, even though the latter achieves aesthetic qualities in Konrad's descriptions.

One thing the arts in Konrad's list have in common is the fact that they can all be counted among the seven *artes mechanicae*, which are described for the first time systematically in Hugh of St. Victor's *Didascalicon* (II, 20–27).[110] While truth and virtue served by the theoretical (theology, mathematics, physics) and practical arts (ethics) are instrumental in overcoming the human deficiency resulting from the Fall in order to restore union with the divine Wisdom, the

pp. 77–110. On the metaphorical field in Middle High German literature see Obermaier, *Von Nachtigallen und Handwerkern*, pp. 262–63, p. 324, pp. 333–34; Patricia Harant, *Poeta Faber: Der Handwerks-Dichter bei Frauenlob: Texte, Übersetzungen, Textkritik, Kommentar und Metapherninterpretationen*, Erlanger Studien, 110 (Erlangen: Palm & Enke, 1997), pp. 163–66; Michael Stolz, *'Tum'-Studien: Zur dichterischen Gestaltung im Marienpreis Heinrichs von Mügeln*, Bibliotheca Germanica, 36 (Tübingen: Francke, 1996), pp. 104–16; Andreas Kraß, *Geschriebene Kleider: Höfische Identität als literarisches Spiel*, Bibliotheca Germanica, 50 (Tübingen: Francke, 2006), pp. 360–74.

107 See Bickert, 'Der Dichter als Handwerker', p. 5.

108 Wolfram von Eschenbach, *Parzival*, ed. by Eberhard Nellmann, trans. by Dieter Kühn, 2 vols, Bibliothek des Mittelalters, 8 (Frankfurt a.M.: Deutscher Klassiker Verlag, 1994), 241, 8–241, 30.

109 See Hübner, who remarks on this line: 'Die Bedeutung ist dabei sicher vom gespannten Bogen hergeleitet' (Gert Hübner, 'Versuch über Konrad von Würzburg als Minnelyriker', in *Artibus: Kulturwissenschaft und deutsche Philologie des Mittelalters und der frühen Neuzeit: Festschrift Dieter Wuttke*, ed. by Stephan Füssel, Gert Hübner and Joachim Knape (Harrasowitz: Wiesbaden, 1994), pp. 63–94 (p. 90, fn. 53).

110 For other categorizations and definitions of the mechanical arts, see F. Krafft, '*artes mechanicae*', in *Lexikon des Mittelalters*, ed. by Bautier and others, I, cols 1063–65.

mechanical arts can at least remedy the burdens of physical existence and are therefore ranked lower, yet not depreciated, by Hugh (*Didascalicon*, I, 5). According to his categorization, shoemaking and the production of clothes would fall under the domain of *lanificium*, which comprises the processing of flexible organic materials, through the employment of diverse instruments such as the needle, spindle or awl, into various products such as clothing, saddles, ropes or baskets. The science of *agricultura*, which includes fieldwork, shepherding, decorative gardening and forestry, relates to the activity of cutting down trees in Konrad's list. Archery is one of many hunting methods mentioned by Hugh when he describes the science of *venatio*, which is divided into gaming, fowling and fishing and encompasses the preparation of all sorts of food and drink. Finally, the knightly tournament and instrumental music can both be counted among the *theatrica*, whose origins Hugh traces back to entertainment in Antiquity such as theatre performance, dancing, sports, instrumental and vocal music and games.[111] Although music is also one of the *artes liberales*, in which instrumental music and singing are grouped together under the lowest category 'instrumental',[112] it seems more in keeping with the classification of the other skills as mechanical arts to subsume music under the art of entertainment in the context of the *Trojanerkrieg* prologue. However, three out of Hugh's seven categories remain unfilled – *armatura*, which includes the production of weapons and armour as well as the construction of buildings; *navigatio*, which concerns all aspects of trade; and *medicina* – so that his system cannot be seen as the guiding principle of Konrad's line-up of skills.

Critical opinions on Konrad's comparison of poetry with other arts have been divided. Based on the classification of Konrad as a poet who works like an urban craftsman,[113] one line of argument reads the attempt to distinguish his work from that of other 'Handwerker' as an indication, 'daß er sich ständisch dieser Gruppe zugeordnet wußte',[114] or as the sign of a 'handwerksmäßige

111 Krafft subsumes 'Ritterspiele' into Hugh's category of 'theatrica' (Krafft, '*artes mechanicae*').

112 Hugh divides the art of music into 'music of the universe' – the harmony of the elements, planets and seasons; 'music of man' – the harmony of the soul and the harmony of the body as well as the harmony between body and soul; and 'instrumental music' (*Didascalicon*, II, 12).

113 See, for example, Gernentz, 'Charakter und Bedeutung', 33, 43. Peters rejects this characterization by pointing out that Konrad in fact shares the 'immer wieder konstatierte Formelhaftigkeit, den stilistisch-thematischen Schematismus und die experimentierfreudige Vielseitigkeit' with courtly authors of the thirteenth century and that his authorial self-representation corresponds to general literary trends (Peters, *Literatur in der Stadt*, pp. 118–19). On this debate see also Brandt, *Konrad von Würzburg*, pp. 201–03.

114 De Boor, *Deutsche Literatur im späten Mittelalter*, p. 31.

Auffassung des Dichtens'.[115] In contrast to this, it has also been argued that Konrad's statement is an attempt to distance poetry from mere crafts.[116] Müller, for example, understands the claim that poetry is the only art which does not rely on instruments as a break with the traditional artisanal concept of art which still informs Konrad's metaphor of the poem as goldsmithery in the *Goldene Schmiede*.[117] Highlighting references to orality in the prologue, he claims: 'Konrads Interesse gilt nicht dem gebildehaften Artefakt, sondern der Performanz. Dichtung ist *rede*, mündlich vorgetragene, akustisch rezipierte Sprache, nicht Schrift'.[118] He points out that in likening his own singing to that of the nightingale, Konrad picks up on a metaphor Gottfried uses to describe lyric poets in his literary excursus (*Tristan*, ll. 4751–820). There, Gottfried distinguishes the natural singing of the nightingales from the culturally determined production of epic texts, which he metaphorizes as dyeing and weaving in the case of Bligger von Steinach. By transferring this qualification to all poets, Müller argues, Konrad distances himself from a 'handwerklich gefärbten Kunstpraxis'.[119] This interpretation is problematic for three reasons.

First, although it is true that Konrad presents his work as singing rather than writing throughout the *Trojanerkrieg* prologue, he does not highlight the immaterial product of poetry as unique but rather the mode of production, the fact that it does not rely on any instruments other than the mouth and the tongue of the poet.[120] If he had intended to emphasize the ephemeral nature of the poetic product he would not have contrasted it to the performance arts of music and jousting but only to those mechanical arts that create material

115 Green, *Vorstudien zum gotischen Stil*, p. 203.

116 See, for example, Brinkmann, *Wesen und Form*, p. 13; Haug, *Literaturtheorie*, p. 358; Obermaier, *Von Nachtigallen und Handwerkern*, p. 336

117 Müller, '*schîn* und Verwandtes', p. 295. On the tradition of artisanal poetry metaphors see Bickert, 'Der Dichter als Handwerker'; Obermaier, *Von Nachtigallen und Handwerkern*, pp. 333–38; Braun, 'Zwischen *ars* und "Kunst"', pp. 77–82.

118 Müller, '*schîn* und Verwandtes', p. 296. Kern, on the other hand, points out discrepancies between the declared autonomy from instruments and the nightingale simile: 'Hier wird eine Selbstgenügsamkeit der "Vokalität" in einer Zeit und in einem Werk imaginiert, das ohne die Materialität der Schrift nicht denkbar wäre. Dass aus der Passage kein positivistischer Beweis für Medialität und Ästhetik der Mündlichkeit zu ziehen ist, die die volkssprachliche Poesie nach wie vor determiniere, belegen die folgenden Verse. Indem sie die Idee der dichterischen Autarkie radikalisieren, blenden sie gerade jene Unmittelbarkeit der Kommunikation aus, die der Theorie zufolge eine Sphäre der Vokalität kennzeichnen müsste' (Kern, *Weltflucht*, p. 435).

119 Müller, '*schîn* und Verwandtes', pp. 296–97. See also Gebert, who points out that Augustine also describes the singing of the nightingale as relying on *natura* instead of *ars* (Gebert, *Mythos als Wissensform*, p. 140).

120 An alternative interpretation of Konrad's emphasis on singing is proposed by Kokott, who suggests that it could be understood as homage to his patron, the cantor Dietrich, who is introduced as a 'singer' (Kokott, *Auftrag und Autonomie*, pp. 246, 286).

artefacts. Brandt remarks that the opinion that Konrad distinguishes poetry from 'handwerklichen Tätigkeiten' is correct in principle but tends to ignore the arts of jousting, archery and forestry.[121] I think that 'Handwerk' is simply an inappropriate category for the discussion of Konrad's *artes* comparison – be it to support the thesis that Konrad presents himself as a craftsman or the opposite thesis that he distances his art from crafts – because it does not include activities like jousting, archery and music in modern usage. In contrast to this, Hugh of St Victor's line-up of the seven mechanical arts also contains performing arts and others that do not produce artefacts.[122]

Second, Müller's interpretation disregards the fact that Konrad uses a variation of precisely the artisanal metaphor with which Gottfried describes Bligger's poetry. It occurs later on in the prologue when he proclaims his intention to glue the cracks in the old book of Troy back together with his rhymes. This will be discussed in more detail below, but it is clear that this metaphor treats the *Trojanerkrieg* as some kind of 'gebildehaftes Artefakt'.[123]

Third, and finally, Müller's interpretation suggests that the employment of artisanal metaphors necessarily points to a concept of poetry as a craft producing a material artefact. That this is not necessarily the case is illustrated by the fact that in the Greek tradition textile metaphors are associated with oral performance – in the Philomela myth, for example, weaving replaces the tongue of the girl.[124] Furthermore, Obermaier correctly emphasizes 'daß die

121 Brandt, *Konrad von Würzburg*, p. 200.

122 At first Hugh glosses the name 'mechanical' for the works of men as 'adulterate' (*Didascalicon*, I, 9; II, 20) because unlike God, who creates out of nothing, the human artificer can merely imitate nature and join together or disjoin things that already exist. He thus highlights the production of artefacts as the domain of the mechanical arts and later quotes a definition to the same effect: 'And mechanics is that science to which they [the ancients] declare the manufacture of all articles to belong' (*Didascalicon*, II, 20, p. 70). Yet, when he enumerates the seven mechanical sciences he also lists skills or professions that do not produce material artefacts, which brings the concept of mechanical art back to the broader definition of relating to the concerns of present life. For accounts that restrict the *artes mechanicae* to manual skills that produce artefacts, e.g. by Dominicus Gundissalinus, see Krafft, '*artes mechanicae*'.

123 Gebert illustrates the fact that the prologue contains 'schriftlichkeitsorientierte' as well as 'mündlichkeitsorientierte' terms with a table of references. He mentions, however, that terms associated with orality become more frequent after the *artes*-discussion (Gebert, *Mythos als Wissensform*, pp. 139–40).

124 Greber explains that metapoetic textile imagery was associated with scripturality only in the Roman culture that developed the *textus*-metaphor (Greber, *Textile Texte*, pp. 27–28). For examples of lyric poets describing their singing as weaving, see Wagner-Hasel, '*Textus* und texere', pp. 26–30. Even though she speculates that the introduction of the metaphor in the fifth century BC may have been inspired by the new practice of writing down poetry on woven papyrus, she states that it is explicitly connected to literacity only in Roman literature (p. 34). However, she also lists examples of weaving representing oral poetry such as Ovid's Arachne myth (pp. 3–4).

Verwendung von Handwerksmetaphorik nicht bedeutet, daß der Dichter sein Tun als ein Handwerk begreift; er hebt lediglich auf eine Analogie zwischen seiner Tätigkeit und der des Handwerkers ab'.[125] She gives several reasons for this statement: for example, the fact that artisanal metaphors are often combined with metaphors that present poetic creation as natural processes[126] – a combination that also characterizes the *Trojanerkrieg* prologue, as will be discussed below. Besides, a metaphor does not just proclaim the similarity of source and target domain but can also serve to underline their essential difference. Thus, the metaphor of goldsmithery is, in fact, perfectly compatible with the oral concept of poetry, as the careful analysis of the *Goldene Schmiede* prologue by Kellner shows:

> Auf den ersten Blick legen diese Bilder [the tongue as a hammer and the heart as the smithy] also nahe, dass die dichterische Produktion als Handwerk gedacht ist, das allerdings im Unterschied zu realen Vorgängen des Schmiedens ganz unabhängig von äußeren Hilfsmitteln vonstatten geht: Gleichsam autark bedarf der Poet nur seines Körpers, seines Herzens, der Zunge und des Mundes, um sein *getihte* (v. 3) hervorzubringen. Der entstehende Text wird – der Bildlogik folgend – nicht auf ein Manuskript notiert, sondern vielmehr im Herzen als dem Inneren des Körpers gebildet und dann durch Mund und Zunge, also als mündlicher, aus dem Körper entlassen.[127]

The oppositions with which Müller discusses the *Trojanerkrieg* prologue – 'handwerklich' versus non-'handwerklich', ephemeral product versus material product – simply do not suit the criteria according to which Konrad distinguishes poetry from other arts. Konrad enumerates noble as well as base disciplines, activities that produce material and ephemeral products, arts that are traditionally associated with poetry as well as others that do not appear in such contexts. They do not conform to a modern notion of craft, but can be classed as mechanical even though there is clearly no attempt to present a systemized *artes* model such as Hugh's. The skills assembled by Konrad do not appear to have any common traits except their dependence on instruments, which seems to be precisely the point of his eclecticism. Their dissimilarity supports his statement that all arts other than poetry, however different they may be in any other respect, rely on tools. It is, furthermore, conspicuous that the system of the Seven Liberal Arts does not play a role in Konrad's *artes* discussion although its inclusion would have provided him with an argument for the supremacy of poetry over artefact-producing crafts. The intellectual

125 Obermaier, *Von Nachtigallen und Handwerkern*, p. 336. See also Brandt, *Konrad von Würzburg*, p. 201.
126 Obermaier, *Von Nachtigallen und Handwerkern*, p. 337.
127 Kellner, 'Meisterschaft', pp. 140–41.

liberal arts were generally considered nobler than the mechanical arts;[128] and poetry, although not constituting a discipline in its own right, was often associated with the language arts of the Trivium.[129] Konrad himself associates poetry with rhetoric in the *Partonopier* prologue, where one of the three purposes of 'rede' and 'sanc' is 'daz diu zunge wirt gespræche sêre von in zwein' (*Partonopier*, ll. 14–15). Nonetheless, in the *Trojanerkrieg* prologue the status of poetry is not enhanced through this relationship. The intellectual nature of poetry does not distinguish it from the other arts, which, in accordance with Hugh's description, are also conceived in the mind first, before they manifest themselves:

> swaz künste man eht öugen sol,
> die müezen hân gerüste,
> mit dem si von der brüste
> ze liehte künnen dringen. (*Trojanerkrieg*, ll. 128–31)[130]

Apart from the fact that the intellectual and immaterial nature of poetry is not the unique characteristic that Konrad chooses to highlight, there is another strong reason why he ignores the system of the liberal arts: although associating poetry with them would endow it with some dignity, it would at the same time undermine its claim to uniqueness, because it would then be part of a group of arts most of which do not rely on instruments either. Konrad's case for the superiority of poetry is therefore highly original but also rather fragile. It depends on his very particular selection of arts and

128 See Ullrich, 'Kunst', p. 571; Krafft, '*artes mechanicae*', col. 1064.

129 On the association of poetry with the liberal arts, see Brandt, *Konrad von Würzburg*, p. 199; Boesch, *Kunstanschauung*, p. 21; Kristeller, *Philosophie, Bildung und Kunst*, p. 173; Viëtor, 'Kunstanschauung', 89, with some Middle High German references; Baldwin, *Medieval Rhetoric*; Faral, *Les arts poétiques*; McKeon, 'Poetry and Philosophy'. See also Schulze, who points out that although poetry is often associated with the Trivium, it is sometimes also explicitly excluded from the realm of philosophy served by the liberal arts in the tradition of Plato (Schulze, 'Stationen der *ars poetica*', p. 95).

130 See also Haupt, who discusses the possible influence of the widely distributed treatise *De diversis artibus* by Theophilus Presbyter (probably Ruger or Roger of Helmarshausen) on the *Straßburger Alexander* and argues that Theophilus ennobles the mechanical arts by emphasizing their intellectual nature (Barbara Haupt, 'Ornament und *vuoge*', in *Interartifizialität*, ed. by Bürkle and Peters, pp. 113–35 (pp. 116–18)). It would therefore be difficult to pinpoint either Hugh's or Theophilus's treatise as the direct model for Konrad's intellectual conception of the mechanical arts. Compare also Geoffrey of Vinsauf, who introduces his *ars poetica* with an analogy between architecture and poetry, which both have to be conceived in the mind first, before being executed (Geoffrey of Vinsauf, *Poetria Nova*, in *Les arts poétiques du XIIe et du XIIIe siècle*, ed. by Faral, pp. 194–262, ll. 43–54. For a translation see Geoffrey of Vinsauf, *The New Poetics*, trans. by Jane Baltzell Kopp, in *Three Medieval Rhetorical Arts*, ed. by James J. Murphy (Berkeley: University of California Press, 1971), pp. 27–108 (p. 34)).

would not withstand any further inquiry that brought up other examples such as the liberal arts.

Another curious aspect of Konrad's representation of arts is the fact that after having elaborated on the exceptional status of poetry, he invokes God as a 'meister aller künste' (*Trojanerkrieg*, l. 259) to inspire his work. This invocation, which defines all arts as God-given, supports Brandt's opinion that it is not poetry's quality as a divine gift that sets it apart from other arts:

> [E]ine *Mittel*aufwertung [findet] durch die Erwähnung ihrer göttlichen Herkunft [...] allein noch nicht statt [...] – denn schließlich kommt ja alles von Gott. [Den Künstler] kennzeichnet, daß Gott ihn überhaupt unterscheidbar gemacht hat – und zwar vor allen Betreibern *aller* anderen Tätigkeiten [...]. Plausibler wird diese Verstehensmöglichkeit noch dadurch, daß über die Qualität der Mittel (*sin* und *mund*) nichts weiter ausgesagt wird. Denn eine Aufwertung über diese Mittel wäre ja theoretisch auch möglich gewesen. Nur teilt der Dichter diese Mittel mit vielen anderen, und ihn unterscheidet auch von daher lediglich, daß es sich dabei um seine einzigen handelt.[131]

In addition to this, the invocation suggests that poetry is the master of all arts not only for the reasons named in the *artes* discussion but also because its proper execution relies on a knowledge of all other arts. Here Konrad could be referring to the liberal arts, like many other Middle High German poets who present them as the indispensable basis for the composition of poetry.[132] In line with the *artes* comparison, however, it seems likely that Konrad articulates a more universal claim by presenting poetry as the art that incorporates all human arts. Such an argument is made by Heinrich von Mügeln, who presents the education in all *artes* – he names more than seven intellectual arts and also associates poetry with practical skills like painting and building – as indispensable for the composition of good poetry. Commenting on this passage, Kellner argues that this capacity to comprise all other arts makes poetry superior, 'denn der Dichter zeigt sich als der Generalist, der den Spezialisten in den verschiedenen *artes* überlegen ist'.[133] If we assume similar implications for Konrad's invocation of the 'meister aller künste', it makes

131 Brandt, *Konrad von Würzburg*, p. 201; similarly Obermaier, *Von Nachtigallen und Handwerkern*, p. 221. For the notion that all human art comes from God, see also Rudolf von Ems, *Barlaam und Josaphat*, ed. by Franz Pfeiffer (Berlin: de Gruyter, 1965), ll. 69–88; and the discussion of this passage by Henrike Manuwald, '*gotes kunst – des tiuvels kunst*: Zum Kunstdiskurs in *Barlaam und Josaphat* Rudolfs von Ems', in *Interartifizialität*, ed. by Bürkle and Peters, pp. 49–68.

132 See Brandt, *Konrad von Würzburg*, p. 199. For examples of Middle High German poems that present the Seven Liberal Arts as the basis for poetry, see Brinkmann, *Wesen und Form*, pp. 14–15, p. 16; Schulze, 'Stationen der *ars poetica*', pp. 97–98.

133 Kellner, 'Meisterschaft', pp. 149–54.

the notion that Konrad categorically rejects a learned, normative concept of poetry in favour of a purely instinctive talent even more questionable.

Konrad does not present a treatise that locates poetry within the framework of contemporary art theories. His argument about the superior status of his discipline may draw on this background, but it does not rely on established categorizations (*artes liberales*, *artes mechanicae*) or interartificial imagery (for example, metapoetic textile metaphors), nor does it have the systematics that would be required of a theory. The points he raises in support of his thesis are not conventional but occasional. They lend coherence to the first part of the prologue by developing the theme of uniqueness foregrounded by the orphan gemstone and the phoenix comparison. The persuasive power of his argument rests on the careful selection and presentation of illustrative examples rather than on logical rigour. The concept of poetry that is presented in this way also defies modern attempts at theoretical systematization. The eclectic arts that Konrad assembles cannot be categorized as 'Handwerk'. Some passages of the prologue emphasize the ephemeral status of poetry while others imagine it as a material product. Individual images or arguments may privilege certain aspects of poetry, but these are frequently undermined by others. This goes to show how important it is to consider the entire prologue rather than isolated passages. It also means that the dichotomies and modern concepts employed to define Konrad's notion of poetry – normativity versus natural talent, crafts versus art, oral versus written poetry – are too static to grasp it.

Renewing the Old Book of Troy

In setting out to write the story of the Trojan War Konrad was confronted with a multitude of sources. Benoît de Sainte-Maure, who discounted Homer and based his French *Roman de Troie* on the supposed eye-witness accounts of Dares Phrygius (*Acta diurna belli Troiani*, late fifth century) and Dictys Cretensis (*Ephemeris belli Troiani*, probably fourth century),[134] had already founded a tradition that would dominate vernacular literature on the Trojan War up to the sixteenth century. Apart from this, many episodes relating to the Trojan War were transmitted in Latin texts that were part of the school curriculum (Ovid, Statius, *Excidium Troiae*, Dares, Dictys, *Ilias latina*). Frequent allusions in Middle High German courtly literature furthermore suggest that the basic events and characters were common knowledge. The literary tradition into which Konrad enters is also highly disparate, as Lienert points out:

134 On these two texts see Stefan Merkle, '*Troiani belli verior textus*: Die Trojaberichte des Dictys und Dares', in *Die deutsche Trojaliteratur: Materialien und Untersuchungen*, ed. by Horst Brunner, Wissensliteratur im Mittelalter, 3 (Wiesbaden: Reichert, 1990), pp. 491–522.

> Im Rahmen der feststehenden großen Handlungslinie waren die Motive hochgradig variabel und offenbar relativ frei kombinierbar. Somit kann von einer 'literarischen Reihe' mittelalterlicher Trojatexte nicht sinnvoll die Rede sein, da der Trojastoff ein Reservoir verschiedener Versionen, Motive, Stofftraditionen darstellt, die im Prinzip gleichzeitig verfügbar waren, nicht nur in geschlossenen Erzählungen, sondern auch in knappen Kompendien, in verstreuten Einzelanspielungen, als Allgemein- und Schulwissen.[135]

Konrad certainly takes up the challenge presented to him by the literary tradition. By combining nearly all available stories relating to the Trojan War that had never before been united in one text, and by adding his own detailed descriptions as well as long speeches and monologues by the characters, he creates a work of monumental proportions. His main source is Benoît: he includes the latter's account in its entirety, up to the point where his own text breaks off, and follows its chronological order. To this basic frame he adds episodes which are not included in Benoît, such as Paris's and Achilles' youth or the cruel deaths of Jason and Hercules taken from other Latin sources: Ovid's *Heroides* and *Metamorphoses*, Statius's *Achilleis*, *Excidium Troiae*, *Ilias latina*, Virgil and Simon Aurea Capra's *Ilias*.[136] However, Konrad's technique of composition is not simply additive, filling the gaps in Benoît's story. The heterogeneous literary tradition means that he has to choose between contradictory accounts of the same events as well. He also leaves out episodes and details that would have obscured the clarity of the narration. Narrative rearrangement, improved motivation and a novel coordination between

135 Lienert, *Geschichte und Erzählen*, p. 33. For an account of the literary tradition of the story of the Trojan War and its central position in courtly literature (as the cradle of knighthood and *minne*), see Klemens Alfen, Petra Fochler and Elisabeth Lienert, 'Deutsche Trojatexte des 12. bis 16. Jahrhunderts: Repertorium', in *Die deutsche Trojaliteratur*, ed. by Brunner, pp. 7–197; and in the same volume Elisabeth Lienert, 'Ritterschaft und Minne, Ursprungsmythos und Bildungszitat: Troja-Anspielungen in nicht-trojanischen Dichtungen des 12. bis 14. Jahrhunderts', pp. 199–243 and *Geschichte und Erzählen*, pp. 30–34. On Konrad's adaptation of his sources, see, for example, Cholevius, *Geschichte der deutschen Poesie*, I, pp. 130–45; Bartsch, *Albrecht von Halberstadt*, pp. xxv–xxiv, pp. lxxxvi–xcv; Dunger, *Die Sage vom trojanischen Krieg*, pp. 43–60; Karl Friedrich Basler, *Konrads von Würzburg 'Trojanischer Krieg', und Benoîts de Ste. Maure 'Roman de Troie'* (Leipzig: Hoffmann, 1910); Clemens Fischer, *Der altfranzösische Roman de Troie des Benoît de Sainte Maure als Vorbild für die mittelhochdeutschen Trojadichtungen des Herbort von Fritslâr und des Konrad von Würzburg*, Neuphilologische Studien, 2 (Paderborn: Schöningh 1883); Cormeau, 'Quellenkompendium oder Erzählkonzept?'; Worstbrock, 'Erfindung der wahren Geschichte'.

136 Lienert explains that while Konrad follows Benoît, Ovid and Statius very closely, sometimes even literally, motifs from the other sources might have been mediated through secondary texts or common knowledge (Lienert, *Geschichte und Erzählen*, pp. 184–85). See also Worstbrock on the difficulty of comparing Konrad's work with Benoît's text, which is transmitted with a great deal of variance (Worstbrock, 'Der Tod des Hercules', p. 274, fn. 3).

different strands of narration through cross-references, prolepses, leitmotifs and thematic correspondences similarly contribute to the coherence of Konrad's composition, which is also influenced by the narrative pattern (episodes are centred on individual protagonists) and motifs of the courtly romance, especially Gottfried's *Tristan*. Lienert sums up this thorough and sovereign reworking of the literary tradition as follows:

> Insgesamt kann man wohl [...] sagen, alles Wesentliche – Stoffauswahl, Komposition, Figurengestaltung, Erzählerrolle, Erzählduktus, Gesamtstruktur und Gesamtdeutungsperspektive – stamme von Konrad. Aber es ist bezeichnend, daß Konrad kennerisch und gelehrt nicht beliebig erfindet, sondern aus dem gesamten ihm zur Verfügung stehenden Fundus der Tradition schöpft und das Vorgefundene nach eigenem zwingendem Konzept verwendet, kombiniert, verändert.[137]

Already Dunger appreciates Konrad's 'freies, selbständiges Schaffen' and the fact that the poet does not stick to one source but 'gestaltet seinen Stoff kunstvoll nach wohldurchdachtem Plane um'.[138] Nonetheless, earlier research has generally criticized a lack of structural and thematic cohesion between the episodes and the text as a whole. Barbara Könneker's judgement on the integration of different narrative threads is particularly damning:

> In der Regel erfüllen diese Episoden innerhalb der Haupthandlung keine Funktion und bleiben für ihr Verständnis ohne Bedeutung, so daß der Sinnzusammenhang immer wieder fast gewaltsam unterbrochen wird und es dem Leser und erst recht natürlich dem Hörer nahezu unmöglich ist, in der Handlungsführung eine gerade fortschreitende Linie zu erkennen bzw. die vielen verstreuten Einzelteile des Romans zu einem Ganzen zusammenzufügen.[139]

Gernentz, however, admires Konrad's 'hervorragende kompositionelle Fähigkeit' to compile a multitude of sources into a seamless whole: 'Alle Nahtstellen zwischen den einzelnen, nach immer neuen Quellen abgefaßten Abschnitten werden durch Zwischenbemerkungen oder erfundene Episoden

137 Lienert, *Geschichte und Erzählen*, pp. 182–222 (p. 222).

138 Dunger, *Die Sage vom trojanischen Krieg*, p. 44.

139 Könneker, 'Erzähltypus', 275. For further negative views on the unity of the *Trojanerkrieg*, see also the introduction in Konrad von Würzburg, *Die Goldene Schmiede*, ed. by Wilhelm Grimm (Berlin: Kleman, 1840), pp. xi–liii (p. xv); Halbach, *Gottfried von Strassburg und Konrad von Würzburg*, pp. 50–69; Green, *Vorstudien zum gotischen Stil*, pp. 46, 58–59, 64–67, 74–75; also de Boor, *Deutsche Literatur im späten Mittelalter*, p. 37; Monecke, *Das Erzählprinzip der 'wildekeit'*, pp. 34–52, 82–83. Monecke appreciates Konrad's attempts to connect the episodes through structuring remarks and prophecies, but is not convinced that the unity of the text is entirely accomplished.

überbrückt oder sogar so verwischt, daß sie nicht mehr spürbar sind'.[140] Cormeau in particular demonstrates that Konrad succeeds in integrating his vast and diverse material into a coherent whole, not only in a formal sense but also by giving it a consistent perspective. Against Gernentz's thesis that the protagonists are passively subjected to an inescapable destiny ('Marionetten eines allmächtigen Schicksals'[141]) he argues that following the narrative principle of the courtly romance their individual motivations in fact frequently drive events, so that a 'tragische Unausweichlichkeit' asserts itself through and against the individual:

> Auf die zwei Parteien des großen Konflikts verteilt [...] kehren sich die Zielrichtungen gegeneinander [...], der Sieg eines jeden der ausgezeichneten Helden bedeutet schließlich den Untergang eines anderen. Gerade dadurch, daß er die individuellen Abläufe an den Schemata des Romans orientiert, aber gegen die Erwartungen scheitern läßt, erreicht Konrad sein Konzept, er gewinnt die Perspektive einer übermächtigen Realität, der das Einzelschicksal unterliegt. [...] Es gibt zwar durchaus die individuelle und kollektive Schuld, doch sie wird als Teilkausalität dem Fatum untergeordnet.[142]

Following Cormeau, Lienert especially emphasizes how fatality asserts itself against the failed attempts of individuals to prevent the catastrophe, be it Priam's plan to have Paris killed, Thetis's efforts to hide Achilles away from the war, or the broken promises of everlasting love: 'Das Ganze ist großteils aus dem Bereich menschlicher Verantwortung herausgenommen. [...] Durch das nebeneinander von übergeordneter Fatalität und individuellen Handlungsspielräumen wird der Eindruck drängender Fatalität auf den ersten Blick abgeschwächt, letztlich aber verstärkt und narrativ verankert'.[143] This interpretation has since been criticized by Worstbrock, who, basing himself on Hercules' admission of personal guilt, sees the catastrophe as something that is caused by the moral failings of individuals: 'Ein Held des *Trojaromans* dessen Handeln den Charakter "tragischer Unausweichlichkeit" hätte, wird noch gesucht'.[144] The excessive vengefulness and *untriuwe* of the protagonists certainly stand in marked contrast to their laudative epithets,

140 Gernentz, 'Charakter und Bedeutung', 32.

141 Gernentz, 'Charakter und Bedeutung', 36–38 (p. 36).

142 Cormeau, 'Quellenkompendium oder Erzählkonzept?', p. 310, pp. 318–19.

143 Lienert, *Geschichte und Erzählen*, pp. 310–13 (pp. 312–13) and 'Der Trojanische Krieg in Basel', pp. 274–76. See also Walter Haug, 'Über die Schwierigkeit des Erzählens in "nachklassischer" Zeit', in *Positionen des Romans im späten Mittelalter*, ed. by Walter Haug and Burghart Wachinger, Fortuna vitrea, 1 (Tübingen: Niemeyer, 1991), pp. 338–65 (p. 351). On the many failed attempts to avert the catastrophe, with special reference to Paris's and Achilles' youth, see also Worstbrock, 'Erfindung der wahren Geschichte'.

144 Worstbrock, 'Der Tod des Hercules', p. 284.

so that their cruel deaths appear as the just punishment for these failings. This logic works even beyond the recurrent narrative pattern of the 'bestrafte Minneverfehlung',[145] as the cruel deaths of the treacherous Peleus and Nessus demonstrate.[146] The narrator even points out possible alternative patterns of behaviour (*Trojanerkrieg*, ll. 13017–67, ll. 17732–72). However, according to Hasebrink this does not mean that the protagonists could really act differently: 'Die Verlagerung der Motivation auf die Figuren trifft bei dem Versuch, sich von Konzepten der Fatalität zu verabschieden, auf die Fatalität des Affekts'.[147] Armin Schulz asserts something along the same lines:

> Immer wieder agieren die Personen auf Basis des feudaladeligen Wertesystems gleichsam wie psychische Automaten, die in ihrer Minne, hinsichtlich ihrer Ehre, als Auslöser ihrer Rache, in bezug auf ihre Sippe etc. nur eines entsprechenden Reizes bedürfen, um geradezu mechanisch affektiv zu agieren.[148]

Another point that speaks against Worstbrock's thesis is the fact that even morally unimpeachable behaviour keeps the wheels of destruction rolling: for example, the fact that the hunters spare the life of the baby Paris whom they are supposed to kill or that Hector refuses to fight his relative Ajax and grants the Greeks a truce.[149] An important contribution to this debate is an article by Kellner, who demonstrates that 'fatality' and 'tragedy' are not the right terms to capture the complicated motivational structure of the text, which is characterized by a 'Vielschichtigkeit der Schicksalsinstanzen'.[150] Classical *fatum*, represented by dreams and prophecies, and Christian *providentia*, represented by divine intervention, 'stehen fugenlos nebeneinander und formieren sich zu einem heterogenen Ensemble'.[151] Both are challenged by

145 Kokott, *Auftrag und Autonomie*, pp. 278–80.

146 Armin Schulz, *Schwieriges Erkennen: Personenidentifizierung in der mittelhochdeutschen Epik*, Münchener Texte und Untersuchungen zur deutschen Literatur des Mittelalters, 135 (Tübingen: Niemeyer, 2008), pp. 488–90.

147 Hasebrink, 'Rache als Geste', p. 221; similarly Martin Pfennig, *'erniuwen': zur Erzähltechnik im Trojaroman Konrads von Würzburg*, Europäische Hochschulschriften I, Deutsche Sprache und Literatur, 1537 (Frankfurt a.M.: Lang, 1995), p. 198; Lienert, *Geschichte und Erzählen*, pp. 313–14.

148 Schulz, *Schwieriges Erkennen*, p. 491; also Lienert, *Geschichte und Erzählen*, pp. 313–14; Pfennig, *Erzähltechnik*, p. 198.

149 See Lienert, *Geschichte und Erzählen*, pp. 311–12; Hasebrink, 'Rache als Geste', pp. 212–14; Müller, 'Blinding Sight', pp. 209–10; Schulz comments 'Die Paradoxie des *Trojanischen Krieges* liegt darin, daß es immer wieder Grundwerte der Adelsgesellschaft sind, die die Mechanik des Untergangs unaufhaltsam vorantreiben' (Schulz, *Schwieriges Erkennen*, pp. 466–67). He also refers to the ambivalent role of *êre*, which will be discussed in Chapter 3.

150 Kellner, 'Kontinuität und Diskontinuität', 94.

151 Kellner, 'Kontinuität und Diskontinuität', 96.

the notion of the coincidental *fortuna* represented by *gelücke* or *geschicht*. Kellner further argues that paradigmatic correspondences – she points out similarities and variations on the same themes in the love stories – create a narrative excess:

> Gegen die Linearität, gegen das Syntagma vom trojanischen Krieg entfaltet sich die Kreativität des Autors im Auserzählen von immer neuen Geschichten, im Generieren von narrativen Möglichkeiten. [...] Durch das Einspeisen von Erzählungen und deren Verästelungen werden allenthalben Alternativen sichtbar, wie die Geschichte von Troja auch anders hätte verlaufen können. [...] Hier manifestiert sich die Aleatorik der *fortuna* und hier muß sich das Telos des trojanischen Niedergangs immer wieder gegen die Alternativen durchsetzen.[152]

The fragmentary status of the text poses a major problem for these interpretations, however, and the last word on this issue may remain to be spoken, as Schulz concludes his overview of the debate with the following remark: 'Die Ereignisse im Text sind durch das partiell problematische Zusammenspiel von kausaler und finaler Motivation insgesamt weitgehend überdeterminiert, und dies erklärt vielleicht auch die anhaltende Forschungsdebatte über die Hierarchie von Fatum und persönlicher Schuld im Text'.[153] Even though the specifics of Konrad's compositional technique are still controversial, it is now generally acknowledged that his integration of different sources is very skilful.[154] The interlacing of the different episodes

152 Kellner, 'Kontinuität und Diskontinuität', 104–05. On the unrealized alternatives as well as the network of variations and correspondences that pervade the text, see also Lienert, *Geschichte und Erzählen*, pp. 227–51, pp. 313–14.

153 Schulz, *Schwieriges Erkennen*, p. 495. See also Toepfer, who analyses the motivational structure of the Medea episode in comparison to its ancient pre-texts (Regina Toepfer, *Höfische Tragik: Motivierungsformen des Unglücks in mittelalterlichen Erzählungen*, Untersuchungen zur deutschen Literaturgeschichte, 144 (Berlin: de Gruyter, 2013), pp. 400–451).

154 Other positive assessments of the accomplished unity are given by Dunger, *Die Sage vom trojanischen Krieg*, p. 44; Basler, *Konrad und Benoît*, pp. 9–32 (although he appreciates only the formal unity); Brandt, *Konrad von Würzburg*, pp. 176–79; Kokott, *Auftrag und Autonomie*, pp. 265–80; Pfennig, *Erzähltechnik*, pp. 78–134 (although he points out some inconsistencies in the temporal structure of the text); Knapp, *Hector und Achill*, pp. 53–87; Franz Josef Worstbrock, 'Die Erfindung der wahren Geschichte: Über Ziel und Regie der Wiedererzählung im *Trojanerkrieg* Konrads von Würzburg', in *Fiktion und Fiktionalität in den Literaturen des Mittelalters: Jan-Dirk Müller zum 65. Geburtstag*, ed. by Ursula Peters and Rainer Warning (Munich: Fink, 2009), pp. 152–74; most recently Gebert, who analyses the narrative strategies that Konrad employs to obscure inconsistencies in the transmission (Gebert, *Mythos als Wissensform*). Schröder, on the other hand, still questions the coherence of the text (Werner Schröder, *Kunstauffassung*, pp. 163, 167, 177; and *Über die Scheu vor der Tragik in mittelalterlicher Dichtung: Jason und Medea im 'Trojanerkrieg' Konrads von Würzburg*, Abhandlungen der Marburger Gelehrten Gesellschaft, 22 (Munich: Fink, 1992), p. 60).

into a tightly knit narrative continuum on various diegetic levels is described in most detail by Lienert:

> Über handlungslogische Verbindungen zwischen den Strängen hinaus sind die Teile (auch Episoden, die zunächst funktionslos erscheinen) dicht miteinander verbunden durch ein Netz von Responsionen und Korrespondenzen, von Parallelen und Kontrasten auf verschiedenen Ebenen: vom grundlegenden Erzählprinzip der sich steigernden Variation, von Leitthemen, Leitmotiven und durchgängigen Figurenkonstellationen über wiederkehrende Szenentypen und strukturelle Muster im kleinen bis zu Leitwörtern und Leitbildern.[155]

The Poet as a Compilator? A Methodological Caveat

Given his highly elaborate mode of adaptation, which creates something new by piecing together old parts, it becomes very interesting to see how Konrad himself reflects on his poetic work. It is, however, important not to project what we know about his actual compositional technique onto his statements in the prologue. Careful consideration of his programmatic exposition may well lead to the conclusion that both are closely related, but such a relation is not at all inevitable. Even if we have to assume that the educated recipient would have been aware of the breadth and disparity of the literary tradition, this does not mean that an author might not choose to obscure the actual state of transmission. Herbort von Fritzlar, for example, who also uses Latin sources besides Benoît, authenticates his work through reference to a linear tradition that preserves the identity of Dares' eye-witness account uncompromised from Greek via Latin to the French version, which is presented as the direct source of his German text:

> Diz buch ist frāzoys vň walsch
> Sin fuge ist gantz vň ane falsch
> Zu kriechen was sin erste stam
> In latin ez dannen quam
> Hīnē ist ez an daz welhishe kvmē
> Daz han ich also vurnvmē
> Tares der aller beste
> Den sturm vō troygē weste
> Wen er da mit was gewesen
> Dˢ screip in vň liz in lesen
> Cornelius den strit las
> Als er in kriechish geschribē was
> Als hat er in inz latin gekart

155 Lienert, *Geschichte und Erzählen*, pp. 227–51 (p. 240).

Sīt ist er tutsche zvngē gelart
Nach der sol ich wirken
[...]
Sint ez aber vō drin zvngen
Mit eime sinne ist her bescribē.[156]

Another example for such a strategy can be found in the main text of the *Trojanerkrieg* itself, as Monecke points out:

> Nahe läge die Vermutung, daß der Dichter [...] mit den Quellen Wucher treibe, daß er viele Stimmen hören, die Belege häufen, Entlegenes, ja Abwegiges vergleichend ausbreiten wolle. Konrad hat in der Tat sorgfältig kompiliert, aber diese Kompilation ebenso sorgfältig verborgen. Seine Gewährsleute im Chor berichten, einander ergänzen, widersprechen, übertrumpfen zu lassen, um dann vielleicht als Schiedsrichter das letzte Wort zu sprechen – eine denkbare Konsequenz der *wilden* Erzählkunst –, das kam Konrad offenbar nicht in den Sinn. Im Gegenteil, er pocht auf Dares. Es ist unwahrscheinlich, daß Konrad diesen Gewährsmann überhaupt benutzt hat.[157]

This obscuring of the different origins of the material and its diversity as well as Konrad's practice of not naming his authorities – other than Dares – is, of course, entirely incompatible with contemporary learned conceptions of *compilatio* such as that of Vincent of Beauvais.[158] In a similar vein to Monecke, Lienert argues that by obscuring his actual compositional technique, Konrad gives the impression that he is narrating the one and only story of the Trojan War, thereby contributing to the authority of his work: 'Der Zusammenhang, den der Autor herstellt, wirkt in sich schlüssig und zwingend, so als gäbe es nur diese eine Möglichkeit des Erzählens. Nirgends – außer in der Polemik gegen den Raub der Rüstung des Patroclus – stellt Konrad verschiedene Versionen nebeneinander'.[159] She argues that despite this appearance of

156 *Herbort's von Fritslâr liet von Troye*, ed. by Karl Frommann, Bibliothek der gesammten deutschen National-Literatur, 5 (Quedlinburg: Basse, 1837), ll. 47–75. On Herbort's strategy of obscuring the disparity of the transmission, see Kellner, 'Poetologie', pp. 235–45.

157 Monecke, *Das Erzählprinzip der 'wildekeit'*, p. 83. Cholevius also points out that Konrad never mentions his sources Ovid and Statius 'sondern ganz wie die anderen von seinem Dares schwatzt' (Cholevius, *Geschichte der deutschen Poesie*, p. 143). Dunger comments on Cholevius's observation that Benoît and other medieval poets writing about the Trojan War also do not mention all the sources they use: 'Und das kann gar nicht wundern; denn wenn sich diese mittelalterlichen Dichter auf irgend eine Quelle berufen, so thun sie das nur, um dadurch die Glaubwürdigkeit des von ihnen Erzählten zu versichern. Für diesen Zweck genügte es vollständig, wenn sie sich auf Dares beriefen' (Dunger, *Die Sage vom trojanischen Krieg*, p. 57).

158 Alastair J. Minnis, 'Late Medieval Discussions of *Compilatio*', *PBB*, 101 (1979), 385–421.

159 Lienert, *Geschichte und Erzählen*, p. 184; see also Cormeau, 'Quellenkompendium oder Erzählkonzept?', p. 304. The poetic strategies that create this impression of coherence from

perfect unity which would have been conveyed to a less informed audience, Konrad's choices for or against a certain version of the story would have been transparent to educated recipients.[160] Although this may be true, it is important to note that Konrad does not present his work as a composite entity in the main text. An interpretation of the concept of retextualization presented in the prologue will therefore have to suspend this knowledge of Konrad's actual method of compilation, which would not necessarily have been known to his contemporary audience, especially not before receiving the actual story.

After he has elaborated on the status of art in society and asserted his determination to keep on composing no matter how little recognition he may receive for his art, Konrad finally turns to the literary project at hand. He cryptically refers to an as yet unnamed deep book on which he has spent considerable time and effort:

> mîn sin der spannet unde dont
> dar ûf mit hôhem flîze,
> daz ich vil tage verslîze
> ob einem tiefen buoche,
> dar inne ich boden suoche,
> den ich doch finde kûme.
> z'eim endelôsen pflûme,
> dar inne ein berc versünke wol,
> gelîchen man diz maere sol,
> des ich mit rede beginne. (*Trojanerkrieg*, ll. 216–25)

The image of the book as a deep river may have been inspired by Geoffrey of Vinsauf, who explains that a chosen subject can be presented in either a concise or an extensive manner, metaphorizing the first option as a brook and the second as a river:

> via namque vel ampla vel arta,
> vel fluvius vel rivus erit; vel tractius ibis,
> Vel cursim salies; vel rem brevitate notabis,
> Vel longo sermone trahes. (*Poetria Nova*, ll. 206–09)

> [For either your path will be broad or narrow, either a river or a rivulet; either you will proceed discursively, or you may skip along hastily; either you will

diverse and often contradictory sources are analysed in Gebert's monograph. He emphasizes the self-referential presentation of myth in the *Trojanerkrieg* and describes its poetics as an 'Erzählmodell innerhalb von Wissensordnungen, deren Gegenstände es zwar absorbiert, sich im Akt des Erneuerns jedoch absolut setzt und seine Fremdreferenz gleichsam zu löschen sucht' (Gebert, *Mythos als Wissensform*, p. 13).

160 Lienert, *Geschichte und Erzählen*, p. 184, p. 193.

> note a thing briefly, or draw it out in an extended treatment. (*The New Poetics*, p. 41)][161]

In this tradition the image of the broad river could allude to Konrad's intention of amplifying ('breiten' (*Trojanerkrieg*, l. 303)) the story. However, the motif of the stream is soon substituted and surpassed by the simile of the grand composition as a wild ocean made up from many different rivers:

> ich wil ein maere tihten,
> daz allen maeren ist ein her.
> als in daz wilde tobende mer
> vil manic wazzer diuzet,
> sus rinnet unde fliuzet
> vil maere in diz getihte grôz. (*Trojanerkrieg*, ll. 234–39)

Despite the reasons for caution discussed above, this simile has frequently been taken as a description of Konrad's actual working method of compiling many different sources into a new coherent composition. Thus Kokott declares: 'Sein selbstbewußter Anspruch ist es, aus einer Vielzahl von Erzählungen und Berichten über Troja ein *getihte grôz* zu komponieren'.[162] Likewise, Kellner, comparing the prologues of the *Trojanerkrieg* and Herbort von Fritzlar's *Liet von Troye*, describes the concept of *erniuwen* articulated in the imagery of Konrad's prologue as that of compilation. She argues that unlike Herbort, who refers to one linear tradition and asserts the uncompromised identity of the story of the Trojan War throughout its different textual reincarnations from Greek to Latin to French and finally to German,[163] Konrad presents his poetic work as a transformation into an entirely novel narrative arrangement from several sources:

> Das Bild von den Flüssen, die sich ins Meer ergießen, steht für *compilatio* in dem Sinne, dass die frühere Überlieferung im Meer des eigenen Textes zum Verschwinden gebracht wird. [...] Es geht nicht mehr darum, die eine Geschichte von Troja in ihrer unverbrüchlichen Identität zu bewahren, das Ziel ist vielmehr die Aufhebung des Früheren in der Überbietung. Im Bild fungiert

161 Geoffrey develops this river metaphor consistently when treating the issue of amplification, speaking of the stream of words flowing in two branches or two streams uniting, when a thought is expressed redundantly, first in a positive and then in a negative form ('Sicque fluunt vocum rivi duo: rivus uterque | Confluit; exundant voces ex duplice rivo' (*Poetria Nova*, ll. 672–73)); and of small springs turning into great rivers ('Flumina magna trahunt ortus de fonte pusillo' (*Poetria Nova*, ll. 688)). The accomplished eloquence of Pope Innocent III is accordingly praised as a fast flowing torrent: 'velox facundia tanquam | Torrens praerapide currens' (*Poetria Nova*, ll. 2077–78).

162 Kokott, *Auftrag und Autonomie*, p. 259.

163 Kellner, 'Poetologie', p. 238.

> das Wasser als Substrat der Kontinuität und als Medium der Entgrenzung zugleich, bruch- und fugenlos verbindet es die verschiedenen Glieder der Tradition zur Einheit.[164]

She thus diagnoses the equivalence of Konrad's poetic programme with his actual working technique. Although her paraphrase captures many aspects of the image very accurately, her emphasis on the novelty of Konrad's work and the common interpretation that Konrad presents himself as a compilator do not appear as inevitable if the knowledge of his actual working technique is suspended. Already Monecke points out that the notion of Konrad's compiling his text from many sources is difficult to reconcile with the reference to one single book, 'daz alte buoch von TROIE' (*Trojanerkrieg*, l. 269), as the basis for his work,[165] a contradiction that Kellner does not account for in her discussion. Read in the wider context of the prologue, the water image – just like the phoenix simile or the renewal of the old book of Troy – is far more ambiguous and expresses concerns that go beyond a technical description of the situation of transmission and a particular mode of retextualization. While Kellner and other interpreters have correctly highlighted the tension between the old and new intrinsic to Konrad's presentation of his project, I believe that the aspects of novelty and difference have been exaggerated in relation to those of tradition and identity; and that ambivalent or contradictory elements of the prologue have often been unduly disambiguated and harmonized. Even though revisiting the frequently discussed passages of the prologue may only lead to a gradual relocation of Konrad's position on the scale between the old and the new, the discussion also aims at exhibiting some of the characteristics of metapoetics in Middle High German literature, which in turn require a readjustment of the interpretative approach. In addition to this, a perspective that is not biased towards discovering reflections of actual compositional techniques in metapoetic statements is open to perceiving aspects which might otherwise have been overlooked because they do not fit the preconceived model. In the case of the *Trojanerkrieg* prologue this particularly concerns the origins and implications of some core metaphors which will be discussed below. Before that, however, the thesis that Konrad presents his work as one of compilation will be investigated in more detail.

164 Kellner, 'Poetologie', p. 250, also 'Kontinuität und Diskontinuität', 85–90; similarly Juergens, 'Umgang mit Geschichte', 435, fn. 10; Hasebrink, 'Rache als Geste', p. 224; Lienert, *Geschichte und Erzählen*, p. 202; Manfred Stuckmann, *Wappenschilderungen und historisch-heraldische Anspielungen in Konrads von Würzburg 'Trojanerkrieg'* (doctoral dissertation, Bergische Universität Wuppertal, 2003), p. 77 (published online at http://elpub.bib.uni-wuppertal.de/servlets/DerivateServlet/Derivate-282/d040301.pdf [accessed 4 April 2016]); Seus, *Heilsgeschichten vor dem Heil?*, pp. 121–22; Gebert, *Mythos als Wissensform*, pp. 145–47.

165 Monecke, *Das Erzählprinzip der 'wildekeit'*, p. 86.

First of all, it is significant that the 'maere' Konrad wants to begin and the 'getihte grôz' he intends to compose are subsumed under the same imagery as that which already characterizes the unnamed book: the metaphor of deep water that the poet has to fathom. Their local position is different – the natural implication is that the 'pflûme' flows into the 'mer' – and their relationship also contains a temporal dimension that corresponds to the relationship between the ancient tradition and the contemporary poet, the old and the renewed book of Troy. Yet the waters of 'buoch', 'getiht' and 'maere' are still the same. The 'maere' is connected with verbs ('beginnen', 'tihten') that present Konrad as the agent of its creation, whereas the 'buoch' he wants to fathom suggests the notion of a single pre-existing entity, be it a written source or the story of the Trojan War itself. Konrad's use of metapoetic terminology bound together by consistent imagery obscures the distinction between the written source, the story and his own work as well as that between the individual parts and the whole – a loss of distinction that is also implicit in the image of flowing water. The ambiguity of his language is particularly striking in his use of the term *maere*, which is employed as a synonym for the deep book (*Trojanerkrieg*, l. 224), denotes his own composition (*Trojanerkrieg*, l. 234) as well as its composite parts (*Trojanerkrieg*, l. 239, l. 235?) and resonates with 'mer' phonetically. Christoph Huber has convincingly demonstrated that *maere* occupies a semantic field that ranges 'zwischen Geschehen und Geschichte, zwischen Stoff und konkretem Erzähltext, zwischen Erzähltradition und bestimmter Quelle, ja materialer Vorlage'.[166] Jürgen Lenerz explains that this vagueness does not differentiate Middle High German metapoetic vocabulary from modern German, but is common to all natural words in contrast to the clear-cut definitions aimed for in scientific terminology. The general meaning (intension) of a natural word has to be broad to remain flexible enough to be applied to different contexts. The actual meaning (extension) is then specified through referential or conceptual shifts. Conceptual shifts can, for example, be created through metaphor or metonymy; they can be conventional or occasional. Lenerz defines the core meaning of *maere* as 'erzählte Geschichte'. It can refer to different stories or to stories in general and be furthermore specified through metonymic conceptual shift:

> Zur Kernbedeutung 'Mitteilung' treten der 'Vorgang des Mitteilens', der 'Inhalt des Mitteilung', sowie dieser Inhalt 'in literarischer Verwendung' und schließlich auch die 'Vorlage'. Vom Akt des Mitteilens verschiebt sich das Konzept auf das 'Medium' der Mitteilung. Dazu gehören weitere konzeptuelle

166 Christoph Huber, 'Wort- und Bildnetze zum Textbegriff im nachklassischen mittelhochdeutschen Roman (Rudolf von Ems, Konrad von Würzburg)', in *Im Wortfeld des Textes*, ed. by Dicke, Eikelmann and Hasebrink, pp. 263–85 (p. 269).

> Verschiebungen, die *Stoff*, *Form*, *Struktur*, *Inhalt* etc der Erzählung betreffen und ihrerseits bewertbar sind.[167]

That such vagueness can, in fact, be an asset to metapoetic reflection is demonstrated by Kellner with reference to Herbort's usage of *sin*, which exemplifies the tension between identity and difference in transmission:

> Durch ihre semantische Offenheit wirken die Begrifflichkeiten wie Scharniere, die von einem Bildfeld gleitend zum nächsten führen. Jene semantische Beweglichkeit können sich dabei gerade poetische Texte zunutze machen, da sie ihre Themen nicht nach Art von Traktaten entfalten und fertige Lösungen anbieten, sondern vielfach in Aporien münden und Probleme in der Schwebe halten.[168]

The same applies to Konrad's usage of *maere*. Rather that reining in the breadth of meaning to a more definitive understanding he exposes different conventional nuances of the word ('Einzelereignis', 'einzelne Episode', 'einzelne Erzählung', 'Gesamtwerk') through conceptional shifts. Lenerz describes this eloquent play with various semantic aspects of a word as typical for poetic expression and emphasizes the cognitive function of displaying the richness and diversity of the associated concept in this way:

> [Die geistreiche Rede] expliziert die verschiedenen Aspekte einer Sache nicht, sondern demonstriert sie durch die in natürlichen Begriffen vorhandene Möglichkeit zur Verschiebung und evoziert sie so im Hörer, der die Komplexität der Sache für sich selber intuitiv rekonstruieren muss, indem er möglichst alle gemeinten Äußerungsbedeutungen entschlüsselt und zu einem komplexen Konzept vereint.[169]

In his discussion of the *Rolandslied* epilogue Peter Strohschneider furthermore emphasizes the semantic ambiguity of metapoetic expression that makes it difficult to reconstruct the actual circumstances of poetic production from it. Instead of deducing such elusive 'historische Faktizitäten' he analyses the 'Sinnbildungsleistungen der Epilogrede über diese Faktizitäten' independently from that 'was sich für Konrads Übersetzungspraxis historisch plausibel

167 Jürgen Lenerz, 'Zum Beispiel *mære*: Bedeutung und Bedeutungsvielfalt aus sprachwissenschaftlicher Sicht', in *Im Wortfeld des Textes*, ed. by Dicke, Eikelmann and Hasebrink, pp. 25–47 (p. 43).

168 Kellner, 'Poetologie', pp. 239–42 (p. 240). She demonstrates that the semantics of *sin* subtly changes throughout the prologue. It refers to each different textual manifestation in different languages, as well as to the unchanged identity of the story and finally even to artistic prowess.

169 Lenerz, '*mære*', pp. 46–47.

machen lässt'.[170] Particularly for the term *buoch*, which also features prominently in the *Trojanerkrieg* prologue as the deep book (*Trojanerkrieg*, l. 219) and the old book of Troy (*Trojanerkrieg*, l. 269), which may or may not be identical with one another and the grand composition (*Trojanerkrieg*, l. 239), he points out a lack of clear (and modern) categorial distinctions and questions: 'Wie verlässlich weiß man denn, dass hier eine Textgeschichte entworfen ist, die Tradierung auffasst als Abfolge von prägnant gegeneinander diskriminierbaren, im Verhältnis von Schrift und Abschrift, von Vorlage und Übersetzung zueinander stehenden Größen?'.[171] The same question could be asked about the *Trojanerkrieg* prologue. There, the 'fluid' shift from source/ story to Konrad's own poetic work, while maintaining the impression of still talking about one and the same thing through the employment of consistent imagery and the multi-faceted recurrence of the term *maere*, implies that they are still essentially identical despite being transformed and in constant flux. In this sense the image recalls the phoenix that remains the same in the process of revival. Consequently, it seems as though the quality of uniting different *maere* is not attributed to Konrad's composition alone, but also characterizes the book – it would certainly explain why it is so deep. Subtle differences in the interpretations of this figurative complex testify to the fact that it undermines clear-cut definitions and attributions: Kellner refers to the 'Metapher von der Entgrenzung der Tradition im Meer der *eigenen* Geschichte'.[172] Cormeau similarly interprets the streams of 'maere' and 'rede' as representing different sources, but identifies the ocean with the pre-existing book instead of Konrad's own work: '[I]hm [erscheint] das *alte buoch*, das er zu erneuern unternimmt, offenbar als ein Kompendium aus verschiedenen Quellen, die wie Flüsse im Meer zusammenfließen'.[173] Kern acknowledges the terminological difficulties of the passage and suggests that rather than representing something that already exists, the book might refer to Konrad's own poetic project, the composition he hopes to accomplish:

> Dabei ist nicht ganz deutlich, was dieses Meer tatsächlich bezeichnet. Offenbar nicht einfach nur das Sujet, sondern das Buch (vgl. 219), nicht im Sinne eines bereits vorliegenden Trojaepos oder Trojaromans, sondern im Sinne der Idee, der Potentialität, die das vorliegende Werk zur aktuellen Gestaltung bringt.[174]

170 Strohschneider, *Höfische Textgeschichten*, p. 283, fn. 42; similarly p. 280.
171 Strohschneider, *Höfische Textgeschichten*, p. 280.
172 Kellner, 'Poetologie', p. 250. This author's emphasis.
173 Cormeau, 'Quellenkompendium oder Erzählkonzept?', p. 303.
174 Kern, *Weltflucht*, p. 436.

Schröder, on the other hand, reads the ocean fed by many rivers as referring to a story made up of many episodes.[175] This alternative interpretation can be supported by Monecke's observation that in the main body of the text Konrad uses the terms *rede* and *maere* to refer to different strands of the narration ('einen Zusammenhang von Einzelgeschehnissen innerhalb des Ganzen') in structuring remarks like this:

> diz maere daz wirt hie geleit
> von ir ungelinge nider,
> wan ich grîf an die rede wider,
> wie man daz kindelîn erzôch. (*Trojanerkrieg*, ll. 5764–67)[176]

The fact that all of these readings are possible demonstrates that each of them is too particular. In any case, the strategically vague figurative expression cannot be read as the precise description of a specific method of retextualization, such as compilation. This notion is also not easily compatible with Konrad's presentation of his sources, especially in comparison with that of other authors. Although Konrad declares at first that he will transfer the old book of Troy from French into German verse (*Trojanerkrieg*, ll. 266–69), he presents a different account of his working process when he describes the genealogy of the story of the Trojan War. Now he declares that he works from both French and Latin:

> DÂRES, ein ritter ûzerwelt,
> der selbe gnuoc vor TROIE streit,
> swaz der in KRIECHISCH hât geseit
> von dirre küniclichen stift,
> daz wart mit endelicher schrift
> ze WELSCHE und ze LATÎNE brâht.
> dâ wider hân ich des gedâht,
> daz ich ez welle breiten
> und mit getihte leiten
> von WELSCHE und von LATÎNE:
> ze TIUTSCHER worte schîne
> wirt ez von mir verwandelt. (*Trojanerkrieg*, ll. 296–307)[177]

Apart from the inversion of the chronology – he names French before Latin – Konrad's account of the genealogy seems rather straightforward.[178] He

175 Schröder, *Kunstauffassung*, p. 167.

176 Monecke, *Das Erzählprinzip der 'wildekeit'*, p. 45. Further references: *Trojanerkrieg*, ll. 11378–79, l. 10215, l. 17326.

177 In the Brussels fragment published by Beckers, 'Brüsseler Bruchstücke', verse 306 reads: '... *czlich in liechtem schine*', which links it more closely to verse 275: *Mit worten lvtter vnd glancz*.

178 Lienert reads this inversion as a reference to the many different sources from which he actually compiled his work: 'Anscheinend geht es Konrad weniger um die Stationen

names only one author, Dares – whom in fact he does not use directly[179] – while leaving his main source Benoît and authorities such as Statius, Ovid and Virgil unnamed. Compared to his main source Benoît, this account of the transmission presents a marked difference. Although Benoît praises Homer's learning, he declares his account untrustworthy because he was born over a hundred years after the events and even his contemporaries considered him mad for having gods fight ordinary men. Dares, on the other hand, participated in the battle himself and recorded the events every day in an unbiased manner. His Greek account was then discovered by Cornelius, who wrote a Latin translation that Benoît pledges faithfully to translate into French.[180] In contrast to this, Konrad does not discuss the shortcomings or merits of individual sources. The authority of his work is not guaranteed through learned critique of sources or a line up of prestigious names, but through its reliance on an uncompromised Dares-tradition, which, despite its incarnation in different anonymous translations, is understood as a single book that is renewed by Konrad, as Monecke points out:

> Konrad [will] seine Quelle als e i n Werk vorgestellt wissen [...]. Er gibt zwar der Wahrheit die Ehre, indem er vermerkt, daß sein Stoff welsch und lateinisch vorliegt. Das soll aber nur besagen, daß zwei Fassungen des e i n e n Originals, eben der griechischen Niederschrift des Dares existieren. [...] Nur dies eine Werk wird als Original angesetzt – *daz alte buoch von Troye* (269) –, an einen Kodex soll ganz konkret gedacht sein. [...] Wie die Wahrheit so gründet auch der epische Stoff in einer einzigen Quelle.[181]

The idea that Konrad presents himself as a compilator becomes even more doubtful if his self-representation is compared with that of his predecessor Rudolf von Ems. In the prologue of his *Alexander* Rudolf explains that the literary transmission is corrupted:

---

der *translatio* (die Stufen *welsche und latîne* sind vertauscht) als um die verschiedenen nebeneinander existierenden Versionen aus denen er *von welsche und von latîne* [...] seine Fassung gestaltet' (Lienert, *Geschichte und Erzählen*, p. 23). She even suggests that Konrad refers to several Latin sources (p. 22, fn. 125). Against this opinion Schmitt argues: 'Konrad fügt seine Dichtung in die Dares-Tradition ein, die auf Lateinisch und Französisch vorliegt. Erst recht kann ich aus dem Vers keinen Hinweis auf zusätzliche lateinische Quellen entnehmen' (Schmitt, 'Autorisierung des Erzählens', p. 196, fn. 38).

179 Lienert, *Geschichte und Erzählen*, p. 186, pp. 182–83.

180 Benoît de Sainte-Maure, *Le Roman de Troie*, ed. by Léopold Constans, 6 vols (Paris: Didot, 1904–1912), ll. 45–144.

181 Monecke, *Das Erzählprinzip der 'wildekeit'*, p. 86, see also p. 36; likewise Schmitt, 'Autorisierung des Erzählens', p. 198. Compare also Strohschneider on the *Parzival* epilogue: 'Vielmehr hält sich in dieser Tradition die âventiur von Parzival als identische durch in einem Wechsel der Sprach- und Schriftformen, der als bloß akzidentieller vorgestellt wird' (Strohschneider, *Höfische Textgeschichten*, p. 45).

in hât manec man genant
und von im âventiure geseit
mit lügen und ouch mit wârheit,
der doch niht rehte hât geseit
von im die rehten wârheit.[182]

He therefore intends to stick to the reliable account of Alexander's teacher Aristotle. However, in the prologue to the third book he states that it is difficult to find the truth in the disparate literary tradition and warns that only texts can be trusted that correspond to Latin sources (*Alexander*, ll. 8045–62). In the prologue to the fourth book he then claims to have pieced together the true story from four reliable and non-overlapping Latin sources (*Alexander*, ll. 12961–13064). One of them is the *Historia de preliis*, whose author Leo is explicitly described as a compilator:

nâch sîner gernder suoche
vant er dô vil buoche
diu er compilierte. (*Alexander*, ll. 13009–11)[183]

Later on Rudolf criticizes the accounts of the German poets who have written about Alexander before him – he names Berthold von Herbolzheim, Lamprecht and Biterolf – as unreliable and incomplete. He explicitly states that he wants to be the origin of the true story in German, which he has reconstructed from different sources, thus presenting himself, as Worstbrock puts it, as a 'Kompilator der neuen Stoffkonstellation':[184]

wan ich in tiutscher zungen wil
ein urhap dirre mære wesn:
als ich die wârheit hân gelesn,
vert ez, als ich hân gedâcht,
sît ich hân zesamene brâht
allez daz diu schrift uns seit

182 Rudolf von Ems, *Alexander*, ed. by Victor Junk, 2 vols, Bibliothek des Literarischen Vereins in Stuttgart, 272, 274 (Leipzig: Hirsemann, 1928–29), ll. 62–66.

183 It is not quite clear whether Rudolf means to say that Leo abandoned this technique once he found the reliable account of Aristotle, or that he only used Aristotle's text as a main guide while adding from other sources as well (*Alexander*, ll. 13012–30).

184 Franz Josef Worstbrock, 'Wiedererzählen und Übersetzen', in *Mittelalter und Frühe Neuzeit: Übergänge, Umbrüche und Neuansätze*, ed. by Walter Haug (Tübingen: Niemeyer, 1999), pp. 128–42 (p. 142). Worstbrock recognizes Rudolf and Konrad as new types of authors: 'Hier zeigt sich eine beachtliche Erweiterung der Verfasserkompetenz über den Artifex hinaus, eine Erweiterung die eine Generation nach Rudolf in Konrads *Trojanerkrieg* weit umfassender noch und dichter noch zur Verschränkung von Kompilator und Artifex treibt' (p. 142). For a detailed discussion of Rudolf's self-representation as a historiographer and compilator see also Schmitt, 'Autorisierung des Erzählens', pp. 189–95.

mit ungelogener wârheit
endehafter mære
von dem wîsen wunderære. (*Alexander*, ll. 15804–12)

Konrad, on the other hand, does not highlight the fact that he used sources outside the Dares tradition to create a sum of all available knowledge about Troy. His textual genealogy obscures his actual compilation technique and, by not even acknowledging the existence of different traditions in the form of a rejection, makes the literary transmission appear much less complex than it really was. There is also no notion of the French and Latin versions compromising the identity of the story: both are described as 'endelich', reliable and/or complete.[185] Furthermore, unlike Rudolf, Konrad does not present himself as the agent who unites all different 'maere' for the first time, but rather as the interpreter of a book and the narrator of a story that are already intrinsically deep.[186] Water and 'maere' flow into the ocean and into the 'getihte grôz' of their own accord. The poet floating on the tempestuous surface appears as subject to these forces, not as their master. The wild and amorphous ocean of the 'grand composition' would also be a highly unorthodox image for the final result of Konrad's poetic efforts because it would contradict the notion of Latin poetics that the poet is supposed to impose order on his subject matter,[187] as well as the contemporary guidelines for compilation that specify *ordinatio* as the central task.[188] Instead, the raging ocean represents the challenge to Konrad's attempts at illumination, the subject matter of 'âventiuren wilde' (*Trojanerkrieg*, l. 283) and the tellingly labelled 'überflüzzeclichen hort von strîte' (*Trojanerkrieg*, ll. 291–92) that is paradoxically supposed to provide moral examples. The challenge attributed to the poet explicitly and repeated three times is that of finding ground in the endless depth of the story (*Trojanerkrieg*, ll. 216–21, ll. 226–29, ll. 240–43) and it is not, despite the need for organization implied in the wildness of the ocean, uniting its waters/'maere' for the first time. The following discussion will

185 See Monecke, *Das Erzählprinzip der 'wildekeit'*, p. 86, pp. 101–02, p. 114; and Schmitt, 'Autorisierung des Erzählens', p. 196. The term is previously associated with the light of true literature (*Trojanerkrieg*, l. 161). Compare also Wolfram's *Parzival*, 827, 5, where *endehaft* denotes the reliability of Kyot's account in contrast to Chrétien's. The fragment of the royal library in Brussels (ms. IV 950, 11) reads 'zv ediler' in *Trojanerkrieg*, l. 300.

186 Compare Schmitt, who also rejects the interpretation of the simile as an expression of a technique of compilation: 'Der Erzähler stellt sein Werk hier jedoch in erster Linie als ein überaus anspruchsvolles Unternehmen vor, wenn er sich zum Ziel setzt, eine Geschichte zu erzählen, die *allen mæren ist ein her*' (Schmitt, 'Autorisierung des Erzählens', p. 198).

187 On this concept of poetic work see Brandt, *Konrad von Würzburg*, p. 197

188 See Minnis, 'Late Medieval Discussions of *Compilatio*'. In contrast to this argument Kern interprets the wild ocean as a programmatic commitment to the aesthetic principle of *wildekeit* (Kern, *Weltflucht*, pp. 437–38).

therefore centre on the metaphor of 'ergründen' before focusing on 'erniuwen', another key word used to describe the process of retextualization.

'ergründen'

Unlike the supposedly implicit concept of compilation the striking metaphor of the tongue as an anchor and the pervasive metaphor of fathoming the waters of the story have received almost no attention in scholarship to date. In the further course of this section, it will be shown that Konrad draws on a rich and diverse tradition of metapoetic water metaphors to express the extraordinary demands of his poetic task.

The challenge Konrad has set himself is to find the ever elusive bottom of the deep book, a cumbersome task that stretches the skills of the experienced poet to the limits:

> ich muoz eht aber lîden
> den kumber, des ich hân gewont.
> mîn sin der spannet unde dont
> dar ûf mit hôhem flîze,
> daz ich vil tage verslîze
> ob einem tiefen buoche,
> dar inne ich boden suoche,
> den ich doch finde kûme. (*Trojanerkrieg*, ll. 214–21)

The metaphor of depth and the attempt to fathom it is then developed further into a simile that likens the story Konrad sets out to narrate to a river so endlessly deep that it could even swallow an entire mountain:

> z'eim endelôsen pflûme,
> dar inne ein berc versünke wol,
> gelîchen man diz maere sol,
> des ich mit rede beginne. (*Trojanerkrieg*, ll. 222–25)

The paradoxical image of trying to find the bottom of something bottomless picks up on and pushes the earlier admission of a personal struggle with a demanding task towards the notion of a mission that is inherently impossible. Nonetheless, in a further contradictory turn, Konrad suggests that he can in fact accomplish his quest for ground by dropping the anchor of his tongue into the deep:

> wil ich den grunt dar inne
> mit worten undergrîfen,
> sô muoz ich balde slîfen
> hie mîner zungen enker. (*Trojanerkrieg*, ll. 226–29)

The beginning of the passage addresses the literary project as a challenge to Konrad's 'sin'. The metaphor of the tongue as an anchor – which is reminiscent of the eccentric metaphor of the tongue as a hammer in the *Goldene Schmiede* (l. 13) – then shifts the emphasis from the intellectual grasp of the subject matter and possibly Konrad's conception of his own work to its realization in words, thus complementing the earlier discussion of the two instruments of the poet, 'sin' and 'mund'/'zunge'.

The anchor metaphor expands the simile of the story as a deep river into a mixed nautical allegory.[189] Whereas the tongue is explicitly identified with the anchor, it remains ambiguous what the boat, whose existence is merely implied, represents. If we were to take Konrad's curious body metaphor seriously, it might be the poet himself, who floats as a boat on the surface of the deep waters of the story. However, in accordance with the characteristic pairing that describes the poet's existence throughout the prologue, the anchor of the tongue would be naturally matched by the boat of the mind ('sin'). Furthermore, this second interpretation corresponds to traditional metapoetic seafaring metaphors. In any case, these two possible interpretations – the poet as a boat; the poet's mind as a boat – are not mutually exclusive but stand in metonymic relationship to one another.

The situation of the poet (or his mind) floating on the surface and trying to fathom the endless depth of his subject-matter appears precarious. This figurative nautical peril corresponds to the hardships ('kumber') of poetic work addressed earlier and to the actual danger the poet faces if he should fail to complete his uniquely demanding task of composing a finite account of an infinite ('endelôs') story:

> mîn lop daz würde krenker,
> ob ich des hie begünde,
> daz ich mit rede niht künde
> z'eim ende wol gerihten. (*Trojanerkrieg*, ll. 230–33)[190]

189 See Quintilian, *The Orator's Education*, ed. and trans. by Donald A. Russell, 5 vols, Loeb Classical Library, 124–27, 494 (Cambridge, MA: Harvard University Press, 2002), 8, 6, 49. Quintilian defines the 'mixed allegory' that combines simile, allegory and metaphor as the noblest form of allegory. Since both semantic realms, the figurative and the literal, are present, this type of allegory can be identified and interpreted more easily than the 'pure allegory', whose detection as a figurative mode of speaking relies on the context. To illustrate the principle of allegory Quintilian gives examples drawing on the source domain of seafaring, such as Horace's allegory of the ship of the Roman state shaken by the public war. Therefore, nautical metaphors and allegories can be described as intrinsically metapoetic (see Stolz, *'Tum'-Studien* pp. 368–69).

190 The overwhelming enormity of the subject matter is also addressed in the main text: *Trojanerkrieg*, ll. 11350–77, ll. 12908–21.

The risk of losing his hard-earned reputation as a writer gains a more existential dimension when the stream turns into the raging ocean of the grand composition:

> ez hât von rede sô wîten flôz,
> daz man ez kûme ergründen
> mit herzen und mit münden
> biz ûf des endes boden kan. (*Trojanerkrieg*, ll. 240–43)

The momentary detachment of the poet's mind on the surface from his tongue anchoring in the deep is superseded by the newly reinstated compound of heart and mouth fathoming the depths together. Konrad's difficulty of finding ground in the deep book is reiterated and identified as a general ('man') rather than a personal problem. It is thus not the inadequacy of the seasoned poet but the enormous scale of the task that is highlighted.

The image of the anchor links Konrad's reflection to the classical metaphor of poetic creation as seafaring, which was widespread in medieval literature, too.[191] In this tradition, the ship represents either the poetic work, or, as in Konrad's case, the mind of the poet. The beginning of a poetic enterprise or of a new chapter is described as setting sail, whereas the completion of the literary task is metaphorized as the arrival at a haven or as furling the sails and/or dropping the anchor, which can also mark the completion of a portion of the work.[192] As in the case of Konrad, who stresses the tempestuousness and depth

191 For the tradition of the metaphor, see Rudolf Drux, 'Des Dichters Schiffahrt: Struktur und Pragmatik einer poetologischen Allegorie', in *Formen und Funktionen der Allegorie*, ed. by Walter Haug (Stuttgart: Metzler, 1979), pp. 38–51; Curtius, *Europäische Literatur*, pp. 138–41. On seafaring as a productive metaphor for human existence in general see Hans Blumenberg, 'Beobachtungen an Metaphern', *Archiv für Begriffsgeschichte*, 15 (1971), 161–214 (pp. 171–90).

192 See for example: 'Atque equidem, extremo ni iam sub fine laborum | vela traham et terris festinem advertere proram' [In fact, were I not, with my task well-nigh done, about to furl my sails and making haste to turn my prow to land] (Virgil, *Eclogues*, *Georgics*, *Aeneid*, ed. and trans. by H. Rushton Fairclough, 2 vols, 2nd rev. edn by G. P. Goold, Loeb Classical Library, 63–64 (Cambridge, MA: Harvard University Press, 1999–2001), *Georgics*, IV, 116–17); 'Pars superat coepti, pars est exhausta laboris. | Hic teneat nostras ancora iacta rates' [Part of my enterprise remains, part is now finished. Here let the anchor be thrown, and hold my bark secure] (Ovid, *The Art of Love and Other Poems*, trans. by J. H. Mozley, 2nd rev. edn by G. P. Goold, Loeb Classical Library, 232 (Cambridge, MA: Harvard University Press, 1979), I, 771–72); 'Sed repetamus opus: mihi nudis rebus eundum est, | Ut tangat portus fessa carina suos' [But let us back to our work! with unveiled matters must I deal, if my weary bark is to reach her haven] (Ovid, *The Art of Love*, III, 747–48); 'mea iam longo meruit ratis aequore portum' [my bark in the wide ocean has already earned her harbour] (Statius, *Thebaid, Achilleid*, ed. and trans. by D. R. Shackleton Bailey, 2 vols, Loeb Classical Library, 207, 498 (Cambridge, MA: Harvard University Press, 2004), *Thebaid*, XII, 809); 'Nunc si forte meis quae sint exordia Musis | scire petis, iam Sidonios emensa labores | Thebais

of the waters, the dangers of such a sea voyage are sometimes emphasized: the sea can be described as rough, full of monsters and cliffs,[193] the ship may be weak or the mariner himself inexperienced.[194] These perils usually represent the difficulty of the literary task and the risk of not being able to complete the work, or of not completing it to the required standard[195] – a danger which Konrad specifies as that of losing his reputation.

The metaphor often appears in connection with invocations addressed to either a patron or a deity. The support or inspiration thus achieved is represented as the wind driving the boat of the poetic work[196] or as the force steering it.[197] Ovid, for example, assigns the role of the navigator to Germanicus, who is a poet himself and to whom he dedicates his *Fasti*: 'excipe pacato, Caesar Germanice, voltu | hoc opus et timidae dirige navis iter' [Caesar Germanicus, accept with brow serene this work and steer the passage of my timid bark] (*Fasti*, I, 3–4). Konrad attributes a similarly important role to his

---

optato collegit carbasa portu' [Now if perchance you would know what my Muse essays, the *Thebaid* has already accomplished her Sidonian labours and furled her sails in longed-for haven] (Statius, *Silvae*, ed. and trans. by D. R. Schackleton Bailey, Loeb Classical Library, 206 (Cambridge, MA: Harvard University Press, 2003), IV, 4, 87–89); 'Jam mare transcurri, Gades in littore fixi' (Geoffrey of Vinsauf, *Poetria nova*, l. 2066) [Now I have crossed the ocean; I have anchored on the shore at Gibraltar (*The New Poetics*, p. 106)].

193 Alcuin invokes the help of Saint Balthere, whose life he is about to narrate: 'placida tu mente teneto, | Et rege nunc nostram pelagi per caerula cymbam | Inter monstra maris, scopulosas inter et undas, | Ut possit portum portans attingere tutum' (Alcuin, *Versus de patribus, regibus et sanctis Euboricensis ecclesiae*, in *Poetae Latini Aevi Carolini Monumenta Germaniae Historiae*, ed. by Ernst Dümmler, 6 vols (Berlin: Weidmann, 1881–1951), I (1881), pp. 169–206, ll. 1321–24) [Kindly guard our boat and steer it now through the blue waters of the ocean past the monsters of the sea and the waves full of cliffs, so that carrying (us) it may reach the safe haven (this author's translation)].

194 For example: 'fluctus an sueta minores | nosse ratis nondum Ioniis credenda periclis?' [Or is my ship, accustomed to sail lesser seas, not yet to be trusted to the perils of the Ionian?] (Statius, *Silvae*, IV, 4, 99–100).

195 See Ovid, *Tristia, Ex Ponto*, trans. by Arthur Leslie Wheeler, 2nd rev. edn by G. P. Goold, Loeb Classical Library, 151 (Cambridge, MA: Harvard University Press, 1988), *Tristia*, II, 329–38. Later, however, the dangers of the sea come to represent the risk of the poet being punished for his work when Ovid comments on the injustice of being exiled for writing about topics that others have written about before without attracting criticism: 'non timui, fateor, ne, qua tot iere carinae, | naufraga servatis omnibus una foret' [I feared not, I admit, that where so many barks plied, one only would be wrecked while all the rest were safe] (Ovid, *Tristia*, II, 469–70).

196 Ovid refers to his inspiration by Venus: 'dum licet et spirant flamina, navis eat' [proceed, my bark, while still though mayest and the breezes blow] (Ovid, *Fasti*, trans. by James George Frazer, 2nd rev. edn by G. P. Goold, Loeb Classical Library, 253 (Cambridge, MA: Harvard University Press, 1989), IV, 18).

197 Thus Statius bewails the death of his father, who taught him the art of poetry: 'labat incerto mihi limite cursus | te sine, et orbatae caligant vela carinae' [Without you my course falters, uncertain my track, befogged the sails of the orphan craft] (*Silvae*, V, 3, 237–38).

patron Dietrich when he addresses him as the person who has *steered* him toward his poetic enterprise:

daz ich ez hebe mit willen an,
dar ûf hât wol gestiuret mich
der werde singer DIETRICH
VON BASEL AN DEM ORTE. (*Trojanerkrieg*, ll. 244–47)[198]

While *stiuren* frequently assumes the more general meaning of 'guiding, helping', it retains its original nautical semantics in the immediate vicinity of the seafaring allegory and is thus remetaphorized. However, unlike Germanicus, who is invoked by Ovid as the guiding force for the entire voyage of the poetic project, Dietrich is responsible only for setting Konrad up on his course, which leaves the poet to fend for himself on the high seas. Only at a later point in the prologue is the image of the lone poet on the raging ocean undermined when Konrad expresses his hope for divine guidance:

wird ich sô wol gehandelt
von götelicher stiure,
daz ich dis âventiure
mac ûf ein ende bringen. (*Trojanerkrieg*, ll. 308–11)

Another tradition that informs Konrad's use of the metapoetic seafaring metaphor is its potential to highlight the different status and demands of specific genres or literary topics – usually in statements of affected modesty. The grander epic themes such as the Trojan War or the history of the Roman Empire are represented by the vast and dangerous open sea that requires big ships or sails,[199] that is, gifted poetic minds, while the lighter genres, such as love poems, are metaphorized as shallow waters that can be navigated with the little barks of modestly talented poets. Horace, for example, opens his ode in praise of the *Pax Augusta* with such a gesture of humility:

Phoebus volentem proelia me loqui
victas et urbis increpuit lyra,
ne parva Thyrrhenum per aequor
vela darem.

198 Gebert points out that this role as a navigator also distinguishes Dietrich from the bat-like audience that lacks orientation (Gebert, *Mythos als Wissensform*, p. 332).

199 Ovid, for example, contrasts the lesser literary pursuits of his youth, which were devoted to the topic of love, to his current, nobler occupation with the seasons and religious rites: 'nunc primum velis, elegi, maioribus itis: | exiguum, memini, nuper eratis opus' [My elegiacs, now for the first time ye do sail with ampler canvas spread: As I remember, up till now your theme was slender] (*Fasti*, II, 3–4).

[When I wanted to sing of battles and the conquest of cities, Phoebus banged on the lyre, to prevent me from setting sail in my tiny craft across the Etruscan Sea.] [200]

Ovid, who employs the metaphor with particular creativity throughout his *Tristia* II, excuses himself for not having written about the Trojan War, the Seven of Thebes and the history of the Roman Empire by claiming not to be gifted enough for these grander themes of literature and more suited instead to the composition of lighter love poems. His limited poetic talent is metaphorized as a boat that may safely sail on the small ponds of lesser literary genres but should not venture onto the high sea of the epic genre: 'non ideo debet pelago se credere, siqua | audet in exiguo ludere cumba lacu' [A skiff ought not to trust itself to the sea just because it ventures to disport itself in a little pool] (*Tristia*, II, 329–30).[201] When he continues that only a gifted poet can narrate the deeds of Caesar, lest the work be overwhelmed by its subject, *materia* appears as the proper equivalent to the sea, while *opus* corresponds to the metaphorical bark that can easily be overwhelmed by the waves: 'divitis ingenii est immania Caesaris acta | condere, materia ne superetur opus' [Only

200 Horace, *Odes and Epodes*, ed. and trans. by Niall Rudd, Loeb Classical Library, 33 (Cambridge, MA: Harvard University Press, 2004), 15, 1–4. Compare Propertius: 'non est ingenii cumba gravanda tui. | alter remus aquas alter tibi radat harenas, | tutus eris: medio maxima turba marist' [The little bark of your genius must not be burdened with a heavy load. With one oar skimming the waters, the other scraping the sand, you will be safe: out in mid-sea occur the roughest storms] (Propertius, *Elegies*, ed. and trans. by G. P. Goold, Loeb Classical Library, 18 (Cambridge, MA: Harvard University Press, 1990), III, 22–24); similarly Statius: 'dic, Marcelle, feram? fluctus an sueta minores | nosse ratis nondum Ioniis credenda periclis?' [Say, Marcellus, shall I bear it? Or is my ship, accustomed to sail lesser seas, not yet to be trusted the perils of the Ionian?] (*Silvae*, IV, 5, 99–100).

201 However, in the further course of his attempt to convince Augustus to lift the sentence of exile Ovid soon undermines this modest stance by reminding him that he has in fact composed noble literature with his *Fasti* and the *Metamorphoses*: 'ne tamen omne meum credas opus esse remissum, | saepe dedi nostrae grandia vela rati' [Yet think not all my work trivial; oft have I set grand sails upon my bark] (*Tristia* II, 547–48). Here it appears that the ship does not represent the poet's talent but his work, for he can choose to put up bigger sails and is not limited by his natural capacity. Concluding his discussion of the *ornatus difficilis* Geoffrey of Vinsauf describes the stylistic devices appropriate to it as sails that the poet may choose: 'Si niti gravitate velis, his utere velis. | Hunc portum teneas, hic fixa sit anchora mentis' (*Poetria nova*, ll. 1061–62) [If you would trust in gravity, use these sails; keep to this harbor; here let the anchor of your mind be fixed (*The New Poetics*, p. 72)]. He also uses the metaphor in his treatment of abbreviation: 'Hac brevitate potes longum succingere thema, | Hac cymba transire fretum' (*Poetria nova*, ll. 702–03) [By means of this brevity you can cinch in an extensive theme; in this small boat you can cross an ocean (*The New Poetics*, p. 58)]. Even though his take on the metaphor is slightly different and focuses on quantitative instead of qualitative aspects of the subject matter, the small size of the boat still emphasizes the vastness of the *materia*.

a rich mind can tell the tale of Caesar's mighty deeds if the theme is not to surpass the work] (*Tristia*, II, 335–36).[202]

In this influential tradition, emphasizing the vastness and depth of the ocean into which he wants to sink the anchor of his tongue means that Konrad presents his subject matter as epic and proclaims the grand status of the story he intends to tell. In fact, he is about to narrate the grandest story of all: 'ich wil ein maere tihten, | daz allen maeren ist ein her' (*Trojanerkrieg*, ll. 234–35). He does not mention the size of his boat, which itself remains implicit, thus passing on a traditional modesty topos, but emphasizes the overwhelming difficulties of his task instead. However, there can be no doubt that his journey on the wild waters of the story is dangerous and that the poet's ship may easily be overwhelmed by the waves of the *materia*.

The classical metapoetic seafaring metaphor was also adopted in exegetical literature, where it refers to the contrast between the literal and the allegorical interpretation of Scripture. At the beginning of one of his homilies Origen, for example, prays to the Holy Ghost for favourable winds so that his ship may safely reach the haven of salvation. While the literal interpretation of the Bible corresponds to a journey close to the shore, the search for a deeper understanding is associated with venturing onto the ocean of secrets with its raging waves.[203]

In Middle High German literature, the metapoetic seafaring metaphor is employed in Heinrich von Mügeln's *Tum*. In the prologue Heinrich proclaims: 'uf genade fischet | min bet in diner güte tich'[204] and describes himself as a sailor on the ocean of the composition: 'uf tichtes mar ich swebe' (*Tum*, 117, 11). Towards the end of the text, he announces that the sail of his poem has almost reached the harbour: 'Zu staden diser schrift | der segel mines tichtes schifft' (*Tum*, 158, 1–2) and asks in the epilogue:

202 A slightly different employment of the metaphor is presented in Quintilian's *The Orator's Education*, 7, 2–4. There, the high sea represents the most difficult task of discussing a formerly untreated aspect of the topic of oration. Starting out with the discussion of easy and frequently treated issues, Quintilian sailed close to the shore alongside many companions. Then, when he tackled the issue of *elocutio*, which had rarely been treated before him, he had already ventured further out to sea and there were only a few companions left around him. Now that he intends to discuss the ethical requirements of the orator, he finds himself swept far out onto the high seas, at a point where even his distinguished predecessor Cicero, with his big and well equipped ship, had furled his sails before.

203 For examples and a detailed discussion, see Hans-Jörg Spitz, *Die Metaphorik des geistigen Schriftsinns: Ein Beitrag zur allegorischen Bibelauslegung des ersten christlichen Jahrtausends*, Münstersche Mittelalter-Schriften, 12 (Munich: Fink, 1972), pp. 137–41.

204 Heinrich von Mügeln, *Tum*, in *Kleinere Dichtungen*, ed. by Karl Stackmann, 3 vols, Deutsche Texte des Mittelalters, 50–52 (Berlin: Weidmann, 1959), II, pp. 147–219 (114, 11–12).

Meit, aller güt inguß,
hab ich nicht blünder sprüche influß
geleitet sam her Tullius,
in dines hoen lobes tich. (*Tum*, 175, 1–4)

These nautical poetry metaphors (conflated with the metaphor of inspiration as influx) gain special complexity through their juxtaposition with other, eschatologically coded water and seafaring metaphors: Heinrich hopes to be rescued from 'todes ünde' and 'jamers flut' (*Tum*, 173, 11–12); and a mixed salvation allegory identifies the ship with the Virgin and 'güte', the mast with the Cross and 'barmung', the sail with Christ and 'genade' and addresses God as the navigator of salvation ('heiles marner') (*Tum*, 174, 1–12). Metapoetic and topical vocabularies thus coincide in the image of seafaring.[205]

A similar religious connotation of Konrad's nautical allegory is implied by the invocation of God as the poet's navigator. The ocean of the story is in turn implicitly associated with the perilous ocean of life, thus endowing the poetic enterprise with an existential importance that transcends mere worldly concerns. The nautical imagery Konrad employs in the *Trojanerkrieg* in a metapoetic context is remarkably similar to his religious imagery in the *Goldene Schmiede*. There, the Virgin is contrasted to the deceptive allure of the siren and likened to the morning star that guides safely into harbour those who are lost on the bottomless ocean of the world:

Maria, muoter unde maget,
diu sam der morgensterne taget
dem wiselosen armen her,
daz uf dem wilden lebermer
der grundelosen werlde swebet:
du bist ein lieht daz iemer lebet,
und im ze sælden ie erschein
swenn ez der sünden agetstein

205 For a detailed discussion, see Stolz, *'Tum'-Studien*, pp. 342–43, pp. 359–69, pp. 369–75, with references to the rich tradition of Christian ship allegories: the Church as a ship navigating the perilous waters of the world to reach the haven of salvation and its many variants and elaborations. An early German example of the allegory can be found in the *Ezzolied*: 'O crux salvatoris. | duo unser segelgerte bist. | disiu werlt elliu ist daz meri. | min trehtin segel unte vere. | diu rehten werch unser segelseil | di rihtent uns die vart heim. | der segel de ist der ware geloube. | der hilfet uns der wole zuo. | der heilige atem. ist der wint! | der vuoret unsih an den rehten sint. | himelriche ist unser heimuot | da sculen wir lenten gote lob' (*Das Ezzolied in der Vorauer Überlieferung*, ed. and trans. by Christoph Lange (Erlangen: Palm & Enke, 2005), ll. 395–406). On this strophe in the context of the Greek and Latin traditions and with further German references, see Hans Neumann, *Die Schiffsallegorie im Ezzoliede* (Göttingen: Vandenhoeck & Ruprecht, 1960); furthermore the commentary by Lange, *Ezzolied*, pp. 211–15.

an sich mit sinen creften nam.
swaz diu syrene trügesam
versenken wil der schiffe
mit süezer dœne griffe,
diu leitest, frouwe, du ze stade;
din helfe uz tiefer sorgen bade
vil mangen hat erledeget. (*Goldene Schmiede*, ll. 139–53)[206]

The metapoetic imagery of the *Trojanerkrieg* prologue is clearly not a straightforward adaptation of the classical seafaring metaphor. There are many parallels that allow Konrad to articulate the risk, the demands and the status of his project, but there are also decisive differences. Instead of conveying the idea of a horizontal journey over the surface of the ocean which is also expressed in the Christian imagery of the ocean of life, the nautical allegory in the *Trojanerkrieg* privileges the notion of vertically fathoming the depth of the waters. It is, after all, the anchor of his tongue rather than the ship on the surface that is made explicit. The goal of the poet's journey is not arrival in a safe haven but the ground of the ocean. While the bottomless depth of the ocean on open sea would represent a threat to the seafaring poet in the classical metaphor and the eschatological simile, it is both menace *and* destination in the *Trojanerkrieg*. Accomplishing the near impossible task would crown his poetic career, whereas failure would cost him his hard-earned reputation. Anchoring in the depths would mean securing the ship, which otherwise would be tossed around helplessly on the wild surface of the waters until it might wreck and sink to the bottomless depths, but it also means staying in the most perilous position in mid-sea and penetrating – not just with the tongue, but also with the heart – into a depth whose bottom may never be found.

The metaphor of fathoming the depth of waters which Konrad conflates with the metaphor of seafaring has a long tradition as an image for biblical exegesis. In his *Confessions* Augustine casts the relationship of the literal and the hidden meaning of the Bible into the metaphor of surface and depth: 'Mira profunditas eloquiorum tuorum, quorum ecce ante nos superficies blandiens parvulis: sed mira profunditas, deus meus, mira profunditas! horror est intendere in eam, horror honoris et tremor amoris' [Wonderful is the depth of thy words, whose surface, see, is before us, gently leading on the little ones: and yet a wonderful deepness, O my God, a wonderful deepness. It is awe to

206 Later, Konrad explains the etymology of *Maria* by likening the Virgin, who is composed of all virtues, to the ocean, which is made up of many rivers (*Goldene Schmiede*, ll. 934–55). The metaphorical association of the Virgin with the ocean is also discussed by Köbele, who draws an analogy between the *Trojanerkrieg* uniting the sum of Troy sources and the *Goldene Schmiede* presenting a sum of Mariological symbolism (Köbele, 'Zwischen Klang und Sinn', p. 312).

look into it; even an awfulness of honour and a trembling of love].[207] Similarly, in the introductory letter to his commentary on Job, Gregory the Great, who also refers to the shipwreck of human life, i.e., of secular concerns from which he took refuge in the safe haven of the monastery, and to the stream of discourse that sometimes needs to be diverted for the purpose of edification, illustrates the different levels of meaning in the Bible with the paradoxical image of a river that is both deep and shallow, where the lamb can walk while the elephant floats:

> Diuinus etenim sermo sicut mysteriis prudentes exerciet, sic plerumque superficie simplices refouet. Habet in publico unde paruulos nutriat, seruat in secreto unde mentes sublimium in admiratione suspendat. Quasi quidam quippe est fluuius, ut ita dixerim, planus et altus, in quo et agnus ambulet et elephas natet.[208]
>
> [For as the word of God, by the mysteries which it contains, exercises the understanding of the wise, so usually by what presents itself on the outside, it nurses the simple-minded. It presenteth in open day that wherewith the little ones may be fed; it keepeth in secret that whereby men of a loftier range may be held in suspense of admiration. It is, as it were, a kind of river, if I may so liken it, which is both shallow and deep, wherein both the lamb may find a footing, and the elephant float at large.][209]

With its different layers of meaning the Bible offers different rewards to different types of reader. While the simple-minded reader remains on the surface of the literal meaning or, according to Gregory, finds some ground of understanding (if not the ultimate bottom) near the surface, the learned exegete finds deeper meaning as he searches beyond. However, the depth only grows greater the more immersed the interpreter becomes. Paradoxically, a deeper understanding creates greater depth rather than leading to arrival at the bottom.[210] It thus seems that Konrad has borrowed the image of the

207 Augustine, *Confessions*, trans. by William Watts, 2 vols, Loeb Classical Library, 26–27 (Cambridge, MA: Harvard University Press, 1912; repr. 1968), XII, XIV.

208 Gregory the Great, *Moralia in Iob*, ed. by Marc Adriaen, 2 vols, Corpus Christianorum, Series Latina, 143 (Turnholt: Brepols, 1979), Ad Leandrvm, 4, 173–78.

209 Gregory the Great, *Morals on the Book of Job*, trans. by Charles Marriott, 3 vols (Oxford: John Henry Parker, 1844–50), I (1844), p. 9.

210 Both references are used in a German sermon by Meister Eckhart in the context of a discussion of allegory (Meister Eckhart, *Deutsche Werke*, ed. and trans. by Niklaus Largier, 2 vols (Frankfurt a.M.: Deutscher Klassiker Verlag, 1993), I, sermon 51. For a discussion of this sermon, see Susanne Köbele, *Bilder der unbegriffenen Wahrheit*: Zur Struktur mystischer Rede im Spannungsfeld von Latein und Volkssprache, Bibliotheca Germanica, 30 (Tübingen: Francke, 1993), pp. 58–63 and the commentary by Largier in Meister Eckhart, *Deutsche Werke*, pp. 1047–50.

search for an ever-elusive bottom in deep waters from this religious tradition, suggesting that if understood and conveyed correctly, his profane subject may offer much more than a sequence of historical events even though it can barely be exhausted. The fact that at first he does not name the deep book he is labouring over only heightens the effect of the allusion to biblical exegesis.

The semantic realm of depth or ground is a traditional metaphor for the ineffable divinity in both Latin and vernacular religious literature. However, as Susanne Köbele points out, the Middle High German vocabulary is much less differentiated than the Latin terminology for the same semantic field. The Middle High German word *grunt* unites many different and even contradictory concepts that have distinct expressions in Latin, ranging from the concrete and local to the abstract. Köbele groups the meanings of the noun into four categories:

> (1) *grunt* als unterste Fläche eines Raumes oder Körpers, überwiegend als Grund von Gewässern (z.B. Meeresgrund, lat. *profundum*), aber auch von Gebäuden (lat. *fundamentum*, *basis*) bzw. in einem übertragenen Sinn (z.B. *grunt des herzen*); *grunt* steht häufig synonym mit *abgrunt* (z.B. *abgrunt der helle*, lat. *abyssus*). (2) *grunt* als Erdboden (lat. *humus*, *fundus*). Damit sind die beiden wesentlichen Bedeutungsstränge genannt. In dem Maße, wie die Vorstellung des Räumlich-Tiefen verblaßt, gewinnt das Wort eine begrifflich-abstrakte Tendenz: (3) *grunt* als Ursprung (*origo*); auch Ursache oder Beweggrund (*causa*), Anfang (*principium*), Vernunftsgrund (*ratio*), Beweisgrund (*argumentum*). (4) *grunt* als Innerstes (*intimum*), Verborgenes (*abditum*), Eigenes (*proprium*), als Wesen (*essentia*).

She furthermore argues that this vagueness or semantic breadth provides the Middle High German term with a special metaphorical productivity that is particularly suited to express paradoxes:

> *grunt* ist immer zugleich imaginierbar als das Innerste, Eigenste, Tiefste, Abgründige, Ursprüngliche, Anfängliche, als das Gründende, Begründende, ja Grundlose. Das mittelhochdeutsche Wort intendiert die Gleichzeitigkeit aller Aspekte und fordert gerade nicht die Entscheidung für einen von mehreren konkurrierenden Aspekten.[211]

Employing Blumenberg's terminology Köbele characterizes *grunt* as a 'Sprengmetapher', a metaphor that exhibits its own inadequacy by uniting polar opposites and undermining the distinction between the concrete image and the abstract concept to which it refers.[212] It can thus hold together

211 Köbele, *Bilder der unbegriffenen Wahrheit*, pp. 174–75, p. 177.

212 Köbele, *Bilder der unbegriffenen Wahrheit*, p. 187. Blumenberg defines the 'Sprengmetapher' as an attempt to articulate 'Unsagbarkeit' itself, as the expression 'der elementaren

contradictory concepts like 'origin' and 'destination', a paradoxical identification that illuminates Konrad's search for ground as a return to the origins, or the essence of the story. What makes the metaphor particularly suited as an ineffability topos, however, is the fact that it can mean 'bottom' as well as 'abyss', a contrast that epitomizes Konrad's impossible and dangerous mission of finding ground in the endless depth of the story.[213] Köbele emphasizes the dynamic quality of the paradoxical metaphor of the 'groundless ground': '*grunt* impliziert die Zuverlässigkeit eines festen Bodens und zugleich (als *abgrunt*) die Unvermeidlichkeit des Scheiterns, wenigstens die Gefährdung. Beide Aspekte überlagern und sprengen einander – der *grunt, der gruntlôs ist*, ist die Pointe dieser paradoxen Zuspitzung'.[214] In the *Trojanerkrieg* prologue a further layer of paradox is added by the conflation of the concepts of height and depth that is represented by the declaration that the waters of the story are deep enough to swallow a mountain. A similar expression can be found in the *Goldene Schmiede*, where Konrad also works with the contrast of height and depth to describe the verbal and intellectual inaccessibility of the Virgin:

> ob iemer uf ze berge flüge
> min rede alsam ein adelar,
> din lob enkünde ich niemer gar
> mit sprüchen überhœhen.
> sus kan din wirde enphlœhen
> so verre sich den sinnen min,
> daz ich den hohen eren din
> niemer mac genahen.
> so min gedanc wil gahen
> uf ze dime werden lobe,

Verlegenheit jeder Theologie, über Gott unentwegt sprechen zu sollen, ohne über ihn etwas zu sagen sich trauen zu dürfen. [...] Es wird eine Intentionalität der Anschauung überdehnt, um ihre Vergeblichkeit in ihr selbst auszusprechen, im Vorgriff zugleich die Zurücknahme des Übergriffs zu vollziehen' (Hans Blumenberg, 'Ausblick auf eine Theorie der Unbegrifflichkeit', in *Theorie der Metapher*, ed. by Anselm Haverkamp (Darmstadt: Wissenschaftliche Buchgesellschaft, 1982), pp. 438–54 (p. 445) (first published in Hans Blumenberg, *Schiffbruch mit Zuschauer* (Frankfurt a.M.: Suhrkamp, 1979), pp. 75–93).

213 Haupt comments with reference to the depiction of underwater life on Enite's saddle that 'meres grunt' could have evoked associations with the abyss in the Bible where monsters like Leviathan (Job 40–41) and other demons (Apocalypse 9.11) as well as the beast of the Apocalypse live (Apocalypse 11.7, 17.8) (Barbara Haupt, 'Literaturgeschichtsschreibung im höfischen Roman: Die Beschreibung von Enites Pferd und Sattelzeug im "Erec" Hartmanns von Aue', in *Festschrift für Herbert Kolb zu seinem 65. Geburtstag*, ed. by Klaus Matzel and Hans-Gert Roloff (Bern: Lang, 1989), pp. 202–19 (p. 213).

214 Köbele, *Bilder der unbegriffenen Wahrheit*, p. 188. See also Kiening, who discusses the creative employment of the metaphor of the dangerous and bottomless depth of the divine mysteries in the *Anegenge* (Kiening, 'Freiräume literarischer Theoriebildung', 426–30).

so sweimet ez dem himel obe
reht als ein flückez vederspil:
swenn aber ich hieniden wil
mit gedanken suochen ez,
so reichet siner tiefe mez
für allez abgründe. (*Goldene Schmiede*, ll. 16–31)[215]

Müller comments: 'Mit der Metapher *grund* wird auf einen Erkenntnisprozess angespielt, der in die tiefsten Zusammenhänge eindringt und so das Ungeformte formt. Wo sich das Marienlob notwendigerweise im Grundlosen verliert, muss das große Werk über Troja zum Grund vorstoßen'.[216] There is no doubt that the subject matters of both texts are categorically different. Nonetheless, given the highly paradoxical nature of the imagery in the *Trojanerkrieg* prologue – fathoming a bottomless abyss; depth as height; danger as security – as well as the religious connotation of the nautical allegory, Müller's strict differentiation of very similar images of inaccessibility seems overstated.

The aporetical structure of the *grunt* metaphor in the *Trojanerkrieg* also becomes evident in the fact that the old book Konrad wants to explore is likened to an 'endelôsen pflûme', whereas the Latin and French texts are descibed as 'endelich' and Konrad intends to bring the story he begins to an 'ende' (*Trojanerkrieg*, l. 233, l. 311). Although there is much to suggest that the identity of the old book (that presumably represents Dares' account) has been preserved in the French and Latin versions and will be preserved in Konrad's restoration, this clear opposition sets them apart again. This difference could mean that the project Konrad undertakes is not so extraordinary after all, because there were clearly people before him, the composers of the Latin and French versions, who managed to bring the seemingly endless expanse of the story to an end. In fact, if the old book can be identified with Dares' account, Dares would presumably have been the first person to achieve this feat. On the other hand, if the dichotomy is read as another expression of ineffability 'endelich' assumes an entirely unconventional connotation of deficiency. In this case any attempt to find ground and an end in the endless depth would be intrinsically flawed and doomed to fail, a reduction of a story which is extraordinary precisely by virtue of being endlessly deep. While this paradoxical structure is essential to Konrad's representation of his poetic task, the contradiction between the endlessness of the old book and the completeness of its textual reincarnations can be resolved if we assume that, in accordance with the exegetical tradition of the image, the bottomless depth of

215 On the biblical tradition of this imagery and for a discussion of this passage from the *Goldene Schmiede* in relation to the praise of Helen, see Chapter 4.

216 Müller, '*schîn* und Verwandtes', p. 297.

the old book does not simply refer to the sheer mass of the historical events, but also to the exploration of its deeper meaning, to the extraction of 'saelic bilde' and 'edel bîschaft' from an overflowing mass of conflict. The texts of the Dares tradition may well preserve a definitive ('endelich') account of the historical events, but it is Konrad who attempts the impossible task of making sense of it all. It has often been argued that while Konrad uses the metaphors *ergründen*, *durchgründen*, *entsliezen* in the traditional exegetical sense in some of his religious works, such as the *Goldene Schmiede*, in the *Trojanerkrieg* they merely mean representing the *materia* in a complete manner.[217] However, the religious associations of the seafaring allegory as well as of other passages such as the bat simile make the employment of the exegetical metaphor *ergründen* seem much less superficial than is often assumed.

'erniuwen'

Another verb Konrad uses to describe his poetic task is often cited as a metapoetic key term in retextualization. Thus Klein states: 'Das programmatische Leitwort für die Neugestaltung überkommener Sujets ist *erniuwen*'.[218] Despite the fact that the metaphors and similes surrounding the verb in the *Trojanerkrieg* have been interpreted as an expression of Konrad's concept of retextualization, the term itself has never been analysed in detail. It will therefore be crucial to establish the general meaning of *erniuwen* (intension) before evaluating its specific meaning in the context of the *Trojanerkrieg* prologue (extension).

Both with and without the prefix (*er*)*niuwen* necessarily refers to an accusative object. This means that the tension between the pre-existing old and the new that is created from it is already intrinsic in the term, in the sense of a reciprocal implication of repetition and transformation, identity and difference. The concept of the renewed is categorically distinguished from the concept of the new in an absolute and original sense. (*Er*)*niuwen* therefore

217 See, for example, Boesch, *Kunstanschauung*, pp. 195–98; Green, *Vorstudien zum gotischen Stil*, p. 82.

218 Dorothea Klein, 'Zwischen Abhängigkeit und Autonomie: Inszenierungen inspirierter Autorschaft in der Literatur der Vormoderne', in *Inspiration und Adaptation: Tarnkappen mittelalterlicher Autorschaft*, ed. by Renate Schlesier and Beatrice Trînca, Spolia Berolinensia, 29 (Berlin: de Gruyter, 2008), pp. 15–39 (p. 16); similarly Franz Josef Worstbrock, '*Dilatatio materiae*', 1; Corinna Laude, 'Quelle als Konstrukt: Literatur und kunsttheoretische Aspekte einiger Quellenberufungen im "Eneasroman" und im "Erec"', in *'Quelle': Zwischen Ursprung und Konstrukt. Ein Leitbegriff in der Diskussion*, ed. by Thomas Rathmann and Nikolaus Wegemann (= *ZfdPh*, 12 (2004)), pp. 209–240 (p. 215). On 'retextualization' as a neutral hypernym for the heterogenous phenomena of treating pre-existing literary material, see the introduction in *Retextualisierung in der mittelalterlichen Literatur*, ed. by Joachim Bumke and Ursula Peters (= *ZfdPh*, 124 (2005)), pp. 1–5.

seems particularly suited to characterizing acts of retelling pre-existing stories or written sources. However, the verb is more frequently employed to denote the resurfacing of usually negative emotions, the regaining of a warrior's strength, or rites of religious renewal such as baptism or confession.[219] Its metapoetic potential is only realized if it refers to specifically literary accusative objects such as *maere* or *buoch*.[220]

The first reference in a metapoetic context can be found in Wolfram's *Parzival* prologue: 'ein mære wil i'u niuwen, | daz seit von grôzen triuwen' (*Parzival*, 4, 9–10). It would certainly be problematic to equate the meaning of *niuwen* with Wolfram's actual technique of retextualization, which is still not fully understood.[221] This is even more the case because the problematic source references in *Parzival* demonstrate yet again that we have to account for significant differences between a poet's statements and his actual practice of retextualization. It would be equally difficult to interpret Wolfram's ambiguous metapoetic metaphors in the prologue or the sum of metapoetic statements dispersed in the main text (for example, the bow simile or the Kyot references) as a precise description of a specific method of retextualization that could serve as a (retrospective) definition of *maere niuwen*. Wolfram, who names neither himself nor his sources in the prologue, is obviously not interested in presenting a clear-cut account of his working technique that would be compatible with the learned terminology of Latin poetics.[222] This does not mean that the semantically vague *maere niuwen* does not gain any specific meaning in the context of the prologue. Wolfram's imagery certainly conveys an idea of which style of narration is to be expected. Thus Bumke suggests: 'Das sprunghafte Erzählen im *Parzival*, von dem im Prolog die Rede war, kann als Gegenprogramm zur Stillehre der Schulpoetik verstanden werden'.[223]

219 See the references in the Middle High German Conceptual Database: <http://mhdbdb.sbg.ac.at/index.en.html> [accessed 4 April 2016].

220 Even the collocation *maere erniuwen* does not always refer to processes of retextualization. In the case of the *Krone* it merely announces the intention of picking up a certain narrative strand again: 'Die mere ich ùch hernùwen wil, | Da von ich vor han geseit' (Heinrich von dem Türlin, *Die Krone*, ll. 12611–12; see also ll. 13021–222).

221 For a summary of research, see Joachim Bumke, *Wolfram von Eschenbach*, 8th rev. edn (Stuttgart: Metzler, 2004), pp. 237–47. Wolfram's intricate play with source references and other metapoetic statements is discussed by Kellner, who interprets them as signals of fictionality that call up the category of retelling to undermine it (Beate Kellner, '*ein mære wil i'u niuwen*: Spielräume der Fiktionalität in Wolframs von Eschenbach Parzival', in *Fiktion und Fiktionalität*, ed. by Peters and Warning, pp. 175–203).

222 Bumke, *Wolfram von Eschenbach*, p. 204.

223 Bumke, *Wolfram von Eschenbach*, p. 205. See also Haug, *Literaturtheorie*, pp. 159–78. He reflects on the interpretative difficulties of Wolfram's metapoetic utterances without denying his 'sich überstürzende[] Bilder[]', their expressive value and coherent meaning (*Literaturtheorie*, p. 164).

Kellner, on the other hand, interprets the statements in the prologue and the *Bogengleichnis* as references to Wolfram's paradigmatic style of narration in which a complicated network of correspondences is superimposed onto the linear succession of events.[224] However, Wolfram's representation of his project of literary renewal in the prologue remains associative and does not produce an accurate description of a process of retextualization that would depict the actual situation of transmission and involve distinct tasks such as *inventio*, *dispositio* and *elocutio*. No matter how influential the prologue might have been, Wolfram's occasional and associative semanticization of the expression *maere niuwen* is not precise enough to coin it as a metapoetic *terminus technicus* referring to a specific concept of retextualization that goes beyond the general meaning of retelling a pre-existing story or source.

That the expression remains open to individual semanticization is demonstrated in the prologue of Stricker's *Karl*, in which the verb *erniuwen* is associated with a very different poetic programme. Unlike in the *Parzival* prologue it is closely connected to the self-introduction of the author. The implicit bipolar time structure of the verb is furthermore emphasized by characterizing the *maere* as old:

> Diz ist ein altez mære.
> nu hât ez der Strickære
> erniuwet durch der werden gunst,
> die noch minnent hovelîche kunst:
> den sol hie mite gedienet sîn.[225]

Der Stricker bases his work on the *Rolandslied* of Konrad der Pfaffe, which he modernizes 'nach dem Muster der höfischen Epik' by introducing pure rhymes, an even metre and a 'flüssigeren Sprachstil'.[226] He also changes the representation of heathens and Christians, deletes some scenes and adds motifs from the Charlemagne and Roland tradition that are not included in his main source.[227] This mode of adaptation, which is compatible with the licence of retextualization (versus invention),[228] corresponds only partly to his statements in the prologue. There he explains that the heroic deeds of Charlemagne are so numerous that a book containing all of them could not

224 Kellner, '*ein mære wil i'u niuwen*'; on the Kyot excursus, see Strohschneider, *Höfische Textgeschichten*, pp. 37–57.

225 Der Stricker, *Karl der Große*, ed. by Karl Bartsch, Bibliothek der gesammten deutschen National-Literatur, 35 (Quedlinburg: Basse, 1857), ll. 115–19.

226 Hans-Joachim Ziegeler, Karl-Ernst Geith and Elke Ukena-Best, 'Der Stricker', in *Verfasserlexikon*, v, cols 417–449 (col. 420).

227 See Ziegeler, Geith and Ukena-Best, 'Der Stricker', p. 421.

228 On these licences, see Worstbrock, '*Dilatatio materiae*'.

be read in half a year. He therefore intends to compose only a short account (*Karl*, ll. 51–69). He addresses an audience that still appreciates 'hovelîche kunst', which could be interpreted as the announcement of a renewal in the courtly style described above. However, disregarding our knowledge of his actual technique of retextualization it could also be read as a quality characterizing the 'altez mære', since 'hoveliche kunst' is presented not as a novel but as a traditional art form ('noch'). Due to the vagueness of *maere* discussed above it remains unclear whether der Stricker understands the act of *niuwen* as reworking one particular source or the story of Charlemagne that is transmitted in several sources. Even the preceeding reference to *diu buoch* relating Charlemagne's deeds does not create clarity on this point, because the plural of this term does not necessarily denote different sources.[229]

Before Konrad von Würzburg there are no more examples for the employment of (*er*)*niuwen* as a term denoting a process of retextualization. In both instances the metapoetic meaning is created in an occasional manner through the syntactic reference to *maere*. While the general semantics – the poetic renewal of a source or story – are the same, the specific meaning of the expression created by the pragmatic context of the two prologues is very different. Neither Wolfram nor der Stricker define the term in the sense of a specific technique of retextualization; instead, the productivity of *niuwen* as a metapoetic term relies on its semantic openness, which can be filled in diverse and associative ways. The rarity of the collocation with *maere* is a further indicator that (*er*)*niuwen* is not an expression with a fixed metapoetic meaning. Such terminologization would also be unusual for Middle High German metapoetic vocabulary, which is generally characterized by pre-theoretical vagueness. Moreover, definitive poetic guidelines for retelling a source or story cannot be deduced from the broad spectum of Middle High German retextualization practice that ranges from translation (*Prose-Lancelot*) to conceptual, stylistic and structural reworking (Wolfram's *Willehalm*) and compilation from different sources (Rudolf's *Alexander*, Konrad's *Trojanerkrieg*) to new compositions from traditional motifs (Stricker's *Daniel*, Ulrich von dem Türlin's *Arabel*).[230] Even the Latin poetics do not treat the reworking of a *materia* consistently. Geoffrey of Vinsauf opens his *Poetria*

229 On the semantics of *buoch*, see Klaus Grubmüller, 'Das *buoch* und die Wahrheit: Anmerkungen zu den Quellenberufungen im *Rolandslied* und in der Epik des 12. Jahrhunderts', in *bickelwort und wildiu mære: Festschrift Eberhard Nellmann zum 65. Geburtstag*, ed. by Dorothee Lindemann, Berndt Volkmann and Klaus-Peter Wegera (Göppingen: Kümmerle, 1995), pp. 37–50.

230 Joachim Bumke, 'Retextualisierungen in der mittelalterlichen Literatur, besonders in der höfischen Epik: Ein Überblick', in *Retextualisierung in der mittelalterlichen Literatur*, ed. by Bumke and Peters, pp. 6–46.

Nova with a discussion of the structure of the content (*dispositio*), which can be either chronological (*ordo naturalis*) or preferably artificial (*ordo artificialis*), before moving on to his much longer treatment of stylistic concerns (*elocutio*), which includes topics such as abbreviation (*abbrevatio*) and extension (*amplificatio*). His predecessor Matthew of Vendôme, on the other hand, barely touches on the subject of structuring a text.[231] The vagueness of Middle High German metapoetic terminology relating to retextualization is thus matched, perhaps even caused, by a lack of implicit or explicit rules on the subject. This means that Konrad's audience will hardly have had a preconceived notion of what exactly is involved in 'renewing' a *maere* or *buoch*. Instead, the specific meaning of the expression had to be inferred from its individual context.

In the *Engelhard* prologue Konrad declares his ambition to restore the lost appreciation of 'triuwe'. The concepts of poetic and moral renewal are closely connected in the first lines of the prologue – 'Ein mære wære guot gelesen, | daz Triuwe niuwe möhte wesen' (*Engelhard*, ll. 1–2) – and in the following statement:

mit herzen und mit munde
wil ich von hôhen triuwen
ein wârez mære erniuwen
ellîche hie ze diute
darumbe daz die liute
ein sælic bilde kiesen dran,
daz si triuwe noch erman
unde in ganze wârheit gebe. (*Engelhard*, ll. 152–59)[232]

The description of the working process of retextualization is kept very minimal: 'ich hân si von latîne | in rîme alsô gerihtet' (*Engelhard*, ll. 212–13). Although the exact source of the story that circulated in Latin, French and German versions is unknown, the names of the protagonists, the structure of the narration as well as the inclusion of the love story and the tournament description are probably Konrad's own contribution.[233] In any case, the description as a mere verse translation does not reflect his actual technique

231 On the uncertain status of *dispositio*, which was sometimes regarded as a sub-category of *inventio* or *elocutio* (on the level of syntactical structure – *compositio*) and whose theoretical treatment was sparse in comparision to that of *inventio* and *elocutio*, see L. Caboli Montefusko and others, 'Dispositio', in *Historisches Wörterbuch der Rhetorik*, ed. by Gert Ueding, 12 vols (Tübingen: de Gruyter, 1994), II, cols 831–66.

232 The coincidence of renewing *triuwe* by renewing a story about *triuwe* is also pointed out by Burkhard Hasebrink, 'Die Ambivalenz des Erneuerns: Zur Aktualisierung des Tradierten im mittelalterlichen Erzählen', in *Fiktion und Fiktionalität*, ed. by Peters and Warning, 205–17 (pp. 214–15).

233 Brandt, *Konrad von Würzburg*, pp. 132–33.

of poetic renewal.[234] Apart from these sparse explicit statements, however, the term *erniuwen* and the concept of retextualization are also specified by the imagery of the prologue. The idea of renewing *triuwe* is associated with terms like *blüemen*, *schîn* and *glast* that pertain to the ethical value of *triuwe* as well as to the aesthetic quality of the renewed poetic artefact. Since Antiquity flowers and radiance have been common metaphors for the office of *elocutio*. Cicero, for example, states about the stylistic device of the metaphor: 'Modus autem nullus est florentior in singulis verbis nec qui plus luminis adferat orationi' [But there is no mode of speech more effective in the case of single words, and none that adds more brilliance to the style].[235] In addition to this, Konrad's elaborate personification of *triuwe*, which is modelled on Gottfried's depiction of the mistreated and impoverished *Minne* (*Tristan*, ll. 12217–357), also reflects on the semantics of *erniuwen*. In the tradition of Boethius and Alan of Lille the disregard for the value represented by the personification is expressed by the poor condition of her formerly precious and radiant gown.[236] Hence, if Konrad succeeds in bringing 'ir lobes trüeben schîn ze liehte wider' (*Engelhard*, ll. 144–45) this poetic and ethical restoration should also restore the beauty of her dress and appearance. The dress motif can therefore be interpreted as an allusion to the common metaphor of *elocutio* as vestment. Already Cicero compares the plain Attic style to a woman in a simple dress who requires neither jewellery nor an elaborate hairstyle or make-up to be beautiful.[237] Classifying the five *officia oratoris* he furthermore describes

234 On the alterity of the medieval concept of translation, see Worstbrock, who argues that the modern concept of translation introduced by Wyle does not just aim at transferring the *materia* into another language but also at preserving the style of the source text (Worstbrock, 'Wiedererzählen und Übersetzen').

235 Cicero, *On the Orator*, trans. by. H. Rackham, 2 vols (Cambridge: Havard University Press, 1942; repr. 1968), III, 166. The metaphor of stylistic devices as flowers is also pervasive in Geoffrey of Vinsauf's *Poetria Nova*; it is sometimes elaborated into gardening allegories: 'Sic igitur cordis digitus discerpat in agro | Rhetoricae flores ejus. Sed floreat illis | Sparsim sermo tuus, variis, non creber eisdem. | Floribus ex variis melior redolentia surgit' (*Poetria Nova*, ll. 1225–28) [In this way, then, the finger of the heart might cull flowers in the field of rhetoric. But let your speech flower sparingly with them, and with a variety, and not be thick with them. That fragrance is better that arises from an assortment of flowers (*The New Poetics*, p. 77)]; also: 'Verborum flores et rerum confer in unum, | Area sermonis ut floreat his specibus | Florum. Surget enim quidam concursus odorum | Et redolet plene permixtus uterque colorum' (*Poetria Nova*, ll. 1584–87) [Unite the flowers of diction and of thought in one, so that the meadow of your speech may bloom with both varieties of flowers. For there arises a certain harmony of fragrances, and it will have a rich odor mixed of both kinds of colors (*The New Poetics*, p. 89)].

236 Boethius, *De consolatio philosophiae: Opuscula theologica*, ed. by Claudio Moreschini (Leipzig: De Gruyter, 2000), I, P1, P3; Alan of Lille, *De planctu naturae*, ed. by Nikolaus M. Häring, *Studi Medievali*, 19 (1978), 797–879, VIII, P4.

237 Cicero, *Brutus*, *Orator*, ed. by H. M. Hubbel, trans. by G. L. Hendrickson, Loeb Classical Library, 342 (Cambridge, MA: Harvard University Press, 1939; repr. 1962), *Orator*, 78–79.

elocutio as the process of decorating and dressing the oration (*On the Orator*, I, 142).[238] The metaphor is also adopted in medieval treatises on poetry. Thus, John of Garland introduces his chapter on *elocutio* in the following way: 'Sequitur de materia nuda uestienda. "Materiam nudam" uoco illam que non est rethorice ampliata neque ornata' [The next subject is dressing up naked matter. I call 'naked matter' whatever is not rhetorically amplified or embellished].[239] Geoffey of Vinsauf uses the metaphor of dressing the (naked) *materia* with the *elocutio* several times, for example when explaining the succession of *dispositio* and *elocutio*: 'Mentis in arcano cum rem digesserit ordo | Materiam verbis veniat vestire poesis' (*Poetria nova*, ll. 60–61) [When a plan has sorted out the subject in the secret places of your mind, then let Poetry come to clothe your material with words (*The New Poetics*, p. 35)].[240] What makes Geoffrey's treatise particularly relevant to the discussion of retextualization is the fact that his *Poetria nova* is indeed a poetics of renewal and variation. Reiterating the necessity of casting existing cognitive content in novel poetic form throughout his work (e.g. *Poetria nova*, ll. 560–61), he also combines the concept of renewal with the dress metaphor, so that his treatise presents a likely model for Konrad's concept of *erniuwen*: 'stude contexere vocum, | Ut rude thema novae formae sibi sumat amictum' (*Poetria nova*, ll. 1683–84) [Strive to weave a fabric of words such that the unadorned theme may take to itself a garment of new beauty (*The New Poetics*, p. 93)].[241]

238 See also the *Rhetorica ad Herennium*, where *elocutio* is described as the means that prevents the product of *inventio* from remaining naked (*nuda*) (*Rhetorica ad Herennium*, ed. and trans. by Harry Caplan, Loeb Classical Library, 403 (Cambridge, MA: Harvard University Press, 1954; repr. 1968), IV, 1–6).

239 John of Garland, *Parisiana Poetria de Arte Prosaica, Metrica, et Rithmica*, ed. and trans. by Traugott Lawler (New Haven: Yale University Press, 1974), IV, 143–45.

240 In l. 1694 he also refers to 'rem nudam'.

241 Elaborating on methods of amplification, Geoffrey also recommends reiterating the same content in various forms – advice that seems to be reflected in the poetics of the *Trojanerkrieg*: 'sententia cum sit | Unica, non uno veniat contenta paratu, | Sed variet vestes et mutatoria sumat' (*Poetria nova*, ll. 220–222) [though your sententia be one single thing, let it not come content with one costume, but rather let it vary its apparel and assume changes (*The New Poetics*, pp. 41–42)]. Similarly: 'Quaelibet induitur duplicem sententia formam' (*Poetria nova*, l. 669) [any statement you please may be dressed in twofold form (*The New Poetics*, p. 57)]. He also uses the dress metaphor to describe the effect of renewal achieved by the employment of metaphor, by changing an old into a new expression of the same content while observing the requirements of aptum: 'Dives honoretur sententia divite verbo, | Ne rubeat matrona potens in paupere panno' (*Poetria nova*, l. 754) [let rich content be dignified by rich expression; do not let a wealthy matron blush in a pauper's gown (*The New Poetics*, p. 69)]; also: 'quae sit sua propria vestis | In simili casu cum videro, mutuor illam | Et mihi de veste veteri transformo novellam' (*Poetria nova*, ll. 767–69) [when I see what its proper apparel is in a similar situation, I change it and transform for myself, out of old clothes, something new (*The New Poetics*, p. 61)]. Other stylistic devices are described as lighter garments woven by art (*Poetria nova*, l. 957).

In Middle High German literature, too, the metaphor of *elocutio* as the dress of the *materia* can be combined with the key word *niuwe* to describe processes of retextualization, for example in a song by Frauenlob:

> Swer der materjen cleit e gab,
> von pfelle, samit rich gewant,
> Duchblümet ende (und) urhab,
> mit sprüchen ganz, vin, rich erkant:
> Danc habe sin herze und sin sin.
> komt aber der materjen such,
> cleide ich sie in ein niuwez tuch.[242]

Likewise, Heinrich von Freiberg praises his predecessor Gottfried as the one who masterfully dressed the 'sin' in 'so richer rede cleit' and the 'materie' in a 'lichte wat'.[243] In this tradition the dress motif in the *Engelhard* prologue presents the act of retextualization addressed by the term *erniuwen* as a stylistic renewal in the sense of *elocutio*: by cladding an old *materia* in a new and radiant – that is, stylistically advanced – dress of words, Konrad intends to restore the lustre to the garb of *triuwe*. This intimate connection between ethics and aesthetics means that although the poetic act of restoration relies on a stylistic update, it is by no means superficial but conforms to the classical requirement of *aptum* that is also expressed in Geoffrey's description of poetic rejuvenation.[244] With regard to the equivalence of content and form as well

242 Frauenlob (Heinrich von Meissen), *Leichs, Sangsprüche, Lieder*, ed. by Karl Stackmann and Karl Bertau, 2 vols, Abhandlungen der Akademie der Wissenschaften in Göttingen, Philologisch-Historische Klasse, 3, 119–120 (Göttingen: Vandenhoeck & Ruprecht, 1981), XIII, 7.

243 Heinrich von Freiberg, *Tristan und Isolde*, ed. by Danielle Buschinger, trans. by Wolfgang Spiewok, Greifswalder Beiträge zum Mittelalter, 16 (Greifswald: Reineke, 1993), ll. 21–29. Compare also the prologue of the *Tum*, where Heinrich von Mügeln asserts the fact that the poet cannot create anything new but has to draw from the river of old art (*Tum*, 112, 1–8). A couple of strophes before this, he expresses this process of retextualization as unpicking the seams of the garment of previous compositions to create a new dress from old material: 'Was e die meister han | den sprüchen wat gesniten an, | die zeist ich wider unde span | daruß ein nuwes tichtes kleit. | des ich uf alde wat, | die nuw min sin geferbet hat, | ufsnide manche slimme nat | mit ungefruter erebeit' (*Tum*, 110, 1–8). However, because of the fluctuating semantics of *sprüche* and *(ge)ticht* in the prologue, it is not quite clear whether Heinrich refers to recasting an old *materia* into a new poetic form, to articulating a new content with traditional poetic forms, or to repurposing old stylistic devices in a novel arrangement to express an old subject matter. While the aspect of dissembling and reorganizing the material of the old garment might call up the notion of *disposition*, the following reference to dying the faded garment with the colours of rhetoric and decorating it with flowers picked from the field of older poetry highlights the aspect of *elocutio* (*Tum*, 111, 1–12).

244 See also Cicero, who despite describing style with metaphors of clothing, decoration and make up insists that it should never become purely superficial: 'His tribus figuris insidere

as to the function of restoration and preservation of a value, Konrad's poetic redressing of *triuwe* resembles the retextualization of legends that Röckelein compares to the treatment of reliquaries and statues:

> Wie man Heiligenfiguren gelegentlich ein neues Gewand anlegte, wie man Heiligenschreine von Zeit zu Zeit überarbeitete, renovierte, veränderte, so wurden auch die Texthüllen der Heiligen immer wieder modernisiert und aktualisiert. Nicht nur in den literarischen Ansprüchen der Reformepochen und im persönlichen Ehrgeiz der Dichter, sondern auch in der Anpassung an den stilistischen Zeitgeist ist eine Ursache für die Praxis der hagiographischen Ré-Ecriture zu sehen.[245]

As in the *Engelhard* prologue, the concept of retextualization associated with the semantically vague term *erniuwen* in the *Trojanerkrieg* has to be inferred by interpreting its figurative context. After praising his patron Dietrich, Konrad finally announces his name and the subject of his work:

> VON WIRZEBURC ich CUONRÂT
> von WELSCHE in TIUTSCH getihte
> mit rîmen gerne rihte
> daz alte buoch von TROIE,
> schôn als ein frischiu gloye
> sol ez hie wider blüejen.
> beginnet sich des müejen
> mîn herze in ganzen triuwen,
> daz ich ez welle erniuwen
> mit worten lûter unde glanz,
> ich büeze im sîner brüche schranz,
> den kan ich wol gelîmen
> z'ein ander hie mit rîmen,
> daz er niht fürbaz spaltet. (*Trojanerkrieg*, ll. 266–79)

Like the image of the ocean fed by many rivers, the aspect of the coherence of the finished poetic artefact expressed in the image of Konrad gluing together the cracks in the old book of Troy has been interpreted as a reflection of Konrad's technique of compiling from many sources, for example by Brandt:

---

quidam venustatis non fuco illitus sed sanguine diffusus debet color' [These three styles should exhibit a certain charm of colouring, not as a surface varnish but as permeating their arterial system] (Cicero, *On the Orator*, III, 199–200). Müller, who studies the history of the dress metaphor, shows that it is often employed to demand an apt relationship between content and style and has at times been used to contrast vain rhetorical ornament to naked truth (Wolfgang G. Müller, *Topik des Stilbegriffs: Zur Geschichte des Stilverständnisses von Antike bis zur Gegenwart* (Darmstadt: Wissenschaftliche Buchgesellschaft, 1981)).

245 Röckelein, 'Vom webenden Hagiographen', p. 110.

> Der Vielzahl und Heterogenität seiner Quellen war sich Konrad durchaus bewußt: er gibt diese Tatsache im Prolog an sein Publikum weiter. Unklar ist, ob er mit *brüchen* [...] fehlende Überlieferungsteile meint (so C. Fischer) oder Nahtstellen, die beim Aufeinandertreffen verschiedener Überlieferungsträger entstehen und die er durch *rîmen* [...], also mit einem *künstlerischen* Mittel beheben will.[246]

Kellner reads the passage in a similar way as referring to the composition of one coherent narrative from a multitude of disparate sources. Despite the change in imagery and despite the fact that a wild, raging ocean is an unlikely candidate for representing sovereign narrative organization, she interprets the image of gluing together the cracks in the old book of Troy as a variation on the image of the ocean fed by many rivers: 'Hier mag man sich noch einmal an das Bild vom Meer erinnern, in welchem die Flüsse ihre Grenzen verlieren und ununterscheidbar werden'. According to her, the term *erniuwen* refers to the composition of a new and coherent poetic artefact from inhomogeneous material: 'Jener [der Vorgang des Erneuerns] besteht letztendlich in der beschriebenen Zusammenführung verschiedenen Materials in einer Weise, die so kunstvoll sein soll, dass keine Risse, Brüche mehr erkennbar seien'.[247] She further argues that the emphasis of this image of renewal does not lie on the truth and identity of the old story that is preserved in Konrad's work, but on the artistry of Konrad's poetry, exemplified by the radiant words and the image of the blossoming flower that unifies the disparate sources and thus creates a 'neuen, eigenen Gesamtzusammenhang'.[248] It is certainly true that the passage is more concerned with the aesthetic quality of Konrad's work than with the explicit proclamation of its historiographic authority – Konrad draws on the same traditional *elocutio* metaphors of flowers and radiance as in the *Engelhard* prologue.[249] However, Kellner's emphasis on the novelty of the

246 Brandt, *Konrad von Würzburg*, p. 175, with reference to Fischer, *Benoît de Sainte Maure*, p. 141; similarly, Dunger, *Die Sage vom trojanischen Krieg*, p. 45; Basler, *Konrad und Benoît*, pp. 12–32; Monecke, *Das Erzählprinzip der 'wildekeit'*, p. 82; Cormeau, 'Quellenkompendium oder Erzählkonzept?', pp. 307–09; Kokott, *Konrad von Würzburg*, p. 259, p. 283; Lienert, *Geschichte und Erzählen*, p. 205; Pfennig, *Erzähltechnik*, pp. 105–06; Stuckmann, *Wappenschilderungen*, p. 75.

247 Kellner, 'Poetologie', p. 251.

248 Kellner, 'Poetologie', p. 252.

249 Since the vocabulary of radiance is pervasive in the text, an additional non-metaphorical reading of the expression 'mit worten lûter unde glanz' could also be as an announcement of retelling the Trojan War employing the very terms *lûter* and *glanz* and their synonyms. In that case, Konrad would be mentioning the words rather than using them. The difference between using and mentioning a word is introduced by Searle, who illustrates it with the following example: 'Socrates was a philosopher versus "Socrates" has eight letters' (John R. Searle, *Speech Acts: An Essay in the Philosophy of Language* (Cambridge: Cambridge University Press, 1969), pp. 72–76). On the etymology and semantic scope of *glanz* and

glued-together artefact is less convincing. The image of gluing together the cracks in the old book of Troy is that of repairing a single, pre-existing literary object rather than of piecing together a new poetic artefact from numerous old and previously unconnected elements. Like the phoenix simile and the water imagery, this metaphorical complex presents the *Trojanerkrieg* as essentially identical with its predecessor. It is the renewed and repaired version of the same old book and therefore possesses the same authority.[250] An explicit affirmation of its historical truth is therefore not necessary. Konrad does not present himself as a compilator designing a new 'Gesamtkomposition' that has never existed before, but as a restorer, who makes the old book blossom *again* (not for the first time!) by gluing its components *back* together.

Emphasizing the unique requirements of his ambitious project and articulating his concept of literary renewal, Konrad employs imagery from diverse semantic realms. The depiction of poetic renewal as an act of gluing with rhymes that will bring about a new flowering of the old book of Troy departs significantly from the previous water imagery and appears also internally incoherent. While Gottfried, in his praise of Heinrich von Veldeke, develops a consistent allegory that metaphorizes the poetic work of Heinrich and his successors as the activities of gardeners (*Tristan*, ll. 4738–50), and Konrad himself employs a tree allegory in *Partonopier* to illustrate the relationship between entertainment and instruction (*Partonopier*, ll. 42–67), the combination of blossoming and gluing in the *Trojanerkrieg* seems rather odd. The variation of the striking *lîm* – *rîm* rhyme suggests that this peculiar juxtaposition of organic and artificial processes is inspired by another passage in Gottfried's literary excursus, namely his praise of Bligger von Steinach, which brings together nature and culture, not in the notion of cultured nature, as in the Veldeke allegory, but in the concept of artifice mimicking nature: 'wie kan er rîme lîmen, | als ob si dâ gewahsen sîn!' (*Tristan*, ll. 4716–17).[251] In

related terms (with reference to the divine; to the sun, stars and fire; and most frequently to objects of the courtly world like weaponry, clothes, castles, as well as knights and ladies) that Konrad uses particularly often and creatively in his work, see Wolfgang Haubrichs, 'Glanz und Glast: Vom inflationären Wortschatz der Sichtbarkeit', in *Sehen und Sichtbarkeit in der Literatur des deutschen Mittelalters: XXI Anglo-German Colloquium London 2009*, ed. by Ricarda Bauschke, Sebastian Coxon and Martin H. Jones (Berlin: Akademie, 2011), pp. 47–64.

250 Strohschneider arrives at a similar conclusion in his interpretation of the *Rolandslied* epilogue that glosses over the distinction between old and new actualizations of the story: 'Das bůch ist eine kompakte Instanz jenseits der Differenzen und des Wandels der Materialitäten, Medien und Praxen' (Strohschneider, *Höfische Textgeschichten*, p. 284).

251 The similarity of Konrad's and Gottfried's lines is also observed by Stuckmann, *Wappenschilderungen*, p. 74. For a recent discussion of Gottfried's horticultural metaphors and his praise of Bligger von Steinach, see Mark Chinca, 'Metaphorische Interartifizialität: Zu Gottfried von Straßburg', in *Interartifizialität*, ed. by Bürkle and Peters, pp. 17–36 (pp.

both cases accomplished poetry is poetry that succeeds in making an artefact that is glued together from several components appear like an organic whole. It is the concept of poetic work as restoration which makes for the subtle yet decisive difference between Gottfried's depiction of Bligger's art and Konrad's self-presentation. Although the fairies in the former can be taken to represent the inspiration of Bligger's composition, there is no notion of retelling an old story. While Bligger glues together his own new artefact from the material of his couplets, Konrad's rhymes are not the parts that make up the poetic artefact, but the glue that holds them together. Another important difference between the two passages is the fact that Konrad exploits the semantic potential of the plant metaphor further than Gottfried. It not only stands for the illusion of organic coherence that characterizes the assembled or restored poetic artefact, but also brings with it the notion of natural decay. The idea that Konrad wants to make the book of Troy blossom again suggests that its former beauty has wilted over time. In this context the attribute of age that would traditionally endow the book of Troy with authority gains an ambivalent status, because it also denotes its deficiency, which in turn necessitates the poetic renewal proposed by Konrad. Moreover, the notion of decay also connects the otherwise distant semantic realms of vegetation and cracks that can be mended with glue, since both natural and artificial objects can be corrupted over time. Konrad's poetic intervention is a pressing matter, not just of restoration but also of conservation, because the process of decay has not halted yet – the cracks will become even bigger unless he glues them with his rhymes. Given the strong emphasis on the aesthetic quality of the restored artefact (blossoming) and the materials of the restoration (shining words), it seems that Konrad's renewal is to be primarily understood as an amplifying ('breiten') stylistic update rather than as filling the gaps and mediating the inconsistencies in different sources.[252] However, as in the *Engelhard* prologue this aesthetic renewal is by no means presented as a menial or superficial task:

25–26, pp. 28–30). Gottfried's metaphor is also picked up by Rudolf von Ems: 'wir tihten und rîmen, | wir wænen daz wir lîmen | niuwan mit der rîme | der hôhen sinne lîme' (Rudolf von Ems, *Alexander*, ll. 3173–76); and by Wirnt von Grafenberg, who – unlike Konrad – seems to address the issue of restructuring the *materia* when translating the story of Litford Gawanides, which is 'ze wild', 'ze krump' and 'ze swære' (ll. 11629–30), from French: 'mîn zunge si verschriete | und begunde si wider lîmen | mit ganzen niuwen rîmen' (Wirnt von Grafenberg, *Wigalois*, ed. by Johannes Marie Neele Kapteyn, trans. by Sabine and Ulrich Seelbach (Berlin: de Gruyter, 2005), ll. 11672–74).

252 Schmitt also emphasizes that Konrad does not present himself as a learned *historiographus* and that the term *erniuwen* expresses primarily an 'ästhetische Neugestaltung' and 'daß ein bekannter Stoff neu – mit Worstbrocks Terminologie: wieder-erzählt wird – und damit in seiner wahrheitsverbürgenden Verbindlichkeit unangetastet bleibt' (Schmitt, 'Autorisierung des Erzählens', pp. 196–97).

it is the glue that holds the story together and will ensure its survival and continued capacity to provide valuable moral lessons – at least until Konrad's own style goes out of date and the flower of the old book wilts again.

A close analysis of the water and gluing metaphors thus demonstrates that they in fact present the *Trojanerkrieg* not as an entirely novel arrangement but as essentially identical with the pre-existing old book, identified with Dares's eyewitness account, and thereby endow Konrad's composition with authority. While the reading of both passages as references to the technique of compilation tends to gloss over the significant differences of the two images, 'ergründen' and 'erniuwen' in fact focus on very different aspects of the process of retextualization. The former addresses an effort to grasp and convey the deep meaning of the story, while the latter describes stylistic concerns. Only together can they provide an appropriate treatment of the challenging subject matter.

The analysis of the *Trojanerkrieg* prologue has demonstrated that it is problematic to generalize individual aspects such as the attitudes expressed in the nightingale simile or the *artes* discussion in order to construct a coherent literary theory, because Konrad's argument is frequently occasional and ad hoc instead of sustained and linear, allusive and associative instead of analytical. Similarly, to read the prologue's multi-faceted metaphors and fluid metapoetic terminology as descriptions of the very specific compositional technique of *compilatio* is a reduction of their complexity, which draws on rich metapoetic traditions and reflects on the antinomies that pertain to the writer's existence and the specificity of his art in a much broader sense. In addition to this, the unusual metaphors, which are drawn from very heterogeneous semantic realms and cannot easily be harmonized, not only thematize the topic of poetry but are themselves highly elaborate examples of the specificity of poetic expression. This latter characteristic lends them a special performative quality: they discuss what poetry is and they show what poetry is.[253] This mode of self-reflexivity, which highlights the core paradoxes of poetry and language in general, without resolving any contradictions or arriving at ultimate and unproblematic definitions, also characterizes the passages that will be analysed in the following chapters. Although many motifs from the prologue – for example, depth and light as ineffability metaphors – will recur, we always have to expect subtle shifts in their employment. While Konrad's interest in the issue of poetry is obvious throughout the text, the elements of his open-ended

253 This argument is made by Gebert: 'Konrads rasch wechselnde Metaphernfolge lenkt [...] die Aufmerksamkeit gleich zu Beginn des Romans auf dessen poetische Faktur – auch das Strukturierungs- und Imaginationspotential von Metaphern und anderer Elemente und Verfahren, aber ebenso auf deren Artifizialität' (Gebert, *Mythos als Wissensform*, p. 13).

reflection cannot be used to reconstruct a coherent 'Kunstauffassung'. Another result of the study of the prologue which will inform the interpretation of the main text is the fact that Konrad draws on imagery that originates in religious contexts. The bat simile presents a model of reception that is akin to the recognition of the divine. Similarly, the tasks of 'ergründen' and navigating the dangerous waters of the story with 'götelicher stiure' suggest an analogy between the interpretation of the Trojan subject matter and the moral lessons to be gained from it on the one hand and biblical exegesis on the other – associations which are foregrounded by expressions like 'wârez lieht' and the initial anonymity of the deep book. These religious connotations can be interpreted as a strategy of 'Selbstauratisierung', to employ a term from Strohschneider, who describes the crucial but nevertheless uneasy relationship between courtly literature and the Bible as the archetype of scripturality:

> In dieser Spannung von Distanz und Nähe zu dem kulturell verbindlichsten Typus von Schriftlichkeit situieren sich die Selbstentwürfe der höfischen Literatur. Man könnte sagen: Sie können nicht und müssen zugleich aber ihren Status als das Andere zur Heiligen Schrift in Szene setzen, weil es zu deren Modell im Grunde keine rechte Alternative gibt und weil sie zugleich doch qua Sakralität nicht in Frage kommt.[254]

Considered in isolation the significance of such repurposing of religious imagery is difficult to ascertain – especially in the case of an industrious professional poet like Konrad, who wrote secular as well as religious texts and might have simply made the most efficient use of his repertoire of figurative expressions – but the following chapters will show that Konrad in fact contextualizes the events of the Trojan War within an eschatological framework.

254 Strohschneider, *Höfische Textgeschichten*, p. 7. One prominent example of these strategies is, of course, Gottfried's *Tristan* prologue with its Eucharistic imagery.

CHAPTER 2

The Apple of Discord

The Apple of Discord is the first object in the *Trojanerkrieg* to be honoured with a lavish description (*Trojanerkrieg*, ll. 1390–529); its details have no model in previous Troy literature.[1] This marvel of workmanship has been soldered together from a golden half and a silver half, yet on closer inspection this dual optics disintegrates into a puzzling mixture of multicoloured sparkles that is obviously inspired by the 'mixtûre', the iridescent polychromy, of the wondrous dog Petitcreiu in Gottfried's *Tristan* (ll. 15818–44).[2] Around the middle of the Apple, presumably dividing the silver from the gold, runs a green band of emeralds, a detail that links the passage to another prominent description, that of Enite's horse in Hartmann's *Erec*, whose black and white halves are divided by a grass-green line.[3] The green band in Konrad's description bears an inscription of multicoloured pearls that specifies the Apple as the prize for the most beautiful among the female guests at the wedding celebration on Mount Olympus. It is further endowed with a magical property that causes it to change its language to address each reader in her own tongue. Another magical feature guarantees the outbreak of conflict: whoever reads the inscription is bound to consider herself the most excellent person and therefore the rightful recipient of the Apple.

1 Lienert, *Geschichte und Erzählen*, p. 43.

2 Monecke, *Das Erzählprinzip der 'wildekeit'*, pp. 176–77.

3 Hartmann von Aue, *Erec*, ed. and trans. by Volker Mertens (Stuttgart: Reclam, 2008), ll. 7311–15. See Hans Jürgen Scheuer, 'Wahrnehmen – Blasonieren – Dichten: Das Heraldisch-Imaginäre als poetische Denkform in der Literatur des Mittelalters', in *Wappen als Zeichen: Mittelalterliche Heraldik aus kommunikations- und zeichentheoretischer Perspektive*, ed. by Wolfgang Achnitz (= *Das Mittelalter*, 11 (2006)), pp. 53–70 (p. 61). On the metapoetic dimension of Hartmann's description see Sonja Glauch, 'Inszenierungen der Unsagbarkeit: Rhetorik und Reflexion im höfischen Roman', *ZfdA*, 132 (2003), 148–76 (pp. 151–55); Haiko Wandhoff, *Ekphrasis: Kunstbeschreibungen und virtuelle Räume in der Literatur des Mittelalters*, Trends in Medieval Philology, 3 (Berlin: de Gruyter, 2003), pp. 157–79; Susanne Bürkle, '"Kunst"-Reflexion aus dem Geiste der *descriptio*: Enites Pferd und der Diskurs artistischer *meisterschaft*', in *Das fremde Schöne*, ed. by Braun and Young, pp. 143–170. Since Enite's saddle bears a pictorial representation of the *lange liet von Troiâ* (l. 7546), Konrad's reference to Hartmann's description effectively closes an intertextual circle.

Konrad motivates the outbreak of the Trojan War in multiple ways: the abduction of Helen is not only caused by Paris's love for her but is also revenge for the first destruction of Troy and the rape of Hesione, which in turn is a reaction to an earlier insult to the Argonauts by the Trojans. The quarrel over the Apple of Discord is the reason why Paris, who is renowned for his precocious wisdom, is called to Mount Olympus. Fitted out by Venus in precious attire that emphasizes his natural beauty and mirrors some aspects of the Apple's appearance – his dress has two colours divided by a green seam decorated with pearls; it bears colours that do not even exist – Paris becomes a dazzling object of desire and competing ownership claims, just like the Apple. The conflict between Jupiter and King Priam of Troy, Paris's unwitting father, leads to a fight between Peleus, the future father of the Greek hero Achilles, and Hector, the principal fighter for the Trojans. This first fight in the story anticipates the Great War, which is presented in the prologue as the fight for Helen, the ultimate desirable object. The Apple is therefore not the sole reason for the Trojan War and is paradigmatically replaced by other desirable objects that cause or perpetuate conflict over the course of the story.[4] Nevertheless, the marvellous Apple of Discord has a special place as the first material 'scheidelsât' (*Trojanerkrieg*, l. 1372), the seed of conflict that sets the events leading up to the Trojan War in motion. It therefore also represents the seed of the *Trojanerkrieg* itself and can be regarded metonymically as the artefactual manifestation of the story. Given this formal and thematic prominence it comes as no surprise that the Apple of Discord has been at the centre of recent interpretations of the *Trojanerkrieg*, which have described it as a *mise en abyme* of the text.[5] This chapter will take this diagnosis as a starting point to discuss the problems of generically attributing metapoetic significance to masterful descriptions, but will ultimately argue that in the case of the Apple of Discord such a reading is in fact justified. After this has been established, it will address the question concerning the ideas which are being conveyed about poetry in general and about the *Trojanerkrieg* in particular. The final section of this chapter will investigate how some details unique to Konrad's description of the Apple foreground the interpretation of the *Trojanerkrieg* within an eschatological framework. First, however, the context of the description will be examined.

4 This connection is pointed out by Bleumer: 'Das Verlangen nach Schönheit bietet [...] zweifellos eine narrative Erklärungsmöglichkeit für das folgende Untergangsgeschehen. Die Schönheit ist stets ein Wert, den die verschiedenen Akteure gegen einen Widerstand begehren und den sie sich selbst zu attribuieren suchen' (Bleumer, 'Zwischen Wort und Bild', p. 117). It has to be noted, though, that in some cases – the Apple of Discord, the Golden Fleece – the desire for the beautiful object appears less important than the desire for the abstract values it represents. This point will be discussed further in Chapter 3.

5 This trend is anticipated by Monecke, who suggests a metapoetic reading of the 'mixture' (Monecke, *Das Erzählprinzip der 'wildekeit'*, pp. 177–78).

Setting the Scene

Apart from a few exceptions – such as the episode of the unsuccessful murder attempt and the abandonment in the forest, which are enriched by sparse yet evocative local colour – the story of Paris's birth and childhood is told with comparatively little scenic elaboration or object description. It is the wedding of Thetis and Peleus on Mount Olympus which presents the first showcase for Konrad's meticulously descriptive style. After introducing the most illustrious gods and goddesses as they arrive at the celebration, Konrad begins to describe the scene in great sensory detail. Animated nature and courtly society decorate the site with their beauty and fill it with sound:

beide bluomen unde wase
zierten anger unde felt.
vil manic keiserlich gezelt
was geslagen ûf den klê,
man dorfte weder sît noch ê
dekeinen plân beschouwen,
den ritter unde frouwen
sô kostbaerlîchen zierten.
ouch spilten unde smierten
rôsen, vîol unde bluot
in manges edelen herzen muot
durch der ougen bürgetor.
in den luft vil hôhe enbor
klanc dâ manic stimme lût.
bluomen, gras, loup unde krût
dâ stuonden wol geferwet
und heten sich gegerwet
in liehten wunneclichen schîn.
diu wilden kleinen vögellîn,
diu sungen ûf den esten
den hofelichen gesten
sô rîlîch in ir ôre,
daz in der himele kôre
möht ir gedoene erklungen sîn. (*Trojanerkrieg*, ll. 1116–39)

The description of the festivities on Mount Olympus is Konrad's own addition to his sources.[6] It is obviously modelled on the description of King Mark's May festival at the beginning of Gottfried's *Tristan*. Konrad does not imitate his predecessor's melodic style, created through numerous repetitions, alliterations, internal rhymes and the like, but like Gottfried he describes

6 Lienert, *Geschichte und Erzählen*, p. 42.

sympathetic anthropomorphized nature in terms of sensory forms of appeal which delight the ears and eyes of the guests, who are further characterized, with Gottfried's key phrase, as noble hearts. In Gottfried's description reciprocal smiles between blossoms and guests illustrate the harmony of courtly society:

> diu süeze boumbluot sach den man
> sô rehte suoze lachende an,
> daz sich daz herze und al der muot
> wider an die lachende bluot
> mit spilenden ougen machete
> und ir allez widerlachete. (*Tristan*, ll. 569–74)[7]

Similarly, Konrad's description of the festival scene peaks in an image of complementary harmony:

> dâ gleiz vil manic fürspan
> und manic edel schapellîn,
> dâ bôt durchliuhteclichen schîn
> diu gimme und daz gesmîde,
> der purper und diu sîde
> ir glanz dar under wâben,
> dar zuo die bluomen gâben
> und diu sunne liehten glast. (*Trojanerkrieg*, ll. 1162–69)[8]

Light is endowed with a tangible quality and solid materiality is dissolved into light when radiance from different sources is woven together into a single dazzling artefact representing an artfully composed unity of culture and nature. Despite the fact that the personified elements of the metaphorical compound are the agents of this process, the uniting act of weaving – which is multiplied in the sense that it involves already woven materials ('purper', 'sîde') – clearly resonates with the traditional metaphor of the poet weaving

7 Kurt Ruh lists a number of stylistic devices that translate 'das in der Semantik der Worte und ihrer Syntax angelegte "Bild" des Frühlings in ein Tonwunder' (Kurt Ruh, *Höfische Epik des deutschen Mittelalters*, 2 vols, Grundlagen der Germanistik, 7, 25 (Berlin: Schmidt, 1967–80), II (1980): *'Reinhard Fuchs', 'Lanzelet', Wolfram von Eschenbach, Gottfried von Straßburg*, p. 260); the harmonious interplay of the court and personified nature in Mark's festival is described by Horst Wenzel in *Hören und Sehen – Schrift und Bild: Kultur und Gedächtnis im Mittelalter* (Munich: Beck, 1995), pp. 403–08. Further details of Gottfried's description that have clearly influenced Konrad's description are, for example: 'diu cleinen waltvogelîn, | diu des ôren vröude sulen sîn, | bluomen, gras, loup unde bluot | und swaz dem ougen sanfte tuot | und edeliu herze ervröuwen sol, | des was diu sumerouwe vol' (*Tristan*, ll. 549–54); and 'diu sælege nahtegal, | daz liebe, süeze vogelîn, | daz iemer süeze müeze sîn, | daz kallete ûz der blüete | mit solher übermüete, | daz dâ manc edele herze van | vröude unde hôhen muot gewan' (*Tristan*, ll. 580–86).

8 A very similar description can be found in *Engelhard*, ll. 2720–27.

a text, or, in this case, Konrad weaving together many different elements to compose a harmonious setting. Apart from foregrounding the metapoetic dimension of the episode on Mount Olympus – not least by focussing on light, goldsmithery and textile work – the metaphor epitomizes the harmony of the courtly celebration which frames the goddesses Juno, Pallas and Venus. Despite the fact that Juno has initially been introduced as the wife of Jupiter and thus assumes the highest rank as the hostess (*Trojanerkrieg*, ll. 1028–29), the goddesses are now presented as equals who form a unity and occupy the throne of supremacy together:

> kein frouwe sich getorste
> mit schoene z'in gemâzen,
> dâ von si z'obrest sâzen
> schôn und gewalteclîchen dô. (*Trojanerkrieg*, ll. 1190–93)

Their splendid appearance and virtue is described collectively as the pinnacle of perfection and they are appreciated by onlookers as a group without differentiation (*Trojanerkrieg*, ll. 1223–37).

In the case of King Mark's festival the public, sensual display of courtliness creates the backdrop against which the secret and potentially unsettling love of Riwalin and Blanscheflur is contrasted[9] – a pattern of celebration and disruption that frequently occurs in courtly romances. Similarly, the ideal scenery of 'hôhe fröude' (*Trojanerkrieg*, l. 1174) on Mount Olympus is the setting for an intrusion that will tear the world of the story apart.[10] The goddess Discord has not been invited by Jupiter and decides to take revenge by causing a dispute that will eventually result in the Trojan War:

> si wolte kriege briuwen
> und alsô bitterliche nôt,
> daz manger sît gelaege tôt. (*Trojanerkrieg*, ll. 1294–96)[11]

Like Cundry, who disturbs the royal banquet in Wolfram's *Parzival*, she arrives on horseback. However, while the Grail sorceress's mount is skinny and burned, Discord rides a radiantly white horse. Furthermore, Cundry's grotesque ugliness stands in marked contrast to her inner 'triuwe' (*Parzival*,

9 See Wenzel, *Hören und Sehen*, pp. 410–12.

10 Lienert remarks that the narrative pattern of the disturbed celebration reappears several times throughout the *Trojanerkrieg*: the identification of Paris as Priam's inauspicious son, for example, happens on Priam's birthday and the wedding of Paris and Helen is interrupted by Cassandra's dark prophecies (Lienert, *Geschichte und Erzählen*, p. 243, fn. 60).

11 On the depiction of Discord, see also Gebert, who highlights the double determination of her actions as a result of her intrinsic nature and a reaction to the insult (Gebert, *Mythos als Wissensform*, pp. 176–79).

312, 3), whereas Discord's outward beauty is at odds with the inner disposition that is expressed by her name:

> DISCORDIÂ geheizen
> was daz wolgetâne wîp,
> mit rîcher waete was ir lîp
> gezieret und befangen,
> doch hete si begangen
> vil dicke wandel unde mein,
> si kunde werren under ein
> mit hazze werde liute.
> 'DISCORDIÂ' ze tiute
> ein missehellung ist genant,
> dâ von der name wol bewant
> was an ir lîbe schoene,
> der nîdic unde hoene
> bî wunneclichem bilde was. (*Trojanerkrieg*, ll. 1254–67)[12]

The description of her horse, beauty and attire, as well as the address to the audience ('seht' (*Trojanerkrieg*, l. 1248)) and the reference to an anonymous intradiegetic centre of perception ('die sach man nider vür daz holz | ûf die plânîe erbeizen' (*Trojanerkrieg*, ll. 1252–53)) suggest a stately entrance by the shamed goddess, a public scene similar to that created by Cundry. It only becomes clear retrospectively that Discordia has actually made herself invisible with a ring containing a magical stone. The paradox of the invisible beauty is accentuated by direct juxtaposition:

> bekleidet si nâch wunsche gienc
> in daz gestüele tougen,

12 Lienert also draws attention to the connection to Cundry, as well as to the thematic similarity to Konrad's Lady World in *Der Welt Lohn* (Lienert, *Geschichte und Erzählen*, p. 43). On the latter text, see Schulz, who points out the paradox that although the reliability of courtly splendour is questioned, the true, rotten nature of Lady World still manifests itself as visual evidence (Schulz, *Schwieriges Erkennen*, pp. 365–69). On the discrepancy between inner value and outer appearance in courtly literature, see Ingrid Hahn, 'Zur Theorie der Personenerkenntnis in der deutschen Literatur des 12. bis 14. Jahrhunderts', *PBB*, 99 (1977), 395–444; and Horst Wenzel, 'Hören und Sehen: Zur Lesbarkeit von Körperzeichen in der höfischen Literatur', in *Personenbeziehungen in der mittelalterlichen Literatur*, ed. by Helmut Brall, Barbara Haupt and Urban Küsters, Studia humaniora, 25 (Düsseldorf: Droste, 1994), pp. 191–218 (pp. 213–15). Müller emphasizes the differences to Cundry: 'Der Auftritt der Discordia hat [...] eine grundsätzlich andere Funktion als der von Unglücksbotinnen wie Lunete oder Cundrie: Diese machen auf einen verborgenen, doch zu bewältigenden Defekt höfischer Harmonie aufmerksam, jene deckt deren heillose Brüchigkeit auf' (Jan-Dirk Müller, *Höfische Kompromisse: Acht Kapitel zur höfischen Epik* (Tübingen: Niemeyer, 2007), p. 312.) See also Schulz, *Schwieriges Erkennen*, p. 460.

sô daz mit sînen ougen
nieman gesehen möhte ir lîp. (*Trojanerkrieg*, ll. 1298–301)

dekeinen man bedûhte,
daz er die frouwen saehe,
diu mit gezierde waehe
gie vor in allen unde stuont. (*Trojanerkrieg*, ll. 1314–17)

Discord's invisibility seems to render the deceptive incongruity of outward appearance and inner disposition redundant. The effect could be described as a reverse personification. Rather than casting an abstract principle into an anthropomorphic form, the person Discord disappears from sensual perception to become the abstract and trans-temporal principle she represents, the invisible force that drives the narrated world into destruction and is still rampant in Konrad's time.[13] In addition to this, the discrepancy between outer and inner qualities does not only serve to qualify Discord's general nature beyond the momentary state of invisibility, but in fact doubly determines her deceitfulness in opposition to the emphasized visuality of the courtly celebration and the ideal of *Kalos kagathos*.[14] Even though the disruption of harmony appears to come from the outside, from somebody excluded from the festivities, Seus convincingly points out that the principle of *krieg* and *strît* represented by Discord is really a central element of the courtly culture represented by Jupiter:

> Als höfischer Agon ist er [der *strît*] der Motor von Heldentaten und Turnieren, verhindert den Stillstand der höfischen Gesellschaft. [...] wenn man beide Personen als Stellvertreter des jeweiligen Prinzips, welches sie zugleich verkörpern, nimmt, so ergibt sich, dass die *hübescheit* (936), die durch Jupiter repräsentiert wird, in ihrem Ursprung, der ja in Jupiter begründet sein soll, gleichsam in ihrem Entstehen schon als Schattenseite mit sich bringt, was sie auszuschließen nicht vermocht hat: den Agon, jedoch nicht als offenen, wie er von Mars verkörpert wird, sondern den verdeckten, wie er durch die sich selbst invisibilisierende Discordia zum Ausdruck gebracht wird, der als Negativform

13 Compare Seus, *Heilsgeschichten vor dem Heil?*, pp. 157–59.

14 On the function of the courtly celebration as visualization of courtly ideals and social status, see Wenzel, *Hören und Sehen*, pp. 180–92, p. 403. Wenzel explains that the sphere of secrecy is an intrinsic part of the courtly culture of visibility since everything that does not correspond to the aristocratic ideal has to be kept hidden (Horst Wenzel, *Höfische Repräsentation: Symbolische Kommunikation und Literatur im Mittelalter* (Darmstadt: Wissenschaftliche Buchgesellschaft, 2005), p. 188). See also Haiko Wandhoff, *Der epische Blick: eine mediengeschichtliche Studie zur höfischen Literatur*, Philologische Studien und Quellen, 141 (Berlin: Schmidt, 1996), pp. 251–58. He describes the invisible as 'the other' of courtly culture. In the case of Discord, secrecy/invisibility is, of course, not an instrument for protecting the illusion of courtly perfection and harmony, but an instrument for disrupting it.

> im *kriec* bzw. in der totalen Zerstörung endet. [...] Das höfische Fest, das eine Gruppe der Besten zusammenbringt, deren Tugend an und für sich ununterscheidbar und damit jenseits der Differenz ist, wird durch Discordia gewaltsam re-differenziert.[15]

Striking at the heart of courtly culture, the deceptive beauty Discord uses an equally beautiful and destructive object to cause a conflict that will expose the ambivalence of its core values: the Apple of Discord.

Metapoetic Descriptions

Lienert opens her monograph on the *Trojanerkrieg* with an interpretation of the Apple of Discord as a microstructural representation of the text's poetics:

> Konrads Discordia-Apfel enthält *in nuce* eine kleine Ästhetik des *Trojanerkriegs*: Glanz und Licht, Farbigkeit und Schillern; Preziosität und irreale Künstlichkeit des Dargestellten; das Zusammenspiel von Detailfülle und strenger Gesamtstruktur, die nur aus der Distanz zu erkennen ist, in der Nahsicht aber sich auflöst in schwer zu fixierende Einzelheiten.[16]

Similarly, Müller sees the Apple of Discord as an object in which the ambivalent structure of the *Trojanerkrieg* is condensed. He describes it as a challenge to its intradiegetic audience which reflects on the extradiegetic challenge of reading the *Trojanerkrieg*:

> Die Beschreibung des Apfels erweist sich als *mise en abyme* des Romans und als Schlüssel seiner Poetik. Er ist klar in zwei Hälften von eindeutiger Farbe geteilt, und das differentielle und Differenz festlegende Medium der Schrift erklärt seine Bedeutung, doch die Schrift stiftet in diesem Fall nicht Ordnung, sondern heillose Verwirrung, und seine Gestalt löst sich in einer oszillierenden Wahrnehmung auf; je nach dem, aus welcher Distanz man ihn betrachtet, wechselt er die Farben. Was aus der Ferne schön und kostbar scheint, verliert aus der Nähe seine Bestimmtheit; man weiß nicht recht, wie es zu beurteilen ist. Der Apfel enthält die Allegorie des Lesens eines Romans, der die Schönheit der höfischen Welt in unerhörtem Glanz feiert und sie zugleich in grässlichem Schlachten untergehen lässt. Was strahlend scheint, verliert bei näherem Zusehen seine Eindeutigkeit.[17]

15 See Seus, *Heilsgeschichten vor dem Heil?*, p. 157, p. 160.

16 Lienert, *Geschichte und Erzählen*, p. 1.

17 Müller, '*schîn* und Verwandtes', p. 301; also 'Blinding Sight', pp. 212–14. See also Bleumer, who describes the iridescence of the Apple as 'weißes Rauschen', an overload of contradictory information that results in the loss of any information value: 'Als Summe der visuellen Möglichkeiten markiert der Apfel [...] ebenso die Grenze der sprachlichen Zeichen wie auch den Versuch, in der Rede von der Farbtotalität die eigene sprachliche Grenze zu

In his discussion of appropriate terminology for the description of medieval texts, Müller himself advises caution when diagnosing a *mise en abyme*. He sees it as a useful term to describe certain poetic techniques that exist in medieval texts yet have no equivalent in contemporary theoretical terminology, but he also mentions the danger of a 'gewisse Beliebigkeit' when *mise en abyme* is understood as an 'universelle[s] Verfahren der konzentrierenden und steigernden Spiegelung einer ästhetischen Ganzheit in einem ihrer herausgehobenen Teile'.[18] However, he does not specify what conditions would have to be fulfilled to avoid such arbitrariness in the identification of this technique, nor does he support his metapoetic interpretation of the Apple of Discord with a detailed analysis of the description.

Although the Apple as a visually ambiguous object that causes conflict undoubtedly encapsulates the duality of beauty and destruction that characterizes the *Trojanerkrieg*, an interpretation of the Apple's description as a *mise en abyme* of the aesthetics of the text would have to demonstrate that it is more than merely the first elaborate example of Konrad's poetic style. The qualities that Lienert enumerates – the emphasis on light, colour, precious materiality, artificiality and an attention to detail that is difficult to reconcile with the overall structure – as well as different forms of visual ambiguity or iridescence also apply to other descriptions in the *Trojanerkrieg*, most importantly that of Helen, as Müller points out himself.[19] This does not contradict the status of the Apple as a *mise en abyme*; after all, it can only be counted as such if it resembles the overall poetics of the text. At the same time, this is where the danger of arbitrariness lies, because one would expect that the aesthetics of a text should be reflected in not just one, but each and every description it contains.

überschreiten' (Bleumer, 'Zwischen Wort und Bild', pp. 119–20 (p. 120)). Scheuer argues that the lack of clear distinction violates the principles of heraldic blazon and arrives at a similar conclusion to Müller's: 'In der heraldisch miniaturisierten Ekphrasis des Apfels verdichten sich so Antagonismus und Dilemmatik, die Grundstrukturen der Discordia, deren maßlose Vergrößerung der Trojanische Krieg selbst ist' (Scheuer, 'Wahrnehmen – Blasonieren – Dichten', pp. 60–62 (p. 62)). Even Monecke identifies the heraldic colour contrasts (*underscheide*) that occasionally transcend themselves with descriptions of iridescence (*mixtûre*) as a key feature of the style of *wildekeit* (Monecke, *Das Erzählprinzip der 'wildekeit'*, pp. 161–66). See most recently Seus, *Heilsgeschichten vor dem Heil?*, p. 165; and Gebert, *Mythos als Wissensform*, p. 133. They also interpret the Apple as a *mise en abyme*.

18 Müller, '*schîn* und Verwandtes', p. 307. On *mise en abyme*, a term that originally refers to a coat-of-arms containing its own miniature, as metaphor for certain forms of poetic self-reflexivity, see Harald Fricke, 'Potenzierung', in *Reallexikon der deutschen Literaturwissenschaft*, ed. by Klaus Weimar, 3 vols (Berlin: de Gruyter, 1997–2003), III (2003), pp. 144–47. See also Wandhoff, who often discusses the function of the description of artefacts as *mise en abyme* (Wandhoff, *Ekphrasis*, especially pp. 7–10).

19 Müller, '*schîn* und Verwandtes', pp. 298–302. See also Lechtermann, 'Figuren der Abhebung', pp. 52–57.

In order to support his reading of the Apple as a miniature of the text Müller states: 'Auch vom Roman könnte man sagen, was vom Apfel gesagt wird: *an im lac hôher künste flîz/ von meisterlicher kûre*'.[20] He thus suggests that the remark has to be read as a form of implicit self-praise, pointing to the author as the *meister* artfully creating the narrated world. This interpretation is supported by the fact that the description of the Apple is indeed Konrad's own invention, which actually makes him its ultimate creator. However, this does not give the Apple a special status within the *Trojanerkrieg* since many of Konrad's detailed descriptions have no model in his sources and often represent masterfully created artefacts, as Lienert points out, concluding that: 'Kunstprodukt heißt jedoch: Produkt von Konrads Kunst'.[21] The term *meister* is indeed employed to refer to poetic artistry, for example in the prologue (*Trojanerkrieg*, l. 6, l. 52), but it is used with reference to all kinds of artefacts on the story level – be they artefacts in a literal sense or natural objects that are metaphorized as artefact – and with such inflationary frequency that it would require further arguments to claim a more than generic metapoetic significance of the term in the case of the Apple of Discord.

A close textual analysis of the description of the Apple is indispensable to supporting a metapoetic interpretation precisely because in some generic sense every poetic description is intrinsically recursive. Thus Lechtermann defines description as a 'doppelte[n] Akt des Zeigens', since every act of showing not only points to something else but also exhibits itself.[22] Similarly, Glauch explains this inherent self-exhibition as a result of the rhetorical function of description and stresses the aspect of competition: 'Wegen ihrer traditionellen Nähe zum *genus demonstrativum* der Rede, also zur epideiktischen Rede, die mehr sich selbst zur Schau stellen, als eine Sache vertreten will, stellt sich die *descriptio* von vornherein dem poetischen Wettbewerb'.[23] Furthermore, Mark Chinca points out that as a formalized rhetorical technique that can be learned and is based on literary models, *descriptio* always showcases literary artistry:

> Wenn die *descriptio* ferner nach den Vorgaben der *ars poetria* ausgeführt wird, was man im Falle klerikal gebildeter Autoren erwarten darf, rücken nicht nur die so beschriebenen Personen oder Sachen, sondern auch die

20 Similarly Kellner: 'Der Apfel ist künstlich, ein Kunstwerk wie Konrads Text, ebenso kostbar und auserlesen' (Kellner, 'Kontinuität und Diskontinuität', 111).

21 Lienert, *Geschichte und Erzählen*, p. 287. See also Glauch, who argues that most objects described in medieval texts are invented so that they exist 'schließlich nicht anders als in der literarischen, erzählten Realität' (Glauch, 'Inszenierungen der Unsagbarkeit', 154).

22 Lechtermann, 'Figuren der Abhebung', p. 51.

23 Glauch, 'Inszenierungen der Unsagbarkeit', 162.

> Beschreibungsverfahren selbst in den Vordergrund und werden zum möglichen Gegenstand der Reflexion.[24]

On this general basis, description lends itself to more overt forms of self-reflection, as Glauch explains:

> Bei der Füllung eines festgefügten Schemas wird jede Variation schnell zur anspielenden Auseinandersetzung mit einem Vorgänger. Sobald die Intertextualität explizit wird und der Verfasser sich bewußt wird, daß sein Text nicht alleine auf der Welt ist, ist die Reflexion über das poetische Selbstverständnis nicht mehr weit.[25]

Bürkle argues that in vernacular literature descriptions frequently give rise to reflection on poetry because they create a pause in the flow of the narrative action. In addition to this, the technique of *amplificatio* that poets used when recasting pre-existing material creates a space ('Spiel-Raum') of artistic licence for such metapoetic endeavours between the constraints of literary tradition. This 'Spiel-Raum' is common to all descriptions, but every individual description utilizes it to a different extent and in different ways.[26] A prime example for this correlation between description, intertextuality and metapoetic reflection can be found in Gottfried's *Tristan*. There, the narrator articulates the difficulty of describing the outer splendour of Tristan and his peers at the knighting ceremony: scenes like these have been described so often before and are 'mit rede alsô zertriben' (*Tristan*, l. 4618) that he can hardly say anything new or better. Instead of trying to outdo his predecessors with an even more artful but conventional description, Gottfried inserts a discussion of literary standards in general, his famous catalogue of Middle High German poets (*Tristan*, ll. 4621–820). Glauch also discusses the heightened metapoetic potential of the description of artefacts (or natural objects metaphorized as artefacts) to which Müller alludes:

> Die *descriptio* pflegt sich auf Gebilde zu richten, die von jemandem geschaffen worden sind. Überwiegend sind es vom Menschen geschaffene Artefakte, oft Kunstwerke, aber selbst Örtlichkeiten und Personen können als Werk eines Meisters dargestellt werden. Dabei verschmilzt in der Formulierung oft der

24 Chinca, 'Metaphorische Interartifizialität', pp. 30–31.

25 Glauch, 'Inszenierungen der Unsagbarkeit', 162; a similar argument is made by Lechtermann, 'Figuren der Abhebung', pp. 49–50.

26 Bürkle, '"Kunst"-Reflexion', p. 145. The description of the saddle of Enite's horse has long been the prime example for the space of artistic self-expression and self-reflection that *descriptio* offers within the restraints of retextualization. See, for instance, Worstbrock's seminal article, '*Dilatatio materiae*'.

> erzählte Entwurf des Werkmeisters mit dem dichterischen Entwurf, dem Akt des Erzählens.[27]

She further emphasizes that due to the established metaphor of poetic composition as textile work the description of garments is particularly prone to metapoetic reflection – another tendency that is exemplified by Gottfried's literary excursus.[28]

Interpretations of certain passages in the *Trojanerkrieg* as implicitly metapoetic often rely on the repetition of certain words or motifs that have previously been associated with poetry. Hasebrink, for example, proposes a metapoetic reading for the description of Medea as laudative speech which 'um so mehr sich selbst lobt, je mehr sie das lobt, was sie zu loben vorgibt'.[29] He emphasizes that both the poet as well as the sorceress perform acts of *erniuwen* and argues that the fact that Medea is 'geblüemet' with virtues (*Trojanerkrieg*, l. 7423) refers to the florid style as Konrad's poetic ideal. He also points out that the comparison of poetry with tailoring in the prologue proves the relevance of the metapoetic *textus* metaphor to Konrad, so that the dress description can legitimately be described as metapoetic. None of these correspondences can be denied, but they remain rather general and would also apply to other garment descriptions in Middle High German literature and to most of Konrad's descriptions. Although Hasebrink's metapoetic interpretation of the Medea episode is generally convincing because he supports his reading with further arguments, it is important to stress that the occurrence of a term or a technique which is used to describe poetry (*erniuwen*, *wîsheit*, *glanz*, *blüemen*, *meisterschaft*, textile production) with reference to story-level elements alone is rarely sufficient to justify a metapoetic reading of that passage. While Discord's act of renewing her old habit of causing war – 'si wolte ir art erniuwen | und ir alten werresite' (*Trojanerkrieg*, ll. 1490–91) – stands in metonymic relationship to the poet's renewing of the old story about the war she provoked,[30] it has to be noted that *erniuwen* does not always carry metapoetic implications in the *Trojanerkrieg*.[31] There are, however, a number of descriptions in the *Trojanerkrieg* – notably of textiles – which expose the narrated world as a product of poetic imagination and language

27 Glauch, 'Inszenierungen der Unsagbarkeit', 154.

28 Glauch, 'Inszenierungen der Unsagbarkeit', 167–68.

29 Hasebrink, 'Rache als Geste', pp. 215–19 (p. 218). He also interprets the description of the golden ram as a passage in which 'die Kunst der Beschreibung mit der Kunst des Gegenstandes parallel gesetzt wird' (p. 225).

30 Compare Gebert: 'Wiederum verweist die Semantik des Erneuerns (vgl. Tr 1490) auf eine Paradoxierung von Bedingung und Aktualisierung, wie sie bereits der Prolog zugespitzt hatte' (Gebert, *Mythos als Wissensform*, p. 179, fn. 169).

31 See *Trojanerkrieg*, l. 6922, l. 21568.

in a very explicit way. Juxtaposing the two metapoetically charged motifs of textile production and forging, the narrator presents himself as the designer of Hector's tunic when describing his shield:

> als ich daz wâpenkleit hie vor
> entworfen und geferwet hân,
> alsô was ouch der schilt getân. (*Trojanerkrieg*, ll. 3768–70)[32]

Helen's dress is 'gelîstet unde gebuochstabet' (*Trojanerkrieg*, l. 20126)[33] and Paris and his attire are 'getihtet' by Wish (*Trojanerkrieg*, l. 3096),[34] while the pearls and gemstones that decorate it are of intellectual, verbal origin:

> ûz tiefer sinne grunde
> erwünschet mit dem munde
> und alsô rehte fîn erdâht. (*Trojanerkrieg*, ll. 2959–61)

This last detail is noted by Green, who states:

> Die Steine, die Konrad soeben geschildert hat, sind also gänzlich unwirklich; die Steigerung, die er in seinem Superlativstil durchgeführt hat, entstammt allein der Phantasie. [...] Jede Realitätswirkung der idealisierenden Schilderung wird also zerstört, und zwar ausdrücklich: das alles war bloß zur Steigerung reiner Phantasie.[35]

Lienert comments similarly that with passages like these Konrad creates a reality 'die nur in seinen Worten existiert'.[36] At the same time this display of poeticity should not be confused with fictionality.[37] In medieval poetics and

32 See Monecke, *Das Erzählprinzip der 'wildekeit'*, pp. 162–63. He sees this passage as an echo of Gottfried's praise of Bligger, in which poets are described as 'verwære' (*Tristan*, l. 4691) and their work as 'entwerfen' (*Tristan*, l. 4713). On colours as a poetry metaphor in Gottfried's literary excursus and in Geoffrey's *Poetria Nova*, see Lambertus Okken, *Kommentar zum Tristan-Roman Gottfrieds von Strassburg*, 3 vols, Amsterdamer Publikationen zur Sprache und Literatur, 57, 58, 81 (Amsterdam: Rodopi, 1984–88), I (1984), pp. 226–30.

33 We can compare this with the poetry metaphor of the 'criecheschen borten' (*Tristan*, l. 4697) in Gottfried's praise of Bligger.

34 On the etymology and semantics of the term *tihten*, which is mostly used in the sense of '(ein literarisches Werk) verfassen', but can also refer to design or creation in general, see Kurt Gärtner, '*tihten/ dichten*: Zur Geschichte einer Wortfamilie im älteren Deutsch', in *Im Wortfeld des Textes*, ed. by Dicke, Eikelmann and Hasebrink, pp. 67–81.

35 Green, *Vorstudien zum gotischen Stil*, p. 10.

36 Lienert, *Geschichte und Erzählen*, pp. 287–88 (p. 288).

37 See, for example, Kraß, who interprets Wirnt von Grafenberg's statement that he has lavished 'sîden', 'borten' and 'gezierde mit worten' onto Florie so that nobody should be envious of her (*Wigalois*, ll. 856–62) as a 'fiktionale Selbstanzeige' (Kraß, *Geschriebene Kleider*, p. 373). He comments: '*gezierde* (lat. *ornatus*) meint sowohl den vestimentären Schmuck, den Florie am Leibe trägt, als auch den rhetorischen Schmuck, mit dem die Schönheit ihrer Kleider sprachlich zur Geltung gebracht wird' (p. 374).

Middle High German literature the poetry metaphors of tailoring, colouring and decorating with gemstones do not refer to invention (the Latin poetics concentrate on the form, not the content of poetry)[38] but to the recasting of the pre-existing *materia*, which is dressed in new clothes and decorated with the colours and stones of rhetorical *ornatus*.

Given the inherent metapoetic potential of *descriptio* and the fact that Konrad's particularly lavish descriptions are undoubtedly highly self-aware showcases of poetic prowess, it is necessary to show which specific signals in the description of the Apple of Discord encourage a metapoetic interpretation and which ideas about poetry they communicate. In the further course of this chapter I shall therefore analyse the various complex and subtle ways in which the description draws attention to the topic of language and presents itself as a materialization of language in general and more specifically as an artefact created by Konrad's words. In this context the unique feature of the Apple's magic inscription will prove to be of particular importance in endowing the passage with metapoetic meaning beyond the self-reflexivity of description in general.

The Apple of Discord as an Allegory of Poetry

In the story the Apple of Discord is a symbol of language, more precisely of praise. It is meant for the 'schoenste' (*Trojanerkrieg*, l. 1455), but it is not the physical looks of the equally beautiful goddesses Juno, Pallas and Venus that are judged but the beauty of the abstract concepts of wealth, wisdom and love which they represent.[39] The beauty contest becomes a contest of rhetorical prowess 'mit worten und mit sinne' (*Trojanerkrieg*, l. 1549).[40] The goddesses praise themselves in a rhetorical fashion to win the Apple; and Paris is accordingly asked to judge the competition by using his ears (*Trojanerkrieg*, ll.

38 See Brinkmann: 'Der Stoff wird als gegeben vorausgesetzt' (Brinkmann, *Wesen und Form*, pp. 46–47 (p. 47)).

39 Gebert discusses the rhetorical dispute of the goddesses in comparison to Konrad's sources and argues that they begin 'zwischen Fremdreferenz und Selbstreferenz zu schweben' because they praise the values they represent as well as themselves as persons (employing deictic personal pronouns like *ich*, *mîn*, *mir*, *mich*) and frequently switch between both types of reference (Gebert, *Mythos als Wissensform*, pp. 124–31 (p. 124)).

40 See Hübner: 'Der Nachweis ontologischer Qualität wird durch die Demonstration rhetorischer Qualität erbracht' (Gert Hübner, *Lobblumen: Studien zur Genese und Funktion der 'Geblümten Rede'*, Bibliotheca Germanica, 41 (Tübingen: Francke, 2000), p. 131). The influence of rhetoric and logic on Konrad's depiction of the goddesses' argumentation is evaluated by Freytag, 'Zur Logik *wilder aventiure*'.

1762–69).[41] Winning abstract *prîs* and *lop* is closely associated with winning the Apple as a material sign of supremacy. The loss of the contest and the Apple is in turn identified with a loss of reputation and verbal praise.[42] Paris finally decides 'daz der apfel sol gezemen | der hôchgelopten minne' (*Trojanerkrieg*, ll. 2768–69) and presents it to Venus with the words:

> erweltiu künigîn,
> enpfâhent diz kleinoete rîch,
> kein frouwe mac iu sîn gelîch
> an êren und an werdekeit,
> der krône ist wol an iuch geleit
> und der apfel schoene:
> ich prîse iuch unde kroene
> mit lobe in allen mînen tagen. (*Trojanerkrieg*, ll. 2798–805)

As the physical sign of superiority the Apple validates the self-praise of Venus and is identified with the metaphorical crown of Paris's praise for her. On the level of the story the Apple of Discord therefore functions as the material equivalent of an immaterial verbal award. The frequent description of the Apple as *prîsant* (gift, trophy) serves to underline this semantic connection between the material and the immaterial prize through the phonetic similarity with the omnipresent *prîs*.[43] The Apple, however, does not only represent the intradiegetic crown of praise for Venus; it is itself crowned by the praise of the narrator:

> enmitten under si zehant
> warfs' einen apfel schoene,
> den ich mit lobe kroene
> vür alle werden epfel noch. (*Trojanerkrieg*, ll. 1390–93)

The Apple is thus presented as an example of Konrad's capacity to praise an object. Its status as an 'object of praise' in this twofold sense is emphasized by the more than casual resemblance between the sentence presenting the Apple as an object of the narrator's praise and the presentation speech of Paris that characterizes the Apple as the material object corresponding to his verbal praise of Venus:

41 See also the passage in *Engelhard* in which Engeltrut chooses between the identical-looking Engelhard and Dietrich based on the sound of their names. The fact that the difficulty of distinguishing the goddesses mirrors the difficulty of distinguishing the colours of the Apple is pointed out by Schulz, *Schwieriges Erkennen*, p. 463 and Bleumer, 'Zwischen Wort und Bild', pp. 121–23.

42 Passages where praise and the Apple are closely associated, even identified, with each other are: *Trojanerkrieg* ll. 1574–87, ll. 1562–69, ll. 1913–46, ll. 2012–16, ll. 2218–19, ll. 2652–53, l. 2881.

43 On the polysemy of *prîs* and *lop* see Chapter 3.

> der krône ist wol an iuch geleit
> und der apfel schoene:
> ich prîse iuch unde kroene
> mit lobe in allen mînen tagen. (*Trojanerkrieg*, ll. 2802–05)

The fact that the Apple is crowned with praise itself and represents the metaphorical crown of praise for Venus at the same time is a striking superimposition of the levels of story and discourse that underlines the metapoetic charge of the passage. The inscription furthermore makes the Apple an object in which language is precious, artefactual materiality and a visual stimulus:

> vil ûzerwelter schrifte vol
> schein der selbe grüene strich,
> wan die buochstaben kostbaerlich
> beschouwen sich dâ liezen.
> von glanzen mergriezen,
> die niht reiner mohten sîn,
> wâren si gefelzet drîn
> und lûhten wunneclîchen dâ,
> si glizzen rôt, gel unde blâ
> ferr ûz der lîsten grasefar. (*Trojanerkrieg*, ll. 1442–51)

The Apple thus exemplifies a feature that Wandhoff has identified as typical for medieval descriptions of artefacts in general, namely the fact that they are often 'schrifthaltig' and that the letters described are usually endowed with a particular iconicity:

> Schon aufgrund der kostbaren Materialien, mit denen eine Inschrift nach Auskunft der Texte geformt ist – in der Regel handelt es sich um Gold oder Edelsteine –, bietet diese einen für den Gesichtssinn äußerst auffälligen und nicht selten auch plastisch vorzustellenden, taktil zu imaginierenden Gegenstand.[44]

Emphasizing the alterity of pre-modern concepts of textuality, Strohschneider argues that the scripturality constitutive for the development of Middle High German courtly literature was still 'unselbstverständlich' among its predominantly illiterate audience, who encountered writing mainly in the form of auratic cult objects such as lavishly ornate Bible codices.[45] Based on these cultural historical circumstances he observes two concepts of textuality in Middle High German literature that differ from the conventional modern

44 Wandhoff, *Ekphrasis*, p. 19.

45 Strohschneider: 'Schriftlichkeit ist für das neue höfische Erzählen konstitutiv und sie ist im gleichen Maße unselbstverständlich' (Strohschneider *Höfische Textgeschichten*, p. 4).

understanding of the text as a transparent medium for something other than itself. According to the first concept the text embodies its contents, it makes them present rather than representing them semiotically, so that the distinction between signifier and signified is collapsed. In the second concept the sensual presence of the text as a material object gains precedence over its function as a linguistic medium or can even block access to its contents completely – Strohschneider contrasts the 'opake[] Materialität von Schrift' to its 'sinntransparente[] Medialität'.[46] The fascination with the materiality of the letters on the Apple does not impair their semiotic function.[47] Nonetheless, the concept of scripturality as something weird and wonderful, even magical, and a heightened sense of its materiality are certainly still encapsulated in the magic inscription – possibly even a sense of the inaccessible revelation that has to be mediated by interpretation or (in this case miraculous) translation.[48] Picking up on Strohschneider's theory, Lieb and Ott emphasize that in pre-typographic societies the materiality of the medium determines to a high degree the contents conveyed. They argue that particularly the depictions of inscriptions in Middle High German literature, which are often very unusual artefacts, can serve to reflect the textual practices of such cultures by momentarily disabling the routine abstraction of texts from their materiality. The intimate connection of the text and its materiality is also the basis for their definition of inscription:

> Von Inschriften ist dann die Rede, wenn das Geschriebene und der Schriftträger eine *gesteigerte Verbindung* eingehen – wenn also die Schrift (und das mit der Schrift Ausgesagte) über das normale Maß hinaus vom Schriftträger mitbestimmt wird. Dies gilt vor allem dann, wenn der Schriftträger selbst eine Bedeutung hat, die sich mit der Bedeutung der Schriftaussage in Verbindung bringen lässt.[49]

46 Strohschneider, *Höfische Textgeschichten*, p. 31. Apart from in his introduction to *Höfische Textgeschichten* (pp. 3–33), Strohschneider also develops this theory in 'Sternenschrift: Textkonzepte höfischen Erzählens', in *Text und Text in lateinischer und volkssprachiger Überlieferung des Mittelalters: Freiburger Kolloquium 2004*, ed. by Eckart Conrad Lutz (= *Wolfram Studien*, 19), pp. 33–58.

47 Gebert speaks of an oscillation or tension between the aesthetic and hermeneutic effects, between the 'Zeichenstatus' and the 'Evidenzeffekt' of the inscription (Gebert, *Mythos als Wissensform*, pp. 185–86).

48 Strohschneider argues that the illiterate aristocratic culture of the time was centred on Scripture, which was venerated as a sacred and charismatic object while its content – coded in the Latin language – was accessible only to a learned minority (Strohschneider, *Höfische Textgeschichten*, pp. 5–6). The idea of the exceptional translation miracle highlights such everyday necessities *ex negativo*.

49 Ludger Lieb and Michael R. Ott, 'Schrift-Träger: Mobile Inschriften in der deutschsprachigen Literatur des Mittelalters', in *Schriftträger – Textträger: Zur materialen Präsenz des Geschriebenen in frühen Gesellschaften*, ed. by Annette Kehnel

In the case of the Apple of Discord this heightened connection consists of the antithesis between its noble materiality and destructive purpose as well as between its puzzling optics and inscription, which mark and undermine distinction at the same time.

In addition to this, the precious letters appear as the epic realization of a poetry metaphor in the prologue. There, Konrad declares his intention to renew the old story of Troy with radiant words (*Trojanerkrieg*, l. 275); here, we find words that literally shine. While metaphor, in the tradition of Quintilian, can be defined as an act of improper naming,[50] which, as a rhetorical device, is confined to the discourse level of the narration, the formalist Dmitrij Tschižewskij defines the 'Realisierung der Metapher' as a process in which metaphorical images become elements of the narrated world.[51] In her monograph on metaphors in Gottfried's *Tristan* Franziska Wessel describes 'realisierte Metaphern' as cases:

> bei denen hinter dem episch in Szene gesetzten Bildspender der bildempfangende Bezugspunkt völlig zurücktritt, so daß es der Kombinationsfähigkeit und -freudigkeit des Lesers überlassen bleibt, ob er die betreffende Szene mit metaphorischem Hintersinn gefüllt sehen oder sie nur im epischen Wortsinn verstehen will.[52]

---

and Diamantis Panagiotopoulos, Materiale Textkulturen, 6 (Berlin: de Gruyter, 2015), pp. 15–36 (p. 18).

50 Quintilian defines metaphor (*translatio*), which he regards as the most common and most beautiful trope, in the following way: 'Transfertur ergo nomen aut verbum ex eo loco in quo proprium est in eum in quo aut proprium deest aut tralatum proprio melius est' [A noun or a verb, then, is 'transferred' from a place in which it is 'proper' to a place in which either there is no 'proper' word or the 'transferred' term is better than the 'proper'] (*The Orator's Education*, 8, 6, 5).

51 Dmitrij Tschižewskij, 'Wiedergeburt des Formalismus? In welcher Art?', in *Immanente Ästhetik – ästhetische Reflexion. Lyrik als Paradigma der Moderne*, ed. by Wolfgang Iser (Munich: Fink, 1966), pp. 297–305 (p. 300); see also Uwe Ruberg, '"Wörtlich verstandene" und "realisierte" Metaphern in der deutschen Dichtung von Veldeke bis Wickram', in *'Sagen mit Sinne': Festschrift für Marie-Luise Dittrich zum 65. Geburtstag*, Göppinger Arbeiten zur Germanistik, 180 (Göppingen: Kümmerle, 1976), pp. 205–20 (p. 216). He cites the fact that Veldeke's Dido describes her lovesickness as a fire burning her just before she throws herself onto the pyre as an example for the interaction of a metaphor and its epic realization in the same text (pp. 210–11). See Heinrich von Veldeke, *Eneasroman*, ed. by Ludwig Ettmüller, trans. by Dieter Kartschoke (Stuttgart: Reclam, 1986; repr. 2007), ll. 2400–03, ll. 2430–40). He also mentions Konrad's *Herzmære* as the realization of common heart metaphors.

52 Franziska Wessel, *Probleme der Metaphorik und die Minnemetaphorik in Gottfrieds von Strassburg 'Tristan und Isolde'*, Münstersche Mittelalter-Schriften, 54 (Munich: Fink, 1984), p. 199. For the phenomenon of the epic realization of poetry metaphors, and the inverse movement of these metaphors describing elements of the story in Gottfried's *Tristan*, see Chinca, 'Metaphorische Interartifizialität', pp. 20–23.

She further explains that metaphors can be recognized objectively because they cause some kind of semantic irritation, leading the reader to assume that they are being used to make him aware of something else. They are thus necessarily perceived as a bipolar phenomenon consisting of a source and a target domain. In contrast to this, realized metaphors do not cause an irritation that rules out taking them literally. They are believable as story-level elements. The narrated scene has the status of epic reality in contrast to metaphors, which are a rhetorical category and thus elements of the discourse.[53] Strictly speaking, a realized metaphor is a metaphor no more, insofar as no act of improper naming is involved. The very process of epic realization removes what is metaphorical about an utterance. It would therefore be more precise to speak of a story-level element that can be recognized as the epic realization of a metaphor rather than of a 'realized metaphor'. Wessel points out that epic realizations of metaphors are 'kaum je objektiv nachweisbar'.[54] Because they are believable as elements of epic reality, the connection to an interpretation beyond the literal is optional and detecting realized metaphors is considered an act of interpretation.[55] Aptly cautious, she lists a number of criteria for the identification of realized metaphors in order to safeguard her interpretation against arbitrariness. The criteria she names are: the importance and position of the passage, for example a scene which appears unduly extended if judged by its role in the course of events; the juxtaposition of realized metaphors with equivalent rhetorical metaphors; correspondence, for example in wording, with rhetorical metaphors in the same text; deviation from the source; and correspondence with topical rhetorical metaphors.[56] Several of these criteria apply to the description of Discord's Apple. Even though it is undoubtedly an important story-level element, its position as the first detailed description and the fact that Konrad deviates from his sources marks out its significance.[57] Furthermore, its elements correspond to traditional metaphors as well as to rhetorical metaphors in the text. Most importantly, however, the sheer number of possible references to poetry metaphors support a metapoetic interpretation of the passage. The inscription on the Apple, in particular, reveals itself on closer inspection to be a point of accumulation where several metaphors are epically realized. The letters on the emerald band are not only radiant; they are also 'gelîmet' (*Trojanerkrieg*, l. 1477). The metaphorical equivalent for the

53 Wessel, *Probleme der Metaphorik*, p. 203.

54 Wessel, *Probleme der Metaphorik*, p. 199.

55 Wessel, *Probleme der Metaphorik*, p. 203.

56 Wessel, *Probleme der Metaphorik*, pp. 207–10.

57 On the significance of descriptions introducing a text as a background for its overall interpretation, see Wandhoff's chapter 'Bild-Eingänge: Ekphrasis als Portal des Textes' (Wandhoff, *Ekphrasis*, pp. 227–69).

process of gluing words or letters can yet again be found in the prologue in the very description of Konrad's poetic aspiration that also contains the metaphor of the radiant words:

> mit worten lûter unde glanz,
> ich büeze im sîner brüche schranz,
> den kan ich wol gelîmen
> z'ein ander hie mit rîmen,
> daz er niht fürbaz spaltet. (*Trojanerkrieg*, ll. 275–79)

As mentioned in the previous chapter, the metaphor of gluing with rhymes is not only an expression of Konrad's literary agenda, but also recalls a prominent poetry metaphor in Gottfried's literary excursus, where Bligger von Steinach is praised for his artistry: 'wie kan er rîme lîmen, | als ob si dâ gewahsen sîn' (*Tristan*, ll. 4716–17). By using the term of 'gluing' that is metapoetically charged through intra- as well as intertextual references Konrad draws attention to the fact that the Apple is not only a creation of skilled workmanship on the level of the story but also an artefact of poetic creation. It is important to emphasize that the inscription on the Apple does not present merely a general repetition of the motifs of radiance and gluing, but rather a very precise epic rendering of the metaphors of radiant and glued *language*. The detailed epic realization thus goes beyond what Müller describes as the 'Zusammenfallen objektsprachlicher und metasprachlich-poetologischer Aspekte' in the word-field of radiance: '*schîn* ist das, was den Gegenstand der Erzählung auszeichnet, und *schîn* ist das, was der Erzähler seiner Erzählung verleiht'.[58] It is also more specific than Hasebrink's casual observation in support of his metapoetic reading of Medea's magic: 'Jason [erhält] Leim [von Medea], mit dem er die Nüstern der feuerspeienden Stiere zukleben kann. Es sei nur angemerkt, daß auch das *lîmen* eine Dichtungsmetapher aus dem Prolog ist'.[59] Through the reference to the metaphors of the prologue, the Apple does not only appear as a product of craftsmanship in the story (craftsmanship that gives language a material form in the inscription), but becomes transparent as an artefactual manifestation of Konrad's own words as well. Therefore, the praise of masterly production cited by Müller can indeed be taken as an indirect self-praise of Konrad in a more specific sense. The Apple is materialized language in various aspects: as an object symbolizing intradiegetic praise; as an object on which real pearls form words; and as a literally radiant artefact that presents itself as the materialization of the metaphorically radiant and gluing words of the poet.

58 Müller, '*schîn* und Verwandtes', p. 297.
59 Hasebrink, 'Rache als Geste', p. 223.

In this self-referential context, even the metapoetic connotation of word-fields that are not explicitly used as metaphors for poetry in the *Trojanerkrieg* is activated. Thus, the pearls of the inscription can be linked to the metaphor of the word as a pearl, which goes back to the allegoresis of the Sermon on the Mount, where the pearl represents the Word of God: 'Do not throw your pearls before swine, or they will trample them underfoot and turn and maul you' (Matthew 7.6).[60] Following this tradition, medieval authors frequently articulate the elitist status of their own works by describing them as pearls.[61] Alan of Lille, for instance, compares his *Anticlaudianus* with a pearl which should not be trampled down by the pigs that represent the unfit audience.[62] Sometimes the pearl can be exchanged for a gemstone. Thus Wirnt von Grafenberg declares in the *Wigalois* prologue that riches (implicitly identified with poetry) which are not shared are wasted, while throwing gold and precious stones among the pigs is not very wise either (*Wigalois*, ll. 75–80).[63] Based on contemporary rhetorical metaphors of this kind, Ohly interprets the pearls and gemstones on the dog leash in the *Jüngere Titurel* as 'konkretisierte Metaphern für die auch inschriftlich auf dem Band stehenden Tugendlehren'.[64]

In another tradition the pearl and the equivalent gemstones are used as metaphors for rhetorical *ornatus*.[65] Matthew of Vendôme explains: 'Siquidem, sicut in constitutione rei materialis ex appositione alicujus margaritae vel emblematis totum materiatum elegantius elucescit, similiter sunt quaedam dictiones, quae sunt quasi gemmarum vicariae, ex quarum artificiosa positione totum metrum videbit festivari' (*Ars versificatoria*, II, 11) [Indeed, as in the forming of a material object the whole material shines more beautifully

60 See also Matthew 13. 45. On the exegetical tradition of interpreting the pearl as the word of God, see Friedrich Ohly, *Die Perle des Wortes: Zur Geschichte eines Bildes für Dichtung* (Frankfurt a.M.: Insel, 2002), pp. 134–88.

61 Ohly provides more examples (Ohly, *Die Perle des Wortes*, pp. 165–71). On the symbolism of the pearl see also Engelen, *Die Edelsteine*, pp. 350–56.

62 'Ab huius igitur operis arceantur ingressu qui, solam sensualitatis insequentes imaginem, rationis non appetunt ueritatem, ne sanctum canibus prostitutum sordescat, ne porcorum pedibus conculcata margarita depereat, ne derogetur secretis, si eorum magestas diuulgetur indignis' (Alan of Lille, *Anticlaudianus*, ed. by R. Bossuat (Paris: Vrin, 1955), p. 56 [Let those be denied access to this work who pursue only sense-images and do not reach out for the truth that comes from reason, lest what is holy, being set before the dogs be soiled, lest the pearl, trampled under the feet of swine be lost (Alan of Lille, *Anticlaudianus*, trans. by James J. Sheridan (Toronto: Pontifical Institute of Mediaeval Studies, 1973), pp. 40–41)].

63 See also Heinrich von dem Türlin, who focuses on the poets instead of the audience and warns that not trying to share wisdom for fear of presenting it inadequately is reproachable: 'Da wirt deu gimme in den mist | Getretten an gewizzen' (*Die Krone*, ll. 26–27).

64 Ohly, *Die Perle des Wortes*, p. 272; similarly Engelen, *Die Edelsteine*, p. 386.

65 For examples see Ohly, *Die Perle des Wortes*, pp. 197–207. On gemstones as metaphors for rhetorical *ornatus* and the wisdom and moral value of poetry, see also Engelen, *Die Edelsteine*, pp. 383–87.

because of the close positioning of some pearl or inlay; similarly, there are some expressions which are, as it were, substitutes for jewels; from skilful positioning of these the whole meter will seem to be celebrating (*The Art of the Versemaker*, p. 64)]. Heinrich von dem Türlin decorates his work 'mit sô guoten steinen' (*Die Krone*, l. 29977), which probably represent rhetorical figures, and Heinrich von Freiberg praises the work of his predecessor Gottfried as 'wol geblumet und wol geberlt' (*Tristan und Isolde*, l. 34).

It is not always possible to draw a clear line between pearl and gemstone metaphors that refer to the valuable content and those that refer to the rhetorical elaboration of the work: precious stones and pearls are valuable because they are beautiful; the value of Scripture can be symbolized through lavishly studded Bible codices; and the ideal of *aptum* demands that the form and content of an utterance ought to correspond to its expression – Gottfried describes Hartmann's poetry as 'cristallîn' precisely because he considers his style and content to be in perfect harmony with one another. Hence it is not easy to determine which tradition is more relevant to the interpretation of the Apple of Discord. After all, the pearls decorate the Apple of Discord *and* constitute the letters communicating its message. The prologue of the *Trojanerkrieg* demonstrates Konrad's familiarity with both metaphorical traditions. Likening good poetry to the orphan gemstone (*Trojanerkrieg*, ll. 20–31) and accusing the bat-like audience of mistaking bad literature for the 'lieht karfunkel' of good literature (*Trojanerkrieg*, ll. 162–69), he appears to refer primarily to the moral value of poetry. The pearl-studded Apple conveying a disruptive message undoubtedly corresponds to the deceptive splendour attracting the bat-like audience. The discrepancy of the Apple's material value and the destruction caused by its message turn the traditional metaphoric association of pearls and gemstones with moral value on its head and violate the ideal harmony between form and content. The metaphors 'worte lûter unde glanz' and 'lîmen', on the other hand, relate mainly to a stylistic updating of the old book of Troy, so that the pearls on the Apple picking up these motifs also draw on the tradition of the pearl as an *elocutio*-metaphor. In this context, the fact that the pearls are colourful can be read as an allusion to the metaphor of the *colores rhetorici*.[66] The inscription made from colourful, radiant and

66 See, for example, the *Rhetorica ad Herennium* with reference to stylistic devices: 'quae si rarae disponentur, distinctam sicuti coloribus [...] reddunt orationem' (IV, 16) [Distributed sparingly, these figures set the style in relief as with colours (*Rhetorica ad Herennium*, pp. 269–70)]; or Geoffrey of Vinsauf, who emphasizes that stylistic devices should not be superficial but conform to the demands of *aptum*: 'Sit brevis aut longus, se semper sermo coloret | Intus et exterius, sed discernendo colorem | Ordine discreto' (*Poetria Nova*, ll. 737–39) [Be it brief or long, let your discourse always "color" itself [i.e., with figures of speech] within and without, the color being chosen by a careful plan (*The New Poetics*, p. 60)].

glued pearls thus comprises epic realizations of various metaphors for poetic language.

It is furthermore significant that the Apple made up of a golden and a silver half is a product of goldsmithery, a craft which prominently features as an *elocutio* allegory in Geoffrey of Vinsauf's *Poetria nova*:

> Hoc facto quasi fungere lege fabrili:
> Ferrum materiae, decoctum pectoris igne,
> Transfer ad incudem studii. Permolliat illud
> Malleus ingenii, cujus luctatio crebra
> Formet ab informi massa peridonea verba.
> Verba, coadjuctis aliis quae verba sequuntur,
> Post conflent folles rationis, nomina verbis
> Verbaque nominibus. (*Poetria nova*, ll. 722–29)

> [In doing this, work as if by the process of a blacksmith: the iron of the subject matter, seethed with the fire of the mind, transfer to the anvil of study. Let the hammer of the intellect, whose close coming to grips may form from the unformed mass words more fit, work it all through. Later, the bellows of reason may fuse verbs (the elements also added which follow verbs) – the nouns to verbs and verbs to the nouns (*The New Poetics*, p. 59).][67]

In the prologue of the *Goldene Schmiede* Konrad famously expresses his desire to forge praise for the Virgin from gold, silver and gemstones in the smithy of his heart and with the hammer of his tongue:

> Ei künde ich wol enmitten
> in mines herzen smitten
> getihte uz golde smelzen,
> und liehten sin gevelzen
> von karfunkel schone drin
> dir, hohiu himelkeiserin!
> so wolte ich diner wirde ganz
> ein lop durchliuhtec unde glanz
> daruz vil harte gerne smiden.
> nu bin ich an der künste liden
> so meisterliche niht bereit,
> daz ich nach diner werdekeit
> der zungen hamer künne slahen,

67 See also: 'Sed ad hoc sudabis pectore toto; | Mentis in incude studiose cude, recude, | Denique quod deceat excude' (*Poetria Nova*, ll. 1614–16) [But to this end you will travail with your whole heart: hammer diligently upon the anvil of your mind, hammer again, and finally strike out something that is fitting (*The New Poetics*, p. 90)].

und minen munt also getwahen
daz er ze dinem prise tüge. (*Goldene Schmiede*, ll. 1–15)[68]

In this wider frame of reference not only the inscription but also the entire Apple can be read as the epic realization of the metaphor of the forged, gem-encrusted poem. Based on the classic definition of allegory as a consistently extended metaphor,[69] the Apple as an object composed of several epic realizations of metaphors for poetry can even be described as an epic allegory of poetry.[70] Since the allegorical meaning of the Apple is not made explicit, it would furthermore be categorized as an epic 'implicative' allegory,[71] whose peculiarities are described by Gerhard Kurz:

> Das Gesagte kann ausschließlich auf der wörtlichen Ebene (dem *sensus litteralis*) verstanden werden, d.h. auf Ebene der Bedeutung, die ohne weiteres verstanden wird. Es ergibt sich ein kohärenter und sinnvoller Zusammenhang, ohne daß man an einen allegorischen Sinn denken müßte.[72]

68 On the *ars ferraria* as a metaphor for the *ars poetica* see Grimm (ed.), *Die Goldene Schmiede*, p. xii; Obermaier, *Von Nachtigallen und Handwerkern*, pp. 321–23; Bickert, 'Der Dichter als Handwerker', pp. 10–11; Harant, *Poeta Faber*, pp. 149–160; Braun, 'Zwischen *ars* und "Kunst"', pp. 79–82. Another famous example is Heinrich von dem Türlin: 'hie mite hat ein ende | diu krone, die min hende | nach dem besten gesmit hant' (*Die Krone*, ll. 29966–68).

69 See Quintilian's influential treatment of allegory in *The Orator's Education*, where he provides the following definition: 'Allegoria, quam inversionem interpretantur, aut aliud verbis, aliud sensu ostendit, aut etiam interim contrarium. Prius fit genus plerumque continuatis tralationibus' [Allegory, which people translate *inversio*, presents one thing by its words and either a different or sometimes even a contrary thing by its sense. The first type generally consists of a succession of Metaphors] (*The Orator's Education*, 8, 6, 44). Quintilian also emphasizes that the orator should stick to the metaphorical field he has chosen and not mix metaphors (*The Orator's Education*, 8, 6, 50). Similar definitions (although with different terminology) are given in the *Rhetorica ad Herennium*, IV, 46; and by Cicero, *On the Orator*, III, 166.

70 In narrative works, it is necessary to distinguish between rhetorical allegories that remain a phenomenon of the discourse level and epic allegories that have the status of reality in the story, for example, the love cave in Gottfried's *Tristan*. On this distinction, see Dietmar Peil, 'Allegorie', in *Metzler Lexikon Literatur- und Kulturtheorie: Ansätze – Personen – Grundbegriffe*, ed. by Ansgar Nünning (Stuttgart: Metzler, 2001), p. 8; Wiebke Freytag, 'Allegorie, Allegorese', in *Historisches Wörterbuch der Rhetorik*, ed. by Gerd Ueding, 9 vols (Tübingen: Niemeyer, 1992–2009), I (1992), cols 330–93 (col. 331).

71 On the distinction between implicative allegories, which contain no hints to further layers of meaning, and explicative allegories, which provide either hints or detailed allegoresis (Quintilian speaks of 'tota allegoria' and 'permixta allegoria' (*The Orator's Education*, 8, 6, 49)), see Peil, 'Allegorie'. In the case of explicative epic allegory, a second dimension of meaning is explicitly attributed to story level elements – as in the case of Gottfried's love cave. For an interpretation of this episode, see the seminal essay by Friedrich Ranke, 'Die Allegorie der Minnegrotte in Gottfrieds *Tristan*', in Friedrich Ranke, *Kleinere Schriften*, ed. by Heinz Rupp and Eduard Studer (Bern: Francke, 1971), pp. 13–30.

72 Gerhard Kurz, 'Zu einer Hermeneutik der literarischen Allegorie', in *Formen und Funktionen*

Like epic realizations of metaphors, the implicative epic allegory does not involve an act of improper naming that causes immediate semantic or pragmatic irritation. There is nothing inherently 'wrong' with the idea of an elaborately crafted object as a prize for the winner of a contest; the reader is not obliged to seek out a further level of signification to make sense of the description of the Apple of Discord. Therefore the detection of an implicative epic allegory is at the reader's discretion and will have to be subject to the same requirements for interpretative caution as the detection of the epic realization of metaphors.

The Apple of Discord as an Aesthetic Object

If the Apple of Discord can legitimately be described as an allegory of poetry or as an accumulation point of several epic realizations of poetry metaphors, the next question is what concept of poetry it articulates. Obermaier explains that artisanal poetry metaphors such as spinning, dyeing, weaving, tailoring, building, painting and forging are particularly suited to expressing the pre-modern concept of poetic creation as retextualization, because all these skills produce artefacts by working with pre-existing materials that they shape or process into something more valuable: 'Diese besondere Art der Tätigkeit – "nicht Urfertigung", sondern Herstellung durch Bearbeitung – bildet das Analogon zwischen dem Handwerk und dem Vorgang des Dichtens'.[73] With regard to goldsmithery, a particularly well regarded profession in the Middle Ages, Obermaier argues: 'Die Schmiedemetaphorik leistet [...] – häufig in Verbindung mit anderen Bildfeldern wie "Redeblumen" und "Redeschmuck" – die adäquate Verbildlichung für den Vorgang der *elocutio*; denn es ist gerade der Goldschmied, der sein "Rohmaterial" besonders fein verarbeitet'.[74] Looking back at the prologue it seems appropriate that Konrad's 'radiant' and 'gluing' poetic language, which beautifies and pieces back together the old book of Troy, should find its epic manifestation in an object whose allegorical meaning points to a conception of poetry as rhetorically ornate retextualization. That this conception is at odds with Konrad's earlier claim that poetry does not require any instruments or material is not an interpretative inconsistency but rather a contrast that already characterizes the prologue itself. Similarly, the contrast between poetry as ephemeral performance art (*sagen* and *singen*) in the prologue and the Apple of Discord

der Allegorie: Symposion Wolfenbüttel 1978, ed. by Walter Haug, Germanistische Symposien: Berichtsbände, 3 (Stuttgart: Metzler, 1979), pp. 12–24 (p. 16).

73 Obermaier, *Von Nachtigallen und Handwerkern*, p. 334.

74 Obermaier, *Von Nachtigallen und Handwerkern*, pp. 153–54.

as a written 'Textkörper' does not appear as drastic if we consider that in the prologue the old book of Troy is already presented as a material artefact that needs to be glued back together. Moreover, any strict distinction of this kind is undermined by the fact that the precious materiality of the Apple is anything but static.

The question as to what makes the Apple of Discord more than just the product of a goldsmith warrants further investigation, because the elements of a metaphor's source domain that resist translation into the terms of the target domain create a semantic excess that points out the unique qualities of the latter. Chinca demonstrates this with reference to the poetological *artes* metaphors in Gottfried's literary excursus:

> Die metaphorische Interartifizialität des Literaturexkurses lässt sowohl die Ähnlichkeit als auch die Unähnlichkeit der Dichtkunst zu den sie metaphorisierenden *artes* erkennen. Die *ars poetria* ist den anderen *artes* insofern ähnlich, als auch sie einen spezifischen Produktionsbereich regelt, in dem der Herstellungsprozess zielgerichtet und fachgemäß nach Normen technischer Kompetenz zu vollziehen ist. [...] Die Unähnlichkeit wird hingegen an der Eigenart der Erzeugnisse deutlich, die weder ganz Artefakt noch ganz Ereignis sind.[75]

While the clearly distinguished gold and silver halves of the Apple appear as rigid materiality, this impression is reversed upon closer inspection; the colours of the 'mixtûre' are dynamic. They are caught up in a perpetual process of rebirth and dispersion, in a dance of eternal 'wandelunge' that challenges perception:

> ein wunderlich mixtûre
> ûz dem rîlichen apfel schein,
> diu was verworren under ein
> von aller hande glaste
> sô sêre und alsô faste,
> daz keiner liehten farwe schîn
> dâ volleclîchen möhte sîn
> und was ir aller teil doch dâ.
> wîz, brûn, rôt, gel, grüen unde blâ,
> diu wurden alliu dâ geborn
> und heten alliu doch verlorn
> dâ ganzen unde vollen glanz,
> sô daz ir keinez was dô ganz,
> noch in volleclicher kür:
> ir schîn was wider unde vür

75 Chinca, 'Metaphorische Interartifizialität', p. 25.

zerdraejet und zersprenget
und alsô gar vermenget
mit wilder temperunge,
daz manic wandelunge
dâ fremdeclîchen lûhte
und iegelichen dûhte
sô maezlich und sô kleine,
als ir dâ vil nâch keine
solte schînen unde wesen. (*Trojanerkrieg*, ll. 1402–25)[76]

The paradox of static materiality and fleeting movement is represented most prominently in the inscription.[77] The material of the pearls and the fact that they are glued onto the Apple, which means that they are permanently fixed to it, implies the stability of language in the aggregate state of a physical artefact, but things are really quite different:

in swelher zungen man daz lesen
wolte bî der selben zît,
diu wart ân allen widerstrît
und in vil kurzen stunden
an den buochstaben funden,
die man dâ stân gelîmet sach.
von hôher künste diz geschach,
daz sich diu geschrift verkêrte
und iegelichen lêrte
dâ finden sîne sprâche. (*Trojanerkrieg*, ll. 1472–81)

In the very special case of the magic inscription, textuality does not mean artefactual immutability and therefore cannot be taken as the polar opposite of ephemeral oral performance. Unlike other magical artefacts in the *Trojanerkrieg* that are created by fairies or dwarfs, the intradiegetic creator of the Apple is never specified – maybe to create a gap that may be filled by

76 On this description see Gebert, who reads it as a 'Exempel der Wahrnehmung' and elaborates: 'Wahrnehmung wird angeregt und komplex gesteigert, so dass sie förmlich kollabiert und nichts mehr zu erkennen gibt [...]. Vor das Objekt der Wahrnehmung schiebt sich hier wie auch in anderen Schönheitsbeschreibungen des *Trojanerkriegs* der Akt der Wahrnehmung und dessen auffällig experimentelle Modalisierung' (Gebert, *Mythos als Wissensform*, p. 180).

77 This paradox also characterizes other prominent inscriptions in Middle High German literature, such as the ephemeral inscription on the grail in Wolfram's *Parzival* or the inscription on the leash in *Titurel*, which is elusive because it is tied to a runaway dog. On these examples see Strohschneider, 'Sternenschrift', pp. 36–37; on *Titurel* see Lieb and Ott, 'Schrift-Träger', pp. 26–28. In the *Trojanerkrieg* the name inscriptions Paris carves into a tree offer a further point of comparison. They are meant to calm Oenone's worries that she may lose Paris, but fail to ensure the stability of their love (*Trojanerkrieg*, ll. 778–803).

Konrad as the creator. Instead, art and mastery themselves figure as the origin of its wonders:

> an im lac hôher künste flîz
> von meisterlicher kûre. (*Trojanerkrieg*, ll. 1400–01)
>
> rîlicher künste soldes
> ein wunder was ûf in geleit. (*Trojanerkrieg*, ll. 1434–35)
>
> von hôher künste diz geschah,
> daz sich diu geschrift verkêrte. (*Trojanerkrieg*, ll. 1478–79; see also ll. 1521–23 quoted below)

The Apple is the epitome of art, an ultimate art that surpasses the product of any ordinary goldsmith. It is a magical artefact and the element of magic seems to cover precisely the semantic excess between the immutable artefact created by a goldsmith and the work of the poet that remains dynamic even as a written artefact. The close connection between poetry and magic in the *Trojanerkrieg* has been observed by several interpreters. Hans Jürgen Scheuer, for example, points out that the art of poetry and the art of magic exercised by both the gods attending the wedding on Mount Olympus and by Medea rely on *wîsheit*. Commenting on the fact 'daz alsô niuwer fünde ursprinc' (*Trojanerkrieg*, l. 884) is said to flow from the hearts of those gods venerated for important inventions, he deduces: 'Der Ausfluss des Herzens, das wie die Seele als *proton organon* der Wahrnehmung zu denken ist, wird zur Quelle *niuwer fünde*, die auf die Inventionskunst des dialektisch geschulten Dichters und seines Phantasmen erzeugenden Wahrnehmungsapparates verweisen'.[78] He argues furthermore that this similarity between magic and poetry is highlighted by the fact that both the poet and Medea, in rejuvenating Jason's father, are performing acts of *erniuwen*: 'Beide lassen sich als Künste verstehen, die Eigenbewegungen hervorrufen oder simulieren können – die magische Arznei am äußeren Erscheinungsbild des lebendigen, die magische Poesie am inneren Vorstellungsbild des phantasmischen Körpers'.[79] Hasebrink, who also emphasizes this connection, elaborates:

78 Scheuer, '*wîsheit*', p. 104. Gebert instead emphasizes the term *meisterschaft* as the link connecting magic and poetry in these episodes: 'Kunstfertige Vollkommenheit (der mythisch vergöttlichten Menschen einerseits, des Erzählers andererseits) und Unverfügbarkeit ihrer Quellen (der Natur einerseits, göttlicher Inspiration andererseits), eigene Exzellenz und heteronomes Empfangen bezeichnen somit eine gemeinsame Matrix, in die analoge Kontrastbeziehungen von Selbstreferenz und Fremdreferenz von Mythographie und Poetik eingetragen werden' (Gebert, *Mythos als Wissensform*, p. 116).

79 Scheuer, '*wîsheit*', p. 104.

> Meister Konrad und Medea, die Meisterin, operieren auf unterschiedlichen narratologischen Ebenen und ohnedies in unterschiedlichen Künsten, doch offensichtlich arbeiten sie mit verwandten methodischen Standards. Schriftkultur, enzyklopädisches Wissen, Artesstudium und Kompilation sind Voraussetzungen einer Transformation, die hier *erniuwen* genannt wird. Dahinter verbirgt sich ein komplexes Modell der *renovatio*, das sich in der Konstruktion der Medea wie in einem Brennglas bündelt.[80]

The association of poetry and magic made by Scheuer and Hasebrink via the term *erniuwen* can be supported by the fact that in his explanation of the *ordo artificialis* Geoffrey of Vinsauf likens poetry to a sorceress:

> ludit [ars] quasi quaedam praestigiatrix,
> Et facit ut fiat res postera prima, futura
> Praesens, transversa directa, remota propinqua;
> Rustica sic fiunt urbana, vetusta novella,
> Publica privata, nigra candida, vilia cara. (*Poetria Nova*, ll. 121–25)
>
> [It plays, as it were, the prestidigitator, and arranges that the last may be the first, the future present, the bias straight, the far near; thus may the rustic be made urbane, the old new, the public private, black white and vile precious (*The New Poetics*, p. 37).]

Scheuer does not refer to this paragraph with regard to the *Trojanerkrieg* but comments on it in a different context:

> Indem Galfreds Vergleich die *ars poetica* mit der *ars magica* engführt, unterstreicht er, worauf es beim Wiedererzählen ankommt: auf die Dynamisierung der inneren Wahrnehmung. Deren bilderzeugende Intensität ist dort am höchsten, wo offensichtliche Unterscheidungen künstlich ins Schwanken gebracht werden und in ihr Gegenteil umkippen, wo – mit anderen Worten – die Form invertiert und ihre *ratio* umgepolt wird.[81]

80 Hasebrink, 'Rache als Geste', p. 226. See also Simone Funkele, who proposes a metapoetic reading of the description of the restored Troy by arguing that the renewal of the city – whose description as a model city and ideal artefact allows Konrad to demonstrate his poetic prowess – resonates with the literary renewal ('erniuwen') of the old book of Troy since both combine and merge different parts into a coherent entity: 'Mit der wiederaufgebauten Stadt findet sich bei Konrad von Würzburg ein eigentlich ahistorisches Gesamtkunstwerk, in der auch ein Bild für das angestrebte Gesamtkunstwerk in nuce gesehen werden darf' (Simone Funkele, 'Die Zerstörung und der Wiederaufbau Trojas in Konrads von Würzburg "Trojanerkrieg"', in *Die zerstörte Stadt: Mediale Repräsentationen urbaner Räume von Troja bis SimCity*, ed. by Andreas Böhn and Christine Mielke (Bielefeld: transcript, 2007), pp. 57–82 (p. 81)). In contrast to Hasebrink and Scheuer, her interpretation does not rely on a repetition of the actual term *erniuwen*.

81 Hans Jürgen Scheuer, 'Sichtbarkeit und Evidenz: Strategien des Vor-Augen-Stellens im Mauritius von Craûn und in der Poetria Nova Galfreds von Vinsauf', in *Sehen und Sichtbarkeit*, ed. by Bauschke, Coxon and Jones, pp. 192–210 (p. 203). Hasebrink refers to

A loss of distinction and the inversion of polar opposites such as vile and precious also characterize the magic Apple. In the case of Medea the similarity between Geoffrey's description of the poet rejuvenating an old expression through the use of metaphors and her pharmaceutical, rejuvenating magic is even more striking:

> Si vetus est verbum, sis physicus et veteranum
> Redde novum. Noli semper concedere verbo
> In proprio residere loco: residentia talis
> Dedecus est ipsi verbo; loca propria vitet
> Et peregrinetur alibi sedemque placentem
> Fundet in alterius fundo: sit ibi novus hospes
> Et placeat novitate sua. Si conficis istud
> Antidotum, verbi facies juvenescere vultum. (*Poetria Nova*, ll. 757–64)

> [If the expression is old, be a physician and make the old veteran a new man. Do not always be willing to allow a word to rest in its usual place; such monotonous lodging is a shame to the word itself; let it avoid its usual haunts, and wander elsewhere and build a pleasing abode on another's side; let it be there a novel guest and give pleasure by reason of its novelty. If you mix this antidote, you will make the face of a word grow young (*The New Poetics*, pp. 60–61).][82]

Thus the connection between poetry and magic seems to be of particular relevance to the *Trojanerkrieg*. Associating the magic Apple with the product of the poet highlights the fact that both arts achieve the paradoxical effect of rendering something static – language as a written artefact – dynamic. Where the prologue focuses on the peculiarities of the production of poetry, the Apple emphasizes the inherent dynamics of poetry as an aesthetic object by stressing the aspect of reception that makes the seemingly static and written artefact come to life:[83] the movement of the beholder stepping closer to investigate the Apple realizes the change of optics from silver-gold to iridescent polychromy;

Geoffrey, *Poetria Nova*, l. 769, as an example for the concept of making something new from something old (Hasebrink, 'Rache als Geste', p. 226).

82 Compare also *Poetria Nova*, ll. 1685–86 and l. 935 on metaphors: 'Renovat talis mutatio verbum' [Such change rejuvenates a word (*The New Poetics*, p. 66)].

83 Following the tradition of Czech Structuralism I distinguish between the poetic work as an artefact (an autonomous sign independent of reception) and the poetic work as an aesthetic object (a communicative sign that receives meaning through reception). In this context, I will use this classification to distinguish in a fundamental fashion between the composed text and the perceived text, without engaging in the Structuralist discussion of the realization of the text in the collective consciousness of a culture (see Jochen-Ulrich Peters, 'Artefakt', in *Reallexikon der deutschen Literaturwissenschaft*, ed. by Harald Fricke, 3 vols (Berlin: de Gruyter, 1997), I, pp. 143–44).

and the reading of the inscription triggers its magic translation, which is described as an actual change of the material inscription. Reception, however, does not only change the Apple itself, but also changes the readers, who have to consider themselves superior to everyone else:

> Der apfel wunneclich gestalt
> von meisterschefte manicfalt
> mit zouber sô gelüppet was,
> swer die geschrift gar überlas,
> diu von im schône lûhte,
> daz den bînamen dûhte,
> daz er sô wunnebaere
> und sô gewaltic waere,
> daz niender lepte sîn genôz. (*Trojanerkrieg*, ll. 1521–29)

This emphasis on poetry as an aesthetic artefact may seem like an extreme departure from the proclaimed independence of the nightingale simile. Once more, this contrast is lessened if we consider that this autonomous stance is already undermined in the prologue: the representation of poetry in the Apple of Discord thus presents a shift in emphasis, but not a real contradiction.

Lienert also attributes particular importance to the Apple's wondrous inscription. Complementing her interpretation of the Apple as a miniature of the text, she reads it as a representation of the reception of the *Trojanerkrieg*:

> Zugleich läßt sich, auf einer Meta-Ebene des Verstehens, kaum eine passendere Chiffre für den *Trojanerkrieg* als Kunstwerk denken: Kunst existiert nur relativ zur Perspektive des Betrachters. Die Schrift, die jedem Leser in seiner eigenen Sprache erscheint, steht für die 'Verschiedenverstehbarkeit' des Kunstwerks als eine diesem inhärente Qualität. Jeder Leser hält fälschlich seine Lesart für die allein richtige; aber das ist nicht die Fehlleistung des Rezipienten, sondern strukturell vorprogrammiert. Die Schrift besagt immer das Gleiche, noch dazu komfortablerweise verdolmetscht, so daß der Rezipient sie scheinbar mühelos verstehen kann: Jeder liest sie dem Wortlaut nach richtig und dem Sinn nach falsch, insofern er fälschlich sich gemeint fühlt.[84]

The meaning of the inscription is generated through its interpretation by the reader; and it is worth emphasizing that this process makes the Apple into an aesthetic object rather than a static artefact independent of its reception. In so doing, it reflects on a general characteristic of poetry. However, Lienert's interpretation of the inscription as a symbol for the 'Verschiedenverstehbarkeit' of the *Trojanerkrieg* relies on a very vague concept of textual ambiguity. First, it

84 Lienert, *Geschichte und Erzählen*, p. 1; a similar argument is offered by Lechtermann, 'Figuren der Abhebung', p. 64.

is problematic to take the maliciously calculated misreading of the inscription as a representation of a benign textual openness. The ambiguity of the inscription pertains to the undefined reference of 'the most beautiful', which leads to conflict only in conjunction with the second magic quality of making each reader feel the most beautiful and thus the single referent of 'the most beautiful' – an interpretation that is incompatible with that of other readers precisely because it is not different but identical and assumes a false exclusivity.[85] In this sense, the Apple works like a mirror that is mistaken for a static image. Its irony is that it is supposed to establish a difference between the indistinguishable goddesses but in making each of them feel distinguished in the same way it eliminates all distinction.[86] It would be hard to map this highly specific ambiguity and its magically enforced misunderstanding – in this sense the inscription is not 'open' at all – onto the reception of the *Trojanerkrieg*. Crucially, there is a decisive distinction between the intra- and the extradiegetic reader of the Apple. Since Konrad presents the inscription as a direct quotation, both readers find the very same message translated into their language – the fact that both Konrad's work and the inscription are translations adds a further layer of correspondence supporting the interpretation of the Apple as *mise en abyme*[87] – but the effect is very different. While the intradiegetic reader cannot realize its ambiguity and

85 See also Gebert, who evaluates the literary tradition of the Apple of Discord and highlights the difference to Konrad's version. While the cause for conflict in other texts is the 'Undeterminiertheit schriftlicher Referenz', the problem in the latter is the 'Hyperreferentialisierung von Schrift' (Gebert, *Mythos als Wissensform*, p. 184), which means: '[N]icht eine für alle Figuren nachvollziehbare regelhafte Zuordnung oder offen zutage tretende Zuordnungsproblematik werden zum Problem, sondern das stillschweigende Gleiten von Referenzen. Das hermeneutische Zauberwerk des Apfels ermöglicht, Sinn und Referenz so zu verfielfältigen, dass sie gar nicht als vielfältig erscheinen' (Gebert, *Mythos als Wissensform*, p. 185). He continues: 'Eine solch prekäre Einschätzung von Schrift schreibt nicht mehr die archaische Schriftkritik des Parisurteils fort, das im Apfel der Discordia das Problem entautorisierter, unkontrollierbarer Polysemie bündelte. Im *Trojanerkrieg* markiert der Apfel der Discodia vielmehr einen medialitätsgeschichtlich neuen Ort, an dem – umgekehrt – das *Gelingen* von Schrifthermeneutik zum Problem geworden ist. Galt der Apfel in der Erzähltradition als Streitobjekt um das richtige Urteil (Wer ist die Schönste?), so wuchern im *Trojanerkrieg* viele richtige Urteile nebeneinander. Nicht die Wiederbelebung des toten Buchstabens durch Referentialisierung bildet somit die Herausforderung der Schrift, sondern ihre Lebendigkeit und Potenz, sich zu wandeln und parallel verstanden werden zu können. Zusammen mit ihrer Medienreflexion setzt diese Kritik des Hermeneutischen die Ausdifferenzierung des Sinnmediums Schrift in einer voll entwickelten Schriftkultur voraus' (Gebert, *Mythos als Wissensform*, p. 187).

86 On this paradox see also Seus, *Heilsgeschichten vor dem Heil?*, p. 165.

87 Compare Seus, who remarks that the fact that the message of the Apple remains the same in different languages relates to medieval concepts of retextualization, in which the *materia* remains the same while the *forma/ artificium* changes (Seus, *Heilsgeschichten vor dem Heil?*, p. 164, fn. 299).

falsely thinks that it refers to her exclusively, Konrad's audience is not affected by its deceptive magic and is informed by the narrator that the inscription is ambiguous in assuring each of its readers of her superior status.[88] The extradiegetic audience recognizes the mirror, where the goddesses see only a portrait of themselves. Moreover, even though the *Trojanerkrieg* as a whole can be described as an ambivalent text, it certainly relies on its readers recognizing the ambivalences it explores rather than exclusively assuming one of several conflicting positions or reading into it whatever they want. Müller, for example, argues that it exposes 'die der höfischen Kultur von Anfang an eingeschriebene Aporie: höchste Vollendung sein zu wollen und doch den Gesetzen der Welt und ihrer Vergänglichkeit anheim gegeben zu sein' and elaborates:

> Die daraus resultierende Ambiguität unterminiert die Geltung der höfisch-ritterlichen Ästhetik, aber sie verweist auch indirekt auf die Maßstäbe, die sie aufzuheben behauptet. Damit steht Konrad mindestens typologisch am Ende der höfischen Epik [...], indem er die Aporien von deren Ansprüchen aufzeigt, des Anspruchs einer Ethik, die auf Gewalt gegründet ist, des Anspruchs einer Ästhetik, die ihre ethischen Maßstäbe nicht aufgeben will.[89]

The gap between the limited perspective of the intradiegetic audience of the Apple of Discord and the superior understanding of the extradiegetic audience encourages Konrad's readers to look out for and appreciate the ambivalences explored in the text. The most decisive difference that sets the Apple and the *Trojanerkrieg* apart is the fact that the radiant beauty of the Apple as a whole is deceptive. It is an evil object whose reception disrupts courtly harmony and causes unsurpassed destruction, whereas the declared purpose of the *Trojanerkrieg*, composed in beautiful, radiant language, is to reaffirm the norms of a virtuous lifestyle and reinstate courtly harmony. If Konrad's work can be identified with the 'wârez lieht' of valuable poetry, the light of the Apple is more akin to the misleading gleaming of rotten wood.[90] In the prologue

88 On this point see Gebert: 'Die Figurenperspektive bestimmt grundsätzliche Konsonanz: "Der Apfel verweist speziell auf mich, auch wenn andere Anderes behaupten". Die Erzählerebene hält hingegen Dissonanzbewusstsein offen: "Dies erging auch jedem anderen Betrachter ebenso"' (Gebert, *Mythos als Wissensform*, p. 187).

89 Müller, '*schîn* und Verwandtes', p. 303.

90 See also Müller: '[T]he light he is talking about [in the prologue], which has to illuminate the immense and confusing *materia*, its branches, its turns in order to clear the nearly incomprehensible, is not the dazzling light that Konrad is effusing on his epic world. For this light does not advance cognition, but blindness' (Müller, 'Blinding Sight', p. 208; similarly, '*schîn* und Verwandtes', p. 297). See also Lienert, who argues that while beauty in the narrated world leads to destruction, the beauty of the text, even when it describes horrible events, is not a self-sufficient 'Ästhetisierung' but a means of 'Leidbewältigung' (Lienert, 'Der Trojanische Krieg in Basel', pp. 277–78).

Konrad outlines his ideal audience as an elite group who are not tricked by an attractive shimmer but possess the 'bescheidenheit' critically to distinguish good from bad poetry as well as good from bad moral examples. In this sense, the reception of the inscription on the Apple is really the antithesis of the reception Konrad envisages for his audience.

While the particulars of the inscription and the *Trojanerkrieg* are thus very different, the fundamental concept of poetry as an aesthetic object represented by the Apple remains relevant to the text as a whole. Unlike Lienert, I would interpret its notion of reception not in the context of a quasi-postmodern textual openness, but more in line with Gottfried's model of poetry, which relies on reception to be actualized or revived: in Gottfried's case literary reception brings the protagonists and the virtues represented by them back to life 'iemer niuwe' (*Tristan*, l. 219, l. 229); in Konrad's case the act of *erniuwen* performed by the poet has to be matched by the realization of the work through reception.

From Pentecost to Babel

In the prologue and at the beginning of the text Konrad does not engage explicitly with the heathendom of the world he depicts. Only after having described Paris's lover Oenone and the participants in Jupiter's courtly celebration as gods does he anticipate the questions of a Christian audience – 'nû möhte iuch nemen wunder, | waz göte waeren bî der zît?' (*Trojanerkrieg*, ll. 858–59) – and counter the implied question with a euhemeristic explanation. The gods are defined as ordinary human beings like his audience and are merely revered as gods because their exemplary virtue and special knowledge of plants and stones enable them to cause 'manic wunder wilde' (*Trojanerkrieg*, l. 869), because they are magicians working with 'gougelwîse' (*Trojanerkrieg*, l. 875), or because they are the inventors of certain cultural techniques. Seus, who analyses Konrad's portrayal of the gods, first points out several inconsistencies: they waver between exemplary, benevolent sages and more sinister magicians who purposefully deceive in order to hide their mortal status and receive offerings. They live in the wilderness and as courtly lords. They are people like you and me but possess exceptional knowledge and skills.[91] More importantly, however, Seus argues that the gods are not presented as spiritual leaders but only as courtly rulers whose power and expertise remain restricted to the secular realm. In this context she reads the narrator's comparison of the birds singing at the wedding

91 Seus, *Heilsgeschichten vor dem Heil?*, pp. 147–54. Gebert points out similar ambivalences in the depiction of the gods (Gebert, *Mythos als Wissensform*, pp. 111–23).

to the celestial choirs (*Trojanerkrieg*, ll. 1135–39) as an indirect pointer to what these worldly gods lack: '[e]in[en] Bezug zur Transzendenz, den weder sie noch andere Figuren der dargestellten Welt herzustellen vermögen'.[92]

Given the fact that the relationship between the heathen narrated world and the Christian culture of reception becomes topical for the first time in this episode, the question arises as to whether the description of the Apple of Discord contains further elements informing the Christian perspective on the pre-Christian story. While it has occasionally been noted that the magic translation recalls the miracle of Pentecost[93] or the pre-Babylonic unity of languages,[94] the fact that it also alludes to the Babylonic confusion of languages has never been mentioned; nor have the implications of these references for the interpretation of the narrated events been discussed. First of all, Konrad's invention of the magic translation seems curious because it serves no real function in the story. Among the gods and goddesses attending the celebration is also Mercury, the messenger of the gods, 'der alle zungen wol vernam' (*Trojanerkrieg*, l. 973) and who is appreciated for his language skills, 'durch daz von sînem munde | flôz aller hande sprâche' (*Trojanerkrieg*, ll. 984–85). However, this motif remains blind: Mercury is not involved in the prominent translation process in the episode.[95] Other than the reference to Mercury's polyglossia, there has been no previous indication that the guests at the festival speak different languages. This makes the introduction of this new feature to the Apple of Discord even more interesting and supports the thesis that it serves a metapoetic function.

As mentioned above, the language miracle of Konrad's Apple is reminiscent of the biblical language miracle of Pentecost:

> When the day of Pentecost had come, they were all together in one place. And suddenly from heaven there came a sound like the rush of a violent wind, and

92 Seus, *Heilsgeschichten vor dem Heil?*, p. 155.

93 See Strohschneider, 'Sternenschrift', p. 46; Gebert, *Mythos als Wissensform*, pp. 184–85.

94 Stuckmann, *Wappenschilderungen*, p. 86.

95 It is striking how little relevance the introduction of the gods on Mount Olympus has to the course of events. The description of Cupid as the servant of love who arrives with his bow and arrows to cause trouble at court (*Trojanerkrieg*, ll. 964–71) is apparently an addition by Konrad (see Lienert, *Geschichte und Erzählen*, p. 42), so it could be assumed that it has been introduced to foreground the lengthy discussion of love in the debate of the goddesses and the beginning of Paris's love for Helen. However, when Paris falls in love with Helen, Cupid has nothing to do with it at all. In the remainder of the story the gods rarely play a role, with the exceptions of Thetis, who attempts to prevent her son Achilles from participating in the war; Mercury, who brings Paris a message from Venus; and Diana and Neptune, who create a sea storm to punish the Greeks (*Trojanerkrieg*, ll. 24005–661). If they play a role, however, their powers surpass those of mere mortals and contradict Konrad's euhemeristic explanation (see Gebert, *Mythos als Wissensform*, pp. 120–23).

> it filled the entire house where they were sitting. Divided tongues, as of fire, appeared among them, and a tongue rested on each one of them. All of them were filled with the Holy Spirit and began to speak in other languages, as the Spirit gave them ability. Now there were devout Jews from every nation under heaven living in Jerusalem. And at this sound the crowd gathered and was bewildered, because each one heard them speaking in the native language of each. Amazed and astonished, they asked, 'Are not all these who are speaking Galileans? And how is it that we hear, each of us, in our own native language? Parthians, Medes, Elamites, and residents of Mesopotamia, Judea and Cappadocia, Pontus and Asia, Phrygia and Pamphylia, Egypt and the parts of Libya belonging to Cyrene, and visitors from Rome, both Jews and proselytes, Cretans and Arabs – in our own language we hear them speaking about God's deeds of power' (Acts 2. 1–11).

The miracle of the outpouring of the Holy Spirit enables Peter to spread the message of Christ among the Jews, addressing each of them in their own language. He thus converts about three thousand souls to Christianity. The event creates harmonious unity: 'All who believed were together and had all things in common' (Acts 3. 44). Mapping the miracle of the Apple of Discord onto the Whitsun miracle, the readers of the Apple, who find their own language in the inscription, would correspond to the Jews of all nations who hear their language spoken by the Apostles. The message of the Apple would accordingly occupy the position of the message of salvation. However, it is quite clear that the Apple is not the equivalent, but rather the reversal of the Whitsun miracle. Where the message of salvation creates unity, the message of the Apple creates discord and war. In this respect, the effect of the Apple's translation miracle is more akin to the first prominent biblical language miracle, the confusion of languages at the Tower of Babel:

> Now the whole earth had one language and the same words. And as they migrated from the east, they came upon a plain in the land of Shinar and settled there. And they said to one another, 'Come, let us make bricks, and burn them thoroughly.' And they had brick for stone, and bitumen for mortar. Then they said, 'Come, let us build ourselves a city and a tower with its top in the heavens, and let us make a name for ourselves; otherwise we shall be scattered abroad upon the face of the whole earth.' And the LORD came down to see the city and the tower, which mortals had built. And the LORD said, 'Look, they are one people, and they have all one language; and this is only the beginning of what they will do; nothing that they propose to do will now be impossible for them. Come, let us go down, and confuse their language there, so that they will not understand one another's speech.' So the LORD scattered them abroad from there over the face of all the earth, and they left off building the city. Therefore it was called Babel, because there the LORD confused the language of all the

> earth; and from there the LORD scattered them abroad over the face of all the earth. (Genesis 11)

Konrad superimposes two biblical language miracles that were traditionally connected in salvation history. In one of his sermons on the day of the Pentecost Augustine interprets the Whitsun miracle as the prefiguration of the unity of the Church and as the antitype of the Tower of Babel:

> That gust was purging their hearts of worldly chaff; that fire was consuming the straw of ancient lusts; those tongues they were speaking in, filled by the Holy Spirit, were prefiguring the Church of the future through the languages of all nations. I mean, just as after the flood the ungodly pride of men built a high tower against the Lord, and the human race was deservedly divided by languages, so that each nation would speak its own language and thus not be understood by the others; so in a similar way the devout humility of the faithful has brought to the unity of the church the variety of their different languages; so that what discord had dissipated charity might gather together, and the scattered members of the human race, as of one body, might be attached to their one head, Christ, and so reunited, and fused together into the unity of the holy body by the fire of love.[96]

In his language miracle, Konrad inverts the coordinates of the biblical miracles: the Apple functions like the Whitsun miracle by making a message accessible to everyone, regardless of his or her mother tongue, but the result of this miracle is not unity but discord, much like the confusion of languages in Babel. The biblical allusions can be seen as intellectual play and as testimony to Konrad's keen interest in the power of language that can cause either discord and destruction – as in the case of the Apple's inscription – or be employed for positive purposes, as in the case of the *Trojanerkrieg*, which, according to the prologue, aims at propagating courtly virtues and thus reinstating courtly harmony. In addition,

96 Augustine, *Sermons on the Liturgical Seasons*, ed. by John E. Rotelle, trans. by Edmund Hill (New Rochelle: New City Press, 1993), Sermon 271: On the Day of Pentecost. See also Sermons 266, 267, 268, 269, 270 and the sermon *De sanctu spiritu*, in *Deutsche Predigten des XIII. und XIV Jahrhunderts*, ed. by Hermann Leyser (Leipzig: Basse, 1883), p. 88. For more references and a summary of Augustine's influential discussions of the Babel and Pentecost events, see Arno Borst, *Der Turmbau von Babel: Geschichte der Meinungen über Ursprung und Vielfalt der Sprachen und Völker*, 4 vols (Stuttgart: Hiersemann, 1957–63), II, 1 (1958–59), pp. 391–404. Borst shows in his detailed study how diverse the interpretation of both biblical events was throughout history. It was, for example, debated whether the original Adamic language (usually thought to be Hebrew) was a perfect divine gift or a limited human invention; whether there were already different, naturally developed languages that merely became unintelligible to one another through the punishment of Babel; whether the Apostles present at the Whitsun miracle really spoke all languages, or just Hebrew, which was miraculously understood by everyone; in the former case, whether each Apostle spoke one of the languages or all of them.

it foregrounds the interpretation of the text. The emotion that disrupts the harmony of the courtly celebration on Mount Olympus is pride, the same vice that leads to the construction of the Tower of Babel.

The eschatological references also permit the staple story element of the Apple of Discord to be read in terms of salvation history, as the Apple that brings sin and misery into the world; and hence the festivities it disturbs are depicted as a state of pre-lapsarian harmony between man and nature. Kellner, whose interpretation of the iridescence and inscription of the Apple of Discord essentially recapitulates the readings of Müller and Lienert,[97] discusses the eschatological dimension of the *Trojanerkrieg*: 'Die Ereignisse um Troja werden im Blick auf den Sündenfall und das Weltgericht gedeutet'.[98] She points out the frequent references to the Apocalypse and Judgement Day (see, for example, *Trojanerkrieg*, l. 17678, l. 23308, l. 23738, ll. 27024–27)[99] and argues that Paris can be seen as a type of Adam, described by Venus as one of the slaves of love:

> ÂDÂM von gotes hende wart
> gebildet und gemachet,
> doch het in sô geswachet
> diu minne schiere und ir gebot,
> daz er begunde wider got
> sô frefellîchen werben,
> daz al sîn künne sterben
> muoste durch die schulde sîn. (*Trojanerkrieg*, ll. 2172–79)

As Adam's love leads to the Fall of mankind, so Paris's love leads to the fall of Troy.[100] In addition, Kellner states: 'Wie der Apfel im Paradies wird auch dieser [the Apple of Discord] zum Objekt von Begierde und zweifellos grundiert die biblische Erzählung vom Sündenfall hier einmal mehr die mittelalterliche

97 Kellner, 'Kontinuität und Diskontinuität', 108–13.

98 Kellner, 'Kontinuität und Diskontinuität', 91–94 (p. 91).

99 See also the list of references collected by Seus, who concludes: 'Diese Stellen zeigen auf, dass auch die dargestellte Welt nicht vollkommen außerhalb des Rahmens des die ganze Welt umspannenden Heilsplanes steht, sondern dass ihr nur der eine Teil dieser Lehre, die spezifische Heilsverheißung, nicht offen steht' (Seus, *Heilsgeschichten vor dem Heil?*, pp. 135–40 (p. 139)).

100 See also Lienert: 'Paris erscheint wie Adam, der sein Geschlecht dem Untergang überantwortet' (Lienert, *Geschichte und Erzählen*, p. 299); and Seus, who emphasizes that the reference to Adam demonstrates that love can cause people to act against God (Seus, *Heilsgeschichten vor dem Heil?*, pp. 169–70). On the topos of the slave of women and the slave of love in general see Rüdiger Schnell, *Causa Amoris: Liebeskonzeption und Liebesdarstellung in der mittelalterlichen Literatur*, Bibliotheca Germanica, 27 (Bern: Francke, 1985), pp. 475–505.

Bearbeitung des antiken Stoffs'.[101] These eschatological allusions are complemented by the fact that the newly rebuilt city of Troy is described as an earthly paradise because of its overwhelming splendour:

> reht als ein irdisch paradîs
> diu stat erwünschet dûhte,
> wan si gar schône lûhte
> von rîchen dingen manger slaht. (*Trojanerkrieg*, ll. 17444–47)

Kellner argues that the tower of Troy, which has been built so lavishly and on such a grand scale because of King Priam's 'frîen übermuot' (*Trojanerkrieg*, l. 17558), is a symbol of *superbia* and concludes: 'Der Turmbau aus Hochmut erinnert an den Turmbau von Babel'.[102] She supports this thesis with reference to the miraculous artificial tree that presents the climax of the wonderful in the description: its root and stem are made from gold, its branches from silver and their leaves from rubies and emeralds which make wonderful sounds when touched. Artificial birds made from gemstones sing in the tree in summer as well as in winter and bring 'hôhe[n] muot' (*Trojanerkrieg*, l. 17599) to their listeners. They have been created 'mit listen' (*Trojanerkrieg*, l. 17594) and 'von nigromanzîe' (*Trojanerkrieg*, l. 17603). Kellner comments:

> Mit dieser Artifizialität erschafft Priamus sich seine Welt gewissermaßen in Akten der *imitatio* göttlicher *creatio*: Er überwindet und übertrifft die Natur. Die künstlichen Vögel ersetzen die natürlichen Vögel nicht nur, ihr Gesang ist zudem vom Rhythmus der Jahreszeiten gelöst. [...] Der Gipfel der antiken Kultur, Troja, dessen gleißende Schönheit paradiesgleich ist, gründet auf Hochmut und schwarzmagischer Kunst, insofern ist es dem Untergang, dem Tod, immer schon verfallen.[103]

101 Kellner, 'Kontinuität und Diskontinuität', 109. See also Friedrich, who argues that the eschatological narrative of man's fall and redemption has been informing narrative structures up to modern times and who demonstrates how medieval German texts modify or even invert the core elements of the story to suit their specific intentions (Udo Friedrich, 'Anfang und Ende: Die Paradieserzählung als kulturelles Narrativ in der *Brandanlegende* und im *Erec* Hartmanns von Aue', in *Anfang und Ende: Formen narrativer Zeitmodellierung in der Vormoderne*, ed. by Udo Friedrich, Andreas Hammer and Christiane Witthöft, Beiträge zu einer kulturwissenschaftlichen Mediävistik, 3 (Berlin: Akademie, 2014), pp. 267–88).

102 Kellner, 'Kontinuität und Diskontinuität', 92.

103 Kellner, 'Kontinuität und Diskontinuität', 93. On the literary tradition of the motif of artificial trees, see also Hartmut Kugler, *Die Vorstellung der Stadt in der Literatur des deutschen Mittelalters*, Münchener Texte und Untersuchungen zur deutschen Literatur des Mittelalters, 88 (Munich: Artemis, 1986), pp. 134–37; and Joachim Bumke, *Höfische Kultur: Literatur und Gesellschaft im hohen Mittelalter*, 10th edn (Munich: dtv, 2002), pp. 18–20. See also Udo Friedrich, 'Überwindung der Natur: Zum Verhältnis von Natur und Kultur im *Strassburger Alexander*', in *Fremdes wahrnehmen – fremdes Wahrnehmen: Studien zur Geschichte der Wahrnehmung in Mittelalter und früher Neuzeit*, ed. by Wolfgang Harms and C. Stephen

Since Troy is the epitome of courtly civilization, the cradle of knighthood and love, two values which become highly problematic in the *Trojanerkrieg*, it also encapsulates the paradox of courtly society: 'Die Schauseite der höfischen Kultur und der Tod bilden zwei Seiten einer Medaille'.[104] An important reference which is not mentioned by Kellner but supports the assumption that the description as the earthly paradise is not just topical occurs much later in the text, when the Trojan forces leave the city for battle:

si [Hector and Troilus] kâmen ûz vür TROIE
vil wol gezieret ûf daz wal.
diu ritterschaft was âne zal,
diu mit in ûz begunde zogen.
als ob der engel schar geflogen
dâ kaemen ûz dem paradîs,
sus kam daz her in alle wîs
geblüemet ûz der feste. (*Trojanerkrieg*, ll. 39176–83)

Not only is Troy described as an earthly paradise – the artificial nature of the tree and the birds present it as the reversal of the garden of Eden, perfect nature created by God – but the fact that it is a city also makes it akin to the heavenly Jerusalem.[105] Like most descriptions by Konrad, the description of Troy emphasizes the luminosity of the city and the preciousness of its materials, gold and gemstones – aspects which are also an important characteristic of the heavenly Jerusalem as it is described in Revelation 21. 18: 'The wall is built of jasper, while the city is pure gold, clear as glass'.[106] Konrad carefully gives

Jaeger (Stuttgart: Hirzel, 1997), pp. 119–36 (pp. 133–36). He discusses the Candacis episode in the *Straßburger Alexander* and argues that its animal-automata do not primarily signify a 'Sündenfall' but 'spiegeln das Selbstverständnis der höfischen Welt, die sich durch die stilisierte Distanz zur Naturwelt definiert' (p. 135). This aspect of accomplished courtly culture is, of course, also important to the *Trojanerkrieg*, but only as an ideal that is revealed to be very problematic.

104 Kellner, 'Kontinuität und Diskontinuität', 94.

105 See Kugler, who shows that the notion of Heaven as paradisiacal garden which was prevalent in the ninth century is successively replaced by the idea of a heavenly city throughout the eleventh and twelfth centuries, possibly because of the rise of actual cities (Kugler, *Vorstellung der Stadt*, pp. 84–88; see also pp. 82–84 and p. 89 on the reinterpretation of the city from a symbol of pagan hubris (e.g. Babylon) to a positive concept as a Christian community).

106 See also Revelation 21. 11, where this radiance is associated with the glory of God. The foundations of the walls are adorned with twelve different kinds of gemstones and the streets are made of gold that is translucent like glass (Revelation 21. 19–21). The streets of Troy are made of marble that is radiant and reflective like a mirror (*Trojanerkrieg*, ll. 17408–15). See Kugler, who points out the similarity of the description to Veldeke's Cartago (*Eneasroman*, ll. 362–413) and to the heavenly Jerusalem (Kugler, *Vorstellung der Stadt*, pp. 133–34). On the description of the heavenly Jerusalem (especially on the aspect of luminosity) in the Bible and in the twelfth-century poem *Das himmlische Jerusalem*, see Ulrich Ernst,

the measurements, number and materiality of its elements: the marble walls of the city measure three days of travel; gold-tipped towers are placed at the distance of a stone's throw from each other and surmount the walls at exactly the same height as the walls surmount the moats; there are seven ornate gates; Priam's tower is located in the middle of the city on top of a rock which measures five hundred fathoms.[107] This precision resembles the description of the heavenly Jerusalem, which despite its transcendent nature is measured by an angel with a golden rod using human measures (Revelation 21. 15–17). More importantly, Konrad states that no grander city had ever been built 'ûf der erden' (*Trojanerkrieg*, l. 17685) or will be seen 'unz an den jungestlichen tac' (*Trojanerkrieg*, l. 17678), that is, not until the heavenly Jerusalem. Another striking reference that demands explanation in this eschatological context and is not discussed by Kellner is the fact that the citizens of Troy are said to be exempt from the Fall of mankind:

> ir hôhen unde ir werden
> burger, die wâren alle
> gefrîget vor dem falle,
> der mannes wirde letzet,
> ez wart nie stat besetzet
> mit frumen liuten alsô wol. (*Trojanerkrieg*, ll. 17686–91)[108]

The last detail that Konrad describes before this conclusive appreciation is the interior decoration of Priam's tower, with its images of the pagan gods that are fashioned in silver and gold. The most precious image, presented under

---

'Illumination und Transluzidität: Vom mythischen Palast zur christlichen Kathedrale: Zu Lichtinszenierungen in poetischen Architekturekphrasen', in *Interartifizialität*, ed. by Bürkle and Peters, pp. 221–45 (pp. 230–36).

107 We can compare this with the precise description of the towering grave of Camilla, which is illuminated by artificial everlasting light (Heinrich von Veldeke, *Eneasroman*, ll. 9385–574); with the description of the vision of the Temple in Ezekiel 40–43, which is measured in even more detail by an angel but is not radiant; and with the description of the carefully measured Temple of Solomon, I Kings 6–7, which is overlaid with gold inside and out. Solomon's Temple is often seen as the prefiguration of the Christian Church (especially of the translucent Gothic cathedral, which is, in turn, supposed to represent the heavenly Jerusalem (see Ernst, 'Illumination und Transluzidität', pp. 227–36). At some points the claim to the definitive measurability of Troy is rejected: the marble of the hall floor is 'ûzer mâze fîn' (*Trojanerkrieg*, l. 17531), just as the moats are 'ûzer mâzen tief' (*Trojanerkrieg*, l. 17361) and the wall 'unmâzen hôch' (*Trojanerkrieg*, l. 17352), which may emphasize Priam's hubris. See also Hugo von Langenstein's *Martina*, in which the height of the wall of the heavenly city is said to be 'ane mez' (Hugo von Langenstein, *Martina*, ed. by Adalbert von Keller, Bibliothek des litteratischen Vereins in Stuttgart, 38 (Stuttgart: Litterarischer Verein, 1856), 275, 53).

108 Manuscript Hs. 998, Nuremberg, Germanisches Nationalmuseum, reads 'gefuret' instead of 'gefrîget'.

a golden canopy with a curtain, is that of Jupiter, who is described as the god of *minne* – one of the great and ambivalent forces of the story. This image of gold and gemstones that is radiant like the sun is positioned so that whenever Priam sits at his dining table he looks right into Jupiter's eyes and whoever enters the building bows before the highest god. Whereas the heavenly city needs no temple, 'for its temple is the Lord God the Almighty and the Lamb' (Revelation 21. 22),[109] the veneration of a pagan idol is at the centre of Troy, which associates its splendour with the empty *luxuria* of Babylon (Revelation 18) that also burned down and with the deceptive splendour of the golden calf. This obviously makes the description of the Trojans as particularly pious people who are exempt from the Fall and the admiring interjection 'swer TROIE alsus hiez machen | der solte leben iemer!' (*Trojanerkrieg*, ll. 17416–17) highly ironic.[110] Troy is indeed the antithesis of the heavenly Jerusalem.[111]

The inscription on the Apple that merges the biblical language miracles of Babel and Pentecost is thus part of a network of biblical allusions which reveal the splendour of the narrated pagan world as empty and even sinful. There is no explicit criticism of its riches, which are, on the contrary, highly praised. Nonetheless, the fatal course of the events and the eschatological allusions undermine this positive assessment. The Trojan and Greek heroes *ante gratiam* certainly have no chance of conversion and of avoiding the catastrophe. Their world and version of courtliness are truly 'heillos' – if they die in war, they go to hell[112] – but Konrad's audience has the opportunity to learn from their story and be different.[113]

109 In the poem *Daz himelrîche*, however, there is a high royal palace in the centre of the heavenly Jerusalem (*Daz himelrîche*, in *Kleinere geistliche Gedichte des 12. Jahrhunderts*, ed. by Albert Leitzmann, 2nd edn (Berlin: de Gruyter, 1929), pp. 20–29 (p. 21); see also Kugler, *Vorstellung der Stadt*, p. 126).

110 Kugler instead comments on *Trojanerkrieg*, ll. 17686–89: 'Dieser Bürgerschaft fehlt zu einer Christengemeinde nicht viel. Befände sie sich nicht im heidnischen Troja, sie könnte leicht als Himmelsgemeinde angesprochen werden' (Kugler, *Vorstellung der Stadt*, p. 134). A lack of Christianity can hardly be described as a negligible factor in resembling a Christian community.

111 See also Seus's interpretation of the 'Kräuterkammer' in Herbort's *Liet von Troye*, which is said to appear like Paradise and contains artwork and apparatuses which obscure the distinction between divine and limited human creation and are associated with devilish influence: 'Somit wird das künstliche Paradies in der Gesamtanschauung zu einem ausgesprochenen Un-Paradies' (Seus, *Heilsgeschichten vor dem Heil?*, pp. 28–31 (p. 30); see also p. 44 on Hector's grave).

112 Seus provides a list of references mentioning Hell as the destination of fallen warriors of both sides (e.g. *Trojanerkrieg*, ll. 12582–83, ll. 31314–15) (Seus, *Heilsgeschichten vor dem Heil?*, pp. 138–39). This fate is, however, made explicit only a few times and in the case of nameless warriors, not for the principal heroes of the story.

113 In contrast to this Müller emphasizes the impossibility of conversion but concludes that courtly splendour can therefore be celebrated 'without any religious remorse' (Müller,

As a composite of several epic realizations of poetry metaphors the Apple of Discord can be interpreted as an allegory of poetry in general which highlights the notions of retextualization and reception. In addition to this, its decidedly self-referential quality as the metonymic representation of the story, as an example of the characteristic amalgamation in the *Trojanerkrieg* of beauty and destruction and as the materialization of Konrad's own radiant and gluing words means that it can also be regarded as a *mise en abyme* of the text. Nevertheless, the identification of the Apple with the *Trojanerkrieg* should not be taken too far. The reception of the inscription can be understood as a model for the reception of the *Trojanerkrieg* only in a very general or inverted sense. In a general sense it highlights the aesthetic aspect of poetry, which is not simply a static artefact but can be revived through reception time and time again. The inscription's misreading and sinister purpose, on the other hand, represents the exact opposite of the intended reception of Konrad's text. In addition to this, the inverted allusion to the language miracles of Babel and Pentecost not only highlights the power of language to cause either harmony or destruction but also points to an eschatological perspective for the overall interpretation of the text. Contrary to the opinion of older research, the Apple of Discord, with its multiple layers of meaning, is testimony to the fact that although Konrad's descriptions are certainly highly self-aware showcases of poetic prowess, they do not remain in the realm of vain self-reflexivity for purely self-sufficient reasons. Instead, the aspects of poetry highlighted in these passages offer a specific model for the reception of the text and are thus intricately linked to the content and didactic purpose of the *Trojanerkrieg*.

'Blinding Sight', p. 215).

CHAPTER 3

Praise

The discussion in the previous chapter has shown that the concept of praise can connect the levels of the story and the discourse in the *Trojanerkrieg* closely: the Apple of Discord is a symbol of intradiegetic praise as well as the subject and even the product of the narrator's praise. Beyond this episode praise plays an important role at the level of the story; its impact is discussed by the characters as well as by the narrator. Furthermore, and crucially, whenever Konrad refers to his poetic task in the main text, he mostly describes it as one of praising the characters or certain excellent objects.[1] This chapter will show how Konrad exploits this connection between praise as a verbal action on the levels of both story and discourse as a way of highlighting metapoetic concerns. To begin with, I shall conduct a semantic analysis of the key terms *prîs* and *lop*, which occur with remarkable frequency throughout the *Trojanerkrieg*, in order to demonstrate how their semantic range and typical metaphorical collocations may be particularly suited to accentuating issues concerning the relationship between words and their referents. The second part of the chapter will focus on the important role of fame as a generator of action, considering in particular how the characters' response to poetic praise in the story presents a negative example for the reception of the *Trojanerkrieg*. The third and final section of this chapter will analyse the special connection between praise and love to explore how Konrad employs the traditional motif of *Fernminne* to reflect upon both the power and the limitations of verbal representation.

Prîs and *lop*

The Middle High German noun *prîs* (verbal form: *prîsen*) was adopted during the Early Middle High German period from the French *pris* ('price',

1 *Trojanerkrieg*, l. 1392, l. 6790, l. 7230, ll. 14636–39, ll. 17552–56, ll. 17672–77, ll. 19684–89, ll. 19694–707, ll. 19936–37, ll. 20026–27, ll. 20034–37, ll. 20130–33, ll. 20282–83, ll. 33114–15, ll. 34908–09, l. 37308, ll. 39282–83. Konrad also expresses concern that the failure to complete his poetic task will weaken his 'lop' (*Trojanerkrieg*, ll. 230–33) and speaks of the difficulty of making his own narration praiseworthy (*Trojanerkrieg*, ll. 11362–69).

'value', 'fame', 'praise'), which was in turn derived from Latin *pretium* ('value', 'price', 'esteem'). It denotes 'excellence/ praiseworthy quality or deed', 'praise/ laudative speech act' and 'reputation/ fame/ public recognition'.[2] The term thus signifies at once the cause/content (excellence), its verbal expression (praise) and the result (prestige). However, since the content of praise can also be already existing prestige – it is often impossible to distinguish whether *prîs* refers to excellence or fame – it is problematic to attribute a definitive order to these aspects. Their conflation in one term is the expression of the circular dynamics of the underlying concept.[3] Although *BMZ* does not list the important meaning 'praise', the entry clearly emphasizes the social and public aspect of the concept: 'die höhere geltung im urtheile anderer; die öffentliche anerkennung einer vortrefflichkeit'.[4] Strictly speaking, there can be no *prîs* in the full social sense of the term in the absence of a (courtly) audience to award and proclaim it publicly. The antonyms of *prîs* are similarly social terms like *schame*.[5]

2 On the etymology and meaning of the term, which soon became fully naturalized with the adjectival, adverbial and nominal derivations *prîslich*, *prîsliche/-en*, *unprîs* and with formulaic expressions such as *ze prîse*, see the entries in Georg Friedrich Benecke, Wilhelm Müller and Friedrich Zarncke (= *BMZ*), *Mittelhochdeutsches Wörterbuch*, 4 vols (Leipzig: Hirzel, 1854–66; repr. Stuttgart: Hirzel, 1990), II, pp. 539–35; Matthias Lexer, *Mittelhochdeutsches Handwörterbuch*, 3 vols (Leipzig: Hirzel, 1872–78; repr. Stuttgart: Hirzel, 1992), II, cols 296–98; Jacob and Wilhelm Grimm, *Deutsches Wörterbuch*, 32 vols (Leipzig: Hirzel, 1854–1954), VII, cols 2086–99; *Kluge: Etymologisches Wörterbuch der deutschen Sprache*, ed. by Elmar Seebold, 24th rev. edn (Berlin: de Gruyter, 2002), p. 719; also the contributions by Eugen Lerch, 'Französisch *priser* – deutsch *preisen* – englisch to *praise* und das Kirchenlatein', *Romanische Forschungen*, 55 (1941), 57–82; Emil Öhmann, 'Der französische Einfluss auf die deutsche Sprache im Mittelalter', *Neuphilologische Mitteilungen*, 6/8 (1931), 195–220, and 'Die Bedeutungsentwicklung von dt. *Preis*, frz. *prix*', *Zeitschrift für Mundartforschung*, 26 (1958), 72–75; Erkki Miettinen, *Zum Mundartlichen Fortleben mhd.-mnd. Lehnwortgutes romanischer Herkunft*, Annales Academiae Scientarium Fennicae: Series B, 126 (Helsinki: Suomalainen Tiedeakatemia, 1962); Bumke, *Höfische Kultur*, p. 117. See also Hübner, who discusses the ambiguity of *pris* with reference to some passages from the *Trojanerkrieg* (Hübner, *Lobblumen*, p. 61). Although *prîs* became a key term in courtly culture and literature, the earliest references occur in religious texts and the term was probably not restricted to the court in spoken Middle High German, either (see Öhmann, 'Der französische Einfluss', 204–07; Bumke, *Höfische Kultur*, p. 118 and Miettinen, *Zum Mundartlichen Fortleben*).

3 Konrad accentuates this self-perpetuating nature of the semantically related *liumet*: 'sîn rede sagebaere | diu wahset unde mêret sich' (*Trojanerkrieg*, ll. 24746–47).

4 *BMZ*, p. 532. See also Grimm, *Deutsches Wörterbuch*, col. 2086, which includes the meaning 'praise': 'die höhere geltung und wertschätzung im urtheile anderer, erworbenes oder gespendetes hohes lob, ehre, ruhm' and whose translation of *prîsen* as 'sehr rühmen und loben und dadurch im urtheile anderer erhöhen' (col. 2093) points to the circular dynamics of the social concept.

5 See, for example, Hartmann's *Iwein*: 'der prîs was sîn, unt mîn diu schame' (Hartmann von Aue, *Iwein*, ed. by G. F. Benecke, K. Lachmann and L. Wolff, trans. by Thomas Cramer, 4th rev. edn (Berlin: de Gruyter, 2001), l. 756); but also 'misseprîs' and 'unprîs' (*Trojanerkrieg*, l.

Like *prîs* the older German word *lop* can designate a praiseworthy quality, the laudative speech act proclaiming it and the resulting public prestige.[6] The notion of publicly recognized excellence furthermore links *prîs* and *lop* to terms like *êre*, *wirde*, *ruom* and *name*, which nonetheless do not usually denote laudative speech acts.[7] The redundant formulation *lob unde êre* appears particularly often in the *Trojanerkrieg*.[8] While it is possible that *prîs* had a more elegant and courtly flavour due to its French origins – it becomes more frequent in thirteenth-century texts like *Der Jüngere Titurel* and *Rennewart* – *prîs* and *lop* usually appear as synonyms in Middle High German literature. Konrad alternates the terms for the sake of variation without discernible semantic distinction (for example, *Trojanerkrieg*, ll. 7642–51) and often uses them in redundant formulations (for example, *Trojanerkrieg*, l. 3092).[9]

17732, l. 19303). Nonetheless, it is possible for knights to win *prîs* in the absence of a courtly audience who admire the heroic deed and praise it. In these cases *prîs* is the projection of future prestige which has its root in the praiseworthy deed and has yet to become publicized. In Arthurian romances this is accomplished by sending defeated knights to Arthur's court or by recounting one's *aventiure* there. In this way Askalon can win *prîs* and Kalogrenant *schame* in their fight at the fountain, although the outcome only becomes public with Kalogrenant's narration of the event many years later at Arthur's court. On this motif in Hartmann's romances, see Haiko Wandhoff, '*Âventiure* als Nachricht für Augen und Ohren: Zu Hartmanns von Aue *Erec* und *Iwein*', *ZfdPh*, 113 (1994), 1–22. In the *Trojanerkrieg*, there are also some instances of private praise (for example, ll. 6204–12, ll. 19542–49, ll. 35387–89).

6 Compare Hübner: 'Das Wort [*lop*] bezeichnet nicht nur den Lobpreis als sprachliches Produkt oder als sprachliche Handlung, sondern auch den Ruhm als Eigenschaft des Gepriesenen' (Hübner, *Lobblumen*, p. 2). References in the *Trojanerkrieg* where *lop* denotes excellence are, for example, ll. 92–93, ll. 30128–29. The Middle High German dictionaries list only the meaning 'praise' for *lop* (BMZ, I, pp. 1020–22; Lexer, *Mittelhochdeutsches Handwörterbuch*, I, cols 1954–55).

7 The public verbal expression of this reputation can certainly be implied, but the verbal mode of publication is not a vital aspect of these concepts. Only the verb *rüemen* denotes a laudative speech act like *prîsen* and *loben* and can also refer to the poetic activity of the *Trojanerkrieg* narrator.

8 For example, *Trojanerkrieg*, l. 4571, l. 4863, l. 6678; *êre* and *prîs* (*Trojanerkrieg*, l. 3188) are less common together; for synonymous employment of *prîs* and *lop* with *wirde* see, for example, *Trojanerkrieg*, l. 8279, l. 10407; with *werdikeit*: *Trojanerkrieg*, l. 7373. Another indicator of semantic proximity is the collocation with the same adjectival predicates: both *êre* and *wirde* are very often described as 'high' (*Trojanerkrieg*, l. 4319, ll. 325–35) and can be *bejaget* (*Trojanerkrieg*, l. 29848); the collocation with 'radiant' is much less common (*Trojanerkrieg*, l. 32377, l. 33141).

9 Konrad nonetheless has a preference for adverbs and adjectives derived from *lop* rather than *prîs*; *lobesam* and *lobelich* are employed with astonishing frequency as generic, positive epithets and attributed mostly to warriors of both parties, to important as well as unimportant characters. Both terms also appear as appreciative epithets in the speech of his characters: *Trojanerkrieg*, l. 115, l. 4064, l. 4356, l. 5110, l. 6022, l. 6502, l. 6651, l. 7505, l. 7653, l. 8364, l. 9134, l. 10281, l. 10322, l. 10913, l.10951, l. 11366, l. 11470, l. 11592, l. 11735, l. 11894, l. 11982, l. 12027, l. 12277, l. 13322, l. 13468, l. 14508, l. 15150, l. 15837, l. 16849,

Although it is often impossible to distinguish between the different but closely related semantic aspects of *lop* and *prîs* (excellence, praise, prestige), there are instances in which the verbal quality is particularly emphasized, for example when a reference occurs in the vicinity of laudative speech acts on the discourse level or on the story level.[10] The verbal and acoustic aspect can also be highlighted explicitly: 'sîn nam und sîn vil werder prîs | hal suoze in wîbes ôren' (*Trojanerkrieg*, ll. 12020–21); 'si lopten in gemeine | mit herzen und mit munde' (*Trojanerkrieg*, ll. 37750–51).

Based on his thesis that feudal lordship in the Middle Ages had to be expressed publicly in a form accessible to the senses because it was not yet fully institutionalized, Wenzel understands *fama, leumund, name* and *lop* – we can doubtlessly add the term *prîs* to this list – as verbal acoustic representations that serve to make 'die *rede* über den Herrscher öffentlichkeitsfähig [...] und über die ganze Reichweite der Herrschaft in Raum und Zeit weitläufig auszubreiten'.[11] This function of making somebody who is physically restricted to one place omnipresent through verbal representation becomes particularly evident in a passage which Wenzel quotes from Hartmann's *Erec*:

ez was eht sô umbe in gewant
daz wîten über elliu lant
was sîn wesen und sîn schîn.
sprechet ir, wie daz mohte sîn?
waz von diu schein der lîp nû dâ,
sô was sîn lop anderswâ.
alsô was sîn diu werlt vol:
man sprach eht niemen dô sô wol. (*Erec*, ll. 10046–53)

l. 16926, l. 17708, l. 17876, l. 17988, l. 18301, l. 18341, l. 20536, l. 20576, l. 21486, l. 21827, l. 22307, l. 22404, l. 23084, l. 24782, l. 24797, l. 25016, l. 25607, l. 26473, l. 26808, l. 26989, l. 29794, l. 30258, l. 30686, l. 31267, l. 32908, l. 35648, l. 35974, l. 36116, l. 36568, l. 37228, l. 37301, l. 37615, l. 39034, l. 40232; *ze lobe* and *nâch lobe* are used in a similar way to adjectives or adverbs denoting 'excellent/ praiseworthy': *Trojanerkrieg*, l. 1183, l. 3032, l. 3712, l. 7289, l. 10026, l. 19923, l. 20211, l. 24165, l. 30912; whereas the phrase *ze prîse* is predominantly used in the sense of 'in honour of/ in order to pay tribute', usually referring to a god or goddess: *Trojanerkrieg*, l. 15143, l. 16189, l. 16402, l. 19460, l. 24567, l. 24638 (*ze/ z'eime lobe* is used with the same meaning in *Trojanerkrieg*, l. 15147, l. 23165, l. 24638, l. 26263). The verb *loben* also frequently occurs with the meaning 'to promise/ to swear' (for example, *Trojanerkrieg*, l. 1838).

10 See, for example, the description of Achilles' fame (*Trojanerkrieg*, ll. 6331–67), which obviously manifests itself as public verbal appreciation, since the praise that the people of Greece lavish upon him collectively ('gemeinlîch und besunder' (*Trojanerkrieg*, l. 6343)) is quoted in direct speech.

11 Wenzel, *Hören und Sehen*, p. 154.

Given this function, it comes as no surprise that the terms *lop* and *prîs* are sometimes collocated with attributes relating to spatial distribution such as 'wide' or 'broad'.[12] Thus, Konrad states of Hecuba: 'man hete wîte erkennet | ir namen und ir hôhen prîs' (*Trojanerkrieg*, ll. 344–45). Of Bacchus he says in a more metaphorical expression: 'BÂCHUS er was geheizen | und schein sîn lop breit unde wît' (*Trojanerkrieg*, ll. 16180–81). The spatial distribution of fame is also emphasized in the episode relating the youth of Achilles:

> Sus manicfaltic wunder
> begienc der helt besunder
> und tet sô frefellichiu dinc,
> daz in des landes umberinc
> mit lobe sîn nam geblüemet fuor. (*Trojanerkrieg*, ll. 6331–35)

In accordance with the general tendency to quantify abstractions metaphorically in terms of verticality,[13] *prîs* and *lop* are often described as 'high'.[14] Since this notion implies that they are visible from afar, it is related to the attributes 'wide' and 'broad' as well as to the association with radiance. The topical nature of this metaphor is proven by numerous references, as well as by lexicalized formulae like *hôchgelopt*. In the *Trojanerkrieg* the attribute 'high' is by far the most common collocation of *lop* and *prîs*.[15] The topical metaphor of high praise can also be elaborated. It can be used to measure praise; thus one

12 Compare also 'des lop was virrec unde wît' (Wolfram, *Parzival*, 43, 5).

13 See George Lakoff and Mark Johnson, who count 'more is up' among the orientational conceptual metaphors that structure cognition by transferring everyday physical experiences onto more abstract target domains: 'If you add more of a substance to a container or pile, the level goes up'; more specifically 'high status is up; low status is down': 'Status is correlated with (social) power and (physical) power is UP [based on the experience 'Physical size typically correlates with physical strength, and the victor in a fight is typically on top']' (George Lakoff and Mark Johnson, *Metaphors We Live By* (Chicago: University of Chicago Press, 1980), pp. 14–24 (pp. 15–16)). See also Walther's humoristic play with the metaphorical length of King Otto's generosity and honour in relation to Otto's actual height (L 26, 33).

14 Compare Hartmann, *Erec*, l. 10040; Wolfram, *Parzival*, 566, 9. The height and breadth metaphor can also be combined and elaborated: 'die zwene jungen recken, die sach man hie mit eren | ir pris die lenge strecken, die breite wit und gen der hoehe keren' (*Albrechts (von Scharfenberg) Jüngerer Titurel*, ed. by Werner Wolf and Kurt Nyholm, 4 vols, Deutsche Texte des Mittelalters, 45, 55, 61, 73, 77, 79 (Berlin: Akademie, 1955–95), 4093, 1–2).

15 References for *hôher prîs*/ *hôhes lop* and the phrase *hôchgelopt*, which is also used as an honorific epithet in the speech of the characters: *Trojanerkrieg*, l. 1823, l. 1827, l. 2107, l. 2627, l. 2769, l. 4574, l. 5480, l. 6596, l. 7911, l. 8154, l. 8245, l. 8506, l. 8705, l. 9423, l. 10155, l. 10832, l. 11730, l. 13174, l. 13277, l. 16189, l. 18528, l. 19633, l. 19687, l. 21610, l. 22074, l. 22999, l. 24002, l. 25211, l. 25585, l. 25651, l. 25668, l. 26423, l. 26991, l. 29867, l. 30071, ll. 30160–61, l. 30491, l. 30552, l. 30637, l. 30860, l. 31154, l. 31297, l. 31411, l. 32113, l. 32125, l. 32375, l. 32513, l. 32615, l. 32778, l. 32893, l. 33104, l. 34630, l. 34910, l. 35558, l. 35955, l. 36232, l. 36764, l. 36793, l. 37877, l. 37911, l. 39915, l. 40168.

person's praise may be higher than another's.[16] Praise can also either grow and rise[17] or be lowered. In the *Trojanerkrieg* Jason declares that his fame would suffer greatly if he acted like a coward and avoided the dangerous task of winning the Golden Fleece. It would be 'pressed down' and 'felled' like a tree: 'mîn lop, daz würde in alle wîs | verdrücket und gefellet nider' (*Trojanerkrieg*, ll. 8280–81; similarly ll. 3366–67, l. 18062).[18] In his description of Hector's fight against Peleus, Konrad even continues the metaphor of 'high praise' *ad absurdum*, thus drawing attention to the topical expression: 'HECTOR, der küene, dô | nâch hôhem prîse tiefe gruop' (*Trojanerkrieg*, ll. 4006–07).

Related to the formulaic metaphor of high praise is the more evocative metaphor of flying praise.[19] Superiority in terms of renown is accordingly expressed as praise that flies higher than that of other people. In the *Trojanerkrieg*, the scalar measurement of praise makes it the subject of competition:

> ACHILLEN dâ ze lande
> nieman irte an sînem lobe,
> sîn prîs der flouc den besten obe
> maniges rîches umberinc. (*Trojanerkrieg*, ll. 6494–97)[20]

The only person who could compete with Achilles' fame is Jason, who is accumulating more and more renown: 'ob allen sînen mâgen | flouc sîn name hôhe enbor' (*Trojanerkrieg*, ll. 6542–43). The results of this rivalry will be discussed in the next section. The metaphor of 'flying fame', which also implies swiftness of circulation,[21] is associated with the more general one of 'flying news (*maere*)'.[22] Both are probably influenced by the tradition of Virgil's

16 Praise of Helen supersedes that of other women (*Trojanerkrieg*, l. 19682, l. 19835).

17 Compare 'iuwer êre wehset alle wîs, | iuwer werdekeit und iuwer prîs, | iuwer vröude und iuwer wunne | diu stîget als diu sunne' (Gottfried, *Tristan*, ll. 1613–16). In this case the metaphor of radiant praise (discussed below) is also evoked.

18 Praise can also be broken off (*abe brechen*): for example, *Trojanerkrieg*, ll. 21532–33, ll. 40296–99.

19 See, for example, *Trojanerkrieg*, l. 4752, ll. 7640–41, ll. 26064–65. See also *Der Winsbecke*, ed. by Moriz Haupt (Leipzig: Weidmannsche Buchhandlung, 1845), 19, 5.

20 Helen's fame (*name*) flies higher than that of other women and is likened to an eagle, which gives it an even more animated and corporeal quality and links it to the *liumet* personification discussed below (*Trojanerkrieg*, ll. 19727–31). See also *Trojanerkrieg*, ll. 1944–46, l. 26065.

21 See also 'sneller dann ein sprintze floc ir beider lop durch manic ore' (*Jüngerer Titurel*, 5778, 3).

22 See, for example: 'Dô flugen disiu mære von schare ze schar' (*Das Nibelungenlied*, ed. by Ursula Schulze, trans. by Siegfried Grosse (Stuttgart: Reclam, 2010), 1587, 1). It is also associated with an initial metonymic exchange of the message for the medium: 'alsus vlouc Morgânes tôt | mit maneger hande clagenôt, | als ob er vlücke wære. | er seite leidiu mære | ûf die bürge und in daz lant. | in dem lande vlouc zehant | niht wan daz eine clagewort' (Gottfried, *Tristan*, ll. 5477–83). This metaphor also appears in the *Trojanerkrieg* when Priam hears about the fall of Troy and his father's death: 'diz maere hin von TROIE kam |

personification of *fama*, an evil, swift-flying monster with feathers and many eyes, ears and tongues.[23] Following Ovid's account of the events at Aulis, Konrad also includes the detail of the personified *fama* informing the Trojans of the impending attack (*Metamorphoses*, XII, 39–63) and adds to it elements of Virgil's *fama* personification and a number of new ideas (*Trojanerkrieg*, ll. 24662–759).[24] Konrad's *liumet* lives high up in the sky from where he can see everything that happens. Many reports fly through the thousand windows of his house, which is populated by his courtiers, who are constantly occupied with spying and gossiping. No secret is safe from the uncontrollable (*wilde*) *liumet*, who wears feathers and flies faster than any bird, spreading truth as well as lies. The detail that the *liumet* is particularly active in witnessing and reporting battles (*Trojanerkrieg*, ll. 24716–25) is Konrad's own addition. It links the business of the *liumet* to Konrad's own task of narrating the Trojan War, with the decisive difference that Konrad's reports ought to be more reliable and pursue benevolent goals while *liumet*'s intention to destroy unity and trigger conflict associates him with Discord:

> zerteilen kan er manic dinc
> und machet zwei von eime.
> [...]
> er ist dar ûf erhitzet,
> daz er stifte manigen zorn. (*Trojanerkrieg*, ll. 24726–31)[25]

---

geriuschet z'in geswinde' (*Trojanerkrieg*, ll. 13120–21); the news of the newly erected tower of Troy flies to the Greeks: 'diz hôrte man ze KRIECHEN sagen, | wan daz maere flouc dâ hin' (*Trojanerkrieg*, ll. 13398–99); 'diu maere wâren dâ geflogen | über al der KRIECHEN lant, | daz mit gewalteclicher hant | HELÊNE was gezücket' (*Trojanerkrieg*, ll. 23394–97). On the metaphor of the flying news, see Werner Wunderlich, '"Der Wesen flüchtigstes, die schnellste aller Plagen": Fama in antiker und mittelalterlicher Sprache und Literatur: Stimme – Gerücht – Ruhm', *Mittellateinisches Jahrbuch*, 39 (2004), 329–70 (pp. 357–58).

23 Virgil, *Aeneid*, ed. and trans. by H. Rushton Fairclough, 2 vols, 2nd rev. edn by G. P. Goold (Cambridge, MA: Harvard University Press, 1999–2000), IV, 173–97 (further occurrences of the personification: VI, 298–99, 666, VII, 390–93, IX, 472–74, XI, 139–41). On the Greek predecessors of *fama*, the deity *pheme* (rumour, reputation) and the personified news *ossa* (voice, sound), see Wunderlich, 'Fama', 329–33.

24 Virgil's demonic Fama is more corporeal and flies around, while Ovid's Fama presides over a house on a mountain top in the middle of the world from where she can see and hear everything – her house is populated by personified true and false rumours. On Konrad's *liumet* personification and its relationship to its predecessors, see *Albrecht von Halberstadt und Ovid im Mittelalter*, ed. by Karl Bartsch, Bibliothek der gesammten deutschen National-Literatur von der ältesten bis auf die neuere Zeit, 38 (Quedlinburg: Basse, 1861), pp. cix–x; Lienert, *Geschichte und Erzählen*, pp. 120–21; Gebert, *Mythos als Wissensform*, pp. 438–39. Gebert observes that Konrad combines the aspect of information-collection from Ovid's depiction with that of information-dissemination, emphasized by Virgil.

25 This similarity is pointed out by Monecke (*Das Erzählprinzip der 'wildekeit'*, p. 49); and is also discussed by Seus (*Heilsgeschichten vor dem Heil?*, pp. 161–62). See also Wunderlich, 'Fama', 334. The latter emphasizes that Fama and Eris (Discord) both develop menacing

In this case *liumet* does not refer to praise but to news in general, but since it is also used with reference to Helen's fame (*Trojanerkrieg*, l. 21072, l. 21086, l. 21526)[26] it can legitimately be discussed in connection with the concept of praise.[27] The portrayal of *liumet* also explains a rather curious insult that Lamedon hurls at Hercules for conquering ('stealing') Troy through a cunning ambush:

> swaz ir hie prîses hânt bejaget,
> der ist alsô gefüege,
> daz in ein mügge trüege
> wol in ir snabel über sê! (*Trojanerkrieg*, ll. 12692–95)

The mosquito that carries Hercules' tiny praise in its beak over the ocean is obviously a comic reversal of the motif of high-flying praise and a parody of the mighty winged *liumet*. Pointing out the structural invisibility of the act and the centre of perception in narrative texts that block out questions like 'To whom does the narrator speak?' or 'Who beholds the events?' – for example by instating God as the omniscient witness and source of inspiration – Gebert argues that the personification *liumet* fills in for the relatively undefined narrator in order to make the narrative paradox invisible: 'Kommunikation zwar anzubieten, aber für Kommunikation selbst nicht zur Verfügung zu stehen'.[28]

Another telling attribute of praise is radiance.[29] Konrad uses this collocation particularly often, not only in the *Trojanerkrieg*.[30] Like the attributes 'wide' and 'broad', radiance suggests a far reaching distribution of praise. Peleus and Hector, for example, fight to make their fame visible in many countries:

---

dynamics from small incidents but does not discuss Konrad's personification, which also includes this detail (*Trojanerkrieg*, ll. 24746–47).

26 Konrad's employment of *liumet* thus mirrors the polyvalence of Latin *fama*, which denotes 'reputation' (*bona fama* as well as *mala fama*) and 'rumour'. Thus *fama* in Virgil's *Aeneis* refers to Dido's good reputation, which is compromised by her love for Aeneas (Virgil, *Aeneis*, IV, 91, 170), as well as to the rumour of her disgrace (see Wunderlich, 'Fama', 333, 337, 341).

27 One obvious similarity between personified rumour and praise is their mode of distribution through flying; one important difference is the association with secrecy ('"nû rûne mir, sô rûne ich dir", | daz sprichet al sîn hofeschar' (*Trojanerkrieg*, l. 24734–35)), which sets morally reprehensible gossip apart from the public discourse of fame. On the depreciation of *rûnen/murmur* as uncourtly and subversive, see Wenzel, *Hören und Sehen*, pp. 151–54; Wunderlich, 'Fama', 350–51.

28 See Gebert, *Mythos als Wissensform*, pp. 415–18, pp. 435–49 (p. 440).

29 Compare Wolfram, *Parzival*, 613, 2; Wolfram, *Willehalm*, 23, 9; 101, 28.

30 Adjectives used in this context are *durliuhtic*, *lieht*, *liehtebernde*, *lûter*, *lûterbære*, *clâr*, *glanz*. Praise can also be brought *ze liehte*: *Trojanerkrieg*, l. 497, l. 2474, l. 3953, l. 3966, l. 6209, l. 6551, l. 10833, l. 14349, ll.16452–54, ll. 19588–89, l. 25341, l. 25584, l. 25785, ll. 27030–31, l. 27355, l. 27852, ll. 27896–99, l. 27931, l. 29836, l. 30169, l. 30226, l. 30383, l. 31291, l. 32176, l. 32615, ll. 33024–25, l. 33135, l. 33365, l. 33463, l. 33795, l. 34207, l. 36595, l. 36619, l. 36835, l. 37001, l. 37887, ll. 39810–11.

si wurben nâch gewinne
mit herzen und mit handen,
durch daz in manigen landen
ir lop ze liehte würde brâht. (*Trojanerkrieg*, ll. 3950–53)

The synaesthetic description of an acoustic mode of representation as something visible emphasizes the function of praise as a substitute for the presence of the praised person or object whose excellence manifests itself visibly: 'Das was man sehen kann, garantiert den Ruhm des Protagonisten, der unlösbar mit seinem Namen und seinem strahlenden Äußeren verknüpft ist; umgekehrt können sein Name und sein sichtbarer Glanz diesen Ruhm und [seine] Taten verbürgen'.[31] Wenzel identifies the *schîn* of fame with the *splendor* of lordship symbolizing noble charisma, divine grace and virtue:

> Durch die Vervielfältigung der Zeichen (Wappen, Kleidung, Architektur) und durch das Herrscherlob wird dieser *schîn* gewährleistet, – auch abgelöst von der physischen Präsenz des Herrn. Die Begriffe *schîn* und *schînen* stellen dabei die Verbindung her zwischen dem appräsentierenden Wort (*lop*) und dem eigentlichen Herrscherkörper, so daß der Herr oder die Dame medial vermittelt im Wort 'erscheinen' können.[32]

Even though the identification of *schîn* with virtue and divine grace is highly problematic in the *Trojanerkrieg*, the splendour of the person still attaches itself to their verbal representation. Thus Paris receives radiant praise from the inhabitants of Citarea ('durchliuhtic unde reine | wart der manicfaltic prîs' (*Trojanerkrieg*, ll. 19588–89)) for his aristocratic beauty and attire, which are described as particularly resplendent by the narrator (*Trojanerkrieg*, ll. 19504–05, l. 19531, ll. 19599–601, ll. 19615–19). Although Paris's praise may be metaphorically radiant and pure in the sense of ornate speech (compare Konrad's 'worte lûter unde glanz' in the prologue), or because the 'durchliuhtic prîs' presented in reported speech contains the very term 'durchliuhtic' (*Trojanerkrieg*, l. 19657), this quality also links the verbal signifier, the radiant praise, to its referent, the radiant Paris.

In a logical extension of the metaphor of radiant praise, the loss of fame can be metaphorized as its darkening: the radiant fame of the young Achilles spreads throughout Greece and beyond: 'sîn prîs durchliuhtic unde grôz | ze KRIECHEN was und anderswâ' (*Trojanerkrieg*, ll. 6338–39), which

31 Schulz (*Schwieriges Erkennen*, p. 374), refering to Konrad's *Turnier von Nantes*: 'Alsus wart er geprîset; | sîn name uns des bewîset | und sîn durchliuhticlicher schîn. | daz schuof er mit der milte sîn | und mit rîlicher hende' (Konrad von Würzburg, *Turnier von Nantes*, in Konrad von Würzburg, *Partonopier und Meliur – Turnei von Nantheiz – Sant Nicolaus – Lieder und Sprüche*, ed. by Karl Bartsch, ll. 1135–39)).

32 Wenzel, *Hören und Sehen*, pp. 155–56.

means that his heroism becomes very visible: 'schouw al diu welt an sîne getât' (*Trojanerkrieg*, l. 6358). This visibility, however, presents a problem for his mother Thetis, who wants to prevent him from participating and dying in the Trojan War. As an infant, she had taken him 'heimlîch unde stille' (*Trojanerkrieg*, l. 5905) to Chiron's cave, which is described as being almost completely inaccessible (*Trojanerkrieg*, ll. 5876–917), but now she worries that the Greeks will hear about his fame and take him to war (*Trojanerkrieg*, ll. 13589–95).[33] Taking Achilles to a remote place is obviously not sufficient to fulfil Thetis's intention of hiding her son from the eyes of the Greek public (*Trojanerkrieg*, ll. 13468–71) since his heroic fame transcends such local restrictions. She also has to prevent him from performing the manly deeds that generate his radiant fame, so forcing him into the role of a girl seems like the perfect plan. Achilles recognizes the threat to his heroic reputation. Not being able to exercise his manly power means that he will become invisible as a hero, not just literally, by hiding his body, but also because his fame will cease to shine forth throughout Greece as his second body:

> mîn lop würd alze tunkel,
> daz gar durchliuhtic schînet,

33 On the episode of Achilles' education by Chiron and the following cross-dressing episode, which is adapted from Statius's *Achilleid*, see Cholevius, *Geschichte der deutschen Poesie*, pp. 138–40; Timothy R. Jackson, 'Außen und Innen bei Konrad von Würzburg: Die Achill-Deidamia-Episode im *Trojanischen Krieg*', in *Personenbeziehungen in der mittelalterlichen Literatur*, ed. by Helmut Brall, Barbara Haupt and Urban Küsters, Studia humaniora, 25 (Düsseldorf: Droste, 1994), pp. 219–49; Lienert, *Geschichte und Erzählen*, pp. 50–54, pp. 81–92; Edith Feistner, '*manlîchiu wîp, wîplîche man*: Zum Kleidertausch in der Literatur des Mittelalters', *PBB*, 119 (1997), 235–60 (pp. 248–51); Lydia Miklautsch, 'Das Mädchen Achill: Männliches Crossdressing und weibliche Homosexualität in der mittelalterlichen Literatur', in *Literarische Leben*, ed. by Meyer and Schiewer, pp. 575–96; Andrea Sieber, '*daz frouwen cleit nie baz gestuont*: Achills Crossdressing im *Trojanerkrieg* Konrads von Würzburg und in der *Weltchronik* des Jans Enikel', in *Genderdiskurse und Körperbilder im Mittelalter: Eine Bilanzierung nach Butler und Laqueur*, ed. by Ingrid Bennewitz and Ingrid Kasten, Bamberger Studien zum Mittelalter, 1 (Münster: Lit, 2002), pp. 49–76, and 'Konfusion der Geschlechter? Zur Sozialisation Achills im *Trojanerkrieg* Konrads von Würzburg', *Der Deutschunterricht*, 55 (2003), 76–89; Kraß, *Geschriebene Kleider*, pp. 285–96; Udo Friedrich, 'Diskurs und Narration: Zur Kontextualisierung des Erzählens in Konrads von Würzburg *Trojanerkrieg*', in *Text und Kontext: Kolloquium 2004*, ed. by Jan-Dirk Müller, Schriften des Historischen Kollegs: Kolloquien, 64 (Munich: Oldenbourg, 2007), pp. 99–120; Müller, *Höfische Kompromisse*, pp. 60–62; Schulz, *Schwieriges Erkennen*, pp. 480–87; Peter Strohschneider, 'Kemenate: Geheimnisse höfischer Frauenräume bei Ulrich von dem Türlin und Konrad von Würzburg', in *Das Frauenzimmer: Die Frau bei Hofe in Spätmittelalter und früher Neuzeit: 6. Symposium der Residenz-Kommisssion der Akademie der Wissenschaften in Göttingen*, Residenzforschungen, 11 (Stuttgart: Thorbecke, 2000), pp. 29–45 (pp. 39–45), Gebert, *Mythos als Wissensform*, pp. 465–72, pp. 504–17.

würd ich dar ûf gepînet,
daz ich verhaele mîne kraft. (*Trojanerkrieg*, ll. 14348–51)[34]

For the question of the representational capacities of language the terms *prîs* and *lop* are particularly instructive because they collapse the message (excellence) and the medium (praise).[35] This identity suggests that the change of medium is not thought to effect a significant distortion and that praise can, in fact, appropriately substitute for the visible physical presence of the praised object or person. The metaphorical attributes of words for praise and fame support this diagnosis. Wenzel explains that the dissemination of honour as praise can be ensured through minstrels who publicize the generosity of a lord or a knight's victory in tournament throughout the realm.[36] The poetic expression of flying fame, however, tends to undermine this actual dependence on human messengers.[37] Instead, fame is presented as an autonomous and animated agent of its own spatial distribution when Paris says that Helen's reputation has flown from her to him: 'der liumet und daz maere, | diu von iu dicke sint geflogen' (*Trojanerkrieg*, ll. 21086–87); and Helen counters with an equivalent formulation: 'mîn liumet und daz maere, | daz von mir fliuget über lant' (*Trojanerkrieg*, ll. 21526–27). These expressions imply an almost physical connection between Helen and her reputation, as though an excellent body emits fame by itself. Likewise the fact that the radiance of the praised object or person attaches itself to their verbal representation and makes them visible even where they are absent suggests a non-arbitrary, indexical relationship between the words and their referents that synaesthetically

34 This fear is confirmed when the seer Calchas bewails the fact that Achilles is hidden under female attire: 'owê, daz man dem helde gît | nû wîbes werc ze handen! | er solte in disen landen | erstrîten liehtebaeren prîs, | nû muoz sîn lop in alle wîs | belîben dort vil tunkel' (*Trojanerkrieg*, ll. 27352–57). Praise can also become extinguished (*Trojanerkrieg*, ll. 40326–31) or dull (*Trojanerkrieg*, ll. 2474–75, l. 16753). See also Konrad's *Engelhard* with reference to Dietrich, who loses his wife, his wealth and his kingdom due to his illness and hides his disfigured body on a beautiful island: 'als ein lieht karfunkelstein | was sîn lop durchliuhtic ê, | daz nû engap niht schînes mê, | wand ez als ein trüebez glas | verdorben und verblichen was' (Konrad, *Engelhard*, ll. 5304–08). The darkness of praise does not refer to publicly proclaimed shame but to a removal from public consciousness. Having become invisible on his island, Dietrich is soon forgotten.

35 Köbele discusses the implications of this coincidence for verse legends as an implicit justification of rhetorical ornamentation against the demands of the *sermo humilis* typical of this genre, as a tension that is created: 'wo im Akt des *wunder tihten* religiöse und ästhetische Rede sich im (demutstopisch gebremsten) Sprechakt des *lop mêren* überlagern, die Legende mit einem, sei es mehr, sei es weniger verborgenen Kunstanspruch auftritt' (Köbele, 'Die Illusion der "einfachen Form"', 365–79 (p. 375)).

36 Wenzel, *Hören und Sehen*, p. 187, p. 191.

37 This is not the case with Hartmann's *vrouwe Melde*, who relies on a squire to inform King Arthur of the honour and fame that Erec earns in tournament (*Erec*, ll. 2516–20).

transcends the divide between the media. Thus Schulz states: 'Wenn man "Ruhm" auch "sehen" kann, werden einzelne Wahrnehmungsbereiche miteinander austauschbar. Sehen und Hören können füreinander einstehen, wo es darum geht, den wahren Wert einer Person zu taxieren'.[38] The notion of indexical, self-distributing praise/fame not only makes the public circulation of excellence automatic and almost instantaneous – the *liumet* is swift like the wind – but can also overcome the difficulties of verbal representation that a human mediator may face. Thus, while the narrator declares himself unable to capture the splendour of the newly erected tower of Troy with his words, its fame can communicate itself as radiance and makes it visible throughout the realm:

> mîn zunge niht ergründen mac
> mit worten sîne koste rîch,
> ez wart ûf erden sîn gelîch
> nie beschouwet noch erkant,
> in manic wildez einlant
> gie durchliuhtic schîn dervon.
> der turn der was ÎLÎON
> geheizen und genennet,
> sîn name wîte erkennet
> von sîme glanzen schîne was. (*Trojanerkrieg*, ll. 17488–97)[39]

The personification *liumet*, as well as the topical metaphors of flying and radiant praise, serve to gloss over the practical questions of who witnesses and who disseminates certain information, how the gap between visual and verbal information is closed. In this regard it will be instructive to explore how Konrad works with a concept of praise/fame that connects the levels of discourse and story in order to highlight issues concerning verbal representation. Although there is a great deal to suggest an intimate relationship between praise and its content, the *liumet* personification also stresses the potential for distortion that becomes relevant where *liumet* refers to Helen's fame. Before treating this topic in the final part of the chapter, however, I shall give an overview of the importance of praise in the story of the *Trojanerkrieg* and show how its representation addresses issues that concern the appropriate reception of heroic poetry.

38 Schulz, *Schwieriges Erkennen*, p. 377.

39 It is, significantly, ambiguous whether 'glanzen schîne', which causes the reputation, refers to the tower itself or to its verbal representation ('name'). The identity of fame and excellence is further emphasized when the metaphor of far-reaching radiance replaces the need for verbal mediation altogether: 'sîn tugent schein sô lieht gevar, | daz man sie vor den besten | sach liuhten unde glesten | in manic rîche verre' (*Partonopier*, ll. 250–53; see also the discussion of this passage by Schulz, *Schwieriges Erkennen*, p. 413).

The Importance of Praise

Praise frequently generates narrative action in the *Trojanerkrieg*. It incites Paris to abduct Helen and the desire to acquire, protect or restore it motivates the key decisions of many characters. The fact that knights actively seek out opportunities to earn *prîs* and *lop* is expressed through the frequent association with the verb *bejagen*, verbs for fighting as well as verbs that emphasize the active striving for renown such as *werben*, or the successful achievement of that renown (*gewinnen*).[40] Gaining a heroic reputation is cited as motivation for fighting in battle speeches (for example, *Trojanerkrieg*, l. 11843, ll. 29815–50, ll. 11704–14) and Ulysses convinces Achilles to leave Deidamia and join the war by appealing to his desire for fame:

> wie mac durchliuhtic unde klâr
> bî reinen guoten wîben
> sîn lop hernâch belîben,
> ob er sich nû sô gar verlît,
> daz er niht suochet einen strît. (*Trojanerkrieg*, ll. 27896–900)[41]

The concern about honour also motivates the first destruction of Troy: when the Argonauts are denied permission to camp on Trojan territory by the old king Lamedon, this insult (*unêre* (*Trojanerkrieg*, l. 7085, l. 7122, l. 7158)) calls for retribution. Hasebrink emphasizes that the conflict, which will eventually lead to the Trojan War, is not motivated by 'Besitzanspruch' but by a violation of the symbolic value of honour,[42] arguing that the need to defend, restore and earn *êre* violently exposes 'die Ambivalenz eines auf "Pazifizierung" zielenden Begriffs des Höfischen'.[43]

40 For example, *bejagen*: *Trojanerkrieg*, l. 3687, l. 4574, l. 6662, l. 6681, l. 11843, l. 12692, l. 25785, l. 29867, l. 30090, l. 30169, l. 31291, l. 33051, l. 33795, l. 36031, l. 36131, l. 37001, ll. 37174–75; *kämpfen, ringen, (er)vehten, (er)strîten, kriegen*: *Trojanerkrieg*, l. 3645, l. 3966, l. 6576, l. 7377, ll. 25874–75, l. 29929, ll. 30160–61, l. 31411, ll. 32176–77, ll. 33134–35, ll. 33612–13, l. 36031, ll. 39232–33; *werben* etc.: *Trojanerkrieg*, l. 25211, l. 25651, l. 25756, ll. 25340–41, l. 37877, ll. 39582–83; *gewinnen*: *Trojanerkrieg*, l. 31911, ll. 32082–83, l. 32096. Compare Hartmann von Aue, *Erec*, l. 2813; *Iwein*, ll. 3522–23, l. 18707.

41 Gebert observes that battle speeches in the second half of the text do not refer to the motivation of revenge as in the first half but focus on the attainment of exemplary heroic honour instead (Gebert, *Mythos als Wissensform*, pp. 291–94). See also Knapp, who remarks: 'Diese Verbindung von Achills ritterlicher Ehre mit seinem Auftrag Hector zu besiegen, ist ein wichtiger neuer Zug in der Fassung Konrads' (Knapp, *Hector und Achill*, p. 64).

42 Although Telamon also cites the opportunity to seize booty as motivation for attacking Troy (*Trojanerkrieg*, ll. 11692–703), this is clearly not the primary reason for the assault on the city.

43 Hasebrink, 'Rache als Geste', p. 214. See also Schulz, who argues that the *Trojanerkrieg* exposes the destructive potential of the rules of feudal interaction, such as *êre* and *minne*,

The psychology of fame and praise is discussed most explicitly in the Jason episode, not only in the context of love, as will be discussed later, but also in the context of competition, hatred and envy. Peleus, Achilles' father, is concerned that his nephew Jason, who acquires considerable praise, might rival his son's status as the most revered Greek hero:

> dar umbe engunde er im des niht,
> daz ieman anders waere
> prîs unde lop gebaere
> denn der hôchgeborne knabe. (*Trojanerkrieg*, ll. 6526–29)

The narrator comments on Peleus's reaction as a general rule that still applies in his own time. Excellence and praise (*werdikeit, lop* and *êre*) will always attract the envy of lesser men, so that hatred is, in fact, desirable as a confirmation of one's achievements (*Trojanerkrieg*, ll. 6583–603).[44] Aware of Jason's ambition for fame, Peleus cunningly turns this very threat to his son's supremacy against his nephew. He begins by duplicitously congratulating Jason on his success and superior reputation, suggesting that his fame is only lacking in one tiny way:

> dû waerest gar gefrîget
> vor aller slahte meine,
> wan daz dir ein vil kleine
> an ganzer wirde bristet:
> ein lop hât sich gefristet
> vor dir in allen dînen tagen,
> ob dû daz möhtest noch bejagen,
> sô waerest dû gar vollekomen
> und für den besten ûzgenomen,
> der iendert lebt ûf erden. (*Trojanerkrieg*, ll. 6656–65)

After Jason has affirmed his keen interest in hunting for 'ganzen prîs' (*Trojanerkrieg*, l. 6681), Peleus reveals this ultimate challenge to be the attainment of the Golden Fleece:

> gewinnest dû die wollen
> von des widers felle,
> dîn lop beginnet helle

without offering a real alternative to them (Schulz, *Schwieriges Erkennen*, pp. 455–97). Cormeau similarly observes that Konrad exposes 'das Zerstörerische eines kompromißlosen Kampfethos' (Cormeau, 'Quellenkompendium oder Erzählkonzept?', p. 319).

44 Compare *Tristan*, ll. 8395–406. Here the exceptionally gifted protagonist attracts the envy of other courtiers and Mark counsels him that this is a necessary by-product, and therefore also a mark, of excellence.

vür alle ritter klingen.
dir ist an allen dingen
gelungen unz an disen tac,
und swie dir nû gelingen mac
an dem rîlichen tiere,
sô muoz dîn name schiere
vür alle künige werden
erhoehet ûf der erden. (*Trojanerkrieg*, ll. 6720–30)

Since everyone who has ever tried to obtain the fleece of the ram, which is protected by a dragon, has died in the attempt, Peleus hopes that Jason will meet the same fate. The emphasis on fame and praise in this episode is Konrad's own invention; the terms *prîs* and *lop* occur with astonishing frequency. In Benoît's account, Peleüs wants to rid himself of his nephew because he fears him as a rival to his throne and lures him to take up the perilous challenge not with the promise of praise but with the promise to make him his heir. In opposition to all his sources, Konrad identifies Jason's uncle with Achilles' father.[45] Hasebrink points out that Konrad's changes turn Jason's quest for rulership into a competition for purely symbolic supremacy which is expressed as praise:

> Peleus fürchtet [...] die Rivalität zwischen beiden um *hôhe wirde*, wie sie sich in *lop*, *prîs* und *rüemen* und damit in Sprache manifestiert. Somit wird die Fahrt Jasons zu einer Aventiure um den stratifikatorischen Rang des Besten, der kommunikativ vermittelt durch die imaginierte Öffentlichkeit und den Grad ihres Rühmens und Preisens festgelegt wird. In diesem Rühmen akkumuliert sich das symbolische Kapital der *êre*, das sich der *ritter* mit seinen selbst schon zu Zeichen geworbenen Taten erwirbt.[46]

He then argues that the association with Peleus's deplorable 'nît' – he is described as 'ungetriuwe' (*Trojanerkrieg*, l. 6580) and 'übele' (*Trojanerkrieg*, l. 6610) – which initiates the quest gives Jason's ambition for fame the negative connotation of a moral defect.[47] The ambivalence of fame that Hasebrink describes can already be observed in the seminal episode of the competition of the goddesses for the Apple of Discord. Like the Golden Fleece, the Apple is an object of dazzling beauty, yet it is not primarily desired for its material or aesthetic value, but for the abstract value of praise and honour it represents.

45 See Lienert, *Geschichte und Erzählen*, pp. 54–55.

46 Hasebrink, 'Rache als Geste', p. 212. Hasebrink also mentions the metapoetic dimension of praise: 'Zugleich verweist diese Rühmung auf die Ebene des Erzählens, auf der sie selbst in einer ausgeweiteten *descriptio* vollzogen wird' ('Rache als Geste', p. 212). However, he does not discuss this matter further.

47 Hasebrink, 'Rache als Geste', p. 214.

Discord disrupts the courtly harmony by introducing a competition for personal symbolic supremacy, the same abstract value that Jason pursues. Like Discord's detrimental gift, Jason's quest has far-reaching consequences. On their journey the Argonauts are insulted by the Trojans and it is this minor cause, a tiny chip in the Greeks' honour, which sets off a chain reaction of retribution between the Greeks and the Trojans:

> dar an sô wart bewaeret wol,
> daz ein maezliche sache
> ze grôzem ungemache
> vil dicke und ofte sich getreit.
> reht als ein michel fiur bereit
> von kleinen funken dicke wirt,
> seht, alsô bringet unde birt
> ein kleiniu schulde grimmen zorn. (*Trojanerkrieg*, ll. 13038–45)

In the Apple of Discord episode the Babel allusion links the striving for praise and honour to the sin of pride; in the Jason episode it is associated with the sin of envy; and while Jason is willing to risk his life for a tiny bit of fame, the Greeks avenge a minor insult ('kleinez dinc' (*Trojanerkrieg*, l. 13019); 'kranke sache' (*Trojanerkrieg*, l. 13022)) with terrible atrocities ('mein unde mort' (*Trojanerkrieg*, l. 12929, l. 12995)) that the narrator condemns as a violation of 'zuht' (*Trojanerkrieg*, ll. 11916–17), 'grôzen ungefuoc' (*Trojanerkrieg*, l. 12956), 'süntlich und unedel' (*Trojanerkrieg*, l. 12959) and which Hercules himself later describes as 'übermuot' (*Trojanerkrieg*, l. 38660).[48]

These examples show that the characters have a keen and even problematically exaggerated awareness of their own fame and that of others. Verbal attacks on an opponent's honour, for example, often centre on the absence of praise or renown. Thus, when the Trojan emissary Antenor demands that King Priam's daughter Hesione be returned, Telamon insults the Trojans by pretending not even to know their king:

> von eime künige sagent ir,
> der PRÎANT sî geheizen,
> des name in disen kreizen
> seltsaene ist unde wilde,
> weizgot, wir hân sîn bilde
> beschouwet selten und gesehen. (*Trojanerkrieg*, ll. 18136–41)[49]

48 See Karl Stackmann, 'Ovid im deutschen Mittelalter', *Arcadia*, 1 (1966), 231–54 (p. 248). He points out that the term *übermuot* characterizes the first destruction of Troy as a deadly sin. On this episode, and the narrator's unusually explicit criticism, see also Lienert, *Geschichte und Erzählen*, pp. 76–81; Worstbrock, 'Der Tod des Hercules', p. 279.

49 See also *Trojanerkrieg*, ll. 12692–95 (discussed above).

That this is understood as an insult to Priam's heroic, even poetic fame becomes clear when Antenor reports back to the Trojan council and rephrases Telamon's reproach to include heroic tales and songs:

> er sprach, daz er bî sîner zît
> unde in allen sînen tagen
> nie von iu gehôrte sagen
> noch gesingen, herre mîn. (*Trojanerkrieg*, ll. 18270–73)

The poetic dimension of fame on the story level is most strikingly expressed when Achilles, disguised as a girl, teaches his unsuspecting playmate and love interest Deidamia to sing a heroic song about himself:

> er lêrte singen einen leich
> die klâren küniginne,
> dâ wart ACHILLES inne
> gerüemet bî der stunde,
> er selbe von ir munde
> mit sange wart geprîset. (*Trojanerkrieg*, ll. 15844–49)

With its erotic connotations this scene is reminiscent of Tristan teaching Isolde in the guise of Tantris and the two lovers' musical pastimes in the *Minnegrotte*.[50] With regard to a hero turning his own story into poetry, however, it also relates to Tristan composing and singing 'den edelen leich Tristanden' (*Tristan*, l. 19201) at the court of Arundel. In both cases there is some confusion about the reference of the names in the songs: in the *Trojanerkrieg* Deidamia does not know that Jocundille is really Achilles and is therefore unaware of the autodiegetic nature of the song; in *Tristan* the listeners falsely assume that his lover Isolde in the song is Isolde of the White Hands. The narrator remarks that the song Tristan composed about his own love story is popular everywhere and will be circulated until the end of the world (*Tristan*, ll. 19202–04). As the first artist to turn his and Isolde's sad story into eternal poetry Tristan thus becomes the original predecessor of Gottfried, who ensures the survival of their fame as exceptional lovers. Similarly, the fact that fame is already a poetic phenomenon on the story level of the *Trojanerkrieg* makes it productive for the purpose of metapoetic reflection, too.[51] The conflation of poetic fame on the story level with the fame that Konrad perpetuates in his own poetic work becomes particularly evident

50 See Gebert, *Mythos als Wissensform*, pp. 420–28. He mentions this intertextual connection and discusses the episode as a complex form of metadiegesis which merges homodiegetic, heterodiegetic and autodiegetic narration.

51 Compare also the scene in which the shepherd who raised Paris claims never to have heard of him: 'ine gehôrte nie | von PÂRÎSE in mînen tagen | weder gesingen noch gesagen' (*Trojanerkrieg*, ll. 5208–10).

in the story of Hercules' death, the narration of which he delegates to one of his characters. The non-chronological placement in the text, which is unusual in the *Trojanerkrieg*, means that both the Greeks and Konrad's readers are informed of Hercules' fate for the first time through Philoctet's story.[52] By presenting the story in the form of direct speech and by matching the knowledge of the extradiegetic audience to that of the intradiegetic audience, Konrad creates a focalized effect that superimposes both positions.

During the truce after the second battle of Troy the Greeks try to escape the horrors of the war by listening to stories:

> nû kam ez eines mâles sô,
> daz die KRIECHEN sâzen
> und leides gar vergâzen
> von hofelichen maeren.
> si wurden ûz ir swaeren
> mit worten und mit rede brâht.
> vil maniges wart von in gedâht,
> der bî den alten zîten
> nâch wirde kunde strîten. (*Trojanerkrieg*, ll. 37866–74)

These stories not only have the quality of courtliness and the subject matter of heroic tales in common with the *Trojanerkrieg* itself, but they also have the same effect of preventing boredom and banishing sorrow (compare *Trojanerkrieg*, ll. 192–205, ll. 20046–54). The episode also demonstrates that fame and its poetic perpetuation as praise serve the function of *memoria*.[53] Nestor, who tells stories about how the Greek heroes earned praise and thus ensures the survival of their fame beyond their death, takes revenge on the dead Hercules by refusing to honour his memory with praise – the key antonyms are *vergezzen* (*Trojanerkrieg*, l. 37885, l. 37902, l. 37924) and *gedenken* (*Trojanerkrieg*, l. 37872, l. 37881, l. 37894, l. 37907) – because he has killed one of his relatives:

> der wirt von mir vermaeret
> mit hôhem prîse niemer,
> vergezzen sol ich iemer
> in herzen unde in muote
> des namen sîn ze guote. (*Trojanerkrieg*, ll. 37910–14)

52 See Worstbrock, 'Der Tod des Hercules', pp. 281–82.

53 On the aspect of *memoria* that links the concept of fame to that of literature, see Wenzel, *Hören und Sehen*, pp. 156–58. The capacity of fame to keep somebody alive is prominently expressed in the *Iwein* prologue, in which the honour and praise that King Arthur earned during his lifetime are said to ensure his afterlife: 'sî jehent er lebe noch hiute: | er hât den lop erworben, | ist im der lîp erstorben, | sô lebet doch iemer sîn name' (Hartmann, *Iwein*, ll. 14–17).

The introduction of Hercules as the killer of Nestor's relative who does not deserve praise already casts the hero in a dubious light: his praiseworthiness is subject to debate.[54] Upon the request of Iolaus, Hercules' son, and the Greeks not to let Hercules remain 'ungeprîset' (*Trojanerkrieg*, l. 37955), Philoctet finally tells the story of his death (*Trojanerkrieg*, ll. 37958–8722).[55] However, an audience expecting to hear Hercules' praises sung would be bitterly disappointed by Philoctet's narration, as Worstbrock points out: it does not present a great hero but a vengeful adulterer who dies on a pyre instead of on the battlefield. While Ovid's Hercules recounts his own heroic deeds before he dies (*Metamorphoses*, IX, 182–99) and is transformed by Jupiter into a constellation, thus transcending his own death, Konrad's Hercules accepts his shameful end as a just punishment for his unfaithfulness towards his wife Dianira and for his exaggerated revenge against the Trojans (*Trojanerkrieg*, ll. 38470–81; ll. 38660–69).[56] Contrary to the common interpretation of Hercules' fate as a story of failure, Gebert proposes an interesting new reading. He demonstrates that in mythographic literature Hercules is often presented as a philosopher overcoming the desires of the body and transcending the divide between *vita contemplativa* and *vita activa*. Konrad similarly presents a hero who distances himself from his previous deeds, which were motivated by affects of desire and anger. Gebert furthermore argues that Hercules' death is stylized according to the religious pattern of conversion. He accuses himself of the sin ('mein' (*Trojanerkrieg*, l. 38665)) of pride ('übermuot' (*Trojanerkrieg*, l. 38660)) and professes regret ('riuwe' (*Trojanerkrieg*, l. 38668)), thus fulfilling the requirements of *confessio* and *contritio cordis*. His terrible death on the pyre recalls hagiographical descriptions of the torments of Christian martyrs – Philoctet describes it as 'strengiu marter' (*Trojanerkrieg*, l. 38508)[57] – and he

54 See Worstbrock, 'Der Tod des Hercules', p. 275.

55 This episode is taken from Ovid's *Metamorphoses* (Ovid, *Metamorphoses*, trans. by Frank Justus Miller, 3rd rev. edn by G. P. Goold (Cambridge, MA: Harvard University Press, 1984), IX (Nestor's refusal to tell of Hercules' deeds appears in Book XII)). It also contains some elements from the *Heroides* (Ovid, *Heroides and Amores*, trans. by Grant Showerman, 2nd rev. edn by G. P. Goold, Loeb Classical Library, 41 (Cambridge, MA: Harvard University Press, 1986), *Heroides*, IX). See Monecke, *Das Erzählprinzip der 'wildekeit'*, pp. 49–50, pp. 157–59; Stackmann, 'Ovid im deutschen Mittelalter', 246–48; Lienert, *Geschichte und Erzählen*, pp. 164–69; Müller, *Höfische Kompromisse*, p. 460.

56 See Worstbrock, 'Der Tod des Hercules', pp. 275–76.

57 Gebert's very specific interpretation of the term 'marter' as 'martyrdom' might be a bit overstated, though, as the terms *marter* and *marterlich* appear quite frequently in the *Trojanerkrieg* as general words for 'suffering' or 'painful' without discernible religious connotation: *Trojanerkrieg*, l. 5595, l. 8612, l. 11680, l. 12982, l. 13133, l. 13205, l. 15995, l. 16004, l. 16725, l. 20699, l. 20854, l. 21271, l. 22581, l. 22658, l. 23280, l. 24570, l. 24596, l. 25383, l. 28638, l. 33748, l. 34039, l. 34564, l. 35477, l. 35526, l. 35544, l. 35705, l. 36490, l. 38801, l. 39439, l. 39581. An exception might be the description of Hector as 'der êren

even heightens his suffering by tormenting his own body as if to do additional voluntary penance for its worldly desires. Asking Philoctet to bury his ashes in an unmarked grave alongside his poisoned arrows that were prophesied to bring about the defeat of Troy, he even attempts to prevent the Greeks from causing any further harm to the Trojans (*Trojanerkrieg*, ll. 38610–84) and to stop the cycle of revenge and destruction by introducing the Christian principle of loving one's enemy. At the same time Gebert carefully notes that this does not make Hercules a proto-saint, because he suffers from a worldly 'angest' (*Trojanerkrieg*, l. 38526) that differentiates him from the transcendent calm of Christian martyrs.[58] Gebert discusses the episode as an example of the text's strategy for rendering narrative problems invisible. In Hercules' case this means that inconsistencies in the mythological hero are not removed but obscured by containing them within the frame of metadiegesis and of narrative patterns such as conversion that are suited to uniting strong differences: 'Die Inkonsistenz der Herculesfigur wird unsichtbar, indem sie als kontemplative Wende sichtbar gemacht wird'.[59] I would, however, argue that another important function of the religious allusions that Gebert detects is to demonstrate what the pagan Hercules lacks in order to transcend his body and overcome death. Not only is he not relieved from 'angest', he also invokes the pagan gods as the agents punishing his deeds (*Trojanerkrieg*, ll. 38664–65) before committing suicide to end his agony. The complete annihilation of his heroic body burnt to ashes is neither transcended by a pagan apotheosis, as in Ovid's pre-text, nor does he have access to Christian redemption. The only afterlife available to Hercules is through heroic fame, a problematic *memoria* that perpetuates the dynamics of revenge he tried to bring to a halt. While Hercules' questionable actions – his vengeful behaviour and unfaithfulness – could provide a negative example of the consequences of such behaviour,

marteraere' (*Trojanerkrieg*, l. 35652) – this is the only occurrence of the term *marteraere* – just before the Trojans praise him as their saviour: 'in sîn eines hende | stêt unser heil und unser trôst. | er hât ûz sorgen uns erlôst | mit hôhen kreften ûzerkorn' (*Trojanerkrieg*, ll. 37644–47). This goes to show that a single word that also appears in religious contexts is rarely sufficient as an indicator of religious connotations unless it is supported by further indicators.

58 Gebert, *Mythos als Wissensform*, pp. 440–59.

59 Gebert, *Mythos als Wissensform*, p. 461. On the definition of metadiegesis, see Genette, *Narrative Discourse*, pp. 231–34. He also remarks that it can function as *mise en abyme*. The metapoetic potential of embedded narratives is also discussed by Haferland and Mecklenburg: 'Sie lenken die Aufmerksamkeit auf einen Aspekt des Erzählten, und sie bedeuten gleichzeitig die Selbstthematisierung des Erzählens' (Harald Haferland and Michael Mecklenburg, 'Einleitung', in *Erzählungen in Erzählungen: Phänomene der Narration in Mittelalter und früher Neuzeit*, ed. by Harald Haferland and Michael Mecklenburg, Forschungen zur Geschichte der älteren deutschen Literatur, 19 (Munich: Fink, 1996), pp. 11–25 (p. 16)).

his own realization of the error of his ways and his compassion for the enemy could present a positive model for emulation. However, the Greeks do not receive Philoctet's story in either of these possible ways. Emphasizing the fact that, regrettably, he did not die on the battlefield, they remember him as Hercules the heroic fighter, not Hercules the reformed advocate of peace. Rather than picking up on the mistakes for which he blamed himself, they begin to praise him as a paragon of knightly honour:

> vil manic fürste rîche
> dô klagete sînen grimmen tôt
> und die vil angstbaere nôt,
> die der getriuwe hete erliten.
> er wart nâch klagebaeren siten
> beweinet von ir gnuogen,
> wan si von im gewuogen
> vil maniger hôher frümekeit.
> si jâhen, daz an in geleit
> waer aller êren überkraft
> und daz er sîne ritterschaft
> mit ellentrîcher staete
> sô wol geblüemet haete. (*Trojanerkrieg*, ll. 38728–40)[60]

Even Philoctet himself seems unaware that he is painting an unflattering picture of the hero. In the beginning, he praises Hercules as a 'helt geblüemet wol mit zuht, | der allen wandel ie verswuor' (*Trojanerkrieg*, ll. 37978–79). He also implicitly condones Hercules' terrible revenge against Iole's father – which is triggered by a violation of his honour ('schande' (*Trojanerkrieg*, l. 38221)), like the first destruction of Troy – by calling the latter 'unstaete' for denying Hercules what he had promised to him (*Trojanerkrieg*, l. 38212), although his refusal to give his daughter to the already married hero seems perfectly justified.[61] The story's strange reception by the Greeks is thus prepared by the depiction of the intradiegetic narrator. In particular Achilles' reaction to the story appears diametrically opposed to its content. The sad tale of Hercules' death refreshes Achilles' grief over the death of Patroclus and he plans to

60 Compare Worstbrock: 'Sie tauchen ihn wieder in den Schein idealer Attribute, der nahezu alle Figuren des *Trojanerkriegs* hüllt [*sic*], was immer sie betreiben. So dissonieren die Erzählung und die Reaktion ihrer Rezipienten, ohne daß ihre Widersprüchlichkeit zu bewußter Geltung käme' (Worstbrock, 'Der Tod des Hercules', p. 282). It is not quite clear whether the epithet 'getriuwe' (*Trojanerkrieg*, l. 38731) represents the opinion of the Greeks, as Worstbrock suggests (p. 282), as a form of free indirect speech, or the position of the narrator.

61 Worstbrock surprisingly seems to attribute this side-taking to the narrator of the *Trojanerkrieg* and claims that Philoctet's narration does not contain any praise for Hercules (Worstbrock, 'Der Tod des Hercules', pp. 278–79, p. 282).

kill Hector and a thousand other Trojans to avenge him (*Trojanerkrieg*, ll. 38846–67). Given the literary tradition, it can reasonably be assumed that the continuation of Konrad's fragment would also have seen Achilles repeating Hercules' mistake of cheating on his wife and paying for it with his life. On the story level this 'vergebliche Erzählung in der Erzählung'[62] represents yet another 'verworfene Alternative'[63] that ultimately serves only to highlight that the protagonists cannot escape the destructive heroic logic of revenge or the passion of sexual desire which Hasebrink has described as the 'Fatalität des Affekts'.[64]

How does this example of problematic poetic *memoria* reflect on the reception of the *Trojanerkrieg* itself? In the prologue Konrad declares that his work provides moral lessons (*Trojanerkrieg*, ll. 260–65, ll. 280–85) by commemorating good and bad deeds alike: 'man hoeret übel unde wol | gedenken hie der liute' (*Trojanerkrieg*, ll. 286–87). Unlike Philoctet, Konrad shows himself acutely aware of the discrepancy between the stereotypically positive attributes that he lavishes upon his morally flawed protagonists and their role in the terrible war. He ends his eulogy of Helen with the words:

> daz sich mîn zunge pînet
> sêr ûf ir lop, daz tuot mir nôt,
> sît daz den bitterlichen tôt
> durch si leit sô manic lîp,
> daz nie durch keiner slahte wîp
> verdarp sô manic hôher man. (*Trojanerkrieg*, ll. 20282–87)

The episode of the metadiegetic cautionary tale whose didactic message is lost on its audience is itself a cautionary tale of how not to receive literature. It is true that the moral lesson of Hercules' death may be less straightforward than it seems, as Müller argues:

> Die naheliegende Folgerung, Liebesverrat werde mit dem Tod bestraft, ist viel zu einfach, denn wer ist eigentlich schuld an diesem Tod? Der liebestolle Nessus? Hercules mit seinem giftigen Pfeil? Der heimtückische Rat? Hercules'

62 Worstbrock, 'Der Tod des Hercules', p. 284.

63 Schulz, *Schwieriges Erkennen*, p. 492, fn. 432.

64 Hasebrink, 'Rache als Geste', p. 221. Apart from the fact that the catastrophic end of the story of the Trojan War is of course well known, this inevitability is also underlined by the fact that the end is inscribed into the narration from the very beginning through numerous prophesies as well as anticipatory remarks made by the narrator. Bleumer describes this as a 'Mechanismus des beobachtenden Nachvollzugs' (Bleumer, 'Zwischen Wort und Bild', pp. 115–17 (p. 117)).

> Untreue? Dianiras *akust* beim Versuch ihn zu halten? Die Geschichte hat keine Moral außer der Botschaft von der Katastrophe des sexuellen Begehrens.[65]

The same can also be said about the text as a whole: the intricate network of personal decisions and coincidences that come together to bring about destruction make it difficult to blame the fatal development on any individual.[66] As Schulz points out, the heroes of the *Trojanerkrieg* behave almost like 'psychische Automaten' who react 'geradezu mechanisch affektiv' to certain triggers and pursue the logic of the feudal value system of love, honour and kinship with the utmost rigour.[67] The example of Hercules shows that there may be moments when these dynamics are called into question and confronted with quasi-Christian ideals of mercy and love for the enemy, but instead of realizing their pacifying potential, they turn into triggers for further violence, as Achilles' reaction to Philoctet's story demonstrates.[68] The fact that the heroes of the *Trojanerkrieg* cannot escape the catastrophe and have no access to religious redemption, however, does not mean that Konrad's contemporary Christian audience are bound by the same limitations and cannot learn from their example. Unlike the Greeks, who praise Hercules uncritically, they are certainly expected to assume a more measured stance of *bescheidenheit* towards his actions and Helen's dangerous beauty. Unlike Achilles, who wants to avenge one death with more than a thousand killings, they can witness the devastating effect of exaggerated retribution from a critical distance and heed Hercules' warning. After all, this lesson is also taught by the narrator himself. Although he is generally very reluctant to judge the events of the story, he condemns inconsiderate revenge repeatedly and emphatically by pointing out that it will lead to ever greater misery, not least for the person taking revenge (*Trojanerkrieg*, ll. 13017–67, ll. 17732–61). Instead he urges his audience not to take insults and injuries to heart and to trust in God: 'man lâze got des walten, | daz man gebüezen niht enkan' (*Trojanerkrieg*, ll. 17762–63). As in the case of the Apple of Discord, where the perspectives of the intra- and the extradiegetic audiences diverge to reveal an ambivalence to the latter that is lost on the former, the problematic response of the intradiegetic audience of the story of Hercules' death encourages the extradiegetic audience to realize the dangers of a feudal logic that is not controlled by a Christian ethics of compassion.

65 Müller, *Höfische Kompromisse*, p. 460.

66 See Lienert, *Geschichte und Erzählen*, pp. 310–14.

67 Schulz, *Schwieriges Erkennen*, p. 491; also Lienert, *Geschichte und Erzählen*, pp. 313–14; Pfennig, *Erzähltechnik*, p. 198.

68 On the transformation of a story of conversion to peace into a trigger for violence, compare Gebert, *Mythos als Wissensform*, pp. 463–65.

Fernminne

Love in Middle High German literature is usually instigated by an act of vision.[69] The literary motif of *Fernminne*, love that is caused by hearsay, has so far primarily been discussed in cultural-historical terms. Wenzel interprets love in Middle High German literature within the framework of an aristocratic culture whose members strive to maintain or, if possible, improve their social status through marriage. In this culture, a person's visible physical but also ethical superiority is an indicator of rank and identifies them as a desirable spouse, but the knowledge of a person's excellence can also be received through the sense of hearing.[70] Wenzel lists several texts, such as *König Rother* and the *Nibelungenlied*, in which *minne* is presented as the direct consequence of acts of *hoeren* or *vernemen*. Even where the beloved person is present, the aural perception of a person's excellence often plays an important role. Wenzel stresses the fact that the verbal representation of a person has to be understood as publicly recognized and articulated superiority – something that would correspond to the terms *prîs* and *lop*:

> Bereits ein erster Überblick über *Minnesangs Frühling* bestätigt, daß der Vorrang der *frouwe* für die Aufnahme des Minnedienstes auch dann konstitutiv wird, wenn er lediglich erkannt ist durch das Wort, – wobei das Wort bezeichnenderweise öffentlich vermittelt ist, der Rang der *frouwe* somit nicht als subjektiv erkannter, sondern als öffentlich anerkannter sittlicher Rang zu verstehen ist.[71]

Müller similarly remarks that love caused by hearsay means 'daß *minne* aus dem individuellen Urteilen und Fühlen herausgenommen und an kollektive Werte gebunden wird'.[72]

A prominent example of the interaction of fame and visual perception in the development of love can be found in Gottfried's *Tristan*. Blanscheflur sees Riwalin excel in knightly combat, but she also hears him praised by the female

69 See, for example, Horst Wenzel, 'Fernliebe und hohe Minne: Zur räumlichen und sozialen Distanz in der Minnethematik', in *Liebe als Literatur: Aufsätze zur erotischen Dichtung in Deutschland: Festschrift für Peter Wapnewski*, ed. by Rüdiger Krohn (Munich: Beck, 1983), pp. 187–208 (p. 190, p. 187); Schleusener-Eichholz, *Das Auge im Mittelalter*, pp. 771–72; Schnell, *Causa amoris*, pp. 241–74; Wolf Gewehr, 'Der Topos "Augen des Herzens" – Versuch einer Deutung durch die scholastische Erkenntnistheorie', *DVjs*, 46 (1972), 626–49 (pp. 638–41); Herbert Kolb, *Der Begriff der Minne und das Entstehen der höfischen Lyrik* (Tübingen: Niemeyer, 1958), pp. 18–38.

70 Wenzel, 'Fernliebe', pp. 190–92.

71 Wenzel, 'Fernliebe', p. 192.

72 Müller, *Höfische Kompromisse*, p. 365.

onlookers (*Tristan*, ll. 699–703). Later Blanscheflur remembers that it was the act of seeing Riwalin (*Tristan*, ll. 990–91) which made her fall in love, but when she recalls the process of falling in love, the step of hearing his public perception precedes that of individual visual perception:

> dô ich sô vil manic edele wîp
> den sînen keiserlîchen lîp
> und sînen ritterlîchen prîs
> mit lobe gehôrte in ballen wîs
> als umbe trîben unde tragen
> und sînes lobes sô vil gesagen
> und ich mit ougen selbe sach
> die tugende, der man von im jach,
> und allez in mîn herze las,
> swaz lobelîches an im was:
> dâ von ergouchete mîn sin,
> hie von geviel mîn herze an in. (*Tristan*, ll. 1027–38)[73]

In his study *Causa Amoris*, Schnell highlights the ethical implications of a love which is not caused by vision but through hearing: in theological literature love *ex visione* is often associated with carnal love (*cupiditas*, *fornicatio*) and contrasted to true love (*caritas*) that is created through *mens* or *ratio*. Even Andreas Capellanus depreciates physical beauty as the cause of love.[74] Despite the fact that love is normally triggered by beauty in courtly literature, it is usually associated with inner quality as well.[75] Schnell therefore sees *Fernminne* as an idealized concept of love, a de-sensualized love that is not based on physical beauty but on virtue and inner qualities. He also interprets it as an internalization of the development of love that is opposed to the sudden intrusion from outside that characterizes the erotic 'Venusminne'.[76] Schnell quotes the example of Blanscheflur and Riwalin as a case of de-sensualized love that is ennobled through the precedence of hearing over seeing.[77] His

73 See also *König Rother*, where Herlint's gaze is initially obstructed by the crowd that gathers around Rother and her love is caused by what these onlookers tell her about his excellence (*König Rother*, ed. and trans. by Peter K. Stein (Stuttgart: Reclam, 2000), ll. 1842–1924). On this episode see Urban Küsters, 'Liebe und der zweite Blick: Wahrnehmungshaltungen in höfischen Liebesbegegnungen', in *Personenbeziehungen in der mittelalterlichen Literatur*, ed. by Brall, Haupt and Küsters, pp. 271–320 (p. 271, p. 284).

74 Andreas Capellanus, *On Love*, ed. and trans. by P. G. Walsh (London: Duckworth, 1982), I, 6.

75 Schnell, *Causa amoris*, pp. 241–52.

76 Schnell, *Causa amoris*, pp. 280–86. See also Wenzel: 'Fernliebe ist zunächst, wenn auch nur übergangsweise völlig spiritualisierte Liebe' (Wenzel, 'Fernliebe', p. 194). We shall instead see that in the *Trojanerkrieg* love instigated by hearsay enters the heart just as violently as love instigated by vision.

77 Schnell, *Causa amoris*, p. 285.

reading, however, disregards the clearly erotic quality of Riwalin's description by the ladies, who focus on the beauty of his knightly body and deduce his aptitude as a lover from it.

Müller agrees with Schnell that *Fernminne* and *cupiditas* are incompatible, but he does not highlight virtue as the primary quality mediated through fame, instead offering a more differentiated perspective that includes the verbal mediation of sensual appeals: 'Die *minne* ist eine Folgeerscheinung von Werterkenntnis. Man liebt im Partner die Vollkommenheit, ob nun, wie meist, überwiegend feudal geprägt, als Stärke und Schönheit, oder, seltener, ethisch akzentuiert, als moralische oder gesellschaftliche (höfische) Tugend'.[78]

Wenzel interprets the literary motif of *Fernminne* as an attempt to harmonize contemporary feudal practices of marriage with the idea of a marriage based on love:

> Nicht als Abschilderung sozialer Realität also, sondern als literarisches Leitbild wird die Fernliebe verständlich: Gerade weil die Verehelichung zweier völlig fremder, bisher einander gänzlich unbekannter Personen das Kalkül der Eheschließung offensichtlich macht und die Vereinnahmung der Frau als Pfand oder Trophäe zuläßt, wird dieser Sachverhalt verklärt als Folge einer primär wirksamen Tugendliebe.[79]

Müller follows this approach. In accordance with the programmatic title of his study *Höfische Kompromisse*, he counts the motif of *Fernminne* among those topical 'Erzählkerne' of courtly epics in which the latent tension of competing values within courtly culture is resolved in the realm of the literary imaginary. Collective demands and individual desires, which may conflict in reality, are harmonized in the literary construct of *Fernminne*: 'Die politische Allianz erscheint nicht als nacktes Interessenbündnis, sondern wird axiologisch überformt, ohne daß ihre politisch-genealogische Bedeutung gemindert würde'.[80]

This cultural-historical approach is criticized by Worstbrock, who rejects the notion that *Fernminne*, already present in the literature of the Romans and a staple of European literature long after the Middle Ages, represents a type of

78 Müller, *Höfische Kompromisse*, p. 365. Küsters is also critical of Schnell's interpretation: 'Schnells grundlegende Unterscheidung von *Visio* Schönheit und Fernliebe Tugend kann ich allerdings für den Adelskontext des *Nibelungenliedes* nicht nachvollziehen' (Küsters, 'Liebe und der zweite Blick', p. 279, fn. 13).

79 Wenzel, 'Fernliebe', p. 196. See also the discussion of Wenzel's approach by Schnell, *Causa amoris*, p. 285, fn. 351a. He remarks that Wenzel's interpretation is limited to thirteenth-century epics that include a bridal quest, whereas *Fernminne* in other texts such as *Minnesang* or courtly romance does not usually serve to idealize a dynastic alliance and can serve different purposes, for example the distinction from sensual love.

80 Müller, *Höfische Kompromisse*, p. 366.

love typical of courtly epics. He points out that the protagonists of the courtly romance do not, in fact, fall in love through hearsay and that Wenzel has to support his thesis instead with examples assembled from the heterogeneous genres of heroic epic, so-called *Spielmannsepik* and *Minnesang*. Worstbrock does not deny that the motif plays an important role in twelfth-century poetry but cautions that its individual occurrences cannot be subsumed into one common denominator. He then goes on to demonstrate that it was in fact far more common as an exordial topos in Latin letters from the early twelfth up to the sixteenth century, where it served the function of *captatio benevolentiae*.[81]

Regardless of whether the motif of *Fernminne* reflects the specific cultural-historical circumstances of Middle High German poetry – in defence of Wenzel against Worstbrock one might argue that a trans-temporal and -cultural motif can be relevant to different audiences for very different and culturally specific reasons – its appeal can also be described in terms of its narrative potential, as Wenzel points out:

> Für den epischen Entwurf ist die Auflösung dieser Spannung, die Überwindung der Distanz, vielfach die Voraussetzung für die Entfaltung der Erzählung insgesamt: Der Spannungsbogen zwischen Werbungsabsicht und Durchsetzung dieses Ziels reicht über die verschiedenen Stationen einer Fahrt, die in ihrem Ablauf konstituierend ist für weite Teile des Textes überhaupt.[82]

This plainly applies in the case of Paris and Helen, because it is his love for the unseen queen that motivates the Trojan prince to abduct her and provoke the Trojan War. What is more, Konrad's romance *Partonopier* not only illustrates how falling in love at a distance equates to hearing reports about the qualities in a partner that make him or her an appropriate spouse, but also shows the inherent narrative tension of the motif which is rendered as the tension between hearing and seeing:

> si jâhen, daz dîn reiniu tugent
> wær alsô vîn und alsô klâr,
> daz du mir stille und offenbâr
> ze manne wol gezæmest,
> und daz du rehte kæmest
> zêren und ze fröuden mir.
> hie von enbran mîns herzen gir,
> daz ich niht lâzen wolte,

81 Franz Josef Worstbrock, 'Fernliebe: Allgemeines und Besonderes zur Geschichte einer literarischen Konstante', in *Projektion – Reflexion – Ferne: Räumliche Vorstellungen und Denkfiguren im Mittelalter*, ed. by Sonja Glauch, Susanne Köbele and Uta Störmer-Caysa (Berlin: de Gruyter, 2011), pp. 137–59.

82 Wenzel, 'Fernliebe', p. 194.

swaz mir geschehen solte,
ich wolte dich mit ougen sehen
und daz wunder selbe spehen,
daz mir von dir wart geseit.
hie mite wart ein kiel bereit
rîlichen unde schône mir. (*Partonopier*, ll. 1833–47)

Words are powerful enough to cause love, but they cannot fully substitute for vision itself. In fact, they trigger a strong desire to see with one's own eyes ('selbe spehen') what has been publicly proclaimed ('si jâhen') about the beloved. This potential of *Fernminne* to generate action – typically a journey – is also demonstrated in a stanza by Meinloh von Sevelingen:

Dô ich dich loben hôrte, dô het ich dich gerne erkant.
durch dîne tugende manige vuor ich welende, unz ich dich vant.
daz ich dich nû gesehen hân, daz enwirret dir niet.
er ist vil wol getiuret, den dû wilt, vrowe, haben liep.
Du bist der besten eine, des muoz man dir von schulden jehen.
sô wol den dînen ougen!
diu kunnen, swen si wellen, an vil güetelîchen sehen.[83]

The praise of the lady triggers the immediate desire to meet her in person and motivates a journey. However, Meinloh's stanza also serves to illustrate that neither the cultural-historical approach nor the treatment of *Fernminne* as a generator of narrative action begins to grasp the full poetic potential of this literary motif. Even though the lover finds his lady's praise justified, the explicit assertion that her presence matches her fame suggests that he might have been disappointed; the accordance of praise and its subject is not a given.[84] The possibility that the praise of a lady may not be justified is also raised in *Kudrun*, where the father of Hartmut, who has fallen in love with the distant Kudrun upon hearing about her beauty, cautions his son that this description may not be accurate: '"wer saget iu daz", sprach Ludewîc, "daz si sô schœne sî?"'.[85] The tension between near and far, hearing and seeing, is a tension that not only produces action, but also serves to highlight the tension between words (praise) and referent (lady). Taking into account that Meinloh's

83 Meinloh von Sevelingen, 'Dô ich dich loben hôrte, dô het ich dich gerne erkant', in *Des Minnesangs Frühling*, ed. by Lachmann and others, 11, 1. Worstbrock suspects that this song might be influenced by the 'Fernminne-Exordium' and general structure of *captatio benevolentiae* in contemporary Latin letters and *artes dictandi* (Worstbrock, 'Fernliebe', pp. 147–51).

84 See Mark Chinca, 'Knowledge and Practice in the Early German Love-Lyric', *Forum for Modern Language Studies*, 33 (1997), 204–16 (p. 212).

85 *Kudrun*, ed. by Karl Bartsch, 5th rev. edn by Karl Stackmann (Wiesbaden: Brockhaus, 1965), 590, 1. For an interpretation of this detail see Müller, *Höfische Kompromisse*, p. 371.

stanza itself constitutes praise of the lady, which likewise may or may not be accurate, the metapoetic potential of a literary motif that relies on the verbal representation of a multisensory presence becomes obvious. Before discussing how Konrad exploits this potential in the case of the *Fernminne* of Paris for Helen, I shall explore how the interaction of praise and love is presented with regard to other relationships in the *Trojanerkrieg*.

Praise and Love in the *Trojanerkrieg*

In the *Trojanerkrieg* there are several examples of praise interacting with vision to create love. When the gods on Mount Olympus begin to praise Paris, whom Venus has dressed in precious garments so that the compound of beautiful body and appropriate dress renders his nobility obvious to everyone, his father Priam develops a strong affection for him:

PÂRÎS wart von der göte schar
geprîset und gehêret,
sîn lop daz wart gemêret
über al des hofes rinc.
'seht', sprâchen si, 'der jungelinc
der wirt ein wunder z'einem man.'
hier under sach in allez an
sîn vater künic PRÎAMUS.
daz in diu frouwe VÊNUS
sô vil gerüemet haete,
dâ von was im der staete
mit herzeclichen triuwen holt. (*Trojanerkrieg*, ll. 3188–99)

As in the case of Riwalin and Blanscheflur, collective appreciation and praise of a person foreground and enhance visual perception by a single person who has a special predisposition to develop stronger feelings for the praised person. Priam sees Paris with different eyes because of their blood relationship:

in lêrte diu natûre daz
und der sippeschefte reht,
daz im der junge süeze kneht
wart übermaezeclîchen trût. (*Trojanerkrieg*, ll. 3204–07)

The similarity of this depiction of parental love to that of romantic love is accentuated through the term *verdenken* (*Trojanerkrieg*, l. 3220), which is the typical reaction to the first overwhelming encounter with the future lover (for example, when Achilles sees Deidamia (*Trojanerkrieg*, ll. 14646–65)). The aural perception of collective praise is added to the kinship that affects the heart through 'der ougen türe' (*Trojanerkrieg*, l. 3215) and thus influences Priam's perception. The development of the inevitable paternal love is thus doubly determined by an aural and a visual trigger.[86]

The episode in which the connection between praise and love is discussed most explicitly by the narrator is the story of Jason and Medea. Although Jason and the Argonauts are at first perceived as strangers when they arrive on Colchis,[87] it soon emerges that Jason's name has reached the island long before he himself:

> JÂSÔNES nam erschollen
> was in dem künicrîche,
> des buten ime gelîche
> man unde wîp dâ werde zuht. (*Trojanerkrieg*, ll. 7364–67)

King Aeëtes treats his guests to a lavish banquet and bestows on his famous guest the special honour of meeting his daughter Medea, whom he has kept for years from the sight of other, no doubt less worthy men. Her father not only calls her to be seen but also to see the visitors herself:

> ir vater si dô wolte
> die geste lân beschouwen (*Trojanerkrieg*, ll. 7454–55)

> des küniges fruht MÊDÊÂ,
> diu saz gezogenlîche dâ
> und nam der werden geste war,
> der kleider wâren liehtgefar
> von golde und von gesteine. (*Trojanerkrieg*, ll. 7597–601)

When she secretly asks who the strangers are, her father introduces Jason as the man 'der lobes vil mit sîner hant | erfohten und erstriten hât' (*Trojanerkrieg*, ll. 7612–13). While Medea did not seem to distinguish between Jason and his peers before, now she is directed by her father to appreciate Jason's individual looks, which verify his reputed excellence: 'nû merke an im lîp unde wât, | wie gar diu vollekomen sint.' (*Trojanerkrieg*, ll. 7614–15). The identification of the man with the name 'Jason' singles him out among his companions and opens up Medea's eyes to the hero, whom she now recognizes as the man whose praise she has heard since her childhood:

86 Schulz argues that this inherently positive value of aristocratic 'Sippenbindung' is another factor that motivates the catastrophe since it results in Paris's return to Troy (Schulz, *Schwieriges Erkennen*, pp. 465–66).

87 Hasebrink emphasizes the 'Fremdheit' of the arriving party, which is constructed through the curious and admiring gaze of the women of Jaconite (Hasebrink, 'Rache als Geste', p. 215).

Des maeres wart diu schoene geil,
si dûhte gar ein hôhez heil,
daz si JÂSÔNEN solte sehen.
ir was sô vil von im verjehen
kürlicher manheit in ir jugent
und hete als endeliche tugent
von im gehoeret in ir tagen
die liute sprechen unde sagen,
daz ir sô liebe nie geschach,
sô daz si den kôs unde sach
mit spilender ougen blicke,
des lop sô rehte dicke
durch ir ôren was geflogen. (*Trojanerkrieg*, ll. 7629–41)

The narrator comments on Medea's suddenly heightened interest in Jason as a typical reaction to praise and thereby complements the earlier discussion of fame as a trigger for envy. Praise makes things desirable that might not be particularly attractive otherwise and can therefore cause ladies to fall in love with men:

ez ist noch wâr und ungelogen,
daz prîs die liute machet wert,
durch lop vil manges wirt gegert,
des man vil sanfte enbaere,
ob niht sîn name waere
geprîset und gerüemet.
lop zieret unde blüemet
mit êren werder manne lîp
und reizet hôchgeborniu wîp
ûf herzeclicher liebe trift.
uns seit der wâren buoche schrift
von werden liuten lobesam,
daz ir süezer guoter nam
sî vil bezzer allenthalp
denn edel unde tiure salp.
Diz wart ouch an JÂSÔNE
bewaeret dicke schône:
sô MÊDÊÂ sînen namen
vil süezen unde lobesamen
hôrt in ir ôren klingen,
sô muoste ir herze ringen
dar nâch, daz si gesaehe
den helt küen unde waehe,
des lop ir ôren dicke traf.
sîn prîs vür aller würze saf

dranc in ir herze tougen.
daz si mit liehten ougen
in sach des mâles unde kôs,
des wart ir fröude grundelôs
und was ir leit zergangen. (*Trojanerkrieg*, ll. 7642–71)[88]

The verbs 'zieren' and 'blüemen', which are typical metaphors for rhetorically ornate praise, imply a visible enhancement of the praised person's beauty. Praise in fact heightens the perception of all the sensory attractions of a man. The synaesthetic aspect of this enhancement through praise is multiplied by the association with ointment and spices that introduces the senses of smell, touch and taste, while the verb 'clingen' highlights the aural appeal of praise. However, although the power of praise to bring about or influence a multitude of sensory stimuli is thus demonstrated, the important and indispensable role of visual perception is emphasized as well. The repeated juxtaposition of *ôren* and *ougen* underlines the complementary relationship in the development of love and the tension that is created in the case of a temporal precedence of the aural perception: Medea's heart yearns to see the man she has heard about. While his *prîs* alone brings about an internalization of Jason's name in Medea's heart, it is the thus anticipated and enhanced vision of him that finally sets her heart on fire:

wan si begunde in bî der zît
als inneclîchen blicken an,
daz von im ir herze enbran
und ir gemüete wart entzunt. (*Trojanerkrieg*, ll. 7674–77)

Müller, who emphasizes the demonic and destructive power of the highly sexualized love in the *Trojanerkrieg*, interprets the scene as a subversion of the motif of *Fernminne* to which it alludes:

> Dieses *lop* ist jedoch nur Vorstufe eines blinden sexuellen Begehrens. Vor dem Hintergrund des Musters [idealisierender Fernliebe] kann die sinnliche Faszination sich umso schärfer abheben. Wenn sie sich sehen, verfallen sie einer verzehrenden Passion (7657–7665), die das Urteil der anderen rücksichtslos beiseiteschiebt.[89]

88 Hasebrink comments on this description: '[D]ie Medialität der Wahrnehmung [fällt] ins Gewicht. Minne ist nicht auf Personalität gegründet, sondern auf *lop* und *êre* und ihrer Verdichtung im Namen' (Hasebrink, 'Rache als Geste', p. 219).

89 Müller, *Höfische Kompromisse*, pp. 452–60 (p. 453); also Schulz, *Schwieriges Erkennen*, pp. 475–76, fn. 370. Green emphasizes the sensual nature of Jason and Medea's love and speaks of a 'mit höfischen Formeln verhüllten Sinnlichkeit' (Green, *Vorstudien zum gotischen Stil*, p. 35). In contrast to this, Schnell notices that Medea does not seem to pay special attention to Jason until she hears his name and interprets this detail in line with his interpretation of *Fernminne* as an idealized love: 'Liebe entflammt nicht beim Anblick des schönen Körpers,

In addition to this, the interplay between praise and vision in the encounter of Medea and Jason could be seen as an exaggerated version, almost a parody, of Blanscheflur's first impression of Riwalin. While praise of Riwalin undoubtedly influences Blanscheflur's perception of him, there is no indication that she might have overlooked his excellence if nobody had pointed it out to her. Similarly, the impact that hearing Paris's praise has on his appreciation by Priam is hinted at only briefly; the blood relationship plays a more important role. Müller argues that the correspondence of the individual and their fame is particularly close in heroic epics: 'Wenn Siegfried im *Nibelungenlied* im Nibelungenland, am Hof Gunthers oder Brünhilds erscheint, erkennt man den Ankömmling, den man vor Augen hat, als den Repräsentanten des Sagenruhms, der den Namen Siegfried trägt'.[90] In contrast to this, Medea is not particularly interested in Jason before she learns who he is, even though the narrator describes Jason as visibly superior to the other Argonauts (*Trojanerkrieg*, ll. 7289–311). Konrad adopts this curious detail from Benoît,[91] but he stresses it much more by adding a new excursus stating that praise can even make things desirable which would not have seemed attractive otherwise. His depiction of the power of praise in the development of love tends to dissociate excellence and praise. Although Jason's praise is, in fact, justified, his excellence is not immediately so evident that the heroic body could be identified with the name that has already reached Colchis. The excursus in particular supports this dissociation in reversing the precedence of excellence over praise. It ought to be *wert*

---

sondern durch die Kunde vom hervorragenden Verhalten eines Menschen' (Schnell, *Causa amoris*, p. 282). On love in the *Trojanerkrieg* in general, see Worstbrock, who argues: 'Minne schafft kein Ethos mehr und ist von keinem Ethos gehalten, die alte Integration von Minne und Ritterschaft wird aufgelöst, das Leben der Figuren damit zerteilt in heterogene Phasen, die sich einander nicht vermitteln. Der Treuebruch aller Liebhaber und die Dissoziation von Minne und Ritterschaft indizieren, daß die im höfischen Roman vordem zentralen Modelle verantworteten Handelns, solche, die dem Ritter *saelde* und der Gesellschaft *vröide* versprachen, zerfallen sind' (Wortsbrock, 'Der Tod des Hercules', pp. 283–84). On this topic see also Kellner, who particularly emphasizes the example of Achilles, whose love for Deidamia conflicts with his desire to fight (Kellner, 'Kontinuität und Diskontinuität', 101–02).

90 Müller, *Höfische Kompromisse*, p. 178; also Jan-Dirk Müller, *Spielregeln für den Untergang: Die Welt des Nibelungenliedes* (Tübingen: Niemeyer, 1998), p. 132. In the seventh *aventiure* of the *Nibelungenlied* the heroic identity of fame and bearer clashes with more courtly, symbolic modes of status visualization: although Siegfried acts as Gunther's subject by helping him to mount his horse, Brunhild only registers his evident physical superiority, which makes him instantly recognizable as Siegfried, and greets him first. On this episode, see also Jan-Dirk Müller, 'Visualität, Geste, Schrift: Zu einem neuen Untersuchungsfeld der Mediävistik', *ZfdPh*, 122 (2003), 118–32 (pp. 129–31); Küsters, 'Liebe und der zweite Blick', p. 285; Horst Wenzel, 'Szene und Gebärde: Zur visuellen Imagination im Nibelungenlied', *ZfdPh*, 111 (1992), 321–43 (pp. 338–39).

91 Schnell, *Causa amoris*, p. 282.

that makes people *prîs*, not, or not primarily, *prîs* that makes people *wert* (*Trojanerkrieg*, l. 7643). While this reversal illustrates the self-perpetuating social dynamics of fame that have been described above, it also presents praise as a value in itself: once established it might grow quite independently from actual excellence and achievements and become hollow, especially if it cannot immediately be confirmed by the praised person's presence.

The episode not only adds another layer to Konrad's ambivalent portrayal of fame; the connection of love and praise also highlights the fact that Paris falls in love with Helen when he hears her praise. In addition to this, there are further correspondences between the two couples. After Paris has revealed his love and intention to abduct her, Helen holds a long monologue about her own fame. She is worried that Paris's plan will destroy it:

> war umbe welt ir mînen prîs
> hie machen wandelbaere?
> mîn liumet und daz maere,
> daz von mir fliuget über lant,
> sint lûter unde reine erkant,
> als wîbes êren wol gezimt,
> dâ von mich iemer wunder nimt,
> wer iuch dar ûf gewîset habe,
> daz ir getürrent brechen abe
> mîn lop mit worten frefelich. (*Trojanerkrieg*, ll. 21524–33)

Her choice of words closely resembles Paris's earlier reference to her 'liumet' and 'maere' that flew from her and caused his desire. Helen thus turns Paris's own words against him – the very praise and reputation that have caused his love present the main obstacle to its fulfilment. At the same time she is not at all surprised that her fame can have such a strong effect:

> bin ich sô rehte wunneclich
> und alsô lûterbaere,
> als al diu welt ze maere
> seit von mînem bilde,
> son ist daz niht ein wilde
> sache und ein seltsaenez dinc,
> ob ein bescheiden jungelinc
> sent nâch mîner minne sich. (*Trojanerkrieg*, ll. 21578–85)

She is well aware that ordinary people praise her beauty throughout the world but coyly doubts that the goddess Venus herself would praise her more highly than wealth and wisdom:

> den êren wart ich nie gelîch
> an lîbe noch an sinne,

daz mînen prîs götinne
mit worten solten blüemen.
daz mich die liute rüemen,
dâ mite dunket mich sîn gnuoc. (*Trojanerkrieg*, ll. 21878–83)[92]

If Venus really has praised her, she continues, her 'lobe süeze' surely presents a trap, because it will cause her considerable trouble (*Trojanerkrieg*, ll. 21886–95). At the same time she cannot deny that she feels flattered by this appreciation: 'iedoch enist mir daz nicht leit, | ob ich si dunke lobes wert' (*Trojanerkrieg*, ll. 21896–97 and similarly ll. 21906–09; cf. *Heroides*, XVII, 127–28). Then again, she also debates the downside of beauty and praise, which lead to increased surveillance and control of women:

ir schoene ist in ein michel pîn
und wirt in von ir lobe wê,
wan man ir hüetet deste mê,
daz ir lîp ist wolgetân;
ir frîheit mügent si niht hân,
dar umbe daz in ist gegeben
êr unde ein hôchgeprîset leben. (*Trojanerkrieg*, ll. 22068–74)[93]

Since widespread praise attracts suitors like Paris it becomes a threat unto itself. The paradox that praise and honour prevent the fulfilment of the desire they cause has come full circle. It is quite ironic that although desire will eventually win the day, Helen's fame will eternally be commemorated precisely because of this.

Helen, however, does not only reflect on her own praise, she also considers Paris's reputation. When he finally reveals his real name and identity to her – he had claimed to be called Alexander before – he advertises his noble descent and the riches of his father's kingdom and the city of Troy that supersede anything Helen's husband has to offer (*Trojanerkrieg*, ll. 21226–61; cf. *Heroides*, XVI, 174–88). Helen, however, is not impressed by his wealth and inherited status and refuses him as an inappropriate suitor. Although he is a Trojan prince and his aristocratic beauty has earned him praise from the Greeks upon his arrival, he lacks heroic reputation. Helen unfavourably compares his repute with that of her previous abductor Theseus, who returned her without having compromised her virtue: 'sîn lop gât vür iuch alle zît, | als ich von sage

92 Cf. Ovid, *Heroides*, XVII, 123–26

93 Compare: 'forma quoque est oneri; nam quo constantius ore | laudamur vestro, iustius ille timet. | quae iuvat, ut nunc est, eadem mihi gloria damno est, | et melius famae verba dedisse fuit' [My beauty, too, is a burden to me; for, the more you men persist in your praise of me, the more justly does he [Menelaus] fear. The glory that is my delight, just now is a bane as well, and it were better I had cheated fame] (Ovid, *Heroides*, XVII, 167–70).

wol vernime' (*Trojanerkrieg*, ll. 21562–63). Paris is certainly no stranger to her, but his reputation is not very good. Thus, Helen repeats the common literary opinion that Paris is a fancy ladies' man rather than a serious warrior before he has even had a chance to prove himself in the Trojan War:

> ir sint zer minne baz gestalt
> denn ir getân ze kampfe sît.
> HECTOR sol fehten alle zît
> für iuch mit grimmen liuten,
> und sulnt ir frouwen triuten,
> daz ist iu wol gebaere. (*Trojanerkrieg*, ll. 22324–29; cf. *Heroides*, XVII, 251–60)

She also knows that his mother's dream prophesied that he would be the cause of Troy's downfall (*Trojanerkrieg*, ll. 22288–301) and that he has abandoned his first lover Oenone (cf. *Heroides*, XVII, 193–200):

> swie kleine ir sîn geloubent,
> mir ist doch iuwer leben kunt,
> ich hân dick und ze manger stunt
> gefrâget iuwer tougen,
> ê daz ich mit den ougen
> iuch saehe bûwen disen kreiz. (*Trojanerkrieg*, ll. 22156–61)

In the depiction of this argument Konrad follows his source, the letters between Helen and Paris in Ovid's *Heroides*, in many details. He deviates slightly, however, to emphasize the lack of Paris's heroic reputation: he does not adopt Paris's boasting about his heroic deeds (*Heroides*, XVI, 353–70) and adds the explicit comparison of Paris's lack of heroic fame with Theseus's reputation. Helen's reservations about Paris on the basis of his bad reputation as a ladies' man and his lack of heroic fame thus present the flip side of the principle with which the narrator had explained Medea's affection for Jason. If widely praised men like Jason appear more desirable, widely defamed men like Paris cannot appear very attractive. However, just as the role of fame as an indicator of actual excellence on which the idea of *Fernminne* relies is subtly destabilized in Medea's case, the reverse principle expressed by Helen's rebuttal is also undermined. Although she has every reason to snub Paris, Helen has actually been deeply in love with him from the moment she laid eyes upon him. While Medea's appreciation for Jason is heightened when she learns who he really is, Helen's love for the beautiful stranger – she explicitly names his beauty as the reason for his appeal to women (*Trojanerkrieg*, ll. 21726–29; cf. *Heroides*, XVII, 93–94) – cannot be diminished by Paris's miserable reputation. The interaction of love and praise in the *Trojanerkrieg* is thus clearly more complex and problematic than the cultural-historical interpretation of the *Fernminne* motif by Wenzel suggests. Müller points out further aspects that render the narrative pattern problematic in Paris's case:

> Doch was scheinbar wie eine gewöhnliche Brautwerbung aussieht, ist von Anfang an mehrfach delegitimiert. Die Brautwerbung ist ein Racheakt. Die Fernliebe auf Grund allgemein gepriesener Tugenden spornt nicht zu einer exorbitanten Rittertat an, sondern zu einem Verbrechen. Helena ist verheiratet; die 'Brautwerbung' begründet nicht eine dynastische Ehe, sondern bedeutet Ehebruch. In ihr triumphiert nicht die Bewährung von Fürst und Land, sondern sie ist Vorwurf zu einer rasenden Leidenschaft. Indem Helena Paris als Lohn von Venus zugesagt ist, riskiert er nicht einmal etwas.[94]

The final section of this chapter will therefore challenge the opinion that Wenzel identifies as the basis of the *Fernminne* concept, namely 'dass die Wahrnehmung der Schönheit direkt über das Ohr erfolgt, weil die Qualität einer Person durch das Hören von ihr (durch die *fama*) angemessen wahrgenommen werden kann'.[95] There are moments of disconnection between the presence of Jason's and Paris's bodies and their reputation: Jason's praise seems more impressive than his appearance and Paris's beauty makes up for his lack of heroic fame. In both cases, this potentially unsettling gap is closed. Medea soon finds the praise she heard about Jason surpassed by the man himself – 'si der tûsent an im fant, | der einez was von im geseit' (*Trojanerkrieg*, ll. 7738–39) – and when Helen watches Paris fight from the walls of Troy she corrects her earlier judgement and praises him for being a good fighter as well as an excellent lover (*Trojanerkrieg*, ll. 35372–89). The question about the correspondence between a person and their verbal representation, however, is an issue that comes to the fore when Paris considers the tension between Helen and her praise.

Helen's Praise

The idea that words can evoke mental images and the illusion of the presence of the verbally represented object, person or event, thereby transcending the medium of language, can be traced back to ancient rhetoric. Already Greek *Progymnasmata* state that ekphrasis effects a kind of seeing through the ear and turns the listener into an observer.[96] The influential *Rhetorica ad Herennium*

94 Müller, *Höfische Kompromisse*, p. 454. On the allusions to the bridal quest motif, see also Schulz: 'Die Ankläge sind massiv (Rat-Szene, Anspielungen auf Kaufmannslist, erste Begegnung bei einer Art Gottesdienst, Identitätslüge, "Kemenatenszene", listige Entführung etc.)' (Schulz, *Schwieriges Erkennen*, p. 470, fn. 356).

95 Wenzel, *Hören und Sehen*, p. 155.

96 For references and an account of the history of ekphrasis, see Fritz Graf, 'Ekphrasis: Die

defines *demonstratio* in a similar way: 'Demonstratio est, cum ita verbis res exprimitur, ut geri negotium et res ante oculos esse videatur' [It is Ocular Demonstration when an event is so described in words that the business seems to be enacted and the subject to pass vividly before our eyes] (*Rhetorica ad Herennium*, IV, 68).[97] It furthermore states that this type of representation is particularly suited to arousing pity and illustrates it with an example that is characterized through descriptive detail, narrative present and direct speech. Quintilian, whose rhetoric was less known in the Middle Ages, calls the same mode of elocution *evidentia* and argues that it heightens the effectiveness of the oration:

> Magna virtus res de quibus loquimur clare atque ut cerni videantur enuntiare. Non enim satis efficit neque, ut debet, plene dominatur oratio si usque ad aures valet, atque ea sibi iudex de quibus cognoscit narrari credit, non exprimi et oculis mentis ostendi.
>
> [It is a great virtue to express our subject clearly and in such a way that it seems to be actually seen. A speech does not adequately fulfil its purpose or attain the total domination it should have if it goes no further than the ears, and the judge feels that he is merely being told the story of the matters he has to decide, without their being brought out and displayed to the mind's eye (*The Orator's Education*, 8, 3, 62).][98]

If the events are presented 'somehow painted in words' and stimulate the visual imagination of the listener through the use of descriptive and vivid detail the quality of *enargeia* is created (8, 3, 61–71). Earlier Quintilian explains that the emotions of the audience can only be stirred if the orator himself is affected

---

Entstehung der Gattung in der Antike', in *Beschreibungskunst – Kunstbeschreibung*, ed. by Gottfried Boehm and Helmut Pfotenhauer (Munich: Fink, 1995), pp. 143–55.

97 Similarly: 'statuit [...] rem totam et prope ponit ante oculos' [it sets forth the whole incident and virtually brings it before our eyes] (*Rhetorica ad Herennium*, IV, 69). On the techniques that create the illusion of 'Augenschein' in ancient rhetoric and in medieval poetic practice, see Gert Hübner, '*evidentia*: Erzählformen und ihre Funktionen', in *Historische Narratologie: Mediävistische Perspektiven*, ed. by Harald Haferland and Matthias Meyer, Trends in Medieval Philology, 19 (Berlin: de Gruyter, 2010), pp. 119–48 (pp. 123–31). He lists the alternative terms *enargeia*, *hypotyposis*, *evidentia*, *sub oculos subiecto* and *illustratio* (p. 123).

98 Quintilian refers to Cicero: 'Nam et commoratio una in re permultum movet et illustris explanatio rerumque quasi gerantur sub aspectum paene subiecto, quae et in exponenda re plurimum valent et ad illustrandum id quod exponitur et ad amplificandum, ut eis qui audient illud quod augebimus quantum efficere oratio poterit tantum esse videantur' [For a great impression is made by dwelling on a single point, and also by clear explanation and almost visual presentation of events as if practically going on – which are very effective both in stating a case and in explaining and amplifying the statement, with the object of making the fact we amplify appear to the audience as important as eloquence is able to make it] (*On the Orator*, III, 202).

emotionally. This can be achieved by identifying with the involved persons and by imagining the related events as 'phantasiai' or 'visiones' 'by which the images of absent things are presented to the mind in such a way that we seem to actually see them with our eyes and have them physically present to us'. This will create *enargeia* which can then be transferred to the audience, 'a quality which makes us seem not so much to be talking about something as exhibiting it. Emotions will ensue just as if we were present at the event itself'.[99]

The notion that a visual image can be mediated through language without compromising its integrity is also suggested by the Latin and vernacular vocabulary in the word field of 'image'. Wandhoff emphasizes that German expressions are particularly vague, since they do not even differentiate between the abstract and immaterial image and the concrete and material picture:

> Das ahd. *bilide* sowie seine mhd. und nhd. Nachfahren *bilde* und *Bild* stehen differenzlos für jedwede materielle und mediale Form der Bildlichkeit ein. Nimmt man diesen sprachlichen Befund ernst, dann gab und gibt es offenbar eine tief verwurzelte Vorstellung vom Bild als einer Entität, die nicht an ein bestimmtes Medium gebunden ist, sondern durch verschiedene Materialien, Künste und Speicher gleichsam 'wandern' kann, ohne dabei ihr Wesen – ihre Bildlichkeit – einzubüßen.[100]

Even the Latin words *imago*, *pictura* and *forma* are rarely distinguished in a consistent manner, so that 'die Grenzen zwischen Urbildern, Abbildern, Spiegelungen, Kunstgemälden, Phantasien und Sprachbildern' remain terminologically open.[101]

The distinction between images that are received through the sense of vision and images that are evoked through verbal description is also undermined in ancient and medieval cognition theory.[102] According to the

99 'per quas imagines rerum absentium ita repraesentantur animo ut eas cernere oculis ac praesentes habere videamur' (*The Orator's Education*, 6, 2, 29); 'quae non tam dicere videtur quam ostendre, et adfectus non aliter quam si rebus ipsis intersimus sequentur' (*The Orator's Education*, 6, 2, 32). Graf sums up the meaning of *enargeia* as follows: 'Enargeia ist mithin die Eigenschaft der Rede, Vergangenes – oder allgemeiner: nicht Gegenwärtiges – innerlich präsent zu machen und dabei scheinbar den Wortcharakter des Textes aufzuheben: das eben meint die Formel "aus Zuhörern Zuschauer machen": an die Stelle der äußeren tritt die innere Schau' (Graf, 'Ekphrasis', pp. 145–46).

100 Haiko Wandhoff, 'Zur Bildlichkeit mittelalterlicher Texte', in *Zur Bildlichkeit mittelalterlicher Texte*, ed. by Haiko Wandhoff (= *Das Mittelalter*, 13 (2008)), pp. 3–23 (pp. 3–4).

101 Wandhoff, 'Zur Bildlichkeit mittelalterlicher Texte', p. 5.

102 See, for example, Mary Carruthers, *The Craft of Thought: Meditation, Rhetoric and the Making of Images, 400–1200* (Cambridge: Cambridge University Press, 1998). An overview of research is provided by Wandhoff, 'Zur Bildlichkeit mittelalterlicher Texte' and *Ekphrasis*, pp. 20–30. The relevance of these theories for Middle High German texts

basic model that Scheuer reconstructs as common knowledge among *clerici* from the twelfth century onwards the brain is divided into three chambers: in the frontal chamber *imaginatio* transforms the information received by the exterior senses (vision, hearing, touch, smell, taste) into phantasms or *imagines* that remain present even when the original object of perception is no longer accessible. In the middle chamber *ratio* processes this information before it can be stored in the back chamber by *memoria*. The vehicle of these phantasms is the element of pneuma that circulates the energy of life throughout the body and the universe. Based on the Aristotelian proposition that the 'soul never thinks without a mental image',[103] which was also taken up by Thomas Aquinas (*Summa theologiae*, I, 89, 1), Scheuer deduces that since perception and cognition are only ever possible through phantasms there is no categorical difference between mental images that are created through vision and those evoked through words:

> Hören und Lesen sind also keine textbezogenen, sondern bildbezogene Tätigkeiten, die Phantasmen generieren. Jede mittelalterliche Poiesis, sie sei skriptural oder piktural überliefert, hat dem Rechnung zu tragen und ist ensprechend durch die Züge einer literarischen Arbeit an den inneren Bildern, den *imagines*, charakterisierbar.[104]

---

is discussed, for example, by Bumke, *Die Blutstropfen im Schnee: Über Wahrnehmung und Erkenntnis im 'Parzival' Wolframs von Eschenbach*, Hermea, 94 (Tübingen: Niemeyer, 2001); and Christina Lechtermann, *Berührt werden: Narrative Strategien der Präsenz in der höfischen Literatur um 1200*, Philologische Studien und Quellen, 191 (Berlin: Schmidt, 2005), pp. 48–77.

103 Aristotle, *On the Soul, Parva Naturalia, On Breath*, trans. by W. S. Hett, Loeb Classical Library, 288 (Cambridge, MA: Harvard University Press, 1936; repr. 1964), *On the soul*, 431a, 16–17.

104 Hans Jürgen Scheuer, '*Numquam sine phantasmate*: Antike in mittelalterlicher Imagination', in *Germanistik in und für Europa: Faszination – Wissen: Texte des Münchener Germanistentages 2004*, ed. by Konrad Ehlich (Bielefeld: Aisthesis: 2006), pp. 381–90 (p. 385), and 'Die Wahrnehmung innerer Bilder im "Carmen Buranum" 62: Überlegungen zur Vermittlung zwischen mediävistischer Medientheorie und mittelalterlicher Poetik', *Das Mittelalter*, 8 (2003), 121–36. Here he argues that 'poetische Formen selbst *visio* herstellen, indem sie den Prozess der Visualisierung vor dem inneren Auge sprachlich anstoßen, lenken und manipulieren' (p. 135). The model of the three ventricles is reflected in Matthew of Vendôme's *Ars versificatoria* (I, 52, 21–24), as well as in vernacular texts like *Der Wälsche Gast* (ll. 8789–8856). The varied adaptation of learned imagination theory in German texts is analysed by Manfred Eikelmann, '*imaginâtio* und *fantasîe*: Entlehnungen des Konzepts der Imagination von Notker bis ins 15. Jahrhundert', in *Archäologie der Phantasie: Vom 'Imaginationsraum Südtirol' zur longue dureé einer 'Kultur der Phantasmen' und ihrer Wiederkehr in der Kunst der Gegenwart*, ed. by Elmar Locher and Hans Jürgen Scheuer (Innsbruck: StudienVerlag, 2012), pp. 185–97.

That these mental images are not just visual, but multisensory and three-dimensional is further specified by Lechtermann.[105] Scheuer sees this theory of imagination not only applied but also self-consciously exposed in various medieval artefacts ranging from explicit references in the *Carmina Burana* to allegorical representations of the 'Wahrnehmungsapparat' in the architecture and wall paintings of Burg Runkelstein to the succession of *âventiuren* in *Daniel von dem Blühenden Tal* and ekphrastic passages in courtly literature, such as the description of Candacis's palace in the *Straßburger Alexander*.[106] This line of interpretation is also pursued by Ellen Strittmatter, who applies it to the works of Hartmann von Aue and highlights the metapoetic potential that is intrinsic to such poetic representations of the cognitive process:

> Die poetische Funktion der Phantasmen ist dabei von ihrer poetologischen Dimension nicht zu trennen. Indem Vorstellungsbilder beim Hörer oder Leser erzeugt werden, die Vermittlungssituation zusätzlich kommentiert und damit ins Bewusstsein der Rezipienten gerückt wird, werden die Strategien und Verfahren der Bildproduktion reflektiert.[107]

Apart from descriptions, this function of reflecting the mediality of the text can also be fulfilled by intradiegetic processes of imagination, even more so if these involve the translation of verbal information about an absent object

105 Lechtermann, *Berührt werden*, pp. 68–73; Wandhoff, 'Zur Bildlichkeit mittelalterlicher Texte', p. 9.

106 Scheuer develops and employs this theory in several articles: 'Die Wahrnehmung innerer Bilder'; 'Bildintensität: Eine imaginationstheoretische Lektüre des Strickerschen Artusromans "Daniel von dem blühenden Tal"', *ZfdPh*, 124 (2005), 23–46; Hans Jürgen Scheuer and Björn Reich, 'Die Realität der inneren Bilder: Candacis Palast und das Bildprogramm auf Burg Runkelstein als Modelle mittelalterlicher Imagination', in *Innenräume in der Literatur des deutschen Mittelalters: XIX. Anglo-German Colloquium Oxford 2005*, ed. by Burkhard Hasebrink, Hans-Jochen Schiewer, Almut Suerbaum and Annette Volfing (Tübingen: Niemeyer, 2008), pp. 101–24. Similarly Wandhoff: 'Wenn aber die entscheidende Rolle den inneren Bildern zukommt, so dass wir medial verkörperte Bilder jedweder Art immer erst durch unseren Wahrnehmungsakt animieren müssen, dann haben die Bilder, die Sprache und Literatur vermitteln, grundsätzlich keinen anderen Status als diejenigen, die die sogenannten visuellen oder bildenden Künste hervorbringen. Die Sprache ist dann lediglich ein weiteres Medium, in dem sich Bilder verkörpern' (Wandhoff, 'Zur Bildlichkeit mittelalterlicher Texte', p. 5). On the basis of this theory of poetically evoked mental images Gebert analyses 'Präsenzeffekte' in the *Trojanerkrieg* (Gebert, *Mythos als Wissensform*, pp. 232–320).

107 Ellen Strittmatter, *Poetik des Phantasmas: Eine imaginationstheoretische Lektüre der Werke Hartmanns von Aue*, Studien zur historischen Poetik, 15 (Heidelberg: Winter, 2013), p. 35. Scheuer also mentions the self-reflexive dimension of such representations: 'Optische und hirnphysiologische Wissenselemente sind keine Metaphern innerhalb eines mittelalterlichen Textes, sie sind vielmehr Explikationen der Medialität des "Textes", der eben nicht einfach Text, sondern Medium zur Aktualisierung und Intensivierung innerer Bilder ist' (Scheuer, 'Die Wahrnehmung innerer Bilder', 128, fn. 14).

into mental images and thus mirror the extradiegetic situation of reception. Processes of perception and cognition associated with *minne* are, furthermore, particularly suited to analysing the depiction of this issue because external vision as well as mental images are crucial steps in the development of love. Thus Strittmatter emphasizes, in the tradition of Agamben, that the development of love was conceptualized as a phantasmatic process, since true passion is not created through external vision but through intense contemplation of a mental image. That love is merely triggered by the first act of vision and has to be complemented by a deep and extended mental occupation with the internalized image in order to grow into true passion is also described in Andreas Capellanus's *De amore* (I, 8–10).[108] The important role that the contemplation of phantasms plays in the context of love is famously demonstrated by Parzival, who remembers Condwiramurs's face when he sees the drops of blood in the snow;[109] or by Riwalin, who falls in love with Blanscheflur after scrutinizing a memorized mental image of her to figure out her feelings. A first internalization of her image is superseded by a second permanent installation of her phantasm in his heart:

ir gruoz, ir rede betrahte er gâr,
ir sûft, ir segen, al ir gebâr
daz marcte er al besunder
und begunde iedoch hier under
ir siuften unde ir süezen segen
ûf den weg der minne wegen:
er kam binamen an den wân,
diu zwei diu wæren getân
durch niht niuwan durch minne.
daz enzunte ouch sîne sinne,
daz si sâ wider vuoren
und nâmen Blanscheflуoren
und vuorten sî mit in zehant
in Riwalînes herzen lant
und crônden si dar inne
im z'einer küniginne. (*Tristan*, ll. 797–812)[110]

108 Strittmatter, *Poetik des Phantasmas*, p. 19. The nexus between imagination and love is also emphasized in Scheuer's works, for example, 'Die Wahrnehmung innerer Bilder', 131–32.

109 The relationship of this scene to contemporary theories of cognition has been discussed by Joachim Bumke, *Die Blutstropfen im Schnee*.

110 On this scene see Küsters, who distinguishes between the first instinctive and charismatic gaze which causes love (*ersehen*) and the second gaze as a rationally controlled tool of cognition (*merken*), usually employed to discover the feelings of the beloved and to communicate one's own emotions (Küsters, 'Liebe und der zweite Blick', pp. 274–75, pp. 289–90, p. 296).

The depiction of Paris's *Fernminne* for Helen therefore presents an interesting experimental arrangement to examine whether the replacement of a visual with a verbal trigger for love can in fact create a mental image of equal validity, as the research discussed above suggests, or whether the ontological gap between words and vision is instead emphasized. In both cases the depiction of the relationship between verbal representation and visual presence would permit a metapoetic reflection on the ability of language to evoke mental images that succeed in transcending medial, spatial, temporal and ontological differences.

When Venus promises Helen to Paris as a reward for awarding her the Apple of Discord, her praise does not contain the strategies typically employed to create *evidentia*, such as descriptive detail or deictic devices. In line with the argument that *Fernminne* is caused by publicly recognized excellence rather than by individual erotic attraction, Venus merely declares Helen's status as the pinnacle of beauty and virtue and describes her in terms of her effect. The fact that her beauty attracts men like the song of a siren attracts ships acts as proof of her objective desirability:

> HELÊNE von der KRIECHEN lant,
> diu schoener ist vil denn alliu wîp,
> diu muoz ir leben unde ir lîp
> an dich mit flîze kêren,
> ist, daz ich hie mit êren
> die sigenuft gewinne.
> diu selbe küniginne
> ist aller frouwen krône,
> si lebt in êren schône
> und in der tugende huote;
> von fleische noch von bluote
> wart nie crêatiure
> sô klâr noch sô gehiure
> sô diu schoene HELÊNE.
> nû sich, wie diu SŶRÊNE
> und ir süezes dônes grif
> ziehe an sich vil manic schif,
> sus kan diz wunnecliche wîp
> mit ir klârheit mangen lîp
> an sich ziehen unde nemen. (*Trojanerkrieg*, ll. 2654–73)

The image of Helen as a siren is certainly influenced by the passage in *Tristan* in which Isolde sings to the Irish court and which contains a similar synaesthetic connection of seeing and hearing:

> Wem mac ich sî gelîchen
> die schœnen, sældenrîchen
> wan den Sŷrênen eine,
> die mit dem agesteine
> die kiele ziehent ze sich?
> als zôch Îsôt, sô dunket mich,
> vil herzen unde gedanken în,
> die doch vil sicher wânden sîn
> von senedem ungemache. (*Tristan*, ll. 8085–93)[111]

In Gottfried's romance the motif of the siren is connected with the metaphor of love as a ship without an anchor and explicitly linked to the perception of Isolde as an auditory phenomenon:

> diu gevüege Îsôt, diu wîse,
> diu junge süeze künigîn
> alsô zôch si gedanken în
> ûz maneges herzen arken,
> als der agestein die barken
> mit der Syrênen sange tuot.
> si sanc in maneges herzen muot
> offenlîchen unde tougen
> durch ôren und durch ougen.
> ir sanc, den s'offenlîche tete
> beide anderswâ und an der stete,
> daz was ir süeze singen,
> ir senftez seiten clingen,
> daz lûte und offenlîche
> durch der ôren künicrîche
> hin nider in diu herzen clanc.
> sô was der tougenlîche sanc
> ir wunderlîchiu schœne,
> diu mit ir muotgedœne
> verholne unde tougen
> durch diu venster der ougen
> in vil manic edele herzen sleich. (*Tristan*, ll. 8106–27)

While Helen's visual appeal ('clârheit') is likened to the aural charm of a siren ('dôn'), Isolde's singing is conversely used as a metaphor for her beauty. Her

111 On Gottfried's siren image, which is probably influenced by Ovid (*The Art of Love*, III, 311–18; *The Remedies for Love*, ll. 789–90), see Ingrid Hahn, *Raum und Landschaft in Gottfrieds Tristan: Ein Beitrag zur Werkdeutung* (Munich: Eidos, 1963), pp. 104–06, p. 145; Wessel, *Probleme der Metaphorik*, pp. 316–24; Manfred Kern, 'Isolde, Helena und die Sirenen: Gottfried von Straßburg als Mythograph', *Oxford German Studies*, 29 (2000), 1–30 (pp. 11–16).

literal, public singing, which reaches the hearts of the audience via their ears, is contrasted to the metaphorical, secret and silent song of her beauty entering through their eyes. The synaesthetic connection of hearing and seeing in *Tristan* reflects the fact that Isolde is indeed presented to the court audience as an audiovisual phenomenon arousing love through singing and beauty. However, unlike Isolde, Helen is not a singer. It might therefore seem that the similarity between her and a siren is much more limited than in Gottfried's employment of the image. Both Helen and the siren exert a fatal attraction, but in very different ways: Helen lures with 'clârheit' and the siren lures with 'dôn'. However, the juxtaposition of the two different modes of attraction in the siren comparison is in fact very instructive. After all, Helen's beauty will only indirectly, in the form of hearsay, lure Paris to Citarea and set off the chain of events leading to the fatal war. Considering that Paris will abduct his wife *über sê* and subsequently cause the embarkation of the Greek fleet, Helen can be linked in a rather literal way to the effect of the siren's song that is said to attract many ships. Helen is an audiovisual phenomenon in a decisively different way from Isolde: she exerts power as a verbalized beauty.

The motif of the desired woman as a siren also appears in Konrad's *Engelhard*. It is Engeltrut's 'wörtelîn', her coy insinuation of her love for Engelhard, which causes his love for her – the exchange of gazes is only a second step in this atypical development (*Engelhard*, ll. 1880–1929).[112] Engelhard recalls this verbal mediation of love when he likens Engeltrut to a siren:

si tuot als diu Sirêne
der stimme ist alsô schœne
daz si mit ir gedœne
an sich die kiele ziuhet
und si dan under diuhet
mit liute und mit getreide.
der wilden meremeide
mîn frouwe sich gelîchet wol.
ir rede süezekeite vol
und ir schœner worte grif

112 On this episode see Küsters, 'Liebe und der zweite Blick', pp. 302–07. He emphasizes that the emphatic first gaze as the traditional cause of love becomes problematic in *Engelhard* and that the communication of love is unusually verbal. Engeltrut cannot choose between the identical looking Dietrich and Engelhard with her eyes alone, but decides on the basis of the sound of their names; the verbal sign of love (*wörtelîn*) precedes the loving gaze as a trigger of love and the assurance of mutual love is established in a dialogue. On the problem of visuality in *Engelhard*, see also Armin Schulz, 'Notwendige Unterscheidungen: Zur Epistemik der Sinne bei Konrad von Würzburg', in *www.germanistik2001.de: Vorträge des Erlanger Germanistentags 2001*, ed. by Hartmut Kugler, 2 vols (Bielefeld: Aisthesis, 2002), I, pp. 129–42, and *Schwieriges Erkennen*, pp. 389–409.

hât under mînes herzen schif
gezogen und gesenket. (*Engelhard*, ll. 2216–27)

There are significant differences between the employment of the motif in *Engelhard* and in the *Trojanerkrieg*: most importantly, it is the praise of Helen, not her own words, that incites Paris's love. However, in both cases the image of the siren is used to highlight the power of words to cause love.[113] In addition, the description of Helen as a siren anticipates her fatal role in the events and carries religious connotations.[114] In the *Goldene Schmiede* (ll. 139–53) the siren represents the temptations of the world and is the antithesis of the Virgin, who, as the morning star, promises rescue from the raging ocean of life.[115]

However brief Venus's praise of Helen may be, especially by Konrad's standards, it is enough to make up Paris's mind. After a short deliberation he cannot but cast his vote in favour of *minne* and at once begins to feel the pain of love:

ze fröuden kêrte er sînen gunst
und ûf die minne hôchgemuot,
diu vür wîsheit und vür guot
durchliuhtic in sîn herze gleiz.
VÊNUS geschuof und ir geheiz
daz wunder an im tougen,
daz er muost âne lougen
nâch hôher minne siechen.
daz HELENÂ von KRIECHEN
geheizen im ze lône was,
des nam er an sich unde las
den willen und die sinne,
daz er gestuont der minne
alsam ir eigenlicher knecht. (*Trojanerkrieg*, ll. 2736–49)

The unconventional trigger of love and the strong effect of Venus's promise are highlighted by the term 'wunder'. Love takes possession of Paris as light that radiates into his heart, which can be seen as a reversal of the simile of Helen as a siren. Together they form a synaesthetic chiasm: the metaphor presents a verbally mediated love as a visual charm and the siren simile presents beauty as a charm to the ears. The fact that an aurally mediated love is communicated

113 Likewise Partonopier falls in love with the invisible Meliur when he recognizes her excellence and beauty through hearing (*Partonopier*, ll. 1536–43, ll. 1590–1623). This lack of visibility, however, represents the deficiency of their illegitimate relationship (see Schulz, *Schwieriges Erkennen*, pp. 409–55).

114 Lienert, *Geschichte und Erzählen*, p. 46, pp. 265–66.

115 In one of Konrad's songs, this role is fulfilled by Christ (*Lieder und Sprüche*, 1, 135–38).

as light, the medium of vision,[116] also mirrors the pivotal role that visual encounters usually play in the development of love, for example when Achilles sees Deidamia:

> sîn [Deidamia's mouth] glast durchliuhtic unde heiz
> ACHILLE durch sîn herze bran,
> er warf in unde stiez in an:
> daz wilde fiur der minne. (*Trojanerkrieg*, ll. 14694–97)

Even though Venus's praise does not contain any information about Helen's individual physical traits, it still manages to evoke a visual impression in Paris's heart, a phantasm of light, and to effect the same emotions that an actual encounter with the radiant Helen would. Without employing the traditional rhetorical devices of *evidentia* the praise effectively substitutes for Helen's visible presence by creating *enargeia*, an illusion of presence that arouses the same emotions as the verbally represented object or event, in a charismatic way. At the same time, there is still a notion of mediation implicit, for it is not Helen herself who radiates into Paris's heart but the abstract power of *minne*. Gebert, who demonstrates convincingly that the representation and role of Helen vary throughout the *Trojanerkrieg*, points out that in this passage she does not appear as the cause but as a subsidiary object of love:

> Helena konkretisiert für Paris [...] zunächst die 'minne', die Venus in Aussicht stellt. Mehrfach streicht der Erzähler sogar heraus, dass Helena für den Jüngling erst sekundär attraktiv wird. Seine affizierbare jugendliche Disposition 'von natûre' und die Macht der Venus zwingen ihn zur Liebe [...], Helena wird lediglich ihr allernächstes Objekt.[117]

It will be a long time before Paris sets eyes upon his beloved. In the meantime, he is often caught up in the contemplation of Helen (*gedenken*, *andaht*). However, unlike in the case of Parzival and Riwalin and, more importantly, unlike the Latin source, Ovid's *Heroides*, in which Paris explicitly sees Helen's vision while awake and in his dreams,[118] Konrad never characterizes Paris's

116 For the importance of light in the process of vision in medieval theories of optics, see David C. Lindberg, *Auge und Licht im Mittelalter: Die Entwicklung der Optik von Alkindi bis Kepler* (Frankfurt a. M.: Suhrkamp, 1987).

117 Gebert, *Mythos als Wissensform*, p. 220.

118 Even though Venus's praise is even shorter in Ovid's account than in Konrad's description – she merely states that Helen is more beautiful than her mother Leda – Paris has obviously formed a mental image of her looks: 'ante tuos animo vidi quam lumine vultus' [I beheld your features with my soul ere I saw them with my eyes] (Ovid, *Heroides*, XVI, 37). See also: 'te vigilans oculis, animo te nocte videbam, | lumina cum placido victa sopore iacent. | quid facies praesens, quae nondum visa placebas?' [It was you that filled my vision as I waked, and you my soul saw in the night, when eyes lie overcome in peaceful slumber. What will you be

thoughts about Helen as an imagination of her looks, but as remembrance of Venus's promise:

> daz HELENÂ von KRIECHEN
> geheizen im ze wîbe was,
> weizgot, des nam er unde las
> gedenke vil ze herzen. (*Trojanerkrieg*, ll. 4368–71)

Nonetheless, his *Fernminne* for Helen is so strong that his memory of Venus's promise immediately replaces his conventional love and presumably visual memory of his first lover Oenone:

> si wart ûz sînem sinne
> gestôzen bî der stunde
> und HELENÂ ze grunde
> dar în versigelt alzehant. (*Trojanerkrieg*, ll. 4388–91; see also ll. 4754–72)

It has often been argued that the recurrent narrative pattern of betrayed love demonstrates that *minne* in the *Trojanerkrieg* relies on the immediate presence of the lovers and follows an out-of-sight-out-of-mind logic.[119] However, in this case it is a much closer lover who is replaced by an invisible and distant rival. Konrad also depicts this unusual dominance of hearing over vision in *Partonopier*, where even the magically enhanced charms of the most beautiful girl in France cannot erase the invisible Meliur from Partonopier's memory for long: 'Obwohl Partonopiers *memoria* an die Geliebte sich nicht auf Bilder stützen kann (wie sie die mittelalterliche Gedächtnistheorie einzig privilegiert), ist diese Bindung stärker als jede Magie'.[120] Whenever Paris's contemplation of Helen is narrated, the verbally mediated nature of his love is kept present, not only by the narrator, but also by Paris himself, who recollects the process of falling in love:

> ich hân geleit in mînen muot
> ir schoene, ir adel und ir tugent
> und hoere sagen von ir jugent
> sô rîcher saelden wunder,

face to face, you who won me yet unseen?] (Ovid, *Heroides*, XVI, 101–103).

119 Schulz states that courtly values in the *Trojanerkrieg* are only upheld within a range of immediate visibility: 'Sie ist von gegenseitiger Präsenz abhängig, was sich etwa beim Motiv des untreuen Liebhabers zeigt, das sich durch den Text zieht: Verfehlung gegenüber anderen Figuren geschehen zumeist in deren Abwesenheit' (Schulz, *Schwieriges Erkennen*, p. 473). Seus comments on love in the *Trojanerkrieg*: 'Diese Einswerdung ist nicht verstetigbar, sie ist auf die Präsenz der Minnenden, auf ihre sichtbare Oberfläche angewiesen' (Seus, *Heilsgeschichten vor dem Heil?*, pp. 176–77).

120 Schulz, *Schwieriges Erkennen*, p. 422.

daz ich durch si besunder
wil mîden alle frouwen.
mich hât ir prîs verhouwen
und ir name reine,
ze herzen und ze beine
bin ich verwundet von ir lobe. (*Trojanerkrieg*, ll. 4416–25)

Paris attributes to Helen's verbal representation, her 'prîs', her 'name' and her 'lop', an extraordinary impact which is metaphorized as a direct violent contact with his body ('verhouwen', 'verwunden'). Even though Helen is still primarily presented as a verbal phenomenon – her praise never fully transcends the medium of language – the verbal representation appears as the perfect substitute for Helen's presence in terms of effect. The tension created through Venus's promise is not presented as that between aural and visual perception, but as that between unfulfilled and fulfilled love. Given the long build-up of tension that extends over seventeen thousand verses, anticipation of the first face-to-face encounter between the two famous lovers Helen and Paris is extremely high.

Paris sees Helen for the first time when she comes to the temple of Venus to greet the strangers who have newly arrived in Citarea. Of all the Trojans Paris is predisposed to see her first:

PÂRÎS, der junge künic rîch,
wart ir zem êrsten innen,
wan si begunde brinnen
und liuhten in sîn ougen
sô ferre sunder lougen,
daz er was der êrste man,
der si von ir kastelle dan
sach komen dô mit ir gezoge:
des wart er als ein regenboge
geferwet von der minne
der glanzen küneginne,
der schoene durch sîn herze brach,
wan dô sîn ouge ir bilde ersach,
dô was zehant diu minne dâ
und tet im kunt, daz HELENÂ
dâ kaeme bî den stunden.
swie selten er die blunden
gesehen hete in sînen tagen,
iedoch begunde im wîssagen
sîn herze tugendebaere,
daz si diu selbe waere,
die VÊNUS im geheizen. (*Trojanerkrieg*, ll. 19782–803)

The first visual encounter is an act of instantaneous recognition. The text emphasizes the fact that although Paris has never set eyes on Helen before, his heart identifies her as the very same person who has been promised to him. Küsters comments: 'Das Sehen [ist] kein äußerer Vorgang: Ihr Bild leuchtet ihm von weitem ein und dringt in sein Herz, da es dem Vorstellungsbild entspricht, das die Prophezeihungen in sein Herz eingeprägt haben'.[121] Rather than with a concrete mental image of Helen's looks, this 'Vorstellungsbild' can only be identified with the phantasm of light which radiates into Paris's heart upon hearing Venus's praise of Helen and which is now identified with the vision of her radiance violently breaking into his heart. Instead of providing a scientific explanation on the basis of cognition theory, the miraculous recognition is explained poetically, through the similarity of the effects of the praise and of the vision, which are expressed by the same metaphors.[122] The love which enters Paris's heart with the vision of Helen is still essentially the same passion that he felt before seeing her:

> swaz ê der werde ritter
> geliten hete riuwe,
> diu wart frisch unde niuwe,
> dô sîn ouge ir lîp gesach. (*Trojanerkrieg*, ll. 20330–33)[123]

Although the first visual encounter is clearly marked as an important event, it does not depict the onset of love as something new, but as the necessary activation of something already present.

At first, Paris's recognition of Helen is instinctive. Only in a second step does he begin to process the overwhelming visual impression intellectually and to equate what he sees with what he has heard about Helen:

> Er dâhte wider sich alsô
> still unde tougenlîchen dô:

121 Küsters, 'Liebe und der zweite Blick', p. 311. He then describes how this successful and charismatic first gaze is contrasted to the complicated and artful identification and communication of love through conscious and unconscious signs in the further course of the episode (pp. 311–17). On the depiction of Paris's and Helen's love (which is modelled on Ovid, *Heroides*, XVI and XVII), see the comparison of both texts by Cholevius, *Geschichte der deutschen Poesie*, pp. 140–42; Bartsch, *Albrecht von Halberstadt*, pp. xxvi–xxxiv; Monecke, *Das Erzählprinzip der 'wildekeit'*, pp. 145–52; Stackmann, 'Ovid im deutschen Mittelalter', 248–51; Schulz, *Schwieriges Erkennen*, pp. 477–80.

122 See also Schulz, *Schwieriges Erkennen*, p. 469. He reads this magical recognition, according to the principle that like is known by like, as a sign that Helen and Paris, the most beautiful man and the most beautiful woman, are a predestined couple.

123 Compare the effect of the vision of Helen on the Greek fighters: 'dô si daz liehte wîp enbor | gesâhen an der zinnen, | dô wurdens' in ir sinnen | ermant ir alten riuwe, | ir smerze wart sô niuwe | und alsô frisch gemachet, | daz von in war geswachet | TROIAERE starkiu ritterschaft' (*Trojanerkrieg*, ll. 34024–31).

'waz frouwen möhte diz gesîn
wan HELENÂ, diu künigîn,
die man ze solde mir gehiez,
dô man den kriec an mich verliez,
der umb den apfel wart getân?
ich wil gelouben sunder wân,
daz si diu selbe frouwe sî,
diu lange mîme herzen bî
gewont mit ganzer staete hât. (*Trojanerkrieg*, ll. 19807–17)

Apart from the instantaneous recognition, which seems to be based on the effect her vision has on him, Paris rationally identifies her not with regard to individual traits, for he knows nothing about her looks specifically, but as the superlative of female beauty, as his following praise of her reveals. He concludes that Venus's portrayal of Helen as the pinnacle of beauty has not been mere rhetorical hyperbole: 'VÊNUS enhât mir niht gelogen, | diu von ir klârheit seite mir' (*Trojanerkrieg*, ll. 19858–59). Now it only remains to be seen whether Venus was right about Helen's virtue:

erfüllet si mîns herzen gir
an ir vil reinen minne klâr,
sô dunket ez mich allez wâr,
swaz mir von ir liutsaelikeit
und von ir tugende ist geseit. (*Trojanerkrieg*, ll. 19860–64)

Although Venus's praise of Helen does not evoke a detailed picture and leaves Paris with an unbearable desire to possess his beloved, its impact on Paris suggests that the praise of Helen is, in fact, a powerful and appropriate substitute for the actual vision whose effects it has anticipated. However, this view, which is supported by Paris's own evaluation, does not remain the ultimate assessment of the representational power of Helen's praise. When Paris finally reveals his identity and his love for Helen, he again recalls that it was Helen's reputation that caused his love:

der liumet und daz maere,
daz mir von iu wart geseit,
hât mich in dise nôt geleit,
daz mîn gemüete brennet.
iuch hât mîn herze erkennet,
ê daz mîn ouge ersaehe
daz wilde wunder waehe,
daz iu von klârheit wart gegeben. (*Trojanerkrieg*, ll. 21072–79)[124]

124 Compare Ovid: 'te prius optavi, quam mihi nota fores. | ante tuos animo vidi quam lumine vultus; | prima tulit vulnus nuntia fama tui. | Nec tamen est mirum, si sic cum polleat arcus, | missilibus telis eminus ictus amo' [You were my heart's desire before you were known to

In contrast to his first impression, which led him to concede that Venus did not lie to him, he has now drastically changed his opinion and, in the tradition of Ovid's Paris, points out the gaping difference between Helen's praise and her physical presence, between what he has heard and what he can see:

ich finde reiner iuwer leben
dann iuwer lop in alle wîs,
sô lûter was niht iuwer prîs
als iuwer lîp und iuwer jugent,
vil groezer ist noch iuwer tugent,
denn iuwer name waere.
der liumet und daz maere,
diu von iu dicke sint geflogen,
hânt sêre mir an iu gelogen,
wan si vil kleiner sint gewesen
dann iuwer zuht vil ûzerlesen
und iuwer liehtiu klârheit.
ich habe an iu die wârheit
erkennet mit den ougen mê,
denne ich rede gehoeret ê
von iu mit den ôren habe.
des krieges kum ich niemer abe,
man finde iu maniger saelde bî,
dann ie von iu gesaget sî
wird unde tugentlicher tât,
wan iuwer lîp gelegen hât
mit sigenuft den worten obe,
diu ie gesprâchen von dem lobe,
daz an iuch wart mit staetekeit
von manigem wîsen man geleit. (*Trojanerkrieg*, ll. 21080–104)[125]

me. I beheld your features with my soul ere I saw them with my eyes; rumour, that told me of you, was the first to deal my wound. Yet, it is not strange if when the bow is so potent, I am in love, stricken by darts that were sped from afar] (*Heroides*, XVI, 36–40).

125 Compare Ovid: 'magna quidem de te rumor praeconia fecit, | nullaque de facie nescia terra tua est; | nec tibi par usquam Phrygia nec solis ab ortu | inter formosas altera nomen habet! | Crede sed hoc nobis! – minor est tua gloria vero, | famaque de forma paene maligna tua est; | plus hic invenio, quam quod promiserat illa, | et tua materia gloria victa sua est' [Fame has indeed made great heralding of you, and there is no land that knows not of your beauty; no other among fair women has a name like yours – nowhere in Phrygia, nor from the rising of the sun! But you must believe me when I tell you this – your glory is less than the truth, and fame has all but maligned your charms; I find more here than the goddess promised me, and your glory is exceeded by its cause] (Ovid, *Heroides*, XVI, 141–48).

While Paris has seen Helen's praise as an adequate representation before, he now sees – maybe because he has overcome the state of just being dazzled by radiance – that her presence surpasses and escapes verbalization. Where there was harmony between Helen and her praise before, there is now a metaphorical war that results in the victory of Helen's corporeal presence over her fame. Interestingly, at this point Venus is no longer addressed as the agent creating or proliferating Helen's praise; her praise is instead personified as *liumet* and *maere*. It is telling that the term *liumet* is only used with reference to the (inadequate) praise of Helen and in the personification, in which the *liumet* is described as being unreliable. It is, furthermore, surprising that Paris now also refers to wise men as the agents of Helen's praise. Although Helen mentions her widespread reputation before, there has never been any suggestion that Paris has heard praise of Helen from anyone but Venus. Instead, the reference to many wise men – not present in the source, which only mentions Venus – is reminiscent of Konrad's earlier appreciation of Helen's literary fame:

> swaz man von frouwen ie gesprach
> an buochen unde an lieden,
> dâ lopten unde schieden
> die wîsen ûz ir schoenen lîp
> vür alliu minneclichiu wîp. (*Trojanerkrieg*, ll. 19722–26)

In the prologue, wisdom is the main quality of the masters of poetry (*Trojanerkrieg*, l. 11, l. 57), which suggests that Paris's assessment is meant to be applied not only to the praise of Helen on the level of the story but also to her literary praise. Furthermore, when Paris declares that words can never adequately represent Helen, it is clearly of relevance that Konrad himself has just sung Helen's praises and given an extraordinarily detailed description of her. If we assume that Konrad actually counted himself among the wise masters of poetry, this connection between story and discourse becomes even stronger. This means that the *Trojanerkrieg* presents itself at this point not just as a story about the Trojan War, but also about the war between words and referents, a hopeless war that the poet has to wage when trying to capture its centre, Helen, in words.

The story of Paris's love for Helen is also a story about the representational capacities and limitations of words. The effect of the praise of Helen on Paris, which anticipates the effect of her beauty, together with his immediate recognition and his judgement that Venus's hyperbolic praise has in fact been appropriate, all prove the power of words to evoke the presence of a person. Eventually, however, Paris declares the impossibility of capturing Helen's presence in words. Following a passage which is at once the single most detailed description of female beauty in Middle High German literature and at the same time strewn with the narrator's declarations of the futility of any effort to praise Helen, Paris's realization can easily be identified as the story-level equivalent of the narrator's ineffability topoi in the discourse. Paris's eyewitness assessment endows these topoi with special authenticity, so that they seem, after all, particularly apt for conveying the essence of the extraordinary beauty that is Helen. A merely rhetorical ineffability becomes an experienced ineffability.

It is true that the single elements of this arrangement are conventional. Paris's remarks are taken from Ovid and Müller comments with reference to the contrast between Helen's praise and her presence: 'Daß ihre Präsenz ihre Fama überbietet [...] gehört noch zum Schema [der *Fernminne*]'.[126] However, the complex interlacing of reflections on the praise of Helen at the levels of story and discourse sets the depiction of the *Trojanerkrieg* apart from the source, which does not include a narratorial description of Helen, and from similar passages in other texts. A good example for comparison is Konrad's *Engelhard*, in which Engelhard and Dietrich are attracted to the Danish court because of the widespread reputation of King Fruote:

> iuwer lop ist flücke
> ûf erden alsô sêre
> daz man siht iuwer êre
> alumbe und umbe sweimen.
> si vert ze Bêheimen,
> ze Ungern und ze Riuzen.
> ouch siht man dâ ze Priuzen
> vast iuwer êre erwahsen.
> Franken unde Sahsen
> hât erfüllet iuwer prîs. (*Engelhard*, ll. 694–703)

Only a moment later, after the king has accepted their request to receive them into his court, the boys assert the inadequacy of even this extraordinary reputation:

> swaz uns von iu wart ie geseit,
> künic vil gewaltec,
> daz hân wir tûsentvaltec
> an iu erfunden unde erkant. (*Engelhard*, ll. 734–37)

Although the basic structure at the story level resembles Paris's experience of Helen in that Engelhard and Dietrich find the person superior to his reputation, the issue does not assume the same metapoetic significance as in

126 Müller, *Höfische Kompromisse*, p. 453, fn. 95. For examples of this motif as an exordial strategy in letters, see Worstbrock, 'Fernliebe', p. 147.

the *Trojanerkrieg*. In the *Engelhard* example there is no build-up of anticipation between the reception of the verbal praise and the actual encounter; and the boys' brief remark does not highlight the issue of verbal representation nearly as much as Paris's elaborate reflection. The scene in the *Trojanerkrieg* builds on a pervasive discourse on the topic of fame and praise and mirrors Paris's reflections on the issue with explicit metapoetic reflections by the narrator.

The concept of praise is central to metapoetics in the *Trojanerkrieg* because it presents an opportunity to draw attention to the representational capacities of language at the level of both story and discourse. As the semantic analysis has shown, the Middle High German terms *prîs* and *lop* are particularly suited to highlighting the relationship between words and their referents since they collapse the distinction between the content (excellence) and the medium (praise). It is particularly their frequent collocation with adjectives suggesting spatial distribution and visibility that characterizes laudative speech as a means by which absent objects and persons can achieve visual presence. The representational power of words is brought to the fore when the act of verbal mediation or the ontological distinction between words and their referents is obscured – for example, when praise is distributed instantaneously and independently of human agents, or when the radiance of a person attaches itself in an indexical manner to his or her praise, making it akin to a charismatic emanation. In addition, praise plays a crucial role in the story because the exaggerated ambition to accumulate the abstract value of *prîs* drives events and finally leads to catastrophe. The metapoetic dimension of praise becomes particularly palpable when it is presented as a poetic phenomenon at the story level, for example, when Achilles teaches Deidamia heroic songs about himself or when Philoctet is asked to praise Hercules and his account is presented in the form of extended metadiegesis. The uncritical reception of Hercules' terrible death, which ought to make the Greeks question the wisdom of excessive revenge but instead incites further aggression, can be interpreted as a cautionary tale about a cautionary tale that goes unheeded. Just as the extreme pursuit of *prîs* is associated with the deadly sins of *invidia* and *superbia*, so the story of Hercules' death carries religious connotations. His depiction as a quasi-saint who renounces his sins of *luxuria*, *superbia* and *ira* in favour of a Christian ethics of compassion highlights what he and the narrated world are lacking: invoking the pagan gods, Hercules cannot transcend the torment of his flesh and overcome his own death. Although there are several instances when compassion is exercised in the text – for example, when the life of baby Paris is spared with the help of divine intervention – these cannot overcome the dynamics of an unchained courtly *agon* and the basic fatality of a society lacking divine grace. The concept of praise is also crucial to the motif of *Fernminne*, since it communicates the publicly recognized excellence of a person and emulates the effect (love) of their physical presence. At the same time the motif can also highlight the tension between praise and its object, when the verbal representation of a person arouses the desire to see him or her with one's own eyes to establish whether he/she really matches his/her reputation. In the *Trojanerkrieg* the issue of the correspondence of praise and person is addressed in several episodes to reveal an implicit tension. While Jason's physical presence initially does not seem to match his praise, Paris's beauty substitutes for his lack of heroic reputation. The story of Paris's *Fernminne* for Helen demonstrates the capacity of praise to evoke the same emotions as the physical presence of the verbally represented person. On the other hand, the ontological gap between Helen and her praise is emphasized by the constant presentation of Paris's lovesickness as an affliction mediated through words and by having Paris himself comment on the fundamental difference between Helen's presence and her verbal representation. This episode also demonstrates the limitations of interpretations relying exclusively on contemporary knowledge of rhetoric and cognition theory: the model of praise effecting a wondrous charismatic presence as a phantasm of light appears to be quite independent of the traditional rhetoric of *evidentia*; and while it has been argued that according to medieval cognition theory there is no categorical difference between mental images evoked through language and mental images evoked through vision, Konrad's stance on this issue is clearly more ambivalent.

CHAPTER 4

Helen

Although the clairvoyants Helenus and Panthus prophesy devastating consequences, the Trojan council agrees to Paris's plan for abducting Helen to shame the Greeks and take revenge for the rape of Hesione (*Trojanerkrieg*, ll. 18942–64). Accompanied by a group of noblemen, Paris sets sail and, with a favourable wind, soon arrives on the island of Citarea. There, the Trojans find a wonderfully ornate temple dedicated to Venus and don their best attire to offer sacrifices to the gods. Paris, who outshines all his men, creates a great stir among the islanders and news of the arrival of the marvellous group and their radiant leader quickly reaches the queen of the realm, who lives in a nearby castle. Curious to see the dazzling strangers with her own eyes, she decides to go down to the temple. At this point Konrad ceremoniously identifies the as yet unnamed queen as Helen. As the cause of the Trojan War anticipated in the prologue (*Trojanerkrieg*, ll. 312–21) and the object of Paris's desire, she has so far remained a figure of significant absence in the text. Now, after nearly twenty thousand verses – almost half of Konrad's fragment – the narration has finally met its thematic centre, the woman who unites the two leitmotifs of the epic, love and war, and epitomizes its pervasive dialectic of beauty and destruction.[1] What follows can undoubtedly be called the poetic core of the *Trojanerkrieg*, the extraordinarily lavish praise and description of Helen, which is even transmitted separately in two *Minnereden*.[2] The passage which

1 Although Lienert concedes that the multitude of narrative strands which do not involve the Greek queen obscure her key position, she still emphasizes Helen's central role in comparison to Benoît (Lienert, 'Helena', 410; *Geschichte und Erzählen*, pp. 219–20). Kellner, on the other hand, argues that the similarity between the text's love stories decentralizes the love between Helen and Paris by making it less special (Kellner, 'Kontinuität und Diskontinuität', 100, 104). A convincing solution to the controversy about Helen's status in the *Trojanerkrieg* is offered by Gebert, who demonstrates that Helen only gradually becomes the centre of the narration, as which she is introduced in the prologue, and fulfils several roles in the meantime. At first she is merely the prize offered to Paris by Venus. Next, she is used as a political tool to take revenge for Hesione's abduction. Only in the second Trojan War does she become the centre of all attention and present herself as the sole reason for the conflict, which was previously depicted as the result of a multitude of causes (Gebert, *Mythos als Wissensform*, pp. 217–24).

2 Lienert, 'Die Überlieferung', p. 327, pp. 347–72, pp. 393–96, pp. 401–02. She also points out that, in contrast to this, the sixteen world chronicles that include excerpts from the

frequently metaphorizes Helen as the object of artistic creation is quite clearly a display of accomplished poetic artistry, designed to compete with and outdo even the most illustrious predecessors, most importantly Gottfried, from whose description of Isolde it obviously draws inspiration.[3] Beyond this self-reflexive potential of *descriptio* per se, the passage is furthermore stylized as the point at which Konrad's metapoetic concerns accumulate. Correspondences to the prologue and to the *Goldene Schmiede* characterize the representation of Helen as the ultimate test of his poetic capacities.

In order to appreciate the metapoetic dimension of the description it is crucial to bear in mind that it is framed by and interlaced with Paris's experience of Helen's presence and his reflections on both the power and the inadequacy of Helen's praise. This chapter will therefore build on the results of the previous one, which demonstrates that Konrad employs the standard story element of Paris's *Fernminne* for Helen in a unique way to draw attention to the mediality of his own text. The intricate connection between story and discourse created by the fact that both Paris and the narrator express the ineffability of Helen's beauty is knitted together even more closely when both Paris and the narrator become her laudators. The first analytical part of this chapter will therefore discuss the effect of this curious doubling and describe the tension that exists between the proclaimed ineffability of the most beautiful woman of all time and her status as a celebrated literary icon whose reputation transcends time and space and successfully emulates the effects of her presence. The relationship of this tension with the paradoxical descriptions of Helen's ontological status as a natural being, as artifice and as the antithesis of artificiality will be analysed in the following section. The next section will identify the sources for Helen's description and discuss the question whether the abundance of detail is meant to create an image in the mind of the reader or results in a-visuality. Opting for a semiotic rather than mimetic reading of the description, the significance of Helen's blinding radiance will then be discussed as an expression of the nexus between beauty and destruction as well as an ineffability metaphor of theological provenance. Finally, the eccentric image of the rainbow-coloured Paris will be interpreted as a concretized metaphor that highlights the limits of metaphorical expression. To create a basis for these discussions a brief overview of the passage's content and its complex structure of repetition and variation will first be given.

Trojanerkrieg concentrate on the 'historiographical' facts of the text instead and show no interest in this rhetorical showpiece.

3 Lienert, *Geschichte und Erzählen*, p. 100. This passage also contains some details from the description of Engeltrut in Konrad's *Engelhard*, ll. 2962–3102.

Summary

Konrad's eulogy of Helen can be divided into three parts. In the first, Konrad praises Helen as the pinnacle of female perfection and places his own portrayal in the context of a long literary tradition (*Trojanerkrieg*, ll. 19684–751). The second part narrates the effect of Helen's beauty on Paris and contains his rhetorically ornate praise of her (an addition to the narrative made by Konrad),[4] which closely resembles her appraisal by the narrator: Helen is superior to all women, who seem like artifice compared to her; she is the ultimate masterpiece of Wish personified; her beauty escapes visual perception (*Trojanerkrieg*, ll. 19782–867). Like Venus's praise of Helen, which declares the Greek queen the peerless crown of all women yet does not contain any concrete details about her looks (*Trojanerkrieg*, ll. 2654–73), the praise of Helen by the narrator and by Paris remains abstract and relative to other women. Both passages not only mirror and validate but also complement one another. The highly mediated account of Helen as an already verbalized phenomenon in the first part draws authority from its reference to a long written tradition and its transtemporal and global vantage point, whereas Paris's immediate reaction to Helen's corporeal presence confirms the narrator's judgements with the authority of an eye-witness report. The third and longest part of the eulogy consists of the actual, concrete description of Helen (*Trojanerkrieg*, ll. 19868–20317). Konrad extends it significantly in comparison to Benoît, who praises Helen as the richest, most beautiful and most intelligent woman without providing any details of her looks.[5] The superlative description of Helen can itself be further subdivided into the description of her body (*Trojanerkrieg*, ll. 19902–20045) and of her exotic attire (*Trojanerkrieg*, ll. 20055–281). It is framed and interwoven with ineffability and modesty topoi: 'daz wol geprîset werde ir nase, | dar zuo bin ich vil gar ze tump' (*Trojanerkrieg*, ll. 19936–37); 'wie möht ich gar besunder | entsliezen ir geferte?' (*Trojanerkrieg*, ll. 20004–05); 'solt ich si prîsen tûsent jâr, | ir lobes kaeme ich z'ende niht' (*Trojanerkrieg*, ll. 20036–37). The transition from body to attire is furthermore marked by reflections on the effect that Helen has on her literary audience, whom she relieves of sorrow and pain (*Trojanerkrieg*, ll. 20046–54). Konrad describes Helen's body *de capite ad calcem*, from her curly golden hair and her beautiful face with black eyebrows, rosy cheeks, red lips and white teeth, to her elegantly shaped white arms and slim waist, down to her straight legs and perfectly formed feet. Helen's extraordinary and strange beauty is completed by her exotic and wondrous attire. Her coat has been woven by a heathen dwarf from India and

4 Lienert, *Geschichte und Erzählen*, p. 100.
5 Lienert, *Geschichte und Erzählen*, pp. 99–100.

is endowed with magic, so that it changes its colour seven times a day from the whitest white to rose-red, thus beautifully mirroring the perfect interplay of red and white on Helen's face. It is decorated with plants and animals which look as though they are alive. Like Helen herself, whose face shows snow in summer and roses even in winter, her coat cools its wearer in summer and warms her in winter. It is lined with the skin of a strange Oriental beast called Dindialus. The narrator explains at some length that Dindialus cannot bear the heat of the sun and because it always seeks out shade it can easily be caught by trappers erecting artificial trees. Its shining skin is multicoloured and has a pleasant odour. Under this coat Helen wears a snugly fitting dress that exposes her blindingly radiant décolleté and is hemmed with the skin of a fish from one of the rivers of Paradise. On her head Helen wears a golden chaplet covered by a silk headscarf.

Re-telling Helen

Both the decision to describe Helen as Paris encounters her for the first time as well as the detailed account of his reaction – especially his soliloquy – create a focalized effect that invites the reader to identify with the experience of the Trojan prince. Although the first part, with its appreciation of Helen as a literary phenomenon, represents a marked transgression of Paris's perspective, this initial focus on Helen as a verbal entity creates an overall structure for the passage that mimics the structure of Paris's encounter with Helen. Like the Trojan prince, who hears Helen's praise before he sees her, the recipient is not immediately confronted with a detailed description of the queen's beauty, but with the narrator's appreciation of Helen's fame:

> wie si genennet waere,
> daz künde ich iu mit rede sâ:
> ez was diu lûter HELENÂ,
> diu PÂRÎSE was gelobet.
> ir lop noch allen frouwen obet
> ze KRIECHEN unde ouch anderswâ. (*Trojanerkrieg*, ll. 19678–83)

Here Konrad obviously plays with the polysemy of the verb *loben*. By juxtaposing it to the noun *lop* he draws attention to the fact that Helen has not only been promised to Paris but that it was her praise that has brought him to Citarea. The pun serves as a reminder that Helen has entered the narration as a verbalized beauty: calling Helen's name means calling up a long tradition of her praise that reaches back into the narrated world itself. In setting out to compose his own praise of Helen, Konrad becomes the successor to Venus, who praised Helen to Paris so effectively that he fell in love with her. Helen is not just a visual phenomenon, an outstanding beauty that Konrad has to capture with words, but exists already as a poetic phenomenon celebrated in books and songs by wise men:

> swaz man von frouwen ie gesprach
> an buochen unde an lieden,
> dâ lopten unde schieden
> die wîsen ûz ir schoenen lîp
> vür alliu minneclichiu wîp.
> Ir name an êren unde an lobe
> fuor ie den besten frouwen obe
> und muoz ouch ob in iemer farn
> gelîch dem wilden adelarn,
> der sweimet in den wolken. (*Trojanerkrieg*, ll. 19722–31)

Helen's literary fame is an all-encompassing phenomenon that transcends time and space as well as cultural and religious boundaries. She is venerated in the writings of Christian priests, Jewish scrolls and the letters of Saracens:

> der pfaffen schrift, der JUDEN rodel
> und aller SARRAZÎNE brief
> diu sagent von dem wunder tief,
> daz von êren und von tugent
> was an ir keiserlichen jugent
> und an ir werden lîp gewant. (*Trojanerkrieg*, ll. 19746–51)

The reference to numerous documents proclaiming Helen's unsurpassed excellence endows Konrad's proclamation of her superior status with authority. At the same time this long literary tradition is also a challenge, although at first it is presented – albeit ironically – as relieving Konrad's poetic burden. Helen's praise is so pervasive that any effort to add his own voice to the chorus appears futile, especially since he claims to lack the skills to do so appropriately:

> man rüemet hie, dort unde dâ
> ir lîp, ir leben unde ir art,
> daz mir der kumber ist gespart,
> daz ich hie sage ir hôhen prîs,
> dar zuo bin ich niht vollen wîs
> an sinne und an vernünste.
> ich dörfte wol der künste,
> der SALOMÔNES herze pflac,
> solt ich den ruom, der an ir lac,
> entsliezen gar ze tiute. (*Trojanerkrieg*, ll. 19684–93)

The topical reference to Solomon, paragon of wisdom and supposed composer of the Song of Songs, emphasizes the extraordinary demands of the task as the ultimate praise of female perfection. In the rhetorical contest of the goddesses on Mount Olympus, the Old Testament king exemplifies wisdom, the principle which is represented by Pallas (*Trojanerkrieg*, ll. 1990–93, ll. 2044–49). He is also mentioned alongside David as a musical composer (*Trojanerkrieg*, ll. 30804–09). However, Solomon's exemplarity is ambivalent because he has also been named by Venus, alongside David, Adam and Samson, as a famous slave of love whose proverbial wisdom was defeated by her power:

> waz möhte SALOMÔNES list
> gehelfen wider mîne kraft?
> mîn lêre diu wart sigehaft
> an sîner hôhen künste grôz. (*Trojanerkrieg*, ll. 2164–67)[6]

Does, therefore, the appropriate praise of Helen require a background of personal experience as a lover? Paris, who has been an 'eigenlicher kneht' (*Trojanerkrieg*, l. 2749) of love since he cast his vote in favour of Venus and whose innate wisdom had no influence on this decision, would then have particular authority as a laudator, an authority that would also reflect back on the narrator whose praise accords with Paris's statements. In addition to this, the association with Solomon's role as a slave of love also foregrounds the darker aspect of Helen's beauty: her ideal poet would be a man who knows what it means to lose his mind because of love.

Konrad's argument that Helen has been praised so often that he does not need to praise her again is reminiscent of Gottfried's refusal to describe the splendour of Tristan and his peers at the investiture ceremony. There, the narrative problem lies with the author's position at the end of a long literary tradition rather than with a lack of talent or the ineffability of the object of

6 Solomon is also depicted in this role in *Partonopier*: 'her Salomôn den schaden kôs | durch diu wîp und ir gebot, | daz er die valschen abgot | mit willen gar muost ane beten' (*Partonopier*, ll. 8892–95). This weakness is also reported by Augustine: like Adam, who was tempted to disobedience by Eve although he knew that he was committing a sin, Solomon was tempted to serve idols by female persuasion despite knowing better (Augustine, *The City of God against the Pagans*, trans. by George E. McCracken and others, 7 vols, Loeb Classical Library, 411–416 (Cambridge, MA: Harvard University Press, 1961–72), XIV, 11). The representation of Solomon in the *Trojanerkrieg* is also discussed by Gebert: 'Salomo wird [...] im Streitgespräch der Göttinnen nacheinander als Exempel brotloser Weisheit (Juno), unverlierbarer Weisheit (Pallas) oder ohnmächtiger Weisheit (Venus) herangezogen, die der Liebe unterliegt – als Exempel aber wird die Salomoreferenz mit einem solchen Aussagehorizont instabil' (Gebert, *Mythos als Wissensform*, p. 131). Gebert also argues that the appropriate interpretation of, and application of examples to a certain life-situation are frequently subject to debate in the *Trojanerkrieg* (Gebert, *Mythos als Wissensform*, pp. 428–34).

description. The poet has to compete against many predecessors, with the added disadvantage that it is difficult to say anything that has not been said before:

> ine weiz, waz ich dâ von gesage,
> daz iu gelîche und iu behage
> und schône an disem mære stê.
> wan bî mînen tagen und ê
> hât man sô rehte wol geseit
> von werltlîcher zierheit,
> von rîchem geræte:
> ob ich der sinne hæte
> zwelve, der ich einen hân,
> mit den ich umbe solte gân,
> und wære daz gevüege,
> daz ich zwelf zungen trüege
> in mîn eines munde,
> der iegelîchiu kunde
> sprechen, alse ich sprechen kan,
> ine wiste wie gevâhen an,
> daz ich von rîcheite
> sô guotes iht geseite,
> mane hæte baz dâ von geseit.
> jâ ritterlîchiu zierheit
> diu ist sô manege wîs beschriben
> und ist mit rede alsô zertriben,
> daz ich niht kan gereden dar abe,
> dâ von kein herze vröude habe. (*Tristan*, ll. 4597–620)

Of course, this difficult starting position as a latecomer, the daunting legacy of the authors praised in the literary excursus (*Tristan*, ll. 4821–58) and the fact that many before him have failed at the same task ('dar an sich alsô manic man | versuochet und verpirset hât' (*Tristan*, ll. 4926–27)) only serve to emphasize Gottfried's eventual triumph in managing to say something new and even better by eloquently rejecting a conventional description of outer splendour in favour of the more appropriate allegorical depiction of Tristan being clothed by his virtues. Likewise, Konrad's early admission of the futility of his poetic efforts in the face of a grand literary tradition is certainly not his last word on the subject. On the contrary, he soon announces his intention to tackle the challenge of paying tribute to Helen, however hopeless his attempts may prove, and begs the benevolent audience to accept his best efforts for the accomplished deed:

des bite ich werde liute,
daz si mir niht verkêren,
ob ich nâch vollen êren
ir lop niht müge ergründen.
ir prîs den wil ich künden
mit worten, als ich beste kan,
dâ sol ein wol bescheiden man
erkennen unde merken bî,
daz mîn gemüete lûter sî
und ich daz beste gerne tuo.
leg ich der werke niht dar zuo,
doch tuon ich reinen willen schîn
und lobe die glanzen künigîn
gern unde wol nâch mîner state. (*Trojanerkrieg*, ll. 19694–707)[7]

The semantic peculiarities of the terms *lop* and *prîs* mean that it is unclear whether Konrad announces his intention to praise Helen's excellence or to extol and increase her already verbalized fame: in fact, he proceeds to do both. The two modes of Helen's existence, as a visual and a verbal phenomenon, are, of course, closely linked. The excellence of her transient (and absent) corporeality is the cause of her transtemporal and omnipresent fame, which in turn proves the excellence of her corporeality. It is remarkable that Helen's ineffable and visually overwhelming beauty does not produce silence but potentially never-ending praise, not only by the narrator and his predecessors, but also by her intradiegetic beholder Paris.

The narrator's commitment to attempting a task that may never be fulfilled recalls his announcement in the prologue of his desire to compose the master of all stories that will push his artistic capacities to its limits and beyond. In fact, the phrasing of this passage suggests that representing Helen appropriately is the ultimate test of his artistic ability and will determine the success of his grand project: 'Konrad verwendet für die inkommensurable Schönheit seiner Heldin nahezu das gleiche Bild [...] wie für die Inkommensurabilität seines ganzen Stoffes'.[8] Again, the strenuous work of the poet is described as 'kumber' (*Trojanerkrieg*, l. 215; l. 19686) and the ever-elusive object of this effort of *ergründen* is metaphorized as a bottomless abyss: 'ir schoene was sô bodenlôs, | daz man niht grundes drinne sach' (*Trojanerkrieg*, ll. 19720–21; also 'wunder tief' (*Trojanerkrieg*, l. 19748, ll. 219–29, ll. 240–43).[9] The

7 In the prologue of the *Goldene Schmiede* Konrad addresses a similar appeal to the Virgin: 'davon du, frouwe, enphahen solt | den guoten willen für diu werc' (*Goldene Schmiede*, ll. 106–07).

8 Lienert, 'Helena', 411.

9 The admission of not being able to fathom Helen's *lop* also recalls earlier ineffability topoi in the descriptions of Medea: 'mit worten ich ir saelde niht | durchgründe noch durchglôse'

metaphor of unfathomable beauty anticipates the destructive effect of Helen's charms, but it is also a metaphor for the poetic risk of Konrad's undertaking, which is similar to the peril of navigating and fathoming the wild and deep ocean of the grand story. In the *Goldene Schmiede* a similar metaphor of the visually unfathomable is closely linked to the expression of poetic ineffability:

du bildær unde exempel,
daran diu werlt ie wunder kos,
din wunder ist so bodemlos
daz aller engel sinne
grundes niht darinne
kiesent noch erreichent.
bi dir ist uns bezeichent
so manec sache wilde,
daz nieman din unbilde
mit worten mac volenden. (*Goldene Schmiede*, ll. 558–67)[10]

Since the bottom of the Virgin's mystery is inaccessible even to the superior senses of the angels, the poet's inability to represent her essential aniconicity ('unbilde') verbally is not a personal failure but an ontological inevitability. A further correspondence between Helen's praise and the poetic task of composing the *Trojanerkrieg* is the paradoxical coupling of unfathomable depth with unreachable height: the mighty river of the story is so endlessly deep that it can swallow the highest mountain (*Trojanerkrieg*, ll. 222–25); and Helen's name flies above the clouds like an eagle and her beauty is so deep that its bottom cannot be seen. In the latter case the reversal from height into depth marks the categorical transition from a visual phenomenon that is now absent into a verbal phenomenon which continues to survive. Together, both images express Helen's utter inaccessibility. However, the combination of two radically opposed images for the same concept also presents the adequate expression of ineffability itself as a poetic challenge. This principle is expressed even more poignantly in the *Goldene Schmiede*, which employs the same oppositional images (high flying eagle; deep ocean) to express not only the ineffability of the Virgin but also the ultimate inadequacy of the spatial ineffability metaphors themselves:

ob iemer uf ze berge flüge
min rede alsam ein adelar,

(*Trojanerkrieg*, ll. 7526–27); and Deidamia: 'diu saelde was sô manicfalt, | der ein wunder an ir lac, | daz ich mit rede niht enmac | ir lop entsliezen noch gezeln' (*Trojanerkrieg*, ll. 14636–39).

10 It is interesting that the Virgin is addressed as a visible example despite being ineffable and unfathomable even to the senses of the angels. She is 'bildær' as well as 'unbilde'.

din lob enkünde ich niemer gar
mit sprüchen überhœhen.
sus kan din wirde enphlœhen
so verre sich den sinnen min,
daz ich den hohen eren din
niemer mac genahen.
so min gedanc wil gahen
uf ze dime werden lobe,
so sweimet ez dem himel obe
reht als ein vlückez vederspil:
swenn aber ich hieniden wil
mit gedanken suochen ez,
so reichet siner tiefe mez
für allez abgründe. (*Goldene Schmiede*, ll. 16–31)[11]

The paradox fundamental to the eulogy of Helen is that she is presented as something that cannot be grasped by words and something that is already a verbal and literary phenomenon which exercises an astonishing power. In the story her reputation has the power to transgress the spatial distance between her and Paris and, as a substitute for her visible corporeal presence, make him fall in love with her. Likewise, her literary fame emulates the impact her beauty has on onlookers. It lifts up the heart and destroys sorrow:

jô wirt noch hiute von ir sage,
sô man si nennen hoeret,
sorg unde leit zerstoeret
eim iegelichen manne,
sîn herze im eine spanne
wirt hôher ûf gerücket,
swâ man ze liehte zücket
ir namen und die saelikeit,
der wunder was an si geleit. (*Trojanerkrieg*, ll. 20046–54)

als von der heizen sunnen
versmelzen muoz der rîfe kalt,

11 The combination of two opposite metaphors of spatial inaccessibility is of biblical origin, for example, Psalm 36. 5–6: 'Your steadfast love, O Lord, extends to the heavens, your faithfulness to the clouds. Your righteousness is like the mighty mountains, your judgements are like the great deep' (compare Job 11. 7–9; Ephesians 3. 18, where God is described as deep and high, long and wide). While the opposition of depth and height suggests mutual exclusivity, the combination with further spatial metaphors expresses God's omnipresence as a limitless extension into all directions (compare: 'dine glanzer reinekeit: | diu was so tief so lanc so breit | und also gar unmazen her, | daz nieman dich getorste mer | besliezen in daz herze sin | wan got, der aller tugende schin | mit hohen eren überobet' (Konrad, *Goldene Schmiede*, ll. 1189–95) – the limitless purity of the Virgin can only be comprehended by God).

sus wart dâ sorge manicfalt
verswendet von ir bilde.
[...]
vil trûrens wart geringet,
dô si kom zuo des tempels tor,
sich lupfte manic herze enbor,
daz in leide was gelegen (*Trojanerkrieg*, ll. 20304–17)[12]

The effect of destroying sorrow and pain is addressed in the prologue of the *Trojanerkrieg* as one of the functions of good poetry (*Trojanerkrieg*, ll. 200–01).[13] In a similar way to Gottfried's Tristan and Isolde, who live on after their deaths through the reception of their story (*Tristan*, ll. 218–40), Helen's excellence survives in the medium of language. Far from being an imperfect re-presentation, her literary praise carries with it the same affective potential as her presence. In some way her fame is, in fact, even superior to her physical presence, because it transcends temporal, spatial and cultural boundaries (*Trojanerkrieg*, ll. 19682–85, ll. 19727–31, ll. 19746–51). Another important difference that elevates Helen's verbal existence above her visual existence – and thus contrasts markedly with Paris's necessarily short-sighted declaration of the superiority of her presence over her praise – is the fact that while both cause pleasure, only the latter causes aggression and destruction. This becomes particularly evident when Helen watches the battle from the walls of Troy and the sight of her incites the Greeks to fight even harder:

si lûhte zuo dem anger hine
den KRIECHEN alsô klâr engegen,
daz si ze stichen und ze slegen
sich deste faster flizzen,
wan si begunden wizzen
mit ougen und mit muote,
daz HELENÂ, diu guote,
ob in saez an der warte:
des wurden si vil harte
von ir gereizet ûf den strît,
si fâhten alle bî der zît
vil harter, dan si tâten vor. (*Trojanerkrieg*, ll. 34012–23)

The devastating effect of her beauty is emphasized even more when it becomes clear that she does not only motivate but also distracts the fighters and thus causes their deaths in a quite immediate way:

12 This effect is even attributed to the sight of her teeth: 'si kunden herzelichez wê | wol mit ir schîne swachen' (*Trojanerkrieg*, ll. 19974–75)

13 Similarly Konrad von Würzburg, *Partonopier*, l. 58, l. 157; Gottfried von Straßburg, *Tristan*, ll. 73–80.

si zwô [Helen and Polixena] vil manigen feigen
dâ mahten ûf der mûre,
der sich an ir figûre
sô lange dô verkapfte,
daz einer ûf in stapfte
und ungewarnet in ersluoc.
si beide tâten schaden gnuoc
des mâles mit ir bilde. (*Trojanerkrieg*, ll. 39268–75)[14]

Lienert comments on this decisive difference between Helen and her literary fame:

> Die Positivbewertungen sind nur ästhetisch zu verstehen: erzählt, nicht erlebt, schlagen Leid und Tod um in Kunst, und als Kunst-Gegenstand sind sie positiv bewertbar, sind sie schön. [...] nur als Kunstgegenstand, als erzählte Figur, als *name* [...] ist sie für die Späteren als Inbegriff des Schönen und Quell der Freude zu würdigen. [...] Kunstgegenstand allerdings ist Helena nicht zum Selbstzweck [...]; Kunst ist d i e Form der Bewältigung von Leid: umgesetzt in Kunst wird das Verderbliche wieder positiv.[15]

Bearing in mind, however, that the Greeks who fail to realize the didactic potential of Hercules' death pay dearly for their blindness, it appears questionable whether Konrad really envisages such a mainly aesthetic reception for his audience, or whether a more tangible moral lesson, as announced in the prologue, would have been proposed had he finished his work. Such a thesis is also supported by the eschatological allusions that cast the narrated world in a very dubious light. In the passage at hand there is certainly a significant change in tone from the contemporary recipient, who simply and possibly superficially delights in the marvels of Helen's legendary fame, to the closing statement by the narrator, who is deeply grieved by the fact that he has to perpetuate the praise of a woman whose unsurpassed excellence became the cause of unsurpassed suffering:

daz sich mîn zunge pînet
sêr ûf ir lop, daz tuot mir nôt,
sît daz den bitterlichen tôt
durch si leit sô manic lîp,

14 On this scene see Müller, *Höfische Kompromisse*, p. 454. He points out, in the tradition of Worstbrock's thesis of the dissociation of love and knighthood (Worstbrock, 'Der Tod des Hercules', pp. 283–84), that Helen's role as a motivation for heroic deeds cites the traditional role of female beauty in courtly romance but turns it into negative destruction; see also Schulz, *Schwieriges Erkennen*, pp. 471–72.

15 Lienert, 'Helena', 419–20; also 'Der trojanische Krieg in Basel', pp. 277–78; *Geschichte und Erzählen*, pp. 320–22.

daz nie durch keiner slahte wîp
verdarp sô manic hôher man. (*Trojanerkrieg*, ll. 20282–87)[16]

If a positive lesson rather than just aesthetic pleasure were to be gained from Helen's tale, her verbalized beauty – the literary fame of a woman who is not only removed in space but also in time so that she cannot cause further conflict – would really be the positive mirror image of her destructive visual beauty. As in the case of the Apple of Discord and the story of Hercules' death, the limited perspective of the pagan world diverges from the informed view of the extradiegetic Christian audience, who are encouraged to assume *bescheidenheit* as a mode of reception, meaning they should be critical of the narrated world and distinguish good from bad examples.

Helen as a Model Beauty

Helen's extraordinary status is emphasized through comparison. The splendour of the radiant queen outshines the beauty of other women, who seem like a dream, a shadow and lifeless pictorial representation next to her:

reht als ein troum und als ein schate,
sus wâren alliu schoeniu wîp,
swâ man ir wunneclichen lîp
begunde rehte schouwen,
si kunde liehte frouwen
mit ir klârheite blenden.
nû seht, wie von den wenden
erschine ein tôt gemaelde blint,
swâ lebende crêâtiure sint,
sus wâren alle farwe
tôt unde erloschen garwe,
sô man ir lebendez bilde kôs. (*Trojanerkrieg*, ll. 19708–19)

The narrator's statement about Helen's appearance is validated by Paris, who repeats it in slight variation. In a formulation that recalls Venus's praise of Helen ('von fleische noch von bluote | wart nie crêatiure | sô klâr noch sô gehiure | sô diu schoene HELÊNE' (*Trojanerkrieg*, ll. 2664–67)), the narrator first admires her as the pinnacle of all corporeal human beings:

16 A different reading is offered by Lienert: '*sit daz*, w e i l sie so unfaßbares Unheil verursacht hat, muß sich der Erzähler um ihr Lob bemühen' (Lienert, 'Helena', 415). It is, of course, correct that Helen only becomes a worldwide literary phenomenon because of her role in the War, but the more natural reading of the passage would be 'because she has caused so much harm it pains me that I have to praise her'.

swaz ie von wîbes molken
ze fleische und ouch ze beine wart,
daz was ein wint an reiner art
biz an daz spilnde wunder,
daz an ir lac besunder
von ûzerwelter klârheit. (*Trojanerkrieg*, ll. 19732–37)

Paris then goes a step further by stating that all of God's creation, apart from his strange and wonderful creation Helen, is 'kunterfeit', an artificial copy, or even deceptive forgery:

swaz got an sîne hantgetât
rîliches wunders hât geleit,
daz allez ist ein kunterfeit
biz an den wunderlichen flîz,
den er ân allen itewîz
an ir figûren hât gewant. (*Trojanerkrieg*, ll. 19818–23)

Applied to God's creation this qualification seems odd, even blasphemous. After all, everything that God creates is by definition original while only man's limited creation could ever be described as forgery or lifeless imitation.[17] Lienert is certainly correct in stating that 'die überschwengliche Hyperbolik weckt den Eindruck einer Vollkommenheit, wie sie real nicht existieren kann', an observation she makes in a section entitled 'Ästhetik des Imaginären'.[18] Nonetheless, it must be clarified that at this point Helen is emphatically distinguished from any notion of the artificial ('tôt gemaelde', 'kunterfeit') or imaginary ('troum'), but is instead depicted as a being of heightened, original reality, a creature of flesh and blood who relates to ordinary women just as God's original creation does to man's dead mimetic artifice. She is also compared to natural phenomena such as roses, lilies, swans, snow and the sun. The hem of her dress, which is made from blue fish skin, may appear artificial but is in fact neither 'getröufet noch gemâlet' (*Trojanerkrieg*, l. 20255) but grown naturally.[19]

17 On the distinction of divine creation *ex nihilo* from human artifice that can only imitate nature and work with existing material, see Hugh of St Victor: 'opus Dei est, quod non erat creare [...]. opus naturae, quod latuit ad actum producere [...]. opus artificis est disgregata coniungere vel coniuncta segregare' (*Didascalicon*, I, 9) [The work of God is to create that which was not [...]; the work of nature is to bring forth into actuality that which lay hidden [...]; the work of the artificer is to put together things disjoined or to disjoin those put together] (*Didascalicon*, p. 55); see also Thomas Aquinas, *Summa theologiae*, I q 45 a 2 c.

18 Lienert, *Geschichte und Erzählen*, p. 285.

19 Gebert interprets this detail as a description that serves to make the tension between 'fremdreferentieller und selbstreferentieller Produktivität' and between art and nature invisible in order to collapse the difference between 'Darstellung und Dargestellte[m]' rather

This puzzling description can be explained on the basis of the Platonic theory of Ideas and its Christian adaptations. Plato does not develop his theory consistently but in many different writings; he also uses diverse expressions for the same concept. The basic model that became extraordinarily influential in Western philosophy, however, is the distinction between the metaphysical and divine ideas and the material world that can be perceived sensually. Crucially, ideas are not understood as mere intellectual abstractions as in Stoic philosophy, but thought to possess a higher reality than the material cosmos. They are the ontologically superior, perfect, immutable, trans-temporal and trans-spatial model for the creation of the transient and imperfect elements of the world of substances, which are hence subsidiary copies. This theory became relevant to Christianity primarily through the works of Augustine, who argues that the ideas exist in God's mind or *logos* and provide the model for all creation. Like Plato, he emphasizes the superior reality of the transcendent ideas and regards them as the true object of knowledge which can only be accessed through the interior senses. According to Augustine, these acts of inner vision depend on divine illumination. Another important source for the reception of the Platonic theory of ideas is the unfinished translation and commentary of the *Timaeus* dialogue by Caldicius.[20] He uses the terms *species* (*principalis/prima*), *archetypa* and *exemplum* (*archetypum/genuinum*) to refer to the ideas which he describes as the thoughts of God the Creator; and the terms *imagines*, *simulacra*, *species* (*nativa*, *sensilis*) to denote the world of Creation that is of a lesser, derived reality. In Christian philosophy the theory of Ideas is often illustrated with the image of God as an *artifex* planning His creation out in His mind before executing it, just like an architect who designs the house before he builds it.[21]

Helen obviously differs from a Platonic Idea in being herself a creation of the *deus artifex* and a sensually perceptible corporeal being, yet she is presented as the idea of beauty in relation to other women, an absolute beauty

---

than exposing it (as I would argue) (Gebert, *Mythos als Wissensform*, pp. 489–90).

20 Other important sources for the medieval reception of Plato's theory are the works of Pseudo-Dionysius the Areopagite, Boethius – especially his description of God creating the world as a copy of the *supernum exemplum* – and Martianus Capella.

21 On the Platonic theorie and its tradition, see H. Meinhardt and others, 'Idee', in *Historisches Wörterbuch der Philosophie*, ed. by Joachim Ritter and Karlfried Gründer, 13 vols (Basel: Schwabe, 1971–2007), IV (1976), cols 55–134 (cols 55–102); Matthias Baltes, 'Idee (Ideenlehre)', in *Reallexikon für Antike und Christentum: Sachwörterbuch zur Auseinandersetzung des Christentums mit der antiken Welt*, ed. by Ernst Dassmann and others, 24 vols (Stuttgart: Hiersemann, 1950–2012), XVII (1996), cols 213–46. An important source for the Platonic theory of Ideas was the dialogue *Timaeus*, for example passages 29–30 (Plato, *Timaeus, Critias, Cleitophon, Menexenus, Epistles*, ed. by R. G. Bury, Loeb Classical Library, 234 (Cambridge, MA: Harvard University Press, 1929; repr. 1966).

that cannot be surpassed. She is the model and they are her imperfect copies. The description of Helen as a 'lebendez bilde' is appropriated from Gottfried's description of Isolde, where it describes the perfect harmony of the exquisitely sewn clothing and the exquisite body of the bearer, which has been turned by the personified Love:

> diu zwei, gedræt unde genæt,
> diu'n vollebrâhten nie baz
> ein lebende bilde danne daz. (*Tristan*, ll. 10954–56)

Gottfried's metaphor highlights the tension between Isolde as a living human being and an artificial product, an ambivalent poetic ontology that presents itself solely to the extradiegetic audience.[22] In contrast to this, the same expression in the *Trojanerkrieg* relates to the impression of an intradiegetic beholder and serves to distinguish Helen from artifice by presenting her as the original *exemplum* of superior reality from which the re-presentations of the other women are derived.[23] As a literary phenomenon and the epitome of beauty, Helen furthermore transcends time and space. She is no longer accessible to the exterior senses but only to the eyes of the mind and her extreme radiance renders her invisible even to her contemporaries: seeing her is indeed a process of illumination.

On the other hand, this depiction of Helen as the transcendent idea of beauty and as a natural beauty contrasts markedly with the repeated metaphorical description of her as an artefact. Her hair is like spun gold, her curls like gold wire, her complexion painted, her waist turned ('gedrât') like Isolde's figure. She is described as the creation of Wish, an agent which suggests Helen's imaginary status and does not seem very different from the dream

22 The opposite case of artifice that appears alive, which could also be described as a *lebendez bilde* (in the description of Helen this applies to the plants and animals depicted on Helen's coat), is discussed by Laude with reference to the saddle cloth of Enite's horse representing mankind: 'geworht von selher meisterschaft | sam si wolde sprechen | und bildes reht brechen' (Hartmann von Aue, *Erec*, ll. 7607–09) (Laude, 'Quelle als Konstrukt', pp. 223–33). She interprets it as a very unconventional concept of masterful artistry that is implicitly identified with Hartmann's poetic creation: 'Diese Transgression, die Überschreitung der Bildhaftigkeit in Richtung auf wirkliche, autonome Lebendigkeit des menschlichen Artefakts und damit auf tatsächliche *creatio* durch den menschlichen *artifex*, ist freilich nur angedeutet, ist im "Als-Ob" [...] allein als Potentialität vorgestellt' (Laude, 'Quelle als Konstrukt', p. 227).

23 On the semantics of *bilde*, see Wandhoff, 'Zur Bildlichkeit mittelalterlicher Texte', pp. 3–4; the semantics of the term in the *Trojanerkrieg* are discussed by Bleumer, 'Zwischen Wort und Bild', pp. 131–33. He distinguishes it from the mimetic 'Abbild' and states: '*bilde* ist im *Trojanischen Krieg* alles, was sich in besonderer Weise der Betrachtung darbietet und eine Verweisbeziehung des Sichtbaren mit einer Bedeutung anknüpft' (Bleumer, 'Zwischen Wort und Bild', p. 132).

quality attributed to the other women. While Helen is initially presented as the model according to which the pictorial re-presentations of the other women are fashioned, she is now described as the ultimate masterpiece of Wish, who constructs her on the basis of many models: 'dô sîn gewalt ir bilde maz, | dô leite er an si manic model' (*Trojanerkrieg*, ll. 19744–45).[24]

A possible source for Konrad's contradictory depiction of Helen might be a myth about the ancient painter Zeuxis that was transmitted in Pliny's *Natural History* and, even more prominently, in Cicero's *De inventione*,[25] one of the main sources of rhetoric in the Middle Ages: asked to decorate the temple of Juno by the wealthy citizens of Croton, Zeuxis decides to paint a picture of Helen that contains all female beauty in one image: 'ut exellentem muliebris formae pulcritudinem muta in se imago contineret, Helenae pingere simulacrum velle dixit' [[H]e [...] said that he wished to paint a picture of Helen so that the portrait though silent and lifeless might embody the surpassing beauty of womanhood]. To achieve this feat, the painter asks to choose models among the most beautiful girls of the city, 'ut mutum in simulacrum ex animali exemplo veritas transferatur' [so that the true beauty may be transferred from the living model to the mute likeness]. He then selects not one, but five models to combine their features into an image of ideal beauty: 'Neque enim putavit omnia, quae quaereret ad venustatem, uno se in corpore reperire posse ideo quod nihil simplici in genere omnibus ex partibus perfectum natura expolivit' [He chose five because he did not think all the qualities which he sought to combine in a portrayal of beauty could be found in one person, because in no single case has Nature made anything perfect and finished in every part].

While this story corresponds to Helen's description as an artefact of Wish based on many models, it appears as an exact inversion of the earlier depiction of Helen as a living model for the lifeless pictorial representations of other women and of Platonic theory, according to which the imperfect creation would be modelled on an idea. This contradiction, however, can be alleviated – if not completely resolved – when the working process of Zeuxis is understood as the re-construction of the original, perfect idea of beauty on the basis of the imperfect creation that derives from it. The tension that remains inherent in the Zeuxis myth and Konrad's portrayal despite this explanation is

24 Being a product of Wish does not categorically set Helen apart from the rest of the narrated world, which is also frequently described as the product of Wish, but presents her as its pinnacle. See Lienert: 'alles was positiv ist, die Schönheit der Frauen und des Paris, der Landschaft wie der Städte und Paläste, ist *wunsch* (vgl. z.B. V. 836–37, 1212–13, 1678–79, 7296, 7555, 14620–21, 19738–43, 19844–51, 26996–97 u.ö.)' (Lienert, 'Helena', 417–18).

25 Cicero, *De inventione, De optimo genere oratorum, Topica*, trans. by H. M. Hubbell, Loeb Classical Library, 386 (Cambridge: Havard University Press, 1949; repr. 1960), *De inventione*, II, 1–3.

one between the idea of beauty as an immaterial and non-artificial entity, the cause of creation instead of its result, and as the sensible creation of an artist. Zeuxis's Helena may surpass the beauty of other women and approximate the perfection of the idea of beauty, but remains a mute and lifeless material object.

In medieval poetics Helen is also a model beauty; in this sense, Matthew of Vendôme offers an example for a description of beauty with a description of Helen (*Ars versificatoria*, I, 56–57). More relevant to Konrad's description, however, is Geoffrey of Vinsauf's model description of an anonymous beauty (ll. 562–621). Although similar individual motifs appear in other Middle High German descriptions, the sum of the many, very detailed correspondences and the overall comprehensiveness suggest that Geoffrey is, in fact, an important source for Konrad's description.[26] Apart from the fact that Geoffrey's beauty provides a model for Helen's extreme luminosity (as will be discussed below), both are described from top to toe with the inclusion of the same details, such as golden hair; forehead; dark eyebrows; a perfect nose; shining eyes; a red and white complexion; full, glowing red lips; nicely shaped snow-white teeth; scented breath; a smooth chin; a radiant neck; slender arms and slim, white fingers; breasts; a slender waist and legs and well shaped feet.[27] Whereas Helen's breath smells of nutmeg, the breath of Geoffey's beauty smells of incense (*Poetria nova*, ll. 577–78), yet both complexions show the same perfectly balanced mixture of red and white that cancels out distinct colours:

ein glanziu farwe reine
was ir gestrichen under
und was diu z'eime wunder
mit wîze und ouch mit rôte
vermischet sô genôte,
daz dâ weder rôt noch wîz
bewaeren mohte sînen flîz
mit volleclichem schîne. (*Trojanerkrieg*, ll. 19944–51)

Aemula sit facies Aurorae, nec rubicundae
Nec nitidae, sed utoque simul neutroque colore. (*Poetria nova*, ll. 571–72)

26 Pastré lists Geoffrey as a possible influence in his footnotes but does not comment on the striking similarities between both descriptions (Jean-Marc Pastré, 'Typologie und Ästhetik: Das Porträt der Helena im *Trojanerkrieg* Konrads von Würzburg', *JOWG*, 5 (1988/1989), 397–408).

27 The only details of Geoffrey's description that Konrad does not include are the relaxed shoulders and the nipples that Geoffrey likens to gemstones. Sometimes the comparisons differ: Geoffrey likens the neck to marble, for instance, and Konrad likens it to ivory. Konrad is generally more verbose, referring to the affective power of Helen's charming beauty more frequently. He also adds some details, such as curls in front of the ears and the dimple in the chin. The order of the details is roughly the same but Konrad is less strictly vertical and describes the breasts later, in the context of the description of the dress.

[Let her face rival the dawn, neither red nor bright, but at once both and neither colour (*The New Poetics*, p. 54).]

Like Konrad, Geoffrey emphasizes the tension between natural and artificial processes of creation. The works of nature are metaphorized as artistic creation while the poet is consistently addressed as the ultimate master of the beauty's creation: 'Praeformet capiti Naturae circinus orbem' (*Poetria nova*, l. 563) [Let Nature's compass describe first a circle for her head (*The New Poetics*, p. 54)]; or 'mentumque polito | Marmore plus poliat Natura potentior arte' (*Poetria nova*, ll. 578–79) [And let Nature, more potent than art, polish her chin more highly than polished marble (*The New Poetics*, p. 54)]. At the end of Geoffrey's description it turns out that the beauty is nameless for a reason: she is not a corporeal woman but the idea of beauty. If Jupiter had seen her he would not have been interested in any of his many lovers, because she encompasses all of them: 'Hanc unam coleret omnesque videret in una' (*Poetria nova*, l. 621) [He would have courted her alone and seen all other women in a single woman (*The New Poetics*, p. 55)]. Krass accordingly identifies the Platonic philosophy behind this description: 'Am Ende zieht Galfrid eine Bilanz, die auf die neuplatonische Ausrichtung seiner Konzeption von Schönheit verweist. Die Dame, deren Portrait soeben en detail vorgestellt wurde, erweist sich als Inbegriff, als *Idee* der Schönheit'.[28]

While Konrad's depiction of Helen as the idea of beauty clearly relies on prominent models, he modifies and functionalizes their elements in a unique way. Drawing attention to the paradox of the artistic re-presentation as the idea of beauty – for an idea is categorically distinguished from its representation – he highlights the poetic dilemma of describing Helen once more. In addition to this, the depiction of Helen as an ontologically unstable construct between natural creation, artificiality and heightened, explicitly non-artefactual reality can be seen as the equivalent to her ambivalent status as a corporeal being in the story and a poetic artefact that transcends time and space as the idea of absolute beauty.

Poetics of Light and Detail

Corresponding to Konrad's announcement to renew the old book of Troy 'mit worten lûter unde glanz' (*Trojanerkrieg*, l. 275) and to amplify it, the abundance of detail and the emphasis on light in his descriptions have long been recognized as the most striking characteristic of his style. Thus Green declares:

28 See Kraß, *Geschriebene Kleider*, p. 156.

> Wir [dürfen] drei Stilmittel als besonders charakteristisch für Konrad bezeichnen – erstens die Lichtfreude, die alle Personen und Gegenstände mit einem schimmernden, unklar-irrealen Glanz bekleidet, zweitens die Farbfreude, die einerseits Konrads Lichtfreude wesensverwandt erscheint, andererseits aber auch seinen Hang zum dritten Stilmittel deutlich kennzeichnet, nämlich seinen Hang zu der gerne beim konkreten Gegenstand verweilenden realistischen Kleinmalerei.[29]

Monecke describes these characteristics as key features of the 'Erzählprinzip der *wildekeit*' (*stilus alienus*), which is further characterized by a preference for the extravagant and exotic, even the monstrous.[30] The description of Helen is undoubtedly the masterpiece of this style. It is not only the longest description of the generally very descriptive *Trojanerkrieg* but also the single most detailed description of female beauty in Middle High German literature, as Pastré emphasizes:

> Mit etwa 25 Angaben übertrifft es an Genauigkeit bei weitem die Porträts der Amurfina, der Blanscheflur, der Isolde, der Helena bei Herbort und der Kamille und hat quantitativ nur in der französischen Maroie aus der Mitte des Jahrhunderts eine Entsprechung (23 Angaben).[31]

Although radiance is possibly the most frequent attribute of all objects and persons in the *Trojanerkrieg*, the description of Helen is clearly the pinnacle of splendour: 'Insgesamt führt [Konrad] so etwa 30 Angaben für das Licht ein, praktisch eine für jedes erwähnte Merkmal, was sein Porträt von allen früheren grundsätzlich unterscheidet'.[32] Pastré interprets the emphasis on light as a reflection of the contemporary association of beauty with light that was influenced by Neo-Platonist concepts such as Albertus Magnus's

29 Green, *Vorstudien zum gotischen Stil*, p. 14.

30 Monecke, *Das Erzählprinzip der 'wildekeit'*, pp. 152–81. See also the sections on 'Ästhetik der Fülle und des Details' and on 'Ästhetik des Lichts und des Schillerns' in Lienert, *Geschichte und Erzählen*, pp. 271–81.

31 Pastré, 'Typologie und Ästhetik', 406. Pastré not only catalogues parallels in Middle High German, French and Latin literature for the details that Konrad describes, but also emphasizes uncommon or completely unprecedented details, such as the golden curls behind the ears or a dimple in the chin. He further points out that the exhaustiveness with which Konrad describes Helen systematically from head to toe differs from the practice of other German authors, who tend to highlight evocative details (Pastré, 'Typologie und Ästhetik', 397–99). For an overview of the descriptions of persons in Middle High German literature, see also Barbara Haupt, 'Der schöne Körper in der höfischen Epik', in *Körperinszenierungen in mittelalterlicher Literatur*, ed. by Klaus Ridder and Otto Langer, Körper, Zeichen, Kultur, 11 (Berlin: Weidler, 2002), pp. 47–73; Kraß, *Geschriebene Kleider*, especially pp. 169–92.

32 Pastré, 'Typologie und Ästhetik', 407. For the emphasis on light and the motif of blinding radiance in the description of protagonists in Konrad's other works, see Schulz, *Schwieriges Erkennen*, pp. 354–455.

resplendita or Thomas Aquinas's *claritas*.[33] As mentioned above, a more immediate influence might be Geoffrey of Vinsauf's model description of beauty. Geoffrey emphasizes the radiance of nearly every detail of the body as well as the attire; splendour encompasses his anonymous lady from head to toe: 'A summo capitis descendat splendor ad ipsam | Radicem' (*Poetria nova*, ll. 598–99) [And thus let beauty [more literally: light] descend from the top of the head to the very roots (*The New Poetics*, p. 55)]. Her neck emits rays of light which penetrate the heart of the beholder, just as Helen's radiant beauty violently enters Paris's heart:

> Ex cristallino procedat gutture quidam
> Splendor, qui possit oculos referire videntis
> Et cor furari. (*Poetria nova*, ll. 582–84)
>
> [From her crystal throat let a kind of radiance go forth which can strike the eyes of the beholder and madden his heart (*The New Poetics*, p. 54).]

Geoffrey's description of the lady's dress is simple compared to Konrad's. For this part of Helen's eulogy Konrad apparently draws on a different Latin model, the description of Nature's dress in Alan of Lille's *De planctu naturae*, which is in turn inspired by Boethius's *De consolatione philosophiae*.[34] Nature's diadem, which represents the firmament and is studded with revolving gemstones whose splendour waxes and wanes (*De planctu naturae*, II, P1, 40–137), resembles the way in which Konrad's descriptions of iridescent colours, for example on the Apple of Discord, are presented as dynamic. More importantly, Nature's dress changes colour from white to red to green:

> Vestis uero, ex serica lana contexta, multiphario protheata colore, puelle pepli seruiebat in usum quam discolorando colorans temporum alteritas multiplici colorum facie alterabat. Que primitus candoris lilio dealbata offendebat intuitum. Secundo, uelut penitentia ducta, quasi laborans in melius, ruboris sanguine purpurata splendebat. Tercio, ad cumulum perfectionis uiroris smaragdo oculis applaudebat (*De plactu naturae*, II, P1, 138–43).
>
> [Her dress, woven from silk-smooth wool, kaleidoscopic in its various colours, served the purpose of a robe of office for the maiden. Changing circumstances, which substituted one hue for another, altered the garment with a varied

33 Pastré, 'Typologie und Ästhetik', 406–07. On the identification of beauty with radiance, which is based on the notion that everything beautiful is a reflection of the divine light, see also Kraß, *Geschriebene Kleider*, pp. 149–57.

34 On Boethius's influence on Alan see Sheridan, 'Introduction', in Alan of Lille, *Plaint of Nature*, trans. by James J. Sheridan, Medieval Sources in Translation, 26 (Toronto: Pontifical Institute of Mediaeval Studies, 1980), pp. 1–64 (pp. 62–63).

display of colour. At first whitened to the brightness of a lily, it dazzled the eyes. Secondly, as though moved to repentance and struggling to amend, it shone forth in a blood red colour. Thirdly, at the peak of perfection, it gladdened the eyes with an emerald green (*Plaint of Nature*, pp. 85–86).]

Perhaps Konrad did not include the mediating green colour because he wanted to emphasize the binary structure of Helen's destructive beauty. Apart from the changing hue of Helen's coat and the representation of plants and animals on it,[35] Alan's description of Nature may also have inspired the motif of blinding radiance. Although luminosity is also a prominent characteristic of Geoffrey's beauty, Alan increases the strength of this feature. He emphasizes the endogenous radiance of Nature's hair (*De planctu naturae*, II, P1, 3–5) and states that the splendour of her garment is eclipsed by the star-like beauty of the maiden: 'Hec uestium ornamenta quamuis sue plenis splendititatis flammarent ardoribus, eorundem tamen splendor sub puellaris decoris sidere paciebatur eclipsim' (*De planctu naturae*, IV, P2, 1–3) [Although the ornaments of these garments are on fire with the full glow of their splendour, their brilliance suffered eclipse by comparison with the star like beauty of the maiden (*Plaint of Nature*, p. 108)].[36] Finally, he says that she in fact shines so brightly that he has to close his eyes: 'Ad cuius pulcritudinis dignitatem inuestigadam, dum tamquam manipulos oculorum radios legarem uisibiles, ipsi tante non audentes maiestatis obuiare decori, splendoris hebetati uerberibus, nimis meticulosi ad palpebrarum contubernia refugerunt' (*De planctu naturae*, IV, P2, 14–17) [When I was concentrating my rays of vision or, if I may say so, the troops of my eyes, to explore the glory of this beauty, my eyes, not daring to confront the splendour of such majesty and dulled by the impact of brilliance, in excessive fear, took refuge in the war-tents of my eyelids (*Plaint of Nature*, p. 109)]. With the probable models for Konrad's description identified, we can now turn to the consideration of the effects of his style that have received considerably more attention. Monecke stated: 'Kein mittelhochdeutscher Erzähler füllt das Auge wie Konrad'.[37] Moreover, Pastré remarks that Konrad's abundance of descriptive detail follows French

35 Nature's dress shows all birds, her coat all animals of the sea and her tunic the land animals and man (at this point her dress is torn to signify the degeneration of mankind); and her shoes are decorated with the different kinds of flowers (*De planctu naturae*, II, P1). Helen's dress also shows plants as well as 'tier', 'vogel' and 'fisch' (*Trojanerkrieg*, l. 20104), but this is a common detail in Middle High German descriptions.

36 Konrad says the same about Helen's décolleté: 'ez kunde wol die sîden, | daz golt und daz gesteine | mit sînem glaste reine | getoeten unde erblenden' (*Trojanerkrieg*, ll. 20234–37). Since Geoffrey has the same detail (*Poetria nova*, ll. 605–13), however, it is impossible to say from whom Konrad took it.

37 Monecke, *Das Erzählprinzip der 'wildekeit'*, p. 179.

examples that aim at clarity and precision – a poetics which he connects to contemporary architectural style: 'Genau wie die gotische Baukunst wollte diese Ästhetik, daß alles gesehen wird, daß also alles auch im Kunstwerk zu sehen ist'.[38] Similarly, Müller explains how these qualities aim at giving the recipient the illusion of immediate visual participation in the narrated world:

> His sumptuous descriptions are *demonstrationes ad oculos*, in the sense of the rhetorical concept of *energeia* (*evidentia*). *Energeia* is aiming at a meticulous and vivid picture of reality. An absent object or scene that is represented linguistically is suggested to be present, in the sense that the reader or listener is made to believe that he or she can actually see them. *Ekphrasis* is the literary equivalent of sight in a culture of visuality.[39]

Konrad's description of sensory appeals is, in fact, not limited to visuality alone, as Cormeau points out: 'Neben die vorherrschenden visuellen Eindrücke tritt die Beschreibung von Tönen, Gerüchen, Fühlbarem und macht manche Verspartie zur synästhetischen Komposition von Sinneswahrnehmungen. Konrad erzählt nicht nur illustrierend, sondern ausmalend-imaginativ'.[40] In contrast to this, Green argues that the excess of detail and light results in diffusion rather than clarity:

> Die Häufung solcher Farbeindrücke in einer Reihe bewirkt bei Konrad kein scharf differenziertes, sondern im Gegenteil ein unbestimmt schillerndes Bild, in dem die funkelnde Buntheit des beschriebenen Gegenstands keinen klaren Umriß mehr erkennen läßt. [...] Der Gegenstand selbst [verschwindet] hinter einem glitzernden Lichtspiel in Unbestimmtheit.[41]

This observation of the a-visual effect of the visual excess is still emphasized in recent studies. Thus Lienert speaks of 'Helenas nicht mehr vorstellbare Schönheit' and explains: 'Die Fülle der Details "überwuchert" den beschriebenen Gegenstand, verwischt das Gesamtbild zu einer nicht mehr vorstellbaren Farbigkeit und zu einem abstrakten Glanz'.[42] Müller similarly qualifies his statement about the visuality of Konrad's style:

> Even though Konrad uses all his rhetorical skills to visualize Helen's beauty it would be difficult to paint her. He gives neither clear contours nor too many details; the listener/reader has only a vague idea of her; instead of being able to gaze, he is overwhelmed by the effects of her shining – as are the

38 Pastré, 'Typologie und Ästhetik', 406.

39 Müller, 'Blinding Sight', p. 208.

40 Christoph Cormeau, 'Überlegungen zum Verhältnis von Ästhetik und Rezeption', *JOWG*, 5 (1988/1989), 95–107 (p. 95); also Lienert, *Geschichte und Erzählen*, p. 275.

41 Green, *Vorstudien zum gotischen Stil*, p. 84.

42 Lienert, *Geschichte und Erzählen*, p. 277.

> protagonists. [...] In Konrad's descriptions the body is dissolved in waves of light. [..] In a paradoxical way the abundant visuality (and sensuality) leads to indistinctiveness.[43]

According to interpretations of this kind, Helen's description is really the perversion of the visual poetics that Wenzel in particular has identified as a key feature of courtly literature. He describes the 'Poetik der Visualität' as the literary equivalent of the semi-oral 'Kultur der Sichtbarkeit' of medieval aristocracy and argues that courtly literature tries to emulate the communicative situation of sensory immediacy and body-oriented interaction through 'poetic strategies of visualization': vivid descriptions which are often narrated as the perception of an intradiegetic audience, or the representation of acts of non-verbal communication which stimulate the visual imagination of the recipient to make up for the absence of actual vision and immediate face-to-face interaction.[44] This interpretative approach is also pursued by Wandhoff,[45] sometimes even in explicit opposition to the notion of poetic self-awareness: 'Verblüffend ist [...], daß diese zutiefst in der klerikalen Schriftkultur verwurzelte Literatur nicht etwa ihre eigene Literarizität reflektiert, sondern vielmehr mit großem Aufwand einen epischen Blick generiert, der sich auf die Interaktionsmuster einer weitgehend schriftlosen Adelsgemeinschaft richtet'.[46]

The description of courtly literature as a poetics of visualization has since been criticized by Peters. She questions, first of all, whether the characteristics of this poetics – the representation of non-verbal acts of communication, the intricate choreography of gazes, the semiotic significance of the body and the rhetorical techniques of creating *evidentia* – really distinguish medieval courtly literature categorically from later literatures.[47] She also warns that

43 Müller, 'Blinding Sight', pp. 211–12; also '*schîn* und Verwandtes', pp. 298–303; similarly Lechtermann, 'Figuren der Abhebung', pp. 53–57. The effect of Konrad's style is described in similar terms by Christoph Huber, 'Brüchige Figur: Zur literarischen Konstruktion der Partonopier-Gestalt bei Konrad von Würzburg', in *Literarische Leben*, ed. by Meyer and Schiewer, pp. 283–308 (p. 293); and Butzmann, *Studien zum Sprachstil*, p. 37. The former comments on the description of Meliur's blindingly radiant beauty (*Partonopier*, ll. 7868–908); the latter on the description of her dress.

44 Wenzel, *Hören und Sehen*, p. 340. Wenzel repeats and elaborates this thesis in many works, for example 'Szene und Gebärde'; 'Hören und Sehen'; 'Visualität: Zur Vorgeschichte der kinästhetischen Wahrnehmung', *Zeitschrift für Germanistik*, N.F., 3 (1999), 549–56.

45 For example, Haiko Wandhoff, 'Zur Poetik der Sichtbarkeit in den höfischen Epen des Mittelalters', *Zeitschrift für Germanistik*, N.F., 3 (1999), 586–97, and *Der epische Blick*.

46 Haiko Wandhoff, 'Iweins guter Name: Zur medialen Konstruktion von adliger Ehre und Identität in den Artusromanen Hartmanns von Aue', in *Mittelalter: Neue Wege durch einen alten Kontinent*, ed. by Jan-Dirk Müller and Horst Wenzel (Stuttgart: Hirzel, 1999), pp. 111–26 (p. 126).

47 Ursula Peters, '"Texte vor der Literatur"? Zur Problematik neuerer Alteritätsparadigmen der Mittelalter-Philologie', *Poetica*, 39 (2007), 59–88 (p. 65). For an overview of this branch of

this perspective assigns to courtly literature a merely affirmative role as a 'one-dimensional archival and mnemonic medium of the nobility's didactic processes of self-fashioning'.[48] Most importantly for our context she argues that descriptions often do not aim at the illusion of immediacy, but, on the contrary, expose their own poeticity:

> [Die] Augenzeugen-Rolle des Lesers/Hörers in der höfischen Epik um 1200 [wird] nicht selten geradezu systematisch konterkariert, am deutlichsten in den ausgreifenden Descriptiones, die angesichts ihrer häufigen Erzähler-Einschübe, ihrer merkwürdigen Abschweifungen und ironischen Kommentierungen keine sehr gelungenen Beispiele dokumentarischer Informationsmedien oder Speicherräume kollektiven Wissens sind, jedenfalls weniger auf die *histoire* des Geschehens als die *discours*-Ebene eines Erzählens höfischer *meisterschaft* zielen. Ihr entscheidender Resonanzboden scheint deshalb eher die Literarizität rhetorischer Kunstprogrammatik zu sein als die kultur- und mediengeschichtlichen Gegebenheiten einer Semi-Oralität an den mittelalterlichen Fürstenhöfen.[49]

Bleumer criticizes the same strand of research for undermining the categorical medial difference between text and image through imprecise terminology and inappropriate analogies. He discusses primarily the term 'Bild', which should not be identified with mimetic representation ('Abbild') and can only ever be attributed metaphorically to the non-visual medium of language.[50] He further

research, see also Müller, 'Visualität, Geste, Schrift'; Bleumer, 'Zwischen Wort und Bild', pp. 141–56.

48 Ursula Peters, 'From Social History to the Poetics of the Visual: Philology of the Middle Ages as Cultural History', *Journal of English and Germanic Philology*, 105 (2006), 185–206 (pp. 200–05, here p. 203).

49 Peters, '"Texte vor der Literatur"', 65–66. See also Wandhoff, who has since adjusted his approach and argues that descriptions and the emphasis on visuality and processes of vision in Middle High German literature do not just reflect an aristocratic culture of visuality but frequently serve as 'besonders markierte Orte poetologischer Reflexion' (Haiko Wandhoff, 'Imaginäre Kopfreisen in die Wunderwelt der *âventiure*, oder: Wenn das Sehen zur Allegorie des Lesens wird: Neue Überlegungen zu Hartmanns *Erec* und *Iwein*', in *Sehen und Sichtbarkeit in der Literatur des Mittelalters*, ed. by Bauschke, Coxon and Jones, pp. 141–59 (p. 142)). He makes a similar argument in *Ekphrasis*, where he states that many descriptions do not aim at lending a visual quality to the poetic artefact, but instead make the discourse opaque, so that they become 'Multiplikator der Diskurse über Kunst und Repräsentation, an denen sich der literarische Text abarbeitet' (Wandhoff, *Ekphrasis*, pp. 11–12); see also 'Zur Bildlichkeit mittelalterlicher Texte', pp. 13–15.

50 Bleumer, 'Zwischen Wort und Bild', pp. 141–56. He also criticizes the reverse convention of describing pictures as 'narrative'; the anachronistic concept of space ('Systemraum' versus 'Aggregatraum') which often underlies the metaphor of the 'Bildraum'; and the inappropriate analogies which are drawn to the virtual spaces of computer technology (he refers to Wandhoff, *Ekphrasis*, pp. 333–39); or the actual multi-mediality of cinema. See

argues that the recipient of the *Trojanerkrieg* is not really expected to visualize the narrated world – whose visual excess defies distinct perception and results in blindness – in his mind as a mimetic representation. Instead he is supposed to recognize the abstract semiotic significance of its descriptions and metaphors, such as the overarching motif of radiance and fire that expresses the nexus between beauty and destruction. This distanced, semiotic reading of visual details in fact requires that the recipient is not fully immersed in the illusion of immediate participation.[51] The disturbance of this illusion that is created not through a denial but an excess of visuality also highlights the mediality of the narration: 'Sollte [...] die Visualität in einer Aporie münden, ist der Rezipient auf die narrative Textualität zurückverwiesen. [...] Man sieht bei einer Lektüre des *Trojanischen Krieges* nicht einfach das Erzählte, man sieht auch und zuerst das Erzählen'.[52]

In addition to this effect of Konrad's descriptive style, the introduction of Helen as an already established verbal, mediated beauty as well as the reflections of the narrator and Paris about the impossibility of praising her

---

also Curschmann, who has similar reservations (Michael Curschmann, 'Interdisziplinäre Beweglichkeit – wie weit reicht sie?', *ZfdPh*, 123 (2004), 109–17 (pp. 111–12, p. 116).

51 Bleumer exemplifies this principle, which only comes into its own when the images of the text 'selbst als sprachliche Zeichen begriffen sind' (Bleumer, 'Zwischen Wort und Bild', p. 129), using the symbolically charged description of the fight between Hector and Peleus: 'Der Kampf ist also in praktischer Hinsicht auf die Handlung eine Auseinandersetzung von Hector und Peleus, aber er ist auch und zuerst ein Kampf der Bilder. Deren Bildhaftigkeit wird allerdings erst erreicht, wenn sie selbst als visualisierte Zeichenkomplexe begriffen werden, die gerade keine direkt sichtbaren Abbildungen von Akteuren sind. Als eine solche Bezeichnung des Sichtbaren liefert die Darstellung also keine Simulation der sichtbaren Welt, sondern eine Stimulation einer Bildvorstellung, die nicht mimetisch, sondern zeichenhaft ist' (Bleumer, 'Zwischen Wort und Bild', p. 133).

52 Bleumer, 'Zwischen Wort und Bild', p. 112. Lechtermann interprets the phenomenon of iridescence in particular as a disturbance of the illusion which enables 'die Ostension medialer Bedingtheit' (Lechtermann, 'Figuren der Abhebung', p. 61). See also Monecke: 'Hyperbolik macht den Ausdruck imperativisch: Vergleichbarkeit wird gesetzt und zugleich unmöglich gemacht. Das ist der Grundsatz der höfischen Erzählkunst, ihr eigentümliches Vergegenwärtigungsprinzip, das nicht gestaltend hinstellt, sondern zum Scheinen bringt. Das Bild wird schwebend zwischen einem Unsagbarkeits- und einem Überbietungstopos heraufgerufen. Es beruhigt sich nicht, kommt nicht zu einer festen Kontur' (Monecke, *Das Erzählprinzip der 'wildekeit'*, p. 178). Gebert, on the other hand, argues that although there are metapoetic aspects in the description of Helen, it still evokes a powerful metal image that renders the inevitable tension between the represented object and the act of representation invisible: 'Was *im* Erzählen *präsent* wird, ist *durch* Erzählen präsent *gemacht*' (Gebert, *Mythos als Wissensform*, pp. 472–595 (pp. 473–74)). He interprets the details, such as blinding light, that irritate and challenge the imagination as 'entfesselte Imaginationsanweisungen' which stimulate cognition and enhance the imaginary presence of the described object (Gebert, *Mythos als Wissensform*, p. 491). I would argue, on the contrary, that this tension is exposed in the description.

appropriately also highlight the issue of poetic representation and the medial gap between words and vision to the extent that any illusion of immediate visual participation in the narrated world is compromised. Helen's praise may succeed in emulating the effects of her presence – Paris falls in love with her; her reputation charms a literary audience just as it does her beholders – but this magical presence is not the presence of a mimetic mental image of her concrete looks. If we suppose then that her radiance is, in fact, not supposed to evoke a mental picture, the next question to be asked must be what her radiance signifies in terms of the semiotic reading that Bleumer suggests.

Helen's Light

In addition to Geoffrey's anonymous beauty and the dress of Alan's Nature, Konrad's emphasis on light, his sun simile and the notion of blinding radiance are also clearly influenced by Gottfried's description of Isolde.[53] When Tristan praises Isolde at Mark's court as 'diu lûtere, diu liehte Îsolt | diu ist lûter alse arâbesch golt' (*Tristan*, ll. 8261–62), who illuminates the world from Dublin and radiates into all hearts, he also declares her superiority over Helen:

> ine geloube niemer mê,
> daz sunne von Mycêne gê;
> ganzlîchiu schœne ertagete nie
> ze Criechenlant, si taget hie. (*Tristan*, ll. 8273–76)[54]

Konrad's exaggeration of Helen's luminosity is therefore obviously an attempt to outdo his revered master Gottfried. Even the fact that Helen extinguishes the light of other women is a response to Tristan's praise, which states the opposite about Isolde:

> mit ir enist kein ander wîp
> erleschet noch geswachet,
> als maneger mære machet:
> ir schœne diu schœnet,

53 Lienert, 'Helena', 411, fn. 6. Gebert furthermore points out an analogy to the description of Enite's white skin shining through her torn dress and emphasizes that the description of Helen contains many layers of intertextuality (Gebert, *Mythos als Wissensform*, pp. 488–89).

54 Kern points out that this mythographic reference would have been understandable only to an educated audience, because Gottfried does not name Helen explicitly. He further argues that the description of Isolde as the 'new sun' has Christological connotations and that the transference of the sun from East to West can be seen as a *translatio amoris* akin to the *translatio imperii, artis et militia* (Kern, 'Isolde, Helena und die Sirenen', 7–10).

si zieret unde crœnet
wîp unde wîplichen namen. (*Tristan*, ll. 8294–99)[55]

The metaphor of Isolde as the sun also expresses her superiority over her mother, the dawn (*Tristan*, ll. 8279–84, ll. 10885–91, ll. 11021–22), and Brangaene, the full moon (*Tristan*, ll. 11080–82).[56] Konrad likens Achilles' lover Deidamia, who outshines the other girls on Scyros, to the full moon that outshines the stars (*Trojanerkrieg*, ll. 14608–13) and Deidamia in turn is superseded by Helen among her ladies, who is likened to the sun leading the stars into the temple of Venus:

si kam reht, als diu sunne
dort her durchliuhteclîchen schine
und mit ir in daz tempel hine
wolt alle sterne wîsen. (*Trojanerkrieg*, ll. 19880–83)

The blinding capacity of Isolde's beauty is first mentioned explicitly in the love grotto episode. When Mark gazes at his wife through a window of the cave he is charmed by the interplay of the actual sunlight with the radiance of the metaphorical sun Isolde:

zwô schœne hæten an der stunt
ein spil gemachet under in zwein:
dâ schein lieht unde lieht in ein.
diu sunne und diu sunne
die hæten eine wunne
und eine hôchzît dar geleit
Îsôte z'einer sælekeit. (*Tristan*, ll. 17580–86)

This vision awakens Mark's desire and causes him to set aside his knowledge of the infidelity of his wife and nephew in favour of a more pleasant self-delusion. The following *huote*-excursus recapitulates this event and describes Isolde's beauty as blinding, exemplifying the proverb 'schœne daz ist hœne' (*Tristan*, l. 17803):

diu wunderlîche schœne
der blüenden Îsôte
diu blante ie genôte

55 Konrad's description of Helen's effect on the beauty of other women is instead more similar to the description of Enite. She outshines the other ladies like the moon outshines the stars: 'sus verswachete ir varwe | die vrouwen begarwe' (Hartmann von Aue, *Erec*, ll. 1782–83).

56 Kern explains that Gottfried describes Helen as the daughter of Aurora – she is really the daughter of Leda – in order to mirror the relationship between the young and the old Isolde (Kern, 'Isolde, Helena und die Sirenen', 6–8).

Marken ûze und innen
an ougen und an sinnen. (*Tristan*, ll. 17804–08)

Although Isolde blinds Mark's eyes as well as his mind, it is ultimately the metaphorical blindness of reason, a blindness of 'well seeing eyes' (*Tristan*, l. 17796) that Gottfried is most interested in, which becomes clear when he contrasts it to literal blindness:

swaz man von blintheit geseit,
sô'n blendet dekein blintheit
als anclîch und als ange
sô geluste unde gelange. (*Tristan*, ll. 17797–800)

Konrad exploits the semantic extension of Gottfried's sun metaphor to the extreme:[57] like the sun herself, Helen's beauty is so radiant that it almost renders her inaccessible to visual perception. When Paris sees her for the first time she burns in his eyes like a direct gaze into the sun: 'si begunde brinnen | und liuhten in sîn ougen' (*Trojanerkrieg*, ll. 19784–85) and colours him like a rainbow:

des wart er als ein regenboge
geferwet von der minne
der glanzen küneginne. (*Trojanerkrieg*, ll. 19790–92)

Helen's capacity to create colour on Paris seems to stand in direct opposition to what has been said about her before: that she can blind the light of other women with her splendour and extinguish all colours (*Trojanerkrieg*, ll. 19712–19). While this effect expresses Helen's superior beauty, the paradox of creating and extinguishing colour simultaneously can be explained as an extension of the sun simile. It describes an everyday phenomenon: the sun illuminates the world and thus brings out its colours, but after a direct gaze into the sun the eyes are so blinded that they perceive the world as black.[58]

Paris asks himself at the sight of Helen: 'wer mac den glanz beschouwen, |

57 The metaphor or simile of the protagonist as a sun is, of course, not unique to Gottfried (see also Hartmann's *Erec*, l. 1717; *Nibelungenlied*, 281, 1–2, Wolfram's *Parzival*, 167, 16–21; 185, 30–186, 6; 228, 1–6) but the way in which Konrad uses it is most similar to the way that Gottfried employs it.

58 There was some debate about the nature of colours, whether they were essential and existed even in darkness, or were accidents of objects that were only created through light (See the discussion by Hans-Joachim Schmidt, 'Was sind Farben? Fragen und Antworten in der Enzyklopädie von Vinzenz von Beauvais', in *Farbe im Mittelalter: Materialität – Medialität – Semantik*, ed. by Ingrid Bennewitz and Andrea Schindler, 2 vols (Berlin: Akademie, 2011), II, pp. 1035—43). In this context, however, it is not important whether light only makes colours visible or actually creates them.

der ûz ir farwe schînet?' (*Trojanerkrieg*, ll. 19830–31). His rhetorical question is mirrored in a statement by the narrator, who points out that the splendour of Helen's attire is not only matched but surpassed by the radiance of her white skin. Her décolleté and neck are so bright that they hurt the eye of the beholder:

> dâ was ein glanz gezogen hin,
> der schein gar durchliuhtic wîz,
> daz sîner blanken farwe flîz
> kein ouge mohte erlîden. (*Trojanerkrieg*, ll. 20230–33)

Based on the Platonic principle that like can only be recognized by like, Helen's capacity to blind, a quality that has previously only been assigned to attire and weapons, underlines the definition of her status as ontologically different to other humans. Even Paris, her destined partner and paragon of male beauty whose description matches hers in many details, not least with regard to luminosity, struggles to bear the violence of her splendour. He correctly anticipates that to the lesser audience of the Trojan citizens, Helen will appear superhuman, a 'feine' or 'götinne' (*Trojanerkrieg*, ll. 21474–80; cf. *Heroides*, XVI, 333–36), but underestimates her effect; she actually appears like the sun herself, an object that could not be more distant, and like an angel:

> si gap sô liehtebernden schîn
> und was ir dinc als ûzerkorn,
> daz die von TROIE wol gesworn
> des heten algemeine,
> daz in diu sunne reine
> mit spilender fröude engegen schine.
> [...]
> man wolte des gelouben,
> daz menschlich crêatiure
> nie würde sô gehiure
> noch sô kürlich als ir lîp,
> man hete si niht für ein wîp,
> man wânde, daz si waere
> ein engel wunnebaere
> und ein durchliuhtic himelbote,
> der von dem almehtigen gote
> waer in daz lant gesendet. (*Trojanerkrieg*, ll. 23052–71)[59]

59 It is unclear whether the Greeks really think that Helen is an angel or whether the passage is just supposed to present rhetorical hyperbole as indirect speech. The unrealistic identification with the sun suggests the latter.

Before Helen, only Paris has been associated with the angelic, for example when the garment he receives from Venus is described as fit for an angel (*Trojanerkrieg*, ll. 2920–29). When he arrives on Citarea the Greeks are so dazzled by his appearance that they think 'er waere ein got und niht ein man' (*Trojanerkrieg*, l. 19613) and he is described to Helen as outshining all his companions by virtue of being 'durchliuhtic als ein engel' (*Trojanerkrieg*, l. 19657; see also ll. 5728–29). The exclusive association of Paris and Helen with angels and gods in the first half of Konrad's fragment marks them out as a predestined couple, but it also serves to highlight their central role in the motivation of the war.[60]

The metaphorical meaning of blindness as a loss of rational thinking that Gottfried discusses in the *huote*-excursus is, of course, also implicit in Konrad's representation of Helen as a blinding beauty. Her presence itself causes Paris to behave like a madman and will eventually lead to senseless destruction. This connection of beauty and destruction is expressed most emphatically when Helen watches the battle from the walls of Troy (*Trojanerkrieg*, ll. 33954–34140). The metaphorical violence of her beauty, which defeats the beautiful Polixena, as well as the radiant armour and weaponry correspond to Helen's own reflections on the fatal effect of her beauty – 'ach got, daz ich ie schoene wart | und ie sô klâren lîp gewan!' (*Trojanerkrieg*, ll. 33968–69) – and to the fact that the vision of her incites the Greeks to fight even harder. The description of Helen extinguishing the splendour of the battle is reminiscent of her outshining other women and making them appear life- and colourless:

> swaz aber glanzes mohte sîn
> ûf der geblüemten heide
> von rîcher ougenweide,
> daz allez was reht als ein wint
> und dûhte gar ze tôde blint
> biz an den schîn aleine,
> den HELENÂ, diu reine,
> dâ kunde mit ir bilde geben.
> dô sich ir glast begunde weben
> in der wâpenkleide glanz,
> dô truoc ir schîn der wirde kranz
> vür allez daz gesmîde.

60 Later in the text this significance is reduced when comparisons to angels are also applied to fighters who play no important role in the story. However, in these cases the similes do not refer to extraordinary corporeal beauty but to precious, radiant armour and attire. Knights of both parties are 'gezieret als engel' (*Trojanerkrieg*, ll. 24860–61, l. 30239, ll. 33488–89, ll. 34592–93, ll. 39176–83). Seus analyses these angelic comparisons and establishes that they do not usually coincide with success in battle (Seus, *Heilsgeschichten vor dem Heil?*, pp. 135–38).

> die gimmen und diu sîde,
> daz silber und daz edel golt,
> daz ûf die heide was geholt,
> daz wart an sîme schîne
> erlöschet, dô diu fîne
> HELÊNE dran begunde sehen.
> si kunde liuhten unde enbrehen
> vür alle die gezierde rîch.
> kein farwe ir schîne was gelîch,
> daz wizzent âne lougen. (*Trojanerkrieg*, ll. 34060–81)

Helen's blinding radiance epitomizes the destructive effect of her beauty but it also encapsulates her utter elusiveness. Helen, the ultimate spectacle, is essentially invisible, just like Helen, the ultimate literary subject, is essentially unspeakable. Her verbal incommensurability is thus not only matched but also explained by her visual incommensurability, which renders the narrator's statements of ineffability more than mere rhetorical topoi.

Monecke argues that the image of the rainbow-coloured Paris represents the reversal of the 'mixtûre' of the Apple of Discord, which he read as an allusion to the *colores rhetorici* or the description of poets as *verwære* respectively: 'Wie im Regenbogen das Licht sich in Farbe zerlegt, so, umgekehrt, faltet sich bei den betrachteten Preziosen die Farbe wieder zusammen zu Licht'.[61] At the same time, the description of Paris as a rainbow also highlights the visual and narrative inaccessibility of Helen again. As though avoiding the gaze into the blinding sun herself, the description focuses on the effect of Helen's radiance on Paris rather than on Helen's radiance itself. Like the sun that enables vision but cannot be beheld directly, Helen's radiance is so overwhelming that it has to be mediated to become manageable not only for the intradiegetic beholder but also for the narrator. The concept of blinding radiance can, of course, only ever be expressed as an effect. Bleumer explains how this principle connects aesthetics with narration:

> Um der unaussprechlichen Schönheit Helenas willen wird nicht nur gestorben, um der unaussprechlichen Schönheit willen wird auch erzählt. Weil die Schönheit nicht direkt wahrgenommen und nicht sprachlich

61 Monecke, *Das Erzählprinzip der 'wildekeit'*, p. 177. The fact that a rainbow is produced when water droplets in the atmosphere reflect the sun was already understood by Aristotle. He argues that the colours – he sees red, green and violet as the primary colours – are created through the diminishing intensity of light that results from the reflection (Aristotle, *Meteorologica*, trans. by H. D. P. Lee, Loeb Classical Library, 397 (Cambridge, MA: Harvard University Press, 1952; repr. 1962), III, 373b–375b). His account remained the basis for explanations until the end of the thirteenth century. On Aristotle's rainbow theory, see Ayden M. Sayili, 'The Aristotelian Explanation of the Rainbow', *Isis*, 30 (1939), 65–83.

> beschrieben, sondern nur durch das Begehren und seine narrativen Folgen begriffen werden kann, geht es nicht um die Visualisierung eines Geschehens, sondern um die Visualisierung eines ebenso narrativen wie ästhetischen Wirkungszusammenhangs.[62]

In theological writing the motif of blinding light is frequently employed as a metaphor for the incommensurability of the divine to human perception and cognition (see Chapter 1). The divine light has to be dimmed – by saints, angels or the Incarnation – to make it commensurable to humans.[63] Konrad shows familiarity with this discourse in the *Goldene Schmiede*: giving birth to Christ, who is described as the sun, the Virgin, who is addressed as the dawn (*Goldene Schmiede*, l. 682), renders divinity accessible to human perception:

> wan diu menschliche forme sin
> gap niht so liehtebernden schin
> uf erden als in himel dort. (*Goldene Schmiede*, ll. 927–29)

The miracle of the Immaculate Conception is likened to a ray of sunshine penetrating a glass window without breaking it (*Goldene Schmiede*, ll. 434–45). The divine becomes flesh through the Virgin just as pure white light assumes the colour of the tinted glass it penetrates:

> diu sunne verwet nach dem glase
> ir claren und ir liehten glanz:
> swa si durch ez schinet ganz,
> ez si gel rot oder bla,
> si wirt nach im gestellet sa
> und in die varwe sin geleit;
> sus was diu luter gotheit
> nach dir geverwet, frouwe guot.
> du striche ir an fleisch unde bluot,
> do Crist, diu ware sunne,
> mit lebelicher wunne
> schein dur dinen ganzen lip,
> also daz du nie mannes wip
> würde und in gebære doch. (*Goldene Schmiede*, ll. 778–91)

Monecke eloquently sums up the significance of pure, blinding light as a metaphor for the invisible and ineffable divinity:

62 Bleumer, 'Zwischen Wort und Bild', p. 140.

63 On blinding radiance, see Schleusener-Eichholz, *Das Auge im Mittelalter*, pp. 146–60, with examples of the motif of blindingly radiant persons or objects in Middle High German literature.

> Es geht um ein oberstes bestimmendes Prinzip, das Reinheit ist, Einhelliges, Ungebrochenes, das dank seiner Lauterkeit strahlt, das Gebrochene, Zerlegte, Gefärbte durchdringt und damit rückführbar macht auf seinen Ursprung. Konrads Goldene Schmiede führt das modellhaft vor. Wir sehen das Verhältnis hundertmal in actu, hier in Beziehung auf den höchsten Gegenstand. Von ihm geht Rede aus und kehrt zu ihm zurück, jeweils die Phasen der Überbietung und der Unfähigkeit durchlaufend, auf dem Weg sich kristallisierend und wieder auflösend. Der Ursprung ist pures Licht, Unsichtbarkeit, Unsagbarkeit.[64]

The prismatic dilution into many colours makes the absolute and invisible light of God visible as the body of Christ. Likewise, the multicoloured Paris renders Helen's blinding radiance both perceptible and speakable and emphasizes its direct inaccessibility at the same time. Konrad undoubtedly adapts the metaphor of incommensurability as blinding light with several of its derivations from the religious context. While he does not assume a direct connection, Green points out the similarity between Konrad's poetic language and the language of the mystics:

> Hier kann von Lichtrealismus nicht die Rede sein, sondern allein von einer Technik, die trotz aller minutiösen Genauigkeit in der Lichtdarstellung letzten Endes doch eine Unbestimmtheit des Bildes erstrebt und auch erreicht, da gerade eine solche Unbestimmtheit die gewünschte Entwirklichung des Ganzen herbeizuführen vermochte. Ein solches Schimmern des lichtdurchfluteten Gegenstands entspricht auch dem Fließenden, Bewegten der Konradschen Schilderung, die, darin der Mystikersprache am nächsten verwandt, durch eine ausgedehnte Häufung der Ausdrücke und Aneinanderreihung der Bilder das stets unsagbar Bleibende durch eine reiche Bilderfülle zu umschreiben versucht; ein Bild verschlingt das andere, sodaß bei aller Häufigkeit und scheinbaren Klarheit der Bilder der Gesamteindruck wie in der Mystik eine bildlose Unbestimmtheit behält, die, bei den Mystikern Ausdruck der göttlichen Unendlichkeit, bei Konrad Ausdruck seines künstlerischen Unendlichkeitsgefühls ist.[65]

Green interprets these correspondences as merely superficial, but they seem, in fact, highly significant to the interpretation of the *Trojanerkrieg*. Another instructive appropriation of religious motifs apart from blinding light as an ineffability topos for the divine is Helen's association with angels, which is based on the common trait of luminosity. The description of angels as radiant is pervasive. Augustine, for example, argues that the angels are the light which God created on the second day and that the division of day from night refers to the separation of the good and the bad angels. The pure angels are not light

64 See Monecke, *Das Erzählprinzip der 'wildekeit'*, p. 178.
65 Green, *Vorstudien zum gotischen Stil*, p. 84.

in themselves but illuminated by the eternal light, the divine Wisdom that created them, whereas the impure angels are darkness because they no longer participate in that light.[66] Pseudo-Dionysius the Aeropagite explains that as purely intellectual beings which occupy the ontological position between man and God, angels are capable of taking in more of His light because they are more similar to the divine principle. However, even among the angels there are different levels of purity and therefore participation. The purest and thus most translucent angels (seraphim, cherubim and thrones) take in and pass down the divine light to the lower, more opaque ones, who can then communicate this dimmed divine truth to mankind, which is unable to perceive it directly.[67] In the *Goldene Schmiede* Konrad himself describes the angels as illuminated (*beliuhtet* (l. 857)) by divine light. It is possible that the term *durchliuhtic* alludes to the function of angels as the transparent messengers of divine light.[68] This role can clearly not be attributed to Helen's destructive radiance. Instead, the association with angels is only called up to undermine the expectation that outward beauty and radiance in particular ought to signify something positive, as in the case of Alexius's angelic radiance that is clearly a radiance from within, signifying his holiness:

> dô schein sîn bilde, wizzent daz,
> durliuhtic als ein glasevaz
> in dem ein lieht ist schône entzunt.[69]

The issue that splendour can be a reliable sign of inner virtue as well as a misleading surface is already addressed in the *Rolandslied*, where Charlemagne's blinding radiance signifies his status as a ruler of divine grace,[70] while Genelun's

66 Augustine, *The City of God*, XI, 9; also XI, 7; XI, 19.

67 Pseudo-Dionysius, *The Complete Works*, trans. by Colm Luibheid (New York: Paulist Press, 1987), *The Celestial Hierarchy*, XI–XIII.

68 Meliur is accordingly described as an 'engelîn, durchliuhtic und durchsihtic' (*Partonopier*, ll. 7884–85).

69 Konrad von Würzburg, *Alexius*, in *Die Legenden: Silvester, Alexius, Pantaleon*, ed. by Paul Gereke, 3 vols, Altdeutsche Textbibliothek, 19–21 (Halle a. S.: Niemeyer, 1925–27), 20, II (1926), ll. 949–51. Although the correspondence of outer beauty and inner value and the primacy of vision in courtly culture are questioned in *Partonopier*, the angelic and even blinding splendour of the noble protagonists (*Partonopier*, ll. 7884–85, ll. 12460–61, ll. 17278–83) eventually proves a reliable sign of their virtuous excellence and their predestination to rule (See Schulz, *Schwieriges Erkennen*, pp. 361–65; pp. 409–55, on both texts). That the reliability of visual signs is an issue even in Konrad's legends is demonstrated by Köbele, who shows that the evidence of the miracle has to prove itself against the implicit suspicion of deceptive sorcery: 'Legenden bestätigen Evidenz, indem sie je neu gegen Evidenz-Verlust anerzählen' (Köbele, 'Die Illusion der "einfachen Form"', 379–395 (p. 373)).

70 Pfaffe Konrad, *Rolandslied*, ed. and trans. by Dieter Kartschoke (Stuttgart: Reclam, 1993), ll. 684–96). On this description see Wenzel, Hören und Sehen, pp. 398–99.

light is deceptive – 'under scœnem schade liuzet, | ez en ist niht allez golt, daz dâ glîzet' (*Rolandslied*, ll. 1958–59) – and has to be destroyed through terrible mutilation in order to restore the correspondence of outer appearance and inner value.[71] It has frequently been argued that the nexus between beauty and destruction that is exemplified not only by Helen and Paris but also by the Apple of Discord and the consistent imagery of radiance and fire[72] undermines the 'Kalokagathieideal' of courtly culture.[73] Schulz, for example, who speaks of an 'ästhetisierende[] Überinszenierung visueller Eindrücke'[74] with a connotative exploitation of the *splendor dei*, asserts: 'Am äußeren Glanz der Protagonisten haftet hier kein Heil, selbst wenn dieser Glanz auf zentrale Adelswerte hin diaphan ist'.[75] The stereotypically ideal epithets that the narrator attributes to the characters contrast with their moral trespasses; and although the characters clearly believe in the correspondence of outer beauty and inner virtue, the cheating heroes in particular undermine this expectation:

> Auf das Urteil des Blicks ist kein Verlaß mehr. Auch hier demontiert der Roman eine Grundprämisse höfischer Kultur: Darauf, daß die Person dauerhaft ihrem idealen sichtbaren Äußeren entspreche, kann man nicht mehr bauen. *Stæte* entzieht sich der Verkörperung in den Präsenz-Epiphanien der 'Realabstraktionen' [...]. Aber es gibt auch nicht den Hauch einer Alternative, um zu einem gesicherten Urteil über den anderen zu kommen.[76]

71 This topic is also discussed by Müller: 'Courtly ideology presupposes a tight link between inner and outer world, the visual and the invisible. Even if visual signs have to be supported by linguistic ones, spoken or written, visuality is a guarantee of truth. The fallacy of the view – a frequent motif in heroic and courtly epics as well as in fabliaux – is always discussed against the background of its reliability, and, if this reliability is called into question, it happens by visual proof [*Tugendproben*]' (Müller, 'Blinding Sight', p. 207).

72 This connection is described in greatest detail by Lienert, 'Helena', 417–19, and *Geschichte und Erzählen*, p. 249, pp. 277–81, pp. 208–09 and passim.

73 See Müller, '*schîn* und Verwandtes', pp. 297–303, *Höfische Kompromisse*, pp. 455–56, and especially 'Blinding Sight', where he argues: '[A]ppearance is deceptive, sight does not lead to insight, but to blindness, in contrast to the otherwise common courtly trust in the harmony of ethic and aesthetic qualities' (p. 215). See also Lechtermann, 'Figuren der Abhebung', pp. 52–60; Kellner, 'Kontinuität und Diskontinuität', 112. Monecke observes that the superlative, radiant beauty of the narrated world does not refer to divine light and could thus be considered *kunterfeit*: 'Weder im Großen die Komposition noch im Kleinen die erzählerische Ausführung sind gehalten durch ein *summum bonum – rehte güete, stæte, edele herze –* , das ihre Echtheit verbürgt. Mögen seine Helden auch mit allen Tugenden verschwenderisch ausstaffiert sein, sie geben nicht wirklich *sælic bilde und edel bîschaft*. Alle hyperbolische Anspannung des *wilden* Stils kann darüber nicht täuschen' (Monecke, *Das Erzählprinzip der 'wildekeit'*, p. 178).

74 Schulz, *Schwieriges Erkennen*, p. 455.

75 Schulz, *Schwieriges Erkennen*, p. 457.

76 Schulz, *Schwieriges Erkennen*, p. 477, also pp. 489–90, p. 495. He further argues that the terrible deaths of the unfaithful Jason and Hercules, which destroy their deceptive beauty

When Helen and Paris are associated with the luminosity of angels, the comparisons thus serve to highlight the fact that they do not participate in divine grace, just like Hercules, who almost becomes a saint but cannot achieve eternal life; or Troy, that is almost like the heavenly Jerusalem, with the small but decisive difference that it venerates pagan gods in its centre and is doomed to be destroyed.

Paris as a Rainbow

The image of the rainbow-coloured Paris is an extension of Gottfried's sun metaphor which could be described as a 'concretized' metaphor. Metaphors can be defined as the cognitive coordination of two distinct semantic fields, the source domain and the target domain. Many of these couplings are topical and may even structure cognition. Like every word, terms used metaphorically (vehicles) are part of a semantic field which influences the productive elaboration of the basic metaphor.[77] Lakoff and Johnson call these basic couplings, which are the basis for most metaphorical expressions and reflect everyday experiences, 'conceptual metaphors' (they use the examples 'argument is war' and 'time is money'). They regard these metaphors as essential cognitive tools that help to structure our conceptual knowledge by transferring the structure of well-known and more concrete source domains to more abstract target domains.[78] In German scholarship these established couplings are usually called 'Bildfeld', a term coined by Harald Weinrich, who names examples such as 'Liebeskrieg', 'Liebesfeuer' or 'Liebeskrankheit'.[79] Very common or even 'dead' metaphors can therefore be re-metaphorized

('An die Stelle des Leuchtens der Personen ist das Leuchten ihrer verbrennenden Körper getreten' (p. 489)), together with the deaths of other characters who reveal themselves as *ungetriuwe*, like Nessus and Peleus, affirm 'die Geltung einer sozialen Epistemik, die vor allem auf Sichtbarkeit gegründet ist, indem es die Abweichung vom Kalokagathiepostulat gewaltsam tilgt. Es läßt aber auch die grundlegende Schwäche dieser Epistemik deutlich hervortreten' (Schulz, *Schwieriges Erkennen*, p. 490). See also Lechtermann, 'Figuren der Abhebung', pp. 57–60.

77 Already medieval poetics recommend the consistent development of a basic metaphor. For references see Gert Hübner, 'Überlegungen zur Historizität von Metapherntheorien', in *Kulturen des Manuskriptzeitalters: Ergebnisse der Amerikanisch-Deutschen Arbeitstagung an der Georg-August-Universität Göttingen vom 17. bis 20. Oktober 2002*, Transatlantische Studien zu Mittelalter und früher Neuzeit, 1 (Göttingen: V&R unipress, 2004), pp. 113–53 (pp. 127–29).

78 Lakoff and Johnson, *Metaphors We Live By*, pp. 3–9.

79 Harald Weinrich, 'Semantik der kühnen Metapher', in *Theorie der Metapher*, ed. by Anselm Haverkamp (Darmstadt: Wissenschaftliche Buchgesellschaft, 1982), pp. 316–39 (p. 336) (first publ. *DVjs*, 37 (1963), 325–44).

or refreshed by employing a non-established neighbour from the same semantic field.[80] In contrast to this, 'concretized' metaphors can be defined as playful, consciously inappropriate elaborations of conceptual metaphors that emphasize the paradox or the absurd with the intention to amuse or irritate.[81] In this sense, concretized metaphors are really anti-metaphors, because they can point out the limits of the explanatory power of the basic metaphor by taking the analogy between source and target domain too far in a very transparent way. Wessel argues that concretized metaphors invite the recipient to reflect on language and its content and defines them as:

> Metaphern, die den Bildspender, ihn mutwillig proprie nehmend, bis zu seiner Konkretisierung weitertreiben, ohne die bildempfangende Ebene gänzlich zu verlassen, so daß die metaphorische Spannung bestehen bleibt und bis zum äußersten gedehnt wird. In dieser sprachlichen Schwebe zwischen ernstem Spiel und gespieltem Ernst besteht der spezifische ästhetische Reiz dieser Figur, der sowohl Mittel höchster Verblüffung sein als auch, im Witz der Verfremdung, Erkenntnis vermitteln kann.[82]

In Konrad's case, key metaphors of the text and of Western civilization are at stake: the metaphor of radiant beauty which further alludes to the metaphor of divine light.[83] His strategy of turning the traditional metaphors against

80 Wessel, *Probleme der Metaphorik*, pp. 70–71.

81 The image of the rainbow-coloured Paris would also qualify as a 'Sprengmetapher' according to Blumenberg's definition: 'Es wird eine Intentionalität der Anschauung überdehnt, um ihre Vergeblichkeit in ihr selbst auszusprechen, im Vorgriff zugleich die Zurücknahme des Übergriffs zu vollziehen' ('Ausblick auf eine Theorie der Unbegrifflichkeit', p. 445). However, it would not count as a 'kühne Metapher' because it is based on an established 'Bildfeld', that of 'radiant beauty', and there are similar metaphors (Helen as a sun) in the context: 'Eine Metapher, die nur eine Stelle in einem von alters her gewußten Bildfeld ausfüllt, kann schwerlich kühn sein. Man mag sich anstrengen, wie man will, in dem Bildfeld noch eine *terra incognita* aufzufinden. Das ist allenfalls eine Kühnheit zweiten Grades' (Weinrich, 'Semantik der kühnen Metapher', p. 336).

82 Wessel, *Probleme der Metaphorik*, p. 199. Hugo Friedrich quotes several instances that could be taken as metaphors turned against themselves, for instance the joking question of how Venus can ignite fire although she is a child of the water, or what he calls 'künstlicher' or 'scherzhafter Trugschluß', if metaphors are used to explain a real-life phenomenon (Hugo Friedrich, *Epochen der italienischen Lyrik* (Frankfurt a. M.: Vittorio Klostermann, 1964), pp. 644–45, p. 661). These metaphors are also closely related to literal readings of metaphors by epic characters (affected or naive) that can be used for comic effect or intentional double entendre, like that of Tristan and Isolde. On this phenomenon see Bickert, 'Der Dichter als Handwerker', pp. 206–10, with examples. He also emphasizes: '[S]tets ist dabei Funktion und Leistung der Sprache selbst mit zur Reflexion aufgegeben' (p. 206).

83 The central role of light metaphors is discussed by Blumenberg in 'Licht als Metapher der Wahrheit' and in many of the contributions in: Christina Lechtermann and Haiko Wandhoff (eds), *Licht, Glanz, Blendung: Beiträge zu einer Kulturgeschichte des Leuchtenden*, Publikationen zur Zeitschrift für Germanistik, N.F., 18 (Bern: Lang, 2008).

themselves by pushing them to absurdity is consonant with learned reflections on metaphor, especially with the tradition of negative theology. Pseudo-Dionysius the Areopagite, for example, introduces his *Celestial Hierarchy* with a discussion of metaphor. Given the fact that in keeping with Platonist tradition he makes pervasive use of light metaphors throughout his treatise, he obviously feels compelled to safeguard his work against a misunderstanding of his imagery. Therefore he emphasizes that whatever he will go on to say about the light of God or the angels must be understood in a strictly metaphorical way because no concept of light will ever capture the true character of the divine and no word or thought can ever be truly analogous to it. He explains that while more dignified and immaterial images like light might obscure the fact that they, too, do not reach true similarity to the divine, obviously inappropriate and undignified sensory and material images encourage the soul not to acquiesce in the representations but to strive for the truth behind them. They work *ex negativo* (*Celestial Hierarchy*, II, 1–4).[84] According to this principle, Konrad turns Gottfried's sun metaphor into an obviously inappropriate simile that openly exhibits its discrepancy with the referent, thus undermining his own light metaphors, which pervade the following description of Helen. This would support the thesis that the recipient is not supposed to imagine Helen as a radiant person but to appreciate the semiotic significance of her light. The fact that Konrad reveals the inadequacy of his own metaphors does not mean that they cannot communicate anything valid at all, however. Helen's beauty is overwhelming and surpasses that of all other women, it affects Paris deeply and, most importantly, it is closely linked to destruction.

In the Christian tradition, the rainbow has mainly positive associations: it is the sign of peace between God and His creation after the Great Flood (Genesis 9. 8–17) and of God's glory (Ezechiel 1. 28); it is the bridge to Heaven at the Last Judgement; and Christ as well as the Virgin are often depicted sitting on a rainbow.[85] Based on the symbolic meaning of the rainbow as a bridge or ladder connecting the worldly to the transcendent realm, Seus argues: 'Paris' Farbe verweist damit zwar auf einen Bereich jenseits der Minne, doch muss dieser für die Welt des *Trojanischen Krieges* unbesetzt bleibt [*sic*]. Durch den Verweis auf die Jenseitssymbolik bezeugt die Paris-Helena-Minne erneut

84 See also Köbele, who gives an overview of the concept of metaphor among mystic authors, especially Meister Eckhart's statement (Sermon 51) of the utter dissimilarity of God to anything that can ever be said about Him (Köbele, *Bilder der unbegriffenen Wahrheit*, pp. 56–68).

85 Werner Bies, 'Regenbogen', *Enzyklopädie des Märchens*, XI (2004), cols 465–70; Victor Stegemann, 'Regenbogen', *Handwörterbuch des deutschen Aberglaubens*, VII (1935–36), cols 586–97.

ihre Defizienz im religiösen Bereich'.[86] Another tradition that might inform Konrad's simile is the proverb 'to build upon a rainbow', which emphasizes the ephemeral status of the beautiful natural phenomenon. Somebody who builds upon a rainbow erroneously bases his actions on an instable foundation and will inevitably fail: 'der uf den bogen regenes zimbert, der kan sich niht lange vristen' (*Jüngerer Titurel*, 4103, 2). The rainbow is therefore also likened to the fleeting and deceptive world in contrast to transcendent eternity:

> Swer umbe dise kurze zît
> die êwigen fröude gît,
> der hât sich selbe gar betrogen
> und zimbert ûf den regenbogen.[87]

Konrad's metaphor can thus be seen as yet another allusion to the principle of deceptive beauty and to the destruction that follows Paris's moment of bliss. Like the tradition that Seus cites, it can, furthermore, underline the lack of transcendent perspectives of the exclusively secular charms of the narrated world. However, this established symbolism of the rainbow only connotes the description of Paris's unusual colour change; it does not help to translate figurative speech into literal speech and to establish which immediate story-level phenomenon this image describes.

Lienert discusses the description of the rainbow-coloured Paris as an example of Konrad's far-fetched and 'broken' metaphors. These make it very difficult to find the *tertium comparationis* and thus create a distancing effect: 'Schlechterdings außerhalb jeder sinnlichen Erfahrung liegt – in vollständiger "Aufhebung der Anschauung" – der Vergleich des Paris mit einem Regenbogen, der nur aus dem intellektuellen Nachvollziehen der Sonnenbildlichkeit um Helena heraus verständlich ist'.[88] While it is true that the eccentric

86 Seus, *Heilsgeschichten vor dem Heil?*, p. 131.

87 *Freidanks Bescheidenheit*, ed. by Wolfgang Spiewok (Leipzig: Reclam, 1985), 1, 7. Further examples for this proverb are collected by Vroni Mumprecht, 'Regenbogen', in *Thesaurus proverbiorum medii aevi*, IX (1999), pp. 237–39.

88 Lienert, *Geschichte und Erzählen*, pp. 286–88 (p. 286). Unfortunately Lienert does not distinguish sufficiently between the unrealistic and the unimaginable: 'Vielfach ist eine der Beschreibung korrelierende Realität nicht vorstellbar. Dies gilt etwa für den Apfel der Discordia, vor allem die unrealistisch lange Inschrift und seine magische Wirkung, für die Beschreibung des neuerbauten Troja, dessen Pracht und Schönheit irreale Dimensionen annehmen, für das Porträt der Helena: Atem duftet nicht nach Muskat; ein Gewand, das die Farbe wechselt, und der Glanz einer schönen Frau, der ein ganzes Schlachtfeld überstrahlt, sind schlechterdings nicht vorstellbar' (Lienert, *Geschichte und Erzählen*, pp. 286–87). Some of Konrad's descriptions, such as Paris's coat of non-existent colours or the curious optics of the Apple of Discord, and even conventional hyperbole such as 'whiter than a lily', truly present a challenge to the imagination. Others, however, although certainly far removed from the reader's everyday experience, are quite easy to imagine because it only requires the

image creates irritation and distance, this has probably more to do with the unfamiliar extension of the conceptual metaphor than with the fact that the point of comparison is any harder to detect – it would be equally difficult to state what Helen really, in literal terms, has in common with the sun. Thus Weinrich points out that the most established 'Bildfelder' – he names 'truth as light' – can be the most difficult to paraphrase in non-metaphorical terms and concludes that, if this is true, 'sich uns die Gewißheit auf[drängt], daß unsere Metaphern gar nicht, wie die alte Metaphorik wahrhaben wollte, reale oder vorgedachte Gemeinsamkeiten abbilden, sondern daß sie ihre Analogien erst stiften, ihre Analogien erst schaffen und somit demiurgische Werkzeuge sind'.[89] In this sense the conceptual metaphor of 'radiant beauty' is simply much more common, so that this problem goes unnoticed, whereas the unfamiliar but equally unrealistic image of the rainbow-coloured Paris exposes it. Lienert's expression 'Aufhebung der Anschauung' is also slightly problematic. Wessel explains in more detail the same effect that Lienert merely diagnoses:

> Auf abstraktester Ebene läßt das Verhältnis von Evidenz und ratio sich folgendermaßen beschreiben: notwendige Bedingung für Evidenz ist das Zurücktreten der (immer a u c h vorhandenen) rationalen Komponente der Metapher ins Unbewußte. Diese 'schauende' Aufhebung der ratio kann sich dann vollziehen, wenn das tertium comparationis einer Metapher [...] auf der Hand liegt und wenn andererseits ein tertium comparationis überhaupt noch unbewußt empfunden wird. 'Weit hergeholte' Metaphern, d.h. metaphorische Neu- und Umprägungen, die kapriziöse Fortspinnung eines Bildfeldes oder gar die Stiftung eines Bildfeldes machen die Frage nach der Einsehbarkeit, rationalen Verstehbarkeit dieser Metapher dringlich. Erst das immer wieder Eingesehene, Vertraute kann schließlich spontan 'angesehen', 'geschaut' werden, kann Atmosphäre, ästhetisches Eigenleben gewinnen.[90]

---

reader to bring together well-known elements of his own realm of experience in unfamiliar combinations. If he knows what nutmeg smells like he will be perfectly capable of imagining breath smelling of it. The same is true for the coat that changes its colour from red to white seven times a day and a woman who is radiant like the sun – they are fantastic yet can easily be visualized. This principle of creating a mental image of things that have never been seen from elements of personal experience is described by Alcuin, who exemplifies the process with the imagination of the heavenly Jerusalem that is based on known cities (Alcuin, *De ratione animae*, in *Patrologia Latina*, ed. by Jaques Paul Migne (Paris, 1844–65), CI (1863), pp. 639–47 (p. 642 B–C)).

89 Weinrich, 'Semantik der kühnen Metapher', p. 331. Similarly Searle, *Speech Acts*, pp. 85–103. This kind of metaphor would correspond to Blumenberg's definition of 'absolute metaphors' as '"Übertragungen", die sich nicht ins Eigentliche, in die Logizität zurückholen lassen' (Hans Blumenberg, *Paradigmen zu einer Metaphorologie*, Suhrkamp Studienbibliothek, 10 (Frankfurt a.M.: Suhrkamp, 2013), p. 14 (first publ. in *Archiv für Begriffsgeschichte*, 6 (1960), 5–142)).

90 Wessel, *Probleme der Metaphorik*, p. 122.

Lienert and Wessel use the term 'Anschauung' or 'Evidenz' as visual metaphors for the immediate grasp of what a metaphor is meant to convey. This, however, can easily lead to confusion with the common description of the vehicle for a metaphor as a 'Bild'. Visuality can thus be attributed to the figurative as well as to the literal side of the metaphor and both implications have to be distinguished carefully.[91] On the one hand, it can be argued that only common, unobtrusive metaphors are compatible with a style of narration that aims at obscuring the boundary between discourse and story and creating the illusion of immediate sensory participation in the narrated world, whereas eccentric metaphors draw attention to the act of narration and therefore disturb this illusion. On the other hand, this does not mean that the latter kind of metaphor cannot have its own kind of 'evidence' – while the image of a rainbow-coloured hero is undoubtedly surreal, it is anything but unimaginable and every reader would be perfectly able to paint Paris according to this description. It certainly does not mean that such metaphors do not have an 'ästhetisches Eigenleben'.

Gebert collects other unconventional metaphors from the *Trojanerkrieg* which he calls 'wilde Metaphern' – for example, the description of Menelaus who turns green like a leek and as yellow as wax when he sees Helen (*Trojanerkrieg*, ll. 34315–17). He distinguishes them from 'Sprengmetaphern' and argues, too, that although they are eccentric, 'Bildlichkeit, Klanglichkeit oder anderweitige Sensorik'[92] always remain in the realm of the imaginable. He interprets them as a poetic strategy of 'Wahrnehmungsstimulation' that re-energizes poetic language:

> Poetische Darstellungsverfahren stehen [...] stets vor der Aufgabe, die Realität der imaginierten Bilder vor Konventionalisierung (und dies heißt zugleich: vor Präsenzverlust) zu schützen. Für alle erzählten Bilder gilt demnach: Was erwartbar ist, wird weniger präsent. Metaphern tragen zentral dazu bei, die Präsenz sprachlich generierter Bilder zu erneuern und lebendig zu halten.[93]

While I agree that these metaphors create 'Präsenzeffekte', I would not follow Gebert's argument that they can be counted among the stylistic devices which make the discourse transparent, for it is not the story – the tenor – that is

91 The tradition of describing metaphors as images, which originated in the eighteenth century, is discussed by Hübner, who points out the difference between the modern *Anschauung* and the classical *evidentia* and cautions against projecting this specifically modern theory of metaphor onto pre-modern metaphors (Hübner, 'Überlegungen zur Historizität von Metapherntheorien', pp. 118–27).

92 Gebert, *Mythos als Wissensform*, p. 267.

93 Gebert, *Mythos als Wissensform*, p. 269. He points out that these metaphors occur mainly in the second half of the text: 'Indem der *Trojanerkrieg* die Präsenzeffekte solcher metaphorischen Erregung über die gesamte Kriegsdarstellung streut, wird die Rezeptionsenergie auf das gesamte Kriegserzählen ausgebreitet'.

made 'sinnlich präsent', as he suggests,[94] but the vehicle on the discourse level that attracts attention and diverts it away from the elements of the narrated world to which it refers.[95] The reader could certainly imagine a rainbow-coloured Paris (although this is not necessary in order to understand the semiotics of Konrad's consistently developed light-imagery), but the visualization of this striking image would not tell him anything about Paris's visual appearance on the level of the story. Since it is difficult to say which actual intradiegetic phenomenon the metaphor describes – it might not even be a visual phenomenon at all but an emotional response – the poetic image of the rainbow-coloured Paris cannot be translated into a mimetic mental image of the actual Paris as an intradiegetic beholder would perceive him. The visual appearance of the story-level Paris completely disappears behind the powerful image of the rainbow-coloured Paris on the discourse level.

Searle explains that in metaphors the 'utterance meaning is arrived at by going through [the] literal sentence meaning', yet, the more common a metaphor is, the less the reader has to dwell on the vehicle. Finally, in the case of dead metaphors, the referential thrust is so strong and established that the reader does not even have to make the detour via the vehicle to reach the tenor anymore, since the 'original sentence meaning is bypassed and the sentence acquires a new literal meaning identical with the former metaphorical utterance meaning'.[96] A refreshed metaphor or a concretized metaphor such as the unconventional image of a rainbow-coloured Paris, on the other hand, would resist this referential thrust and develop some degree of aesthetic autonomy. In this respect, Konrad's eccentric metaphor resembles the modern collision metaphors described by Karsten Harries in which 'the image is so strong that the vehicle seems to emancipate itself from the tenor' and may even obscure what is vehicle and what is tenor.[97] The discourse thus draws attention to itself; it becomes opaque, rather than immediately referring to the narrated world beyond. Harries interprets collision metaphors as a struggle against the inevitable referentiality of language. By destroying the close, preconceived union between vehicle and tenor typical of established metaphors they 'reveal the usually-passed-over inadequacy of language'.[98] When it becomes unclear

94 Gebert, *Mythos als Wissensform*, p. 315

95 It has to be conceded that the metaphors listed by Gebert are not as eccentric as the rainbow-coloured Paris; their utterance meaning generally seems easier to detect. However, while they do not necessarily block access to the story level, they still command attention as images in their own right and emphasize the discourse.

96 Searle, *Speech Acts*, p. 115.

97 Karsten Harries, 'Metaphor and Transcendence', in *On Metaphor*, ed. by Sheldon Sacks (Chicago: University of Chicago Press, 1979), pp. 71–88 (p. 77); see also Harries 'The Many Uses of Metaphor', in the same volume, pp. 165–72.

98 Harries, 'The Many Uses of Metaphor', p. 171. He also argues that 'as members of a community

to what the metaphor refers, it gains an almost self-sufficient presence: 'The collision of images helps to decompose familiar reality, to reduce it to poetic material. Out of the fragments of the world the poet creates his own poetic world.'[99]

There is certainly some debate concerning the question of whether medieval metaphors can be interpreted by employing such modern theories: Udo Friedrich, for example, mentions Konrad's light metaphors in the *Trojanerkrieg* as an example of the accomplished employment of metaphors contained 'im Horizont eines epochenpezifischen Bildarchivs'[100] and Konrad's *Goldene Schmiede* as an example of how metaphorical topoi can be combined, varied and exploited in creative and complex ways within the constraints of this tradition. At the same time he is very careful not to equate this variation of traditional metaphors with the 'Originalitätsanspruch moderner Metapherntechnik [...], die in der Vorstellung von der Arbitrarität der Zeichen und im Verlust des Sprachvertrauens, der Inadäquatheit von Zeichen und Bezeichnetem gründen.'[101] However, he concedes that metapoetic metaphors in Middle High German poetry can concern scepticism towards the representational power of language: 'Über die Metapher kann Dichtung auch auf sich selbst reflektieren und die Möglichkeiten und Grenzen von Sprache ausloten.'[102] He even identifies some metaphors, 'durch die sich die dichterische Sprache von der Wirklichkeit emazipiert, um auf ihr autonomes Potential zu verweisen.'[103] Gert Hübner is particularly critical about interpreting pre-modern metaphors on the basis of modern image and interaction theories according to which the associations evoked by the coupling of two distinct semantic realms are potentially endless and cannot be paraphrased or substituted for by a literal expression. He argues that classical rhetoric and medieval poetics such as Geoffrey's *Poetria nova* frequently attribute very definitive meaning to metaphorical expressions by translating them in proper speech: 'Die rhetorische Metapherntheorie ist der

we are necessarily caught up in already-established and taken-for granted ways of speaking and seeing. We understand things without having made them our own. The adequacy of words is taken for granted' (Harries, 'Metaphor and Transcendence', p. 87). Harries further argues: 'Semantic collision helps to dissolve this too intimate union. As language gains a certain autonomy we are forced to recognize the usually forgotten distance that separates words and things' (Harries, 'The Many Uses of Metaphor', p. 77).

99 Harries, 'Metaphor and Transcendence', p. 81. See also Hutcheon on the general metapoetic charge of such defamiliarization: 'The laying bare of literary devices in metafiction brings to the reader's attention those formal elements of which, through over-familiarization, he has become unaware' (Hutcheon, *Narcissistic Narrative*, p. 24).

100 Friedrich, 'Historische Metaphorologie', p. 198.

101 Friedrich, 'Historische Metaphorologie', p. 203.

102 Friedrich, 'Historische Metaphorologie', p. 197.

103 Friedrich, 'Historische Metaphorologie', p. 198.

Ausdruck der Einschätzung, daß die Metapher eine bestimmte Eigenschaft hervorhebt, die das eigentlich gemeinte ontologisch hat und die auf einen Begriff gebracht werden kann'.[104] The only exception he makes are metaphors for the divine which can never represent their referent appropriately or be substituted for by literal expressions:

> Hier benötigt man die Interaktionstheorie, und zwar gerade in ihrer extremsten Form, der Unähnlichkeitstheorie, weil die hergestellte Analogie keine Bedeutung substituiert, sondern eine Bedeutung konstruiert. Das liegt, etwas flapsig gesagt, daran, daß manche mittelalterlichen Ansichten über das Verhältnis zwischen Sprache und Gott gewisse Ähnlichkeiten mit modernen Ansichten über das Verhältnis zwischen Sprache und Welt haben.[105]

However, if this concept of metaphor exists in pre-modern religious writing, I would argue that it can also be transferred onto secular poetry, from the inconceivable and unspeakable divine as light onto inconceivable and unspeakable beauty as light.

There is, of course, also the possibility of taking literally the descriptions of Helen as a beauty of sun-like radiance and of the rainbow-coloured Paris. The reader can assign them either to a fantastic world that is utterly removed from his own reality (*vremede, wilde*) and in which these things can be true, or read them as a metaphor for more natural phenomena. After all, the concretized metaphor is basically a metaphor taken literally, only in an ironic way – a transgression that is meant to assert the boundary between the metaphorical and the literal. Monecke observes that Konrad plays with this boundary, mainly through hyperbolic insistence, when he describes how Helen watches the fighters and affects their performance in battle. Monecke argues that the descriptive metaphor of Helen's radiance is taken literally and extended into narration: 'Man sieht, wie der Topos epische Substanz angezogen, wie er, durch Variierung und Kontrastierung, sich zu einem Stück Erzählung organisiert hat. Freilich ist er nicht als causa prima zu verstehen'.[106] In practice, the distinction between a more naturalistic metaphorical reading and a fantastical literal reading of Helen's radiance is difficult to draw, since the reader cannot simply measure the statements against the background of his own reality, in which even the notion of a golden ram may cause semantic irritation and prompt a metaphorical interpretation.[107] Thus Schnell argues that it is often difficult to

104 Hübner, 'Überlegungen zur Historizität von Metapherntheorien', p. 153.

105 Hübner, 'Überlegungen zur Historizität von Metapherntheorien', p. 138. For a more detailed response to Hübner's categorical rejection of the interaction theory for the interpretation of secular, pre-modern metaphors see Friedrich, 'Historische Metaphorologie', pp. 188–203.

106 Monecke, *Das Erzählprinzip der 'wildekeit'*, p. 132.

107 On the process of identifying metaphors see Searle, *Speech Acts*.

decide whether transcendent causes of love – for example Love personified – are supposed to be understood literally or figuratively.[108] Even if a reader chose to interpret the descriptions of Helen's radiance in a completely literal manner, it has to be noted that this fantastic reality remains restricted to the realm of the descriptions and to the moments of Helen's epiphany. For as ungraspable and blindingly radiant as she is to her beholders in these moments, in the remainder of the story she functions as a natural human being whom people can see and with whom they can interact. Paris does not need sunglasses when he talks to her.

We can safely discard the notion that the eulogy of Helen aims at creating the illusion of immediate visual participation. The excess of detail and references to light make it difficult to construct a clear mental image of her. Even if this were possible – Lienert and Bleumer sometimes overstate the unimaginable – the considerations of Helen's status as a literary phenomenon, as well as the ineffability topoi that are validated by Paris's eyewitness judgement, highlight the medial gap between the words and their object. In addition, the concretized metaphor of the rainbow-coloured Paris – and by extension the metaphor of light – exposes its own inadequacy in representing that to which it refers. The discourse becomes opaque and the extravagant metaphors obscure the 'view' of the narrated world. On the other hand, the verbal praise of Helen succeeds in capturing her essence insofar as it emulates the effects of her presence: Paris falls in love without ever having seen her and her literary audience is charmed, just like her intradiegetic beholders. In some sense, her literary reputation is even superior to her dangerous presence because it transcends time, space and cultural boundaries and may actually have a beneficial didactic effect. Moreover, the key motif of light emancipates itself from the narrated world, which means that its semiotic status becomes more obvious but also that it gains autonomous presence and creates a surreal poetic world. The iridescent epiphany of the radiant Helen is really the epiphany of Konrad's 'worte lûter unde glanz'.

108 Schnell, *Causa amoris*, pp. 188–97.

CONCLUSION

des krieges kum ich niemer abe,
man finde iu maniger saelde bî,
dann ie von iu gesaget sî
wird unde tugentlicher tât,
wan iuwer lîp gelegen hât
mit sigenuft den worten obe,
diu ie gesprâchen von dem lobe,
daz an iuch wart mit staetekeit
von manigem wîsen man geleit. (*Trojanerkrieg*, ll. 21096–104)

Konrad's *Trojanerkrieg* is not only a text about the Trojan War but also a text about the war between words and their referents, an existential poetic struggle to contain the endless, fathom the bottomless and speak the ineffable. Contrary to what may be expected from such ineffability topoi, this poetic war is never quite decided – neither in favour of the poet, so that he may rise all the more impressively above the daunting challenge, nor in favour of the narrated world, which may sparkle all the more dazzlingly the more it resists verbalization. Instead, Konrad reworks the commonplaces of metapoetic concern so thoroughly that they become highly productive tools of enquiry into the unique quality and function of poetry. This metapoetic discourse pervades the entire text, focuses on various aspects of poetry and expresses itself in many different ways, both explicitly and implicitly, on the level of the story as well as of the discourse. Particularly the paradox of Helen as both an ineffable beauty and a powerful literary presence serves to tease out the specific medial limitations of poetry as well as its unique power. Konrad's poetics therefore present an instructive example with which to reassess the picture scholarship has painted of the Middle Ages as a culture of visuality whose literary artefacts strive to set the world they represent before the eyes of the beholder.

On the other hand, the *Trojanerkrieg* is not just a text about the war between words and their referents, but also a text about the Trojan War.[1] Contrary to

1 See Köbele's criticism of interpretations that over-emphasize metapoetic aspects of medieval texts or attribute a purely aesthetic quality to them: '"Rein ästhetisches Sprachspiel" kann jedenfalls für die spätmittelalterliche Lyrik schon allein deswegen nicht stimmen, weil diese Sprache keine ist, die mit dem Selbstbezug ihren Gegenstand verlöre, sondern, auch in Extremfällen von Künstlichkeit und Dunkelheit, den Zeichenstatus nicht abwirft, ihn vielmehr in den Hintergrund treten läßt' (Susanne Köbele, *Frauenlobs Lieder: Parameter*

the criticism that early scholarship levelled against the text, namely that the form is dissociated from the content, Konrad's self-conscious artistry is not purely self-sufficient, but intricately linked to the story. In fact, the connection between both goes well beyond turning destruction into aesthetically pleasing poetry, as Lienert suggests. This becomes particularly evident in metapoetic passages that intimate certain ways of receiving the text. Modern interpreters all too often gloss over a text's explicit self-identification as didactic, discarding such statements as mere topoi of legitimization. Another reason might be that to a modern reader didacticism can seem like a patronizing reduction of complexity. However, unless we find good arguments to the contrary, we should take seriously Konrad's statement that the *Trojanerkrieg* provides good and bad examples that can help the discerning reader to lead a virtuous life, even though there is little explicit narratorial judgement in the main text. The bat simile in the prologue not only portrays the bad audience but also carves out a picture of the ideal reader *ex negativo* as someone who possesses *bescheidenheit*, the ability to distinguish between good and bad (examples) and who is not misled by deceptive splendour.[2] Reception within the narrated world frequently figures as a negative example which contrasts with the reception envisaged for the *Trojanerkrieg*. Thus the intradiegetic reader of the inscription on the Apple of Discord must fail to recognize its ambiguity and the sinister purpose behind its dazzling appearance, whereas the recipient of the *Trojanerkrieg* is aware of this ambivalence, which exemplifies the essential nexus between beauty and destruction. While the Greeks fail to realize the didactic potential of the story of Hercules' death, the recipient of the *Trojanerkrieg* is surely not expected to delight uncritically in the splendour of the narrated world, but to recognize the destructive principle of exaggerated revenge and the emptiness behind the façade of courtly epithets. Whereas the characters are so dazzled by Helen's light that they run into destruction, the spatially and temporally detached audience can instead read this light in a semiotic way and draw a positive, salvific lesson from it. Far from being patronizing or simplistic, Konrad does not explain these lessons but relies on

---

einer literarischen Standortbestimmung, Bibliotheca Germanica, 43 (Tübingen: Francke, 2003), pp. 231–34 (p. 232)).

2 With reference to the prologue of the Old French *Partonopeu* romance, which argues that even the worst heathen text can still provide good and bad examples to the reader who is able to distinguish between them, see Hübner, '*evidentia*', p. 144. He cautions against dismissing such statements out of hand as superficial common places: 'Natürlich kann man zeigen, wo und weshalb sich gerade die Partonopeu-Geschichte der Funktion entzieht, Generalisierungen exemplarisch zu belegen; man kann aber ebenso zeigen, wo und wie der gelehrte Dichter mit seiner Bearbeitung dem Prinzip zur Geltung verhilft, auf das Befolgen von Normen den Erfolg des Handelnden und auf ihre Missachtung den Misserfolg folgen zu lassen'.

the discriminating reader to look beyond the dazzling surface of the narrated world and make his own judgement.

Konrad is as clearly influenced by the masters of the so-called *Blütezeit* as he was influential for his late-medieval successors. Although his metapoetic positions appear quite original and even revolutionary – the nightingale simile as an articulation of literary autonomy; the *artes* discussion as a renouncement of poetry as craft – they are in fact compatible with contemporary opinions and can contribute to charting the field of possible conceptualizations of textuality, language and poetry in his cultural context. Although the cultural historical specificity of Konrad's brand of metapoetics could only be demonstrated through a diachronously comparative study, there are further respects in which it might be representative of Middle High German literature. This concerns, of course, the typical spaces of metapoetic reflection such as prologues and descriptions, but also characteristic poetic practices and modes of discourse such as retextualization or exemplariness. Another feature that Konrad's explicit metapoetic statements have in common with those of other Middle High German authors is the fact that they are frequently expressed in the form of topical utterances of ineffability and modesty. It has been shown that Konrad employs great creativity in adapting these conventional forms to suit his own purposes and to endow them with renewed authenticity. The frame of reference from which Konrad draws the material for his metapoetic expressions is also very specific: there are frequent intertextual references to Middle High German and Latin poetry as well as to Latin poetics and more specialized Neo-Platonic and theological discourses. In addition to the obvious fact that the *Trojanerkrieg* is based on a multitude of Latin sources, these references, along with the possibility that the clerical patron Dietrich represents at least the elite part of Konrad's audience that was sufficiently educated to appreciate these connections, challenge the general advice for interpreting medieval German texts that is given by Schulz. He argues that the context of cultural knowledge used as a frame for interpretation should be kept very general: 'Die relevanten Kontexte [dürfen] nicht besonders speziell angesetzt werden [...]. Sonst begibt man sich in die Gefahr der Überinterpretation. [...] Es sollte beim Interpretieren darum gehen, den Ball möglichst flach zu halten'. He also distances vernacular poetry from learned Latin literature: 'Oft sind die Beziehungen zwischen den gelehrten Wissensbeständen und der höfischen Laienliteratur gar nicht besonders eng'.[3] It is granted that one ought to proceed from the general to the specific and that vernacular literature is characterized by 'Konterdiskursivität', which means that it does not simply reflect learned

3 Armin Schulz, *Erzähltheorie in mediävistischer Perspektive*, ed. by Manuel Braun, Alexandra Dunkel and Jan-Dirk Müller (Berlin: de Gruyter, 2012), pp. 23–24.

concepts in a discursive way but adapts them playfully and poetically. However, if the main goal of interpretation should be to keep the ball on the ground, we might miss the most interesting aspects and most playful counter-discourses of many texts, not least the *Trojanerkrieg*. Moreover, I cannot follow Schulz in attributing to the story a clear priority over the discourse:

> Die Ebene des wörtlichen Geschehens, der *histoire* mit ihrer dargestellten Welt, die aus Räumen, Zeiten, Ereignissen und Figuren besteht, [ist] immer demjenigen übergeordnet, was ein Erzähltext 'Durch die Blume' aussagt. Der 'Don Quixote' von Cervantes mag eine Parodie auf die zeitgenössischen Ritterromane sein, aber in erster Linie erzählt er selbst eine Geschichte, diejenige des Ritters von der traurigen Gestalt.[4]

Since discourse and story can only ever be separated as abstract analytical categories, while in reality the one cannot exist without the other, I see no reason for this hierarchy of interpretative importance. After all, how accurate would an interpretation of *Don Quixote* be that did not take its parodic status into account; and how could its parodic status be established without reference to its story? In the *Trojanerkrieg* meaning is clearly generated through the complex interplay of story and discourse, through explicit as well as implicit means. This has become particularly evident in the discussion of the connection between the plot structure of *Fernminne* and the discourse-level reflections on verbal representation.

Apart from the light that an investigation of Konrad's metapoetics can shed on the peculiarities of Middle High German poetics and its discursive contexts in general, there are also some methodological principles that can be generalized beyond the scope of this work: the systematic distinction between the analytical categories of actual and proclaimed methods of composition; avoidance of the disambiguization of multi-faceted figurative expressions; the differentiation between passages with pronounced metapoetic significance

4 Schulz, *Erzähltheorie*, p. 26. He also argues that modern narratological instruments are too complex to describe the discourse of Middle High German texts while they are not developed enough to analyse their story level (*Erzähltheorie*, pp. 1–3). The exclusion of Latin contexts and the imbalance between analyses of phenomena at the levels of both story and discourse in Schulz's study, which is intended as a general narratological introduction to the interpretation of medieval German texts, are also criticized by Hübner: 'Das abschließende Kapitel 7 läßt auf 366 Seiten *histoire*-Narratologie 30 Seiten *discours*-Narratologie folgen' (Gert Hübner, 'Armin Schulz: Erzähltheorie in mediävistischer Perspektive', *ZfdPh*, 132 (2013), 445–450 (p. 447)). In contrast to this, Hübner's narratological study *Erzählform im höfischen Roman* demonstrates how the evaluative structure of texts can be shaped by the discourse even against plots that suggest a different judgement (Gert Hübner, *Erzählform im höfischen Roman: Studien zur Fokalisierung im 'Eneas', im 'Iwein' und im 'Tristan'*, Bibliotheca Germanica, 44 (Tübingen: Francke, 2003)). On the possibility of a contrast between 'Sinnangebote' coded in the *discourse* to those coded in the *histoire*, see also Hübner, '*evidentia*', pp. 143–44.

and a more general opacity of the discourse created through a self-consciously elaborate style and the recurrence of certain word fields (such as radiance) with reference to story-level elements as well as in metapoetic contexts.

The investigation of the sources for Konrad's metapoetic imagery has demonstrated that he frequently draws on a religious frame of reference, a result that has also proven relevant to the overall interpretation of the text. The relationship between spiritual and secular literature in the Middle Ages has long been a central subject of scholarly investigation and is still very relevant in recent discourse. The discussion encompasses a broad variety of phenomena ranging from structural analogies of cognitive and narrative patterns, shared vocabulary and imagery, to the transmission of religious and profane texts in the same codices.[5] Even though the distinction between the transcendent and the worldly realms and the ontological priority of the former is central to the Christian Middle Ages, the boundaries between the spiritual and the secular are not clear-cut but represent opposite poles on a scale with many possible positions in between. Burghart Wachinger speaks of a 'geistlich-weltlichen Mischkultur des Mittelalters', whose various permutations are also reflected in its literary artefacts.[6] The relationship can be described as one of complex mutual influence, tension and analogy:

5 An early overview of the interferences between both spheres is given by Max Wehrli, 'Roman und Legende im deutschen Hochmittelalter', in Max Wehrli, *Formen mittelalterlicher Erzählung* (Atlantis: Zürich, 1969), pp. 155–76. The examples he covers – the hybrid courtly legend *Gregorius*; the grail society in Chrétien's and Wolfram's *Parzival*-romances; the Eucharistic allusions in Gottfried's *Tristan* – have since remained central to the debate. Apart from numerous independent studies on individual texts and aspects of this field of research, this issue has also been treated in several conference volumes: *Geistliches in weltlicher und Weltliches in geistlicher Literatur des Mittelalters*, ed. by Christoph Huber, Burghard Wachinger and Hans-Joachim Ziegeler (Tübingen: Niemeyer, 2000); *Literarische und religiöse Kommunikation in Mittelalter und Früher Neuzeit: DFG-Symposion 2006*, ed. by Peter Strohschneider (Berlin: de Gruyter, 2009); *Literarische Säkularisierung im Mittelalter*, ed. by Susanne Köbele and Bruno Quast (Berlin: de Gruyter, 2014).

6 Burghart Wachinger, 'Einleitung', in *Geistliches in weltlicher und Weltliches in geistlicher Literatur*, ed. by Huber, Wachinger and Ziegeler, pp. 1–15. He argues that these antonyms are, in fact, relative, so that the line between them cannot be clearly drawn: 'Für einen Konventualen lebte ein Weltpriester weltlich, für einen strengen Observanten auch der gemäßigte Konventuale' (Wachinger, 'Einleitung', p. 5). Müller illustrates this fluidity in literature with reference to the recurrent narrative pattern of the *moniage*: after a successful life as a secular lord and warrior a hero becomes a monk, but his heroic nature remains present and can be revived if necessary; both lifestyles retain their validity (Müller, *Höfische Kompromisse*, pp. 158–69). Köbele argues emphatically against a generalized interpretation of *Minnesang* as purely secular which levels the differences between individual artists and the productive tension between explicit and implicit modes of expression (Köbele, *Frauenlobs Lieder*, pp. 228–40). See also Susanne Köbele and Bruno Quast, 'Perspektiven einer mediävistischen Säkularisierungsdebatte: Zur Einführung', in *Literarische Säkularisierung*, ed. by Köbele and Quast, pp. 9–20.

> Bei aller systematischen Unterscheidung greift die sich in der zweiten Hälfte des 12. Jahrhunderts erst formierende volkssprachliche literarische Kommunikation [...] auf Figurationen religiöser Kommunikation zurück, sei es auf Schrift- sei es auf Lesekonzepte. [...] Umgekehrt schließt sich religiöses Erzählen über Erzählschemata und andere dezidiert intertextuelle Verweise literarischer Kommunikation an.[7]

In this field of research Konrad von Würzburg represents a particularly interesting type of author. As the most versatile poet of the Middle High German period, one who probably had a basic clerical education but was not ordained,[8] he composed hagiographic as well as courtly narratives; and lyric poetry about courtly love and courtly values as well as about religious topics like the Trinity, the Incarnation and, of course, the Virgin. In addition, a tension between both spheres not only characterizes his oeuvre as a whole, but also individual texts. A clear separation of his work into religious and worldly texts is further undermined by the fact that Konrad mentions clerical patrons for texts with secular subject matters, such as the provost Berthold von Tiersberg in *Heinrich von Kempten* and the cantor Dietrich an dem Orte in the *Trojanerkrieg*, as well as influential lay people from the Basel elite for some of his legends, such as Johannes von Bermeswil and Heinrich Isenlin in *Alexius* and Johannes von Arguel in *Pantaleon*.[9] Thus Strohschneider lists the hybrid aspects of the *Alexius* – the vernacular language, the four-beat rhyming couplets typical of courtly epics, the description of the world that Alexius renounces as an aristocratic and knightly one – and concludes that the text was probably not meant to be received in an institutionalized cultic-ritualistic context.[10] He also notices that the protagonist is described in a metaphorical language, 'welche die Semantiken des Rittertums umcodiert und auf den Heiligen anwendet: er ist *gotes kempfe*'.[11] Müller, who devotes one chapter of his *Höfische Kompromisse* to the question of how the conflicting demands

7 Bruno Quast, 'Einleitung II. Sektion: Rede – Text – Schrift', in *Literarische und religiöse Kommunikation*, ed. by Strohschneider, pp. 285–91 (pp. 286–87). On the influence of religious notions of textuality on vernacular conceptions, see also Strohschneider, *Höfische Textgeschichten*, pp. 3–8.

8 Brandt grants to Konrad the educational level of the *trivium*, a comprehensive knowledge of classical Latin and Middle High German poetry as well as additional expertise in the subjects of law and theology (Brandt, *Konrad von Würzburg*, p. 66). The unusually early adoption of the Latin term *prologus* with the foreign accusative inflection 'prologum' (*Trojanerkrieg*, l. 261) could be read as a strategy of Konrad to present himself as a learned author. On the adoption of the Latin term into German see Grimm, *Historisches Wörterbuch*, XIII, col. 2164.

9 A brief overview of the patrons of Konrad's work is given by Brandt, *Konrad von Würzburg*, pp. 70–80.

10 Strohschneider, *Höfische Textgeschichten*, pp. 132–33.

11 Strohschneider, *Höfische Textgeschichten*, p. 146.

of spiritual and worldly lifestyles are negotiated in Middle High German literature – for example, the Christian ideal of virginity versus the feudal necessity to produce legitimate heirs – also analyses Konrad's *Alexius* in this context. He argues that the emphasis on nobility and the continuing relevance of family ties contrast with the ascetic rejection of these values in favour of devotion to God.[12] The courtly narrative *Engelhard*, by contrast, contains typical motifs of a legend, such as the miracle, the appearance of an angel and the presentation of the children as martyrs.[13] The mutual permeability of the spiritual and worldly sphere in Konrad's *Goldene Schmiede* is discussed by Köbele. She argues that Konrad's peculiar play on the repetition of sounds and words links even highly disparate elements in an unexpected way, so:

> dass sich für die Gegenstands- und Meta-Ebene, für die religiösen und ästhetischen Sachverhalte äquivoke Kategorien ergeben: als wäre das, was den Dichter qualifiziert (*wilde rede*), dieselbe unzugängliche *wildekeit* wie die, über die er spricht (das *wilde wunder* der Inkarnation in Maria).[14]

In this way the text oscillates between explicit assertions of the categorical difference between Konrad's poetic language and its divine referent on the one hand and the subliminal suggestion of their identity on the other. Konrad's inclination towards repetition also means that not only the intra- but also the intertextual boundaries between religious, metapoetic and secular discourse become permeable. Köbele highlights a number of correspondences between the *Goldene Schmiede* and the *Trojanerkrieg*, such as the water imagery or the integrative key terms *wunder* and *wilde*, and comments: 'Ein anderer Effekt von Konrads repetitiver Klangkunst, die die Symmetrieachsen immer wieder unsichtbar macht, scheint die in seinem Œuvre so auffällige Austauschbarkeit der Diskurse "weltlich-geistlich". Das wäre ein eigenes Thema.'[15]

While a comprehensive treatment of Konrad's entire body of work could not be attempted in the scope of this study, the analysis of metapoetic imagery has gone some way towards addressing the lacuna identified by Köbele by demonstrating the influence of theological traditions on the *Trojanerkrieg* and its frequent analogies to the *Goldene Schmiede*. However, even though

12 Müller, *Höfische Kompromisse*, pp. 120–23.

13 Brandt, *Konrad von Würzburg*, p. 138, pp. 141–42.

14 Köbele, 'Zwischen Klang und Sinn', pp. 304–05.

15 Köbele, 'Zwischen Klang und Sinn', p. 313, fn. 36. There are also poems by Konrad in which it remains unclear whether they praise a mortal lady or the Virgin. See Köbele, *Frauenlobs Lieder*, p. 221; Gert Hübner, 'Versuch über Konrad von Würzburg als Minnelyriker'. This issue has also been investigated in a conference paper by Frieder Schanze which has unfortunately remained unpublished (Wachinger, 'Einleitung', p. 8; Köbele, *Frauenlobs Lieder*, p. 233, fn. 38).

these analogies can be established, the important question remains as to how to interpret them. It could be argued that as a particularly prolific author of religious as well as secular texts, Konrad merely exercises economic rationality by recycling certain expressions in various texts without intending to transfer the associations of their original content as well. These interpretative difficulties are discussed in detail by Köbele and Quast, who identify the 'Stellenwert religiöser Allusionen und Metaphern' as a 'Schlüsselproblem'. They argue that literary phenomena of transference from the spiritual onto the secular are characterized by a heightened 'Unbestimmtheitspotential':

> Denn literarische Texte privilegieren ihrerseits übertragene (evokative, allusive, implizite) Sprechakte mit dem Effekt spezifischer Referenzunsicherheiten, die die Entscheidung verunsichern, ob das Säkulare das Religiöse jeweils ergänzt, transformiert, verabschiedet oder substituiert. Gerade in literarischen Texten kann der angespielte religiöse Sprechakt im indirekten Mitteilungsmodus des literarischen Textes fallweise ganz verschwinden.[16]

Even when the connection is obvious – for example, when Paris is likened to an angel – it seems to be a matter of perspective as to whether this should be classed as a 'Verweltlichung des Sakralen' or a 'Sakralisierung des Profanen'.[17] Green opts for the former possibility of a purely superficial adoption: 'Die Verweltlichung der religiösen Begriffe [ist] auch mit einer Preisgabe des religiösen Gefühls verbunden [...]. Konrads religiöser Wortschatz dient also nur noch der Idealisierung seiner Gestalten'.[18] Taken in conjunction with his criticism of the *Trojanerkrieg* for an 'Überwucherung des Inhalts durch die losgelöste, eigengesetzlich gewordene Form',[19] this position can be taken as a negative version of Karlheinz Stierle's concept of secularization as 'Transzendenzentzug' in favour of literary 'Ästhetisierung'. According to Stierle's teleological model, in the first stage of Christianization self-sufficient and secular ancient art, in which the picture of a lamb represents a lamb, becomes a subsidiary tool for the expression of the transcendent in which the picture of a lamb represents Christ. A secondary secularization then occurs when art is relieved of this function as a vehicle for religion and gains aesthetic independence. Thus secularization leads to a new, emphatic concept of self-sufficient art which Stierle describes as a 'weltimmanente Transzendenz des Ästhetischen'.[20] He illustrates this development with the

16 Köbele and Quast, 'Perspektiven einer mediävistischen Säkularisierungsdebatte', p. 16. Similarly, Köbele, *Frauenlobs Lieder*, p. 230, p. 237.

17 Köbele and Quast, 'Perspektiven einer mediävistischen Säkularisierungsdebatte', p. 20.

18 Green, *Vorstudien zum gotischen Stil*, pp. 76–83 (p. 78).

19 Green, *Vorstudien zum gotischen Stil*, p. 50.

20 Karlheinz Stierle, 'Säkularisierung und Ästhetisierung im Mittelalter und in der frühen

history of rhyme, which is elaborated in liturgical texts as a cultic mode of expression that gestures towards something beyond itself, but is then also employed in texts with secular subject matters. Another example of particular relevance to Konrad's use of religious vocabulary, because it associates a protagonist with a divine being, is a passage from the *Chevalier de la charrette* in which Lancelot kneels in front of Guenièvre's bed and worships her, since he does not believe in any holy body as much as in hers. Stierle argues that the association of adulterous love with religious experience approaches blasphemy, thereby heightening the potency of the secular and diminishing that of the transcendent: 'Die in der Tilgung der Transzendenz erscheinende säkulare Welt bringt aus sich selbst eine sekundäre Transzendierung hervor, die ihrerseits auf die christliche Sprache der Transzendierung zurückgreift und diese so metaphorisch depotenziert'.[21]

Köbele and Quast not only criticize the notion of worldly transcendence as contradictory and ambiguous, but also question whether the employment of religious vocabulary and imagery in secular contexts necessarily weakens the validity of the transcendent: 'Dass Bildrede im Mittelalter nicht immer schon, wie neuzeitlich gern missverstanden wird, eine Schwächung, eine metaphorische Depotenzierung dessen ist, worauf sie zurückgreift ("bloße Metapher"), sondern im Gegenteil gerade dessen Potenzierung sucht, sollte [...] im Auge behalten werden'.[22] How, then, are we supposed to understand religious elements in the *Trojanerkrieg*? Do they effect a merely superficial secularization of religious imagery that is thereby stripped of its original spiritual content or, on the contrary, a quasi-sacred idealization of the narrated world? Bearing in mind the specificity of literary allusions described by Köbele and Quast, a third possibility would be the oscillation between difference and identity on a spectrum between both.

For some instances of religious allusion in the *Trojanerkrieg* Rainer Warning's influential concept of 'connotative exploitation' provides a helpful model for interpretation. He defines connotation as a secondary meaning in addition to the primary meaning of an utterance's denotation. While the latter is lexicalized, the former can also be conventionalized to a certain degree, but is generally less semantically stable and depends on specific cultural-historical

Neuzeit', in *Ästhetik – Religion – Säkularisierung*, ed. by Silvio Vietta and Herbert Uerlings, 2 vols (Munich: Fink, 2008), I, *Von der Renaissance zur Romantik*, pp. 55–74 (p. 60).

21 Stierle, 'Säkularisierung und Ästhetisierung', p. 60. See also Wehrli, 'Roman und Legende', p. 175. He considers alternative implications of the clear contrast between the adulterous love of Tristan and Isolde and the religious allusions in Gottfried's *Tristan*: 'Das Wunder, wie es nun vom Roman usurpiert wird, ist entweder die Manifestation einer unbekannten oder gar widergöttlichen Macht, oder es ist zum leeren, erfurchtslos übertragbaren Motiv geworden'.

22 Köbele and Quast, 'Perspektiven einer mediävistischen Säkularisierungsdebatte', p. 17.

contexts of knowledge for its interpretation. Unlike the hierarchically ordered semantics of denotation, connotative elements in a text are not connected in a systematic way but through recurrence, which stabilizes the connotative meaning successively, possibly even retrospectively, with the result that their interpretation is less controlled: 'Häufig werden die poetischen Effekte gerade über das bewußte Spiel mit dem unsystematischen Status der Konnotatoren gesucht. Die Konnotation wird in solchen Fällen eingesetzt mit dem Ziel, bestimmte Interpretationshypothesen zu provozieren und zugleich ihre systematische Einlösbarkeit zu verweigern'.[23] Warning highlights metaphor in particular as a device for playfully heightening an utterance's complexity of meaning and for exposing its connotative dimension. He exemplifies the principle of connotative exploitation with reference to the art of the troubadours. Even though the lady is revered as the quasi-divine, inaccessible one whose grace is longed for, she remains the object of worldly sexual desire and does not replace God. Nonetheless, the established extra-textual reference system of religion helps to articulate and legitimize the novel role concept of secular courtly love by endowing it with quasi-religious dignity: 'Gegen die Nichtidentität des Gehalts steht die formale Identität der sprachlichen Artikulation, die auch für den neuen Gehalt die Verbindlichkeit des Religiösen reklamiert'.[24]

Köbele has since differentiated Warning's model with regard to Frauenlob's secular and Mariological poetry. These are connected particularly closely, as is also suggested by their occasional transmission in juxtaposition. She argues that the metaphoric expressions and recurring rhymes for erotic and spiritual love respectively are in fact so similar that they undermine the clear distinction between both spheres. Even on the level of the individual poem the boundary between the target and the source domain is frequently obscured. Rather than understanding metaphor as an implied comparison or short allegory, Köbele defines it as a device that multiplies an utterance's contexts and as a paradoxical mode of expression that asserts and undermines difference at the same time. In Warning's terms this means that the distinction between denotation and connotation is not clear-cut and that the opposition of spiritual and secular cannot be reduced to analogous systems of reference:

23 Rainer Warning, 'Lyrisches Ich und Öffentlichkeit bei den Trobadors', in *Deutsche Literatur im Mittelalter: Kontakte und Perspektiven: Hugo Kuhn zum Gedenken*, ed. by Christoph Cormeau (Stuttgart: Metzler, 1979), pp. 120–59 (p. 137). See also the short definition in Rainer Warning, 'Imitatio und Intertextualität: Zur Geschichte lyrischer Dekonstruktion der Amortheologie: Dante, Petrarca, Baudelaire', in *Ästhetischer Schein*, ed. by Willi Oelmüller, Kolloquium Kunst und Philosophie, 2 (Paderborn: Schöningh, 1982), pp. 168–207.

24 Warning, 'Lyrisches Ich und Öffentlichkeit', p. 140.

> 'Konnotative Ausbeutung' suggeriert einen unumkehrbaren Prozeß und eine klare Hierarchie. Wo es sich, wie bei Frauenlob, um wechselseitig aufeinander bezogene, nicht eindeutig hierarchisierte, vielmehr perspektivisch umschlagende Verweissysteme handelt, träfe eher das metaphorische Gegenteil zu, 'Bereicherung' statt 'Ausbeutung', 'symbiotisch' statt 'parasitär' – und bliebe die gleiche Hilfskonstruktion.[25]

She further argues that such correspondences do not necessarily point to analogies with the purpose of endowing the secular with quasi-religious dignity, but can also postulate identity, in the case of Frauenlob that of love as a universal principle transgressing all boundaries.

For the interpretation of the *Trojanerkrieg* there are several important consequences to be drawn from Warning's and Köbele's explanations. Since metapoetic meaning in general – not only in the form of religious allusions – is frequently allusive, the concept of connotation is relevant to this study in a more general sense. First of all, in order to detect connotation the cultural-historical context of an utterance has to be reconstructed. This has been attempted in this study by investigating the Latin and vernacular traditions of key metaphors. Second, connotations are not systematic but stabilized through recurrence and form what Warning calls a 'connotative axis'. It has been demonstrated that although metapoetics in the *Trojanerkrieg* does not constitute a coherent literary theory, the full significance of individual metapoetic passages can only be understood if they are recognized as part of a far-reaching network of correspondences between key images (for example, light and depth) as well as between the levels of story and discourse (the consistent emphasis on praise). Third, the concept of metaphor as an agent for heightening the complexity of an utterance's meaning and for multiplying its contexts describes very well the way in which Konrad's imagery opens up many perspectives that often cannot be pinned down and resist harmonization. Finally, it has to be considered carefully whether religious allusions, especially when they occur in the form of metaphors, suggest a structural analogy, a more substantial similarity or even identity.

In the case of religious allusions in the prologue – the association of the text with divine light and the exegetical metaphor *ergründen* – Warning's concept seems to capture quite well their function of dignifying the *Trojanerkrieg* and providing models for articulating particular aspects of reception and interpretation through reference to an established concept of religious textuality. Given the didactic purpose of the text, however, these

25 Susanne Köbele, 'Umbesetzungen: Zur Liebessprache in den Liedern Frauenlobs', in *Geistliches in weltlicher und Weltliches in geistlicher Literatur*, ed. by Huber, Wachinger and Ziegeler, pp. 213–35.

allusions could also serve to point out that the text indeed provides salvific lessons for its audience because a virtuous lifestyle in the world can have beneficial effects beyond this world. In the case of Helen's eulogy, the fact that Konrad employs ineffability and incommensurability topoi from spiritual traditions – for example, the metaphor of blinding light – demonstrates how connotative exploitation can provide a model for articulating challenging contents: the unspeakable and absolute beauty. At the same time it allows Konrad to endow these topoi with renewed authenticity by associating them with the religious discourse in which ineffability is not just rhetorical but ontological.[26]

However, where religious allusions or explicit transfers do not refer to the discourse level, to the *Trojanerkrieg* as a poetic artefact, but to the narrated world, Warning's and Köbele's models do not offer sufficient explanation. What meaning should we derive from the fact that the Apple of Discord functions like the miracles of Pentecost and Babel, that Troy resembles the heavenly Jerusalem, that Hercules dies like a Christian martyr, that Paris and Helen are likened to angels and that Helen is described in similar words to the Virgin? I would argue that this special kind of exploitation of the religious reference-system both connotatively and denotatively does not suggest similarity but asserts dissimilarity instead. In being 'almost' like their Christian counterparts, it becomes all the more evident in which ways Konrad's characters are unlike them. The Apple of Discord inverts salvation history; Hercules will not transcend his terrible death; in bringing pain and suffering into the world Helen and Paris are more akin to Adam and Eve than to divine beings; and Troy resembles the empty splendour of Babylon more than the godly radiance of the eternal city. In some respects, this interpretation is similar to that suggested by Green, who observes that the laudative epithets appear hollow. While he reads this as a symptom of inconsequential aestheticism, I believe that this emptiness is in fact programmatic and meaningful. In this sense, the system of religious references does not serve to blur the boundary between immanence and transcendence – a possible effect of connotative exploitation discussed by Köbele – but to draw the line all the more clearly. The Trojan world is doomed and even good intentions must fail because it is a world *ante gratiam*. The fact that pre-Christian heroes can hardly be blamed for not being Christian and are obviously not eligible for salvation does not mean that they cannot serve as warning examples of what can happen if feudal *agon* and

26 See Haug: 'Die topische Behauptung, daß man mit seiner Kunst der Größe und Bedeutung des Gegenstandes nicht gerecht zu werden vermöge, [wird] unter christlichen Prämissen zutiefst wahr' (Haug, *Literaturtheorie*, p. 22).

courtly splendour are not kept in check by Christian virtues and of the futility of human ambition without divine grace.[27]

27 While Seus (in *Heilsgeschichten vor dem Heil?*) and Kellner (in 'Kontinuität und Diskontinuität') have both proposed a Christian perspective for the interpretation of the text, the most recent argument against this reading has been made by Lienert in her review, 'Olga Seus: *Heilsgeschichten vor dem Heil?*', *PBB*, 136 (2014), 713–15. Although she qualifies as highly relevant the question of how Christian writers judge the pre-Christian cultures that appear as the epitome of courtliness, she is not satisfied with Seus's treatment of this issue. Lienert raises a number of justified concerns – the lack of methodological reflection and contextualization within contemporary discourses – and rejects Seus's conclusions: 'Troja geht nicht unter, weil es höfisch ist [...], und auch nicht weil "keine christliche Norm das Höfische vor sich selbst schützt" [...], sondern weil der Stoff den Untergang der Stadt vorgibt' (Lienert, 'Olga Seus', 715). This argument, which seems to reject the notion that different retextualizations can make sense of the same sequence of events in very different ways, is very odd. Even if the story alone were to determine the moral assessment of the narrated world, which is clearly not the case, the fall of Troy would probably have to be interpreted in the sense of a 'Tun-Ergehen-Zusammenhang'. Later, however, Lienert acknowledges the difference between a predetermined plot and the narrative motivation of individual texts, something which makes her argument against Seus's thesis even more puzzling: 'Nach den erzählten Ursachen des Untergangs und nach der expliziten und impliziten Bewertung der untergehenden Welt und ihrer Figuren ist durchaus zu fragen' (Lienert, 'Olga Seus', 715). Although I cannot follow Seus in all the details of her argument and would also criticize her for focussing mostly on explicit occurrences of religious vocabulary, I largely agree with her conclusions.

BIBLIOGRAPHY

Editions and Translations

Alan of Lille, *Anticlaudianus*, ed. by R. Bossuat (Paris: Vrin, 1955)

— *Anticlaudianus*, trans. by James J. Sheridan (Toronto: Pontifical Institute of Mediaeval Studies, 1973)

— *De planctu naturae*, ed. by Nikolaus M. Häring, *Studi Medievali*, 19 (1978), 797–879

— *Plaint of Nature*, trans. by James J. Sheridan, Medieval Sources in Translation, 26 (Toronto: Pontifical Institute of Mediaeval Studies, 1980)

Albrecht von Halberstadt und Ovid im Mittelalter, ed. by Karl Bartsch, Bibliothek der gesammten deutschen National-Literatur von der ältesten bis auf die neuere Zeit, 38 (Quedlinburg: Basse, 1861)

Albrechts (von Scharfenberg) Jüngerer Titurel, ed. by Werner Wolf and Kurt Nyholm, 4 vols, Deutsche Texte des Mittelalters, 45, 55, 61, 73, 77, 79 (Berlin: Akademie, 1955–95)

Alcuin, *De ratione animae*, in *Patrologia Latina*, ed. by Jaques Paul Migne (Paris, 1844–65), CI (1863), pp. 639–47

— *Versus de patribus, regibus et sanctis Euboricensis ecclesiae*, in *Poetae Latini Aevi Carolini Monumenta Germaniae Historiae*, ed. by Ernst Dümmler, 6 vols (Berlin: Weidmann, 1881–1951), I (1881), pp. 169–206

Andreas Capellanus, *On Love*, ed. and trans. by P. G. Walsh (London: Duckworth, 1982)

Aristotle, *The Metaphysics*, trans. by Hugh Tredennick, Loeb Classical Library, 271 (Cambridge, MA: Harvard University Press, 1933; repr. 1968)

— *Meteorologica*, trans. by H. D. P. Lee, Loeb Classical Library, 397 (Cambridge, MA: Harvard University Press, 1952; repr. 1962)

— *On the Soul, Parva Naturalia, On Breath*, trans. by W. S. Hett, Loeb Classical Library, 288 (Cambridge, MA: Harvard University Press, 1936; repr. 1964)

Augustine, *The City of God against the Pagans*, trans. by George E. McCracken and others, 7 vols, Loeb Classical Library, 411–16 (Cambridge, MA: Harvard University Press, 1961–72)

— *Confessions*, trans. by William Watts, 2 vols, Loeb Classical Library, 26–27 (Cambridge, MA: Harvard University Press, 1912; repr. 1968)

— *Sermons on the Liturgical Seasons*, ed. by John E. Rotelle, trans. by Edmund Hill (New Rochelle: New City Press, 1993)

Benoît de Sainte-Maure, *Le Roman de Troie*, ed. by Léopold Constans, 6 vols (Paris: Didot, 1904–12)

The Bible (Anglicized Edition) (Cambridge: Cambridge University Press, 2007)

Boethius, *De consolatio philosophiae: Opuscula theologica,* ed. by Claudio Moreschini (Leipzig: de Gruyter, 2000)

Bonaventure, *Itinerarium Mentis in Deum*, ed. by Quaracchi, trans. by Philotheus Boehner (Mansfield, OH: The Franciscan Institute, 2002)

Cicero, *Brutus, Orator*, ed. by H. M. Hubbel, trans. by G. L. Hendrickson, Loeb Classical Library, 342 (Cambridge, MA: Harvard University Press, 1939; repr. 1962)

— *De inventione, De optimo genere oratorum, Topica*, trans. by H. M. Hubbell, Loeb Classical Library, 386 (Cambridge, MA: Havard University Press, 1949; repr. 1960)

— *On the Orator*, trans. by H. Rackham, 2 vols, Loeb Classical Library, 348–49 (Cambridge, MA: Harvard University Press, 1942; repr. 1968)

Clement I, in *The Apostolic Fathers*, trans. by Kirsopp Lake, 2 vols (Cambridge, MA: Harvard University Press, 1912–13; repr. 1965), II, pp. 1–121

Deutsche Predigten des XIII. und XIV. Jahrhunderts, ed. by Hermann Leyser (Leipzig: Basse, 1883)

Meister Eckhart, *Deutsche Werke*, ed. and trans. by Niklaus Largier, 2 vols (Frankfurt a.M.: Deutscher Klassiker Verlag, 1993)

Das Ezzolied in der Vorauer Überlieferung, ed. and trans. by Christoph Lange (Erlangen: Palm & Enke, 2005)

Frauenlob (Heinrich von Meissen), *Leichs, Sangsprüche, Lieder*, ed. by Karl Stackmann and Karl Bertau, 2 vols, Abhandlungen der Akademie der Wissenschaften in Göttingen, Philologisch-Historische Klasse, 3, 119–20 (Göttingen: Vandenhoeck & Ruprecht, 1981)

Freidanks Bescheidenheit, ed. by Wolfgang Spiewok (Leipzig: Reclam, 1985)

Geoffrey of Vinsauf, *Poetria Nova*, in *Les arts poétiques du XIIe et du XIIIe siècle*, ed. by Edmond Faral (Paris: Librairie Ancienne Honoré Champion, 1924), pp. 194–262

— *The New Poetics*, trans. by Jane Baltzell Kopp, in *Three Medieval Rhetorical Arts*, ed. by James J. Murphy (Berkeley: University of California Press, 1971), pp. 27–108

Gottfried von Straßburg, *Tristan*, ed. by Walter Haug and Manfred Günter Scholz, trans. by Walter Haug, Bibliothek des Mittelalters, 10 (Berlin: Deutscher Klassiker Verlag, 2011)

Gregory the Great, *Moralia in Iob*, ed. by Marc Adriaen, 2 vols, Corpus Christianorum, Series Latina, 143 (Turnholt: Brepols, 1979)

— *Morals on the Book of Job*, trans. by Charles Marriott, 3 vols (Oxford: John Henry Parker, 1844–50)

Der Grosse Alexander aus der Wernigeroder Handschrift, ed. by Gustav Guth, Deutsche Texte des Mittelalters, 13 (Berlin: Weidmann, 1908)

Hartmann von Aue, *Erec*, ed. and trans. by Volker Mertens (Stuttgart: Reclam, 2008)

— *Iwein*, ed. by G. F. Benecke, K. Lachmann and L. Wolff, trans. by Thomas Cramer, 4th rev. edn (Berlin: de Gruyter, 2001)

Heinrich von Freiberg, *Tristan und Isolde*, ed. by Danielle Buschinger, trans. by Wolfgang Spiewok, Greifswalder Beiträge zum Mittelalter, 16 (Greifswald: Reineke, 1993)

Heinrich von Mügeln, *Tum* in *Kleinere Dichtungen*, ed. by Karl Stackmann, 3 vols, Deutsche Texte des Mittelalters, 50–52 (Berlin: Weidmann, 1959), II, pp. 147–219

Heinrich der Teichner, *Gedichte*, ed. by Heinrich Niewöhner, 3 vols, Deutsche Texte des Mittelalters, 44, 46, 48 (Berlin: Akademie, 1953–56)

Heinrich von dem Türlin, *Die Krone*, ed. by Fritz Peter Knapp and others, 2 vols, Altdeutsche Textbibliothek 112, 118 (Tübingen: Niemeyer, 2000–05)

Heinrich von Veldeke, *Eneasroman*, ed. by Ludwig Ettmüller, trans. by Dieter Kartschoke (Stuttgart: Reclam, 1986; repr. 2007)

Heinzelein von Konstanz, *Von den zwein Sanct Johansen*, ed. by Franz Pfeiffer (Leipzig: Weigel, 1852)

Herbort's von Fritslâr liet von Troye, ed. by Karl Frommann, Bibliothek der gesammten deutschen National-Literatur, 5 (Quedlinburg: Basse, 1837)

Vom Himmelreich, in *Kleinere geistliche Gedichte des 12. Jahrhunderts*, ed. by Albert Leitzmann, 2nd edn (Berlin: de Gruyter, 1929), pp. 20–29

Horace, *Odes and Epodes*, ed. and trans. by Niall Rudd, Loeb Classical Library, 33 (Cambridge, MA: Harvard University Press, 2004)

Hugh of St Victor, *Didascalicon*, ed. by C. H. Buttimer, Catholic University of America Studies in Medieval & Renaissance Latin, 10 (Washington, DC: The Catholic University Press, 1939)

— *Didascalicon*, trans. by Jerome Taylor (New York: Columbia University Press, 1961)

Hugo von Langenstein, *Martina*, ed. by Adalbert von Keller, Bibliothek des litteratischen Vereins in Stuttgart, 38 (Stuttgart: Litterarischer Verein, 1856)

John of Garland, *Parisiana Poetria de Arte Prosaica, Metrica, et Rithmica*, ed. and trans. by Traugott Lawler (New Haven, CT: Yale University Press, 1974)

König Rother, ed. and trans. by Peter K. Stein (Stuttgart: Reclam, 2000)

Pfaffe Konrad, *Rolandslied*, ed. and trans. by Dieter Kartschoke (Stuttgart: Reclam, 1993)

Konrad von Würzburg, *Engelhard*, ed. by Paul Gereke, 3rd rev. edn by Ingo Reiffenstein (Tübingen: Niemeyer, 1982)

— *Die Goldene Schmiede*, ed. by Wilhelm Grimm (Berlin: Kleman, 1840)

— *Die Goldene Schmiede*, ed. by Edward Schröder (Göttingen: Vandenhoeck & Ruprecht, 1926)

— *Heinrich von Kempten, Der Welt Lohn, Das Herzmaere*, ed. by Edward Schröder, trans. by Heinz Rölleke (Stuttgart: Reclam, 2000)

— *Klage der Kunst*, in *Kleinere Dichtungen Konrads von Würzburg*, ed. by Edward Schröder, 3 vols (Berlin: Weidmann, 1924–26; repr. 1970), III (1970)

— *Die Legenden: Silvester, Alexius, Pantaleon*, ed. by Paul Gereke, 3 vols, Altdeutsche Textbibliothek, 19–21 (Halle a. S.: Niemeyer, 1925–27)

— *Partonopier und Meliur - Turnei von Nantheiz - Sant Nicolaus - Lieder und Sprüche*, ed. by Karl Bartsch (Wien: Braunmüller, 1871)

— *Trojanerkrieg und die anonym überlieferte Fortsetzung*, ed. by Heinz Thoelen and Bianca Häberlein (Wiesbaden: Reichert, 2015)

Kudrun, ed. by Karl Bartsch, 5th rev. edn by Karl Stackmann (Wiesbaden: Brockhaus, 1965)

Pfaffe Lambrecht: *Alexanderroman*, ed. and trans. by Elisabeth Lienert (Leipzig: Reclam, 2007)

Der Marner, ed. by Philipp Strauch (Berlin: de Gruyter, 1965)

Matthew of Vendôme, *Ars versificatoria*, in *Les arts poétiques du XIIe et du XIIIe siècle*, ed. by Edmond Faral (Paris: Librairie Ancienne Honoré Champion, 1924), pp. 106–93

— *Ars versificatoria (The Art of the Versemaker)*, trans. by Roger P. Parr (Milwaukee: Marquette University Press, 1981)

Der Meißner, 'Zurechtweisung', in *Mittelalter: Texte und Zeugnisse*, ed. by Helmut de Boor, 2 vols (Munich: Beck, 1965), I, pp. 899–900

Des Minnesangs Frühling, ed. by Karl Lachmann and others, 38th rev. edn by Hugo Moser and Helmut Tervooren (Stuttgart: Hirzel, 1988)

Das Nibelungenlied, ed. by Ursula Schulze, trans. by Siegfried Grosse (Stuttgart: Reclam, 2010)

Ovid, *The Art of Love and Other Poems*, trans. by J. H. Mozley, 2nd rev. edn by G. P. Goold, Loeb Classical Library, 232 (Cambridge, MA: Harvard University Press, 1979)

— *Fasti*, trans. by James George Frazer, 2nd rev. edn by G. P. Goold, Loeb Classical Library, 253 (Cambridge, MA: Harvard University Press, 1989)

— *Heroides and Amores*, trans. by Grant Showerman, 2nd rev. edn by G. P. Goold, Loeb Classical Library, 41 (Cambridge, MA: Harvard University Press, 1986)

— *Metamorphoses*, trans. by Frank Justus Miller, 3rd rev. edn by G. P. Goold, 2 vols, Loeb Classical Library, 42–43 (Cambridge, MA: Harvard University Press, 1984)

— *Tristia, Ex Ponto*, trans. by Arthur Leslie Wheeler, 2nd rev. edn by G. P. Goold, Loeb Classical Library, 151 (Cambridge, MA: Harvard University Press, 1988)

Plato, *Timaeus, Critias, Cleitophon, Menexenus, Epistles*, ed. by R. G. Bury, Loeb Classical Library, 234 (Cambridge, MA: Harvard University Press, 1929; repr. 1966)

Propertius, *Elegies*, ed. and trans. by G. P. Goold, Loeb Classical Library, 18 (Cambridge, MA: Harvard University Press, 1990)

Pseudo-Dionysius, *The Complete Works*, trans. by Colm Luibheid (New York: Paulist Press, 1987)

Quintilian, *The Orator's Education*, ed. and trans. by Donald A. Russell, 5 vols, Loeb Classical Library, 124–27, 494 (Cambridge, MA: Harvard University Press, 2002)

Reinmar von Zweter, *Gedichte*, ed. by Gustav Roethe (Leipzig: Hirzel, 1887; repr. Amsterdam: Rodopi, 1967)

Rhetorica ad Herennium, ed. and trans. by Harry Caplan, Loeb Classical Library, 403 (Cambridge, MA: Harvard University Press, 1954; repr. 1968)

Rudolf von Ems, *Alexander*, ed. by Victor Junk, 2 vols, Bibliothek des Literarischen Vereins in Stuttgart, 272, 274 (Leipzig: Hirsemann, 1928–29)

— *Barlaam und Josaphat*, ed. by Franz Pfeiffer (Berlin: de Gruyter, 1965)

Seifrits Alexander, ed. by Paul Gereke, Deutsche Texte des Mittelalters, 36 (Berlin: Weidmann, 1932)

Seuse, Heinrich, *Deutsche Schriften*, ed. by Karl Bihlmeyer (Stuttgart: Minerva, 1907; repr. 1961)

Statius, *Silvae*, ed. and trans. by D. R. Schackleton Bailey, Loeb Classical Library, 206 (Cambridge, MA: Harvard University Press, 2003)

— *Thebaid, Achilleid*, ed. and trans. by D. R. Shackleton Bailey, 2 vols, Loeb Classical Library, 207, 498 (Cambridge, MA: Harvard University Press, 2004)

Der Stricker, *Karl der Große*, ed. by Karl Bartsch, Bibliothek der gesammten deutschen National-Literatur, 35 (Quedlinburg: Basse, 1857)

— *Kleinere Gedichte von dem Stricker*, ed. by Karl August Hahn, Bibliothek der gesammten deutschen National-Literatur von der ältesten bis auf die neuere Zeit, 18 (Quedlinburg: Basse, 1839)

Thomas Aquinas, *The Summa Theologica*, ed. by Daniel J. Sullivan, trans. by Fathers of the English Dominican Province (Chicago: Encyclopaedia Britannica, 1952)

Thomas of Cantimpré, *Liber de natura rerum*, ed. by H. Boese (Berlin: de Gruyter, 1973)

Thomasin von Zirclaria, *Der Wälsche Gast*, ed. by Heinrich Rückert (Berlin: de Gruyter, 1965)

Ulrich von Etzenbach, *Alexander*, ed. by Wendelin Toischer (Tübingen: Litterarischer Verein Stuttgart, 1888)

Virgil, *Eclogues, Georgics, Aeneid*, ed. and trans. by H. Rushton Fairclough, 2 vols, 2nd rev. edn by G. P. Goold, Loeb Classical Library, 63–64 (Cambridge, MA: Harvard University Press, 1999–2001)

Walther von der Vogelweide, *Spruchlyrik*, ed. and trans. by Günther Schweikle (Stuttgart: Reclam, 1994)

Der Winsbecke, ed. by Moriz Haupt (Leipzig: Weidmannsche Buchhandlung, 1845)

Wirnt von Grafenberg, *Wigalois*, ed. by Johannes Marie Neele Kapteyn, trans. by Sabine and Ulrich Seelbach (Berlin: de Gruyter, 2005)

Wolfram von Eschenbach, *Parzival*, ed. by Eberhard Nellmann, trans. by Dieter Kühn, 2 vols, Bibliothek des Mittelalters, 8 (Frankfurt a.M.: Deutscher Klassiker Verlag, 1994)

— *Willehalm*, ed. and trans. by Joachim Heinzle, Bibliothek des Mittelalters, 9 (Frankfurt a.M.: Deutscher Klassiker Verlag, 1991)

Secondary Literature

Alfen, Klemens, Petra Fochler and Elisabeth Lienert, 'Deutsche Trojatexte des 12. bis 16. Jahrhunderts: Repertorium', in *Die deutsche Trojaliteratur: Materialien und Untersuchungen*, ed. by Horst Brunner, Wissensliteratur im Mittelalter, 3 (Wiesbaden: Reichert, 1990), pp. 7–197

Baldwin, Charles Sears, *Medieval Rhetoric and Poetic: Interpreted from Representative Works* (New York: Macmillan, 1928; repr. Gloucester, MA: Smith, 1959)

Baltes, Matthias, 'Idee (Ideenlehre)', in *Reallexikon für Antike und Christentum: Sachwörterbuch zur Auseinandersetzung des Christentums mit der antiken Welt*, ed. by Ernst Dassmann and others, 24 vols (Stuttgart: Hiersemann, 1950–2012), XVII (1996), cols 213–46

Basler, Karl Friedrich, *Konrads von Würzburg 'Trojanischer Krieg', und Benoît de Ste. Maure 'Roman de Troie'* (Leipzig: Hoffmann, 1910)

Beckers, Hartmut, 'Brüsseler Bruchstücke', *Zeitschrift für deutsches Altertum und deutsche Literatur*, 124 (1995), 319–27

Benecke, Georg Friedrich, Wilhelm Müller and Friedrich Zarncke, *Mittelhochdeutsches Wörterbuch*, 4 vols (Leipzig: Hirzel, 1854–66; repr. Stuttgart: Hirzel, 1990)

Bickert, Hans Günter, 'Der Dichter als Handwerker: Zu Herkunft und Bedeutung einiger Begriffe der Dichtungstheorie', in *Sprache in Vergangenheit und Gegenwart: Beiträge aus dem Institut für Germanistische Sprachwissenschaft der Philipps-Universität Marburg*, ed. by Wolfgang Brandt and Rudolf Freudenberg, Marburger Studien zur Germanistik, 9 (Marburg: Hitzeroth, 1988), pp. 1–14

Bies, Werner, 'Regenbogen', in *Enzyklopädie des Märchens: Handwörterbuch zur historischen und vergleichenden Erzählforschung*, ed. by Kurt Ranke and others, 13 vols (Berlin: de Gruyter, 1977–2009), XI (2004), cols 465–70

Bleuler, Anna Kathrin, *Überlieferungskritik und Poetologie: Strukturierung und Beurteilung der Sommerliedüberlieferung Neidharts auf der Basis des poetologischen Musters*, Münchener Texte und Untersuchungen zur deutschen Literatur des Mittelalters, 136 (Tübingen: Niemeyer, 2008)

Bleumer, Hartmut, '"Historische Narratologie"? Metalegendarisches Erzählen im *Silvester* Konrads von Würzburg', in *Historische Narratologie: Mediävistische Perspektiven*, ed. by Harald Haferland and Matthias Meyer, Trends in Medieval Philology, 19 (Berlin: de Gruyter, 2010), pp. 231–61

— 'Zwischen Wort und Bild: Narrativität und Visualität im *Trojanischen Krieg* Konrads von Würzburg (Mit einer kritischen Revision der Sichtbarkeitsdebatte)', in *Zwischen Wort und Bild: Wahrnehmungen und Deutungen im Mittelalter*, ed. by Hartmut Bleumer and others (Cologne: Böhlau, 2010), pp. 109–56

Blumenberg, Hans, 'Licht als Metapher der Wahrheit: Im Vorfeld der philosophischen Begriffsbildung', *Studium Generale*, 10 (1957), 432–47

— *Paradigmen zu einer Metaphorologie*, Suhrkamp Studienbibliothek, 10 (Frankfurt a.M.: Suhrkamp, 2013) (first publ. in *Archiv für Begriffsgeschichte*, 6 (1960), 5–142)

— 'Beobachtungen an Metaphern', *Archiv für Begriffsgeschichte*, 15 (1971), 161–214

— 'Ausblick auf eine Theorie der Unbegrifflichkeit', in *Theorie der Metapher*, ed. by Anselm Haverkamp (Darmstadt: Wissenschaftliche Buchgesellschaft, 1982), pp. 438–54 (first publ. in Hans Blumenberg, *Schiffbruch mit Zuschauer* (Frankfurt a.M.: Suhrkamp, 1979), pp. 75–93)

Boesch, Bruno, *Die Kunstanschauung in der mittelhochdeutschen Dichtung von der Blütezeit bis zum Meistersang* (Bern: Haupt, 1936; repr. Hildesheim: Olms, 1976) de Boor, Helmut, *Die Deutsche Literatur im späten Mittelalter: Zerfall und Neubeginn*, Geschichte der deutschen Literatur von den Anfängen bis zur Gegenwart, III, i (Munich: Beck, 1962)

Borst, Arno, *Der Turmbau von Babel: Geschichte der Meinungen über Ursprung und Vielfalt der Sprachen und Völker*, 4 vols (Stuttgart: Hiersemann, 1957–63)

Brandt, Rüdiger, *Konrad von Würzburg*, Erträge der Forschung, 249 (Darmstadt: Wissenschaftliche Buchgesellschaft, 1987)

Braun, Manuel, 'Zwischen *ars* und "Kunst": Zum Verhältnis der "Künste" in der Sangspruchdichtung und im Meistergesang', in *Interartifizialität: Die Diskussion der Künste in der mittelalterlichen Literatur*, ed. by Susanne Bürkle and Ursula Peters (= *Zeitschrift für deutsche Philologie*, 128 (2009)), pp. 69–91

Braun, Manuel, and Christopher Young (eds), *Das fremde Schöne: Dimensionen des Ästhetischen in der Literatur des Mittelalters*, Trends in Medieval Philology, 12 (Berlin: de Gruyter, 2007)

Brinkmann, Hennig, *Zu Wesen und Form mittelalterlicher Dichtung* (Halle a.S.: Niemeyer, 1928; repr. Darmstadt: Wissenschaftliche Buchgesellschaft, 1979)

— 'Der Prolog im Mittelalter als literarische Erscheinung: Bau und Aussage', *Wirkendes Wort*, 14 (1964), 79–105

Brunner, Horst, 'Konrad von Würzburg', in *Die deutsche Literatur des Mittelalters: Verfasserlexikon*, 2nd rev. edn (Berlin: de Gruyter, 1978–2008), V (1985), cols 272–304

— 'Zugang zu Konrad von Würzburg', *Jahrbuch der Oswald von Wolkenstein-Gesellschaft*, 5 (1988/1989), 15–21

Bumke, Joachim, *Mäzene im Mittelalter: Die Gönner und Auftraggeber der höfischen Literatur in Deutschland: 1150–1300* (Munich: Beck, 1979)

— *Die Blutstropfen im Schnee: Über Wahrnehmung und Erkenntnis im 'Parzival' Wolframs von Eschenbach*, Hermea, 94 (Tübingen: Niemeyer, 2001)

— *Höfische Kultur: Literatur und Gesellschaft im hohen Mittelalter*, 10th edn (Munich: dtv, 2002)

— *Wolfram von Eschenbach*, 8th rev. edn (Stuttgart: Metzler, 2004)

— 'Retextualisierungen in der mittelalterlichen Literatur, besonders in der höfischen Epik: Ein Überblick', in *Retextualisierung in der mittelalterlichen Literatur*, ed. by Joachim Bumke and Ursula Peters (= *Zeitschrift für deutsche Philologie*, 124 (2005)), pp. 6–46

Bumke, Joachim, and Ursula Peters (eds), *Retextualisierung in der mittelalterlichen Literatur* (= *Zeitschrift für deutsche Philologie*, 124 (2005))

Burdach, Konrad, *Reinmar und Walther von der Vogelweide: Ein Beitrag zur Geschichte des Minnesangs* (Leipzig: Hirzel, 1880)

Bürkle, Susanne, '"Kunst"-Reflexion aus dem Geiste der *descriptio*: Enites Pferd und der Diskurs artistischer *meisterschaft*', in *Das fremde Schöne: Dimensionen des Ästhetischen in der Literatur des Mittelalters*, ed. by Manuel Braun and Christopher Young, Trends in Medieval Philology, 12 (Berlin: de Gruyter, 2007), pp. 143–170

— 'Einleitung', in *Interartifizialität: Die Diskussion der Künste in der mittelalterlichen Literatur*, ed. by Susanne Bürkle and Ursula Peters (= *Zeitschrift für deutsche Philologie*, 128 (2009)), pp. 1–16

Bürkle, Susanne, and Ursula Peters (eds), *Interartifizialität: Die Diskussion der Künste in der mittelalterlichen Literatur* (= *Zeitschrift für deutsche Philologie*, 128 (2009))

Butzmann, Hans, *Studien zum Sprachstil Konrads von Würzburg* (Würzburg: Werkbund, 1930)

Caboli Montefusko, L. and others, 'Dispositio', in *Historisches Wörterbuch der Rhetorik*, ed. by Gert Ueding, 2 vols (Tübingen: de Gruyter, 1994), cols 831–66

Carruthers, Mary, *The Craft of Thought: Meditation, Rhetoric and the Making of Images, 400–1200* (Cambridge: Cambridge University Press, 1998)

Chinca, Mark, 'Knowledge and Practice in the Early German Love-Lyric', *Forum for Modern Language Studies*, 33 (1997), 204–16

— 'Metaphorische Interartifizialität: Zu Gottfried von Straßburg', in *Interartifizialität: Die Diskussion der Künste in der mittelalterlichen Literatur*, ed. by Susanne Bürkle and Ursula Peters (= *Zeitschrift für deutsche Philologie*, 128 (2009)), pp. 17–36

Cholevius, Carl Leo, *Geschichte der deutschen Poesie nach ihren antiken Elementen*, 2 vols (Leipzig: Brockhaus, 1854–56), I (1854): *Von der christlich-römischen Cultur des Mittelalters bis zu Wieland's französischer Gräzität*

Cormeau, Christoph, 'Quellenkompendium oder Erzählkonzept? Eine Skizze zu Konrads von Würzburg *Trojanerkrieg*', in *Befund und Deutung: Zum Verhältnis von Empirie und Interpretation in Sprach- und Literaturwissenschaft: Festschrift für Hans Fromm*, ed. by Klaus Grubmüller and others (Tübingen: Niemeyer, 1979), pp. 303–19

— 'Überlegungen zum Verhältnis von Ästhetik und Rezeption', *Jahrbuch der Oswald von Wolkenstein-Gesellschaft*, 5 (1988/1989), 95–107

Coxon, Sebastian, *The Presentation of Authorship in Medieval German Narrative Literature: 1220–1290* (Oxford: Clarendon, 2001)

Cramer, Thomas, '*Solus creator est deus*: Der Autor auf dem Weg zum Schöpfertum', *Daphnis*, 15 (1986), 261–76

Curschmann, Michael, 'Interdisziplinäre Beweglichkeit – wie weit reicht sie?', *Zeitschrift für deutsche Philologie*, 123 (2004), 109–17

Curtius, Ernst Robert, *Europäische Literatur und lateinisches Mittelalter*, 2nd rev. edn (Berlin: Francke, 1954)

Drux, Rudolf, 'Des Dichters Schiffahrt: Struktur und Pragmatik einer poetologischen Allegorie', in *Formen und Funktionen der Allegorie*, ed. by Walter Haug (Stuttgart: Metzler, 1979), pp. 38–51

Dunger, Hermann, *Die Sage vom trojanischen Krieg in den Bearbeitungen des Mittelalters und ihren antiken Quellen* (Leipzig: Vogel, 1869)

Ehlert, Trude, 'Zu Konrads von Würzburg Auffassung vom Wert der Kunst und von der Rolle des Künstlers', *Jahrbuch der Oswald von Wolkenstein-Gesellschaft*, 5 (1988/1989), 79–94

Ehrismann, Gustav, *Geschichte der deutschen Literatur bis zum Ausgang des Mittelalters*, 2 vols (Munich: Beck, 1918–35)

Eifler, Günter, 'Publikumsbeeinflussung im strophischen Prolog zum *Tristan* Gottfrieds von Strassburg', in *Festschrift für Karl Bischof zum 70. Geburtstag*, ed. by Günter Bellman, Günter Eifler and Wolfgang Kleiber (Cologne: Böhlau, 1975), pp. 357–89

Eikelmann, Manfred, '*imaginâtio* und *fantasîe*: Entlehnungen des Konzepts der Imagination von Notker bis ins 15. Jahrhundert', in *Archäologie der Phantasie: Vom 'Imaginationsraum Südtirol' zur longue dureé einer 'Kultur der Phantasmen' und ihrer Wiederkehr in der Kunst der Gegenwart*, ed. by Elmar Locher and Hans Jürgen Scheuer (Innsbruck: StudienVerlag, 2012), pp. 185–97

Engelen, Ulrich, *Die Edelsteine in der deutschen Dichtung des 12. und 13. Jahrhunderts*, Münstersche Mittelalter-Schriften, 27 (Munich: Fink, 1978)

Ernst, Ulrich, 'Illumination und Transluzidität: Vom mythischen Palast zur christlichen Kathedrale: Zu Lichtinszenierungen in poetischen Architekturekphrasen', in *Interartifizialität: Die Diskussion der Künste in der mittelalterlichen Literatur*, ed. by Susanne Bürkle and Ursula Peters (= *Zeitschrift für deutsche Philologie*, 128 (2009)), pp. 221–45

Essen, Erika, *Die Lyrik Konrads von Würzburg* (Marburg: Bauer, 1938)

Faral, Edmond (ed.), *Les arts poétiques du XIIe et du XIIIe siècle* (Paris: Librairie Ancienne Honoré Champion, 1924)

Feistner, Edith, '*manlîchiu wîp, wîplîche man*: Zum Kleidertausch in der Literatur des Mittelalters', *Beiträge zur Geschichte der deutschen Sprache und Literatur*, 119 (1997), 235–60

Fischer, Clemens, *Der altfranzösische Roman de Troie des Benoît de Sainte Maure als Vorbild für die mittelhochdeutschen Trojadichtungen des Herbort von Fritslâr und des Konrad von Würzburg*, Neuphilologische Studien, 2 (Paderborn: Schöningh 1883)

Fischer, Hubertus, and Paul-Gerhard Völker, 'Konrad von Würzburg: *Heinrich von Kempten*: Individuum und feudale Anarchie', in *Literaturwissenschaft und Sozialwissenschaften 5: Literatur im Feudalismus*, ed. by Dieter Richter (Stuttgart: Metzler, 1975), pp. 83–130

Frank, Armin P., 'Theorie im Gedicht und Theorie als Gedicht', in Armin P. Frank, *Literaturwissenschaft zwischen Extremen: Aufsätze und Ansätze zu aktuellen Fragen einer unsicher gemachten Disziplin* (Berlin: de Gruyter, 1977), pp. 131–69, pp. 188–93

Freytag, Wiebke, 'Zur Logik *wilder aventiure* in Konrads von Würzburg Paris-Urteil', *Jahrbuch der Oswald von Wolkenstein-Gesellschaft*, 5 (1988/1989), 373–94

— 'Allegorie, Allegorese', in *Historisches Wörterbuch der Rhetorik*, ed. by Gerd Ueding, 9 vols (Tübingen: Niemeyer, 1992–2009), I (1992), cols 330–93

Fricke, Harald, 'Potenzierung', in *Reallexikon der deutschen Literaturwissenschaft*, ed. by Klaus Weimar, 3 vols (Berlin: de Gruyter, 1997–2003), III (2003), pp. 144–47

Friedrich, Hugo, *Epochen der italienischen Lyrik* (Frankfurt a.M.: Vittorio Klostermann, 1964)

Friedrich, Udo, 'Überwindung der Natur: Zum Verhältnis von Natur und Kultur im *Strassburger Alexander*', in *Fremdes wahrnehmen – fremdes Wahrnehmen: Studien zur Geschichte der Wahrnehmung in Mittelalter und früher Neuzeit*, ed. by Wolfgang Harms and C. Stephen Jaeger (Stuttgart: Hirzel, 1997), pp. 119–36

— 'Diskurs und Narration: Zur Kontextualisierung des Erzählens in Konrads von Würzburg *Trojanerkrieg*', in *Text und Kontext: Kolloquium 2004*, ed. by Jan-Dirk Müller, Schriften des Historischen Kollegs: Kolloquien, 64 (Munich: Oldenbourg, 2007), pp. 99–120

— 'Anfang und Ende: Die Paradieserzählung als kulturelles Narrativ in der *Brandanlegende* und im *Erec* Hartmanns von Aue', in *Anfang und Ende: Formen narrativer Zeitmodellierung in der Vormoderne*, ed. by Udo Friedrich, Andreas Hammer and Christiane Witthöft, Beiträge zu einer kulturwissenschaftlichen Mediävistik, 3 (Berlin: Akademie, 2014), pp. 267–88

— 'Historische Metaphorologie', in *Literatur- und Kulturtheorien in der Germanistischen Mediävistik: Ein Handbuch*, ed. by Christiane Ackermann and Michael Egerding (Berlin: de Gruyter, 2015), pp. 169–211

Funkele, Simone, 'Die Zerstörung und der Wiederaufbau Trojas in Konrads von Würzburg "Trojanerkrieg"', in *Die zerstörte Stadt: Mediale Repräsentationen urbaner Räume von Troja bis SimCity*, ed. by Andreas Böhne and Christine Mielke (Bielefeld: transcript, 2007), pp. 57–82

Gärtner, Kurt, '*tihten/ dichten*: Zur Geschichte einer Wortfamilie im älteren Deutsch', in *Im Wortfeld des Textes: Worthistorische Beiträge zur Bezeichnung von Rede und Schrift im Mittelalter*, ed. by Gerd Dicke, Manfred Eikelmann and Burkhard Hasebrink, Trends in Medieval Philology, 10 (Berlin: de Gruyter, 2006), pp. 67–81

Gebert, Bent, *Mythos als Wissensform: Epistemik und Poetik des 'Trojanerkriegs' Konrads von Würzburg*, spectrum Literaturwissenschaft, 35 (Berlin: de Gruyter, 2013)

Genette, Gérard, *Narrative Discourse: An Essay in Method* (Ithaca: Cornell, 1972)

Gerhardt, Christoph, 'Der Phönix auf dem dürren Baum ('Historia de preliis', cap. 106)', in *Natura loquax: Naturkunde und allegorische Deutung vom Mittelalter bis zur frühen Neuzeit*, ed. by Wolfgang Harms and Heimo Reinitzer, Mikrokosmos: Beiträge zur Literaturwissenschaft und Bedeutungsforschung, 7 (Frankfurt a.M.: Lang, 1981), pp. 73–108

Gernentz, Hans Joachim, 'Konrad von Würzburg: Charakter und Bedeutung seiner Dichtung', *Weimarer Beträge*, 7 (1961), 27–45

Gervinus, Georg Gottfried, *Geschichte der poetischen National-Literatur der Deutschen*, 5 vols (Leipzig: Engelmann, 1835–42), I (1835): *Von den ersten Spuren der deutschen Dichtung bis gegen das Ende des 13. Jahrhunderts*

Gewehr, Wolf, 'Der Topos "Augen des Herzens" – Versuch einer Deutung durch die scholastische Erkenntnistheorie', *Deutsche Vierteljahrsschrift für Literaturwissenschaft und Geistesgeschichte*, 46 (1972), 626–49

Glauch, Sonja, 'Inszenierungen der Unsagbarkeit: Rhetorik und Reflexion im höfischen Roman', *Zeitschrift für deutsches Altertum und deutsche Literatur*, 132 (2003), 148–76

Graf, Fritz, 'Ekphrasis: Die Entstehung der Gattung in der Antike', in *Beschreibungskunst – Kunstbeschreibung*, ed. by Gottfried Boehm and Helmut Pfotenhauer (Munich: Fink, 1995), pp. 143–55

Greber, Erika, *Textile Texte: Poetologische Metaphorik und Literaturtheorie: Studien zur Tradition des Wortflechtens und der Kombinatorik*, Pictura et poesis, 9 (Cologne: Böhlau, 2002)

Green, Dennis Howard, *Konrads 'Trojanerkrieg' und Gottfrieds 'Tristan': Vorstudien zum gotischen Stil in der Dichtung* (Waldkirch: Waldkircher Verlagsgesellschaft, 1949)

Grimm, Jacob and Wilhelm, *Deutsches Wörterbuch*, 32 vols (Leipzig: Hirzel, 1854–1954)

Gruber, J., and J. Engemann, 'Phoenix', in *Lexikon des Mittelalters*, ed. by Robert-Henri Bautier and others, 10 vols (Munich: Artemis & Winkler, 1980–99), VI (1993), cols 2106–07

Grubmüller, Klaus, 'Das *buoch* und die Wahrheit: Anmerkungen zu den Quellenberufungen im *Rolandslied* und in der Epik des 12. Jahrhunderts', in *bickelwort und wildiu mære: Festschrift Eberhard Nellmann zum 65.*

Geburtstag, ed. by Dorothee Lindemann, Berndt Volkmann and Klaus-Peter Wegera (Göppingen: Kümmerle, 1995), pp. 37–50

Haferland, Harald and Michael Mecklenburg, 'Einleitung', in *Erzählungen in Erzählungen: Phänomene der Narration in Mittelalter und früher Neuzeit*, ed. by Harald Haferland and Michael Mecklenburg, Forschungen zur Geschichte der älteren deutschen Literatur, 19 (Munich: Fink, 1996), pp. 11–25

Hahn, Ingrid, *Raum und Landschaft in Gottfrieds Tristan: Ein Beitrag zur Werkdeutung* (Munich: Eidos, 1963)

— 'Zur Theorie der Personenerkenntnis in der deutschen Literatur des 12. bis 14. Jahrhunderts', *Beiträge zur Geschichte der deutschen Sprache und Literatur*, 99 (1977), 395–444

Halbach, Kurt Herbert, *Gottfried von Strassburg und Konrad von Würzburg: 'Klassik' und 'Barock' im 13. Jahrhundert: Stilgeschichtliche Studie*, Tübinger Germanistische Arbeiten, 12 (Stuttgart: Kohlhammer, 1930)

Harant, Patricia, *Poeta Faber: Der Handwerks-Dichter bei Frauenlob: Texte, Übersetzungen, Textkritik, Kommentar und Metapherninterpretationen*, Erlanger Studien, 110 (Erlangen: Palm & Enke, 1997)

Harries, Karsten, 'Metaphor and Transcendence', in *On Metaphor*, ed. by Sheldon Sacks (Chicago: University of Chicago Press, 1979), pp. 71–88

— 'The Many Uses of Metaphor', in *On Metaphor*, ed. by Sheldon Sacks (Chicago: University of Chicago Press, 1979), pp. 165–72

Hasebrink, Burkhard, 'Rache als Geste: Medea im *Trojanerkrieg* Konrads von Würzburg', in *Literarische Leben: Rollenentwürfe in der Literatur des Hoch- und Spätmittelalters: Festschrift für Volker Mertens zum 65. Geburtstag*, ed. by Matthias Meyer and Hans-Jochen Schiewer (Tübingen: Niemeyer, 2002), pp. 209–30

— 'Die Ambivalenz des Erneuerns: Zur Aktualisierung des Tradierten im mittelalterlichen Erzählen', in *Fiktion und Fiktionalität in den Literaturen des Mittelalters. Festschrift für Jan-Dirk Müller*, ed. by Ursula Peters and Rainer Warning (Munich: Fink, 2009), pp. 205–17

Haubrichs, Wolfgang, 'Glanz und Glast: Vom inflationären Wortschatz der Sichtbarkeit', in *Sehen und Sichtbarkeit in der Literatur des deutschen Mittelalters: XXI Anglo-German Colloquium London 2009*, ed. by Ricarda Bauschke, Sebastian Coxon and Martin H. Jones (Berlin: Akademie, 2011), pp. 47–64

Haug, Walter, 'Über die Schwierigkeit des Erzählens in "nachklassischer" Zeit', in *Positionen des Romans im späten Mittelalter*, ed. by Walter Haug and Burghart Wachinger, Fortuna vitrea, 1 (Tübingen: Niemeyer, 1991), pp. 338–65

— *Literaturtheorie im deutschen Mittelalter: Von den Anfängen bis zum Ende des 13. Jahrhunderts*, 2nd rev. edn (Darmstadt: Wissenschaftliche Buchgesellschaft, 1992)

Haupt, Barbara, 'Literaturgeschichtsschreibung im höfischen Roman: Die Beschreibung von Enites Pferd und Sattelzeug im "Erec" Hartmanns von Aue', in *Festschrift für Herbert Kolb zu seinem 65. Geburtstag*, ed. by Klaus Matzel and Hans-Gert Roloff (Bern: Lang, 1989), pp. 202–19

— 'Der schöne Körper in der höfischen Epik', in *Körperinszenierungen in mittelalterlicher Literatur*, ed. by Klaus Ridder and Otto Langer, Körper, Zeichen, Kultur, 11 (Berlin: Weidler, 2002), pp. 47–73

— 'Ornament und *vuoge*', in *Interartifizialität: Die Diskussion der Künste in der mittelalterlichen Literatur*, ed. by Susanne Bürkle and Ursula Peters (= *Zeitschrift für deutsche Philologie*, 128 (2009)), pp. 113–35

Heinzle, Joachim, *Geschichte der deutschen Literatur von den Anfängen bis zum Beginn der Neuzeit*, 3 vols (Königstein i.T.: Athenäum, 1984–2004), II (1984): *Vom hohen bis zum späten Mittelalter: Wandlungen und Neuansätze im 13. Jahrhundert (1220/30–1280/90)*

Huber, Christoph, Burghart Wachinger and Hans-Joachim Ziegeler (eds), *Geistliches in weltlicher und Weltliches in geistlicher Literatur des Mittelalters* (Tübingen: Niemeyer, 2000)

— 'Brüchige Figur: Zur literarischen Konstruktion der Partonopier-Gestalt bei Konrad von Würzburg', in *Literarische Leben: Rollenentwürfe in der Literatur des Hoch- und Spätmittelalters: Festschrift für Volker Mertens zum 65. Geburtstag*, ed. by Matthias Meyer and Hans-Jochen Schiewer (Tübingen: Niemeyer, 2002), pp. 283–308

— 'Wort- und Bildnetze zum Textbegriff im nachklassischen mittelhochdeutschen Roman (Rudolf von Ems, Konrad von Würzburg)', in *Im Wortfeld des Textes: Worthistorische Beiträge zur Bezeichnung von Rede und Schrift im Mittelalter*, ed. by Gerd Dicke, Manfred Eikelmann and Burkhard Hasebrink, Trends in Medieval Philology, 10 (Berlin: de Gruyter, 2006), pp. 263–85

Hübner, Gert, 'Versuch über Konrad von Würzburg als Minnelyriker', in *Artibus: Kulturwissenschaft und deutsche Philologie des Mittelalters und der frühen Neuzeit: Festschrift Dieter Wuttke*, ed. by Stephan Füssel, Gert Hübner and Joachim Knape (Harrasowitz: Wiesbaden, 1994), pp. 63–94

— *Lobblumen: Studien zur Genese und Funktion der 'Geblümten Rede'*, Bibliotheca Germanica, 41 (Tübingen: Francke, 2000)

— *Erzählform im höfischen Roman: Studien zur Fokalisierung im 'Eneas', im 'Iwein' und im 'Tristan'*, Bibliotheca Germanica, 44 (Tübingen: Francke, 2003)

— 'Überlegungen zur Historizität von Metapherntheorien', in *Kulturen des Manuskriptzeitalters: Ergebnisse der Amerikanisch-Deutschen Arbeitstagung an der Georg-August-Universität Göttingen vom 17. bis 20. Oktober 2002*, Transatlantische Studien zu Mittelalter und früher Neuzeit, 1 (Göttingen: V&R unipress, 2004), pp. 113–53

— '*evidentia*: Erzählformen und ihre Funktionen', in *Historische Narratologie: Mediävistische Perspektiven*, ed. by Harald Haferland and Matthias Meyer, Trends in Medieval Philology, 19 (Berlin: de Gruyter, 2010), pp. 119–48

— 'Armin Schulz: Erzähltheorie in mediävistischer Perspektive', *Zeitschrift für deutsche Philologie*, 132 (2013), 445–450

Hünemörder, Christian, 'Fledermaus', in *Lexikon des Mittelalters*, ed. by Robert-Henri Bautier and others, 10 vols (Munich: Artemis, 1977–99), IV (1989), cols 540–41

Hutcheon, Linda, *Narcissistic Narrative: The Metafictional Paradox* (New York: Methuen, 1980)

Jackson, Timothy R., 'Außen und Innen bei Konrad von Würzburg: Die Achill-Deidamia-Episode im *Trojanischen Krieg*', in *Personenbeziehungen in der mittelalterlichen Literatur*, ed. by Helmut Brall, Barbara Haupt and Urban Küsters, Studia humaniora, 25 (Düsseldorf: Droste, 1994), pp. 219–49

Jaffe, Samuel, 'Gottfried von Straßburg and the rhetoric of history', in *Medieval Eloquence: Studies in the Theory and Practice of Medieval Rhetoric*, ed. by James J. Murphy (Berkeley: University of California Press, 1978), pp. 288–318

Juergens, Albrecht, 'Über den Umgang mit Geschichte in Konrads von Würzburg *Trojanerkrieg*-Fragment', *Jahrbuch der Oswald von Wolkenstein-Gesellschaft*, 5 (1988/1989), 431–42

Käppel, Lutz, 'Phoenix [5]', in *Der neue Pauly: Enzyklopädie der Antike*, ed. by Hubert Cancik and Helmuth Schneider, 16 vols (Stuttgart: Metzler, 1996–2003), IX (2000), cols 937–38

Kellner, Beate, '*daz alte buoch von Troye* [...] *daz ich ez welle erniuwen*: Poetologie im Spannungsfeld von "wiederholen" und "erneuern" in den Trojaromanen Herborts von Fritzlar und Konrads von Würzburg', in *Im Wortfeld des Textes: Worthistorische Beiträge zur Bezeichnung von Rede und Schrift im Mittelalter*, ed. by Gerd Dicke, Manfred Eikelmann and Burkhard Hasebrink, Trends in Medieval Philology, 10 (Berlin: de Gruyter, 2006), pp. 231–62

— '*ein mære wil i'u niuwen*: Spielräume der Fiktionalität in Wolframs von Eschenbach *Parzival*', in *Fiktion und Fiktionalität in den Literaturen des Mittelalters: Festschrift für Jan-Dirk Müller*, ed. by Ursula Peters and Rainer Warning (Munich: Fink, 2009), pp. 175–203

— 'Meisterschaft: Konrad von Würzburg – Heinrich von Mügeln', in *Interartifizialität: Die Diskussion der Künste in der mittelalterlichen Literatur*, ed. by Susanne Bürkle and Ursula Peters (= *Zeitschrift für deutsche Philologie*, 128 (2009)), pp. 137–62

— 'Konrads von Würzburg *Trojanerkrieg*: Kontinuität und Diskontinuität zwischen Antike und Mittelalter', *Poetica*, 42 (2010), 81–116

Kern, Manfred, 'Isolde, Helena und die Sirenen: Gottfried von Straßburg als Mythograph', *Oxford German Studies*, 29 (2000), 1–30

— *Weltflucht: Poesie und Poetik der Vergänglichkeit in der weltlichen Dichtung des 12. bis 15. Jahrhunderts*, Quellen und Forschungen zur Literatur- und Kulturgeschichte, 54 (Berlin: de Gruyter, 2009)

Kiening, Christian, 'Freiräume literarischer Theoriebildung: Dimensionen und Grenzen programmatischer Aussagen in der deutschen Literatur des 12. Jahrhunderts', *Deutsche Vierteljahrsschrift für Literaturwissenschaft und Geistesgeschichte*, 66 (1992), 405–49

Klein, Dorothea, 'Zwischen Abhängigkeit und Autonomie: Inszenierungen inspirierter Autorschaft in der Literatur der Vormoderne', in *Inspiration und Adaptation: Tarnkappen mittelalterlicher Autorschaft*, ed. by Renate Schlesier and Beatrice Trînca, Spolia Berolinensia, 29 (Berlin: de Gruyter, 2008), pp. 15–39

Kluge: Etymologisches Wörterbuch der deutschen Sprache, ed. by Elmar Seebold, 24th rev. edn (Berlin: de Gruyter, 2002)

Knapp, Gerhard P., *Hector und Achill: Die Rezeption des Trojastoffes im deutschen Mittelalter: Personenbild und struktureller Wandel*, Utah Studies in Literature and Linguistics, 1 (Bern: Lang, 1974)

— 'Die bedingte Metapher: Ein Beitrag zum frühneuhochdeutschen Roman', in *Kommunikative Metaphorik: die Funktion des literarischen Bildes in der deutschen Literatur von ihren Anfängen bis zur Gegenwart*, ed. by Holger A. Pausch, Studien zur Germanistik, Anglistik und Komparatistik, 20 (Bonn: Bouvier, 1976), pp. 61–80

Köbele, Susanne, *Bilder der unbegriffenen Wahrheit: Zur Struktur mystischer Rede im Spannungsfeld von Latein und Volkssprache*, Bibliotheca Germanica, 30 (Tübingen: Francke, 1993)

— 'Umbesetzungen: Zur Liebessprache in den Liedern Frauenlobs', in *Geistliches in weltlicher und Weltliches in geistlicher Literatur*, ed. by Christoph Huber, Burghart Wachinger and Hans-Joachim Ziegeler (Tübingen: Niemeyer, 2000), pp. 213–35

— *Frauenlobs Lieder: Parameter einer literarischen Standortbestimmung*, Bibliotheca Germanica, 43 (Tübingen: Francke, 2003)

— 'Die Illusion der "einfachen Form": Über das ästhetische und religiöse Risiko der Legende', *Beiträge zur Geschichte der deutschen Sprache und Literatur*, 134 (2012), 365–404

— 'Zwischen Klang und Sinn: Das Gottfried-Idiom in Konrads von Würzburg *Goldener Schmiede* (mit einer Anmerkung zur paradoxen Dynamik von Alteritätsschüben)', in *Alterität als Leitkonzept für historisches Interpretieren*, ed. by Anja Becker and Jan Mohr, Studien und Quellen, 8 (Berlin: Akademie, 2012), pp. 303–33

Köbele, Susanne, and Bruno Quast, 'Perspektiven einer mediävistischen Säkularisierungsdebatte: Zur Einführung', in *Literarische Säkularisierung im Mittelalter*, ed. by Susanne Köbele and Bruno Quast (Berlin: de Gruyter, 2014)

— (eds), *Literarische Säkularisierung im Mittelalter* (Berlin: de Gruyter, 2014)

Kokott, Hartmut, 'Ein Autor zwischen Auftrag und Autonomie: Konturen eines neuen Konrad von Würzburg-Bildes', *Jahrbuch der Oswald von Wolkenstein-Gesellschaft*, 5 (1988/1989), 69–77

— *Konrad von Würzburg: Ein Autor zwischen Auftrag und Autonomie* (Stuttgart: Hirzel, 1989)

Kolb, Herbert, *Der Begriff der Minne und das Entstehen der höfischen Lyrik* (Tübingen: Niemeyer, 1958)

Könneker, Barbara, 'Erzähltypus und epische Struktur des Engelhard: Ein Beitrag zur literaturhistorischen Stellung Konrads von Würzburg', *Euphorion*, 62 (1968), 239–77

Krafft, F., '*artes mechanicae*', in *Lexikon des Mittelalters*, ed. by Robert-Henri Bautier and others, 10 vols (Munich: Artemis & Winkler, 1980–99), I (1980), cols 1063–65

Kraß, Andreas, *Geschriebene Kleider: Höfische Identität als literarisches Spiel*, Bibliotheca Germanica, 50 (Tübingen: Francke, 2006)

Kristeller, Paul Oskar, *Humanismus und Renaissance*, ed. by Eckhard Keßler, trans. by Renate Schweyen-Ott, 2 vols (Munich: Fink, 1974–76), II (1976): *Philosophie, Bildung und Kunst*

Kugler, Hartmut, *Die Vorstellung der Stadt in der Literatur des deutschen Mittelalters*, Münchener Texte und Untersuchungen zur deutschen Literatur des Mittelalters, 88 (Munich: Artemis, 1986)

Kurz, Gerhard, 'Zu einer Hermeneutik der literarischen Allegorie', in *Formen und Funktionen der Allegorie: Symposion Wolfenbüttel 1978*, ed. by Walter Haug, Germanistische Symposien: Berichtsbände, 3 (Stuttgart: Metzler, 1979), pp. 12–24

Küsters, Urban, 'Liebe und der zweite Blick: Wahrnehmungshaltungen in höfischen Liebesbegegnungen', in *Personenbeziehungen in der mittelalterlichen Literatur*, ed. by Helmut Brall, Barbara Haupt and Urban Küsters, Studia humaniora, 25 (Düsseldorf: Droste, 1994), pp. 271–320

Lakoff, George and Mark Johnson, *Metaphors We Live By* (Chicago: University of Chicago Press, 1980)

Laude, Corinna, 'Quelle als Konstrukt: Literatur und kunsttheoretische Aspekte einiger Quellenberufungen im "Eneasroman" und im "Erec"', in '*Quelle*': *Zwischen Ursprung und Konstrukt. Ein Leitbegriff in der Diskussion*, ed. by Thomas Rathmann and Nikolaus Wegemann (= *Zeitschrift für deutsche Philologie*, 12 (2004)), pp. 209–40

Lechtermann, Christina, *Berührt werden: Narrative Strategien der Präsenz in der höfischen Literatur um 1200*, Philologische Studien und Quellen, 191 (Berlin: Schmidt, 2005)

— 'Figuren der Abhebung: Schillerndes Erzählen im *Trojanischen Krieg*', in *Deixis und Evidenz*, ed. by Horst Wenzel and Ludwig Jäger, Scenae, 8 (Freiburg: Rombach, 2008), pp. 43–64

Lechtermann, Christina, and Haiko Wandhoff (eds), *Licht, Glanz, Blendung: Beiträge zu einer Kulturgeschichte des Leuchtenden*, Publikationen zur Zeitschrift für Germanistik, N.F., 18 (Bern: Lang, 2008)

Leipold, Inge, *Die Auftraggeber und Gönner Konrads von Würzburg: Versuch einer Theorie der 'Literatur als soziales Handeln'* (Göppingen: Kümmerle, 1976)

Lenerz, Jürgen, 'Zum Beispiel *mære*: Bedeutung und Bedeutungsvielfalt aus sprachwissenschaftlicher Sicht', in *Im Wortfeld des Textes: Worthistorische Beiträge zur Bezeichnung von Rede und Schrift im Mittelalter*, ed. by Gerd Dicke, Manfred Eikelmann and Burkhard Hasebrink, Trends in Medieval Philology, 10 (Berlin: de Gruyter, 2006), pp. 25–47

Lerch, Eugen, 'Französisch *priser* – deutsch *preisen* – englisch to *praise* und das Kirchenlatein', *Romanische Forschungen*, 55 (1941), 57–82

Lexer, Matthias, *Mittelhochdeutsches Handwörterbuch*, 3 vols (Leipzig: Hirzel, 1872–78; repr. Stuttgart: Hirzel, 1992)

Lieb, Ludger and Michael R. Ott, 'Schrift-Träger: Mobile Inschriften in der deutschsprachigen Literatur des Mittelalters', in *Schriftträger – Textträger: Zur materialen Präsenz des Geschriebenen in frühen Gesellschaften*, ed. by Annette Kehnel and Diamantis Panagiotopoulos, Materiale Textkulturen, 6 (Berlin: de Gruyter, 2015), pp. 15–36

Lienert, Elisabeth, 'Helena – thematisches Zentrum von Konrads von Würzburg *Trojanerkrieg*', *Jahrbuch der Oswald von Wolkenstein-Gesellschaft*, 5 (1988/1989), 409–20

— 'Die Überlieferung von Konrads von Würzburg *Trojanerkrieg*', in *Die deutsche Trojaliteratur: Materialien und Untersuchungen*, ed. by Horst

Brunner, Wissensliteratur im Mittelalter, 3 (Wiesbaden: Reichert, 1990), pp. 325–405

— 'Ritterschaft und Minne, Ursprungsmythos und Bildungszitat: Troja-Anspielungen in nicht-trojanischen Dichtungen des 12. bis 14. Jahrhunderts', in *Die deutsche Trojaliteratur: Materialien und Untersuchungen*, ed. by Horst Brunner, Wissensliteratur im Mittelalter, 3 (Wiesbaden: Reichert, 1990), pp. 199–243

— 'Der Trojanische Krieg in Basel: Interesse an Geschichte und Autonomie des Erzählens bei Konrad von Würzburg', in *Literarische Interessenbildung im Mittelalter: DFG-Symposion 1991*, ed. by Joachim Heinzle, Germanistische Symposien Berichtsbände, 14 (Stuttgart: Metzler, 1993), pp. 266–79

— *Geschichte und Erzählen: Studien zu Konrads von Würzburg 'Trojanerkrieg'*, Wissensliteratur im Mittelalter, 22 (Wiesbaden: Reichert, 1996)

— *Deutsche Antikenromane des Mittelalters*, Grundlagen der Germanistik, 39 (Berlin: Schmidt, 2001)

— 'Olga Seus: *Heilsgeschichten vor dem Heil?*', *Beiträge zur Geschichte der deutschen Sprache und Literatur*, 136 (2014), 713–15

Lindberg, David C., *Auge und Licht im Mittelalter: Die Entwicklung der Optik von Alkindi bis Kepler* (Frankfurt a.M.: Suhrkamp, 1987)

Lutz, Eckart Conrad, *Rhetorica Divina: Mittelhochdeutsche Prologgebete und die rhetorische Kultur des Mittelalters*, Quellen und Forschungen zur Sprach- und Kulturgeschichte der germanischen Völker, 82 (Berlin: de Gruyter, 1984)

Manuwald, Henrike, '*gotes kunst – des tiuvels kunst*: Zum Kunstdiskurs in *Barlaam und Josaphat* Rudolfs von Ems', in *Interartifizialität: Die Diskussion der Künste in der mittelalterlichen Literatur*, ed. by Susanne Bürkle and Ursula Peters (= *Zeitschrift für deutsche Philologie*, 128 (2009)), pp. 49–68

McCulloch, Florence, *Medieval Latin and French Bestiaries*, University of North Carolina Studies in the Romance Languages and Literatures, 33 (Chapel Hill: University of North Carolina Press, 1960)

McKeon, Richard, 'Poetry and Philosophy in the Twelfth Century: The Renaissance of Rhetoric', in *Critics and Criticism: Ancient and Modern*, ed. by R. S. Crane (Chicago: University of Chicago Press, 1952), pp. 297–318 (first publ. in *Modern Philology*, 43 (1946), 217–34)

Meinhardt, H. and others, 'Idee', in *Historisches Wörterbuch der Philosophie*, ed. by Joachim Ritter and Karlfried Gründer, 13 vols (Basel: Schwabe, 1971–2007), IV (1976), cols 55–134

Merkle, Stefan, '*Troiani belli verior textus*: Die Trojaberichte des Dictys und Dares', in *Die deutsche Trojaliteratur: Materialien und Untersuchungen*, ed. by Horst Brunner, Wissensliteratur im Mittelalter, 3 (Wiesbaden: Reichert, 1990), pp. 491–522

Miettinen, Erkki, *Zum Mundartlichen Fortleben mhd.-mnd. Lehnwortgutes romanischer Herkunft*, Annales Academiae Scientarium Fennicae: Series B, 126 (Helsinki: Suomalainen Tiedeakatemia, 1962)

Miklautsch, Lydia, 'Das Mädchen Achill: Männliches Crossdressing und weibliche Homosexualität in der mittelalterlichen Literatur', in *Literarische Leben: Rollenentwürfe in der Literatur des Hoch- und Spätmittelalters. Festschrift für Volker Mertens zum 65. Geburtstag*, ed. by Matthias Meyer and Hans-Jochen Schiewer (Tübingen: Niemeyer, 2002), pp. 575–96

Minnis, Alastair J., 'Late-Medieval Discussions of *Compilatio*', *Beiträge zur Geschichte der deutschen Sprache und Literatur*, 101 (1979), 385–421

Minnis, Alastair J., and Alexander Brian Scott (eds), *Medieval Literary Theory and Criticism c.1100–c.1375: The Commentary Tradition*, 2nd rev. edn (Oxford: Clarendon, 1991)

Monecke, Wolfgang, *Studien zur epischen Technik Konrads von Würzburg: Das Erzählprinzip der 'wildekeit'*, Germanistische Abhandlungen, 24 (Stuttgart: Metzler, 1968)

Müller, Jan-Dirk, *Spielregeln für den Untergang: Die Welt des Nibelungenliedes* (Tübingen: Niemeyer, 1998)

— 'Visualität, Geste, Schrift: Zu einem neuen Untersuchungsfeld der Mediävistik', *Zeitschrift für deutsche Philologie*, 122 (2003), 118–32

— '*schîn* und Verwandtes: Zum Problem der "Ästhetisierung" in Konrads von Würzburg *Trojanerkrieg* (Mit einem Nachwort zu Terminologie-Problemen der Mediävistik)', in *Im Wortfeld des Textes: Worthistorische Beiträge zur Bezeichnung von Rede und Schrift im Mittelalter*, ed. by Gerd Dicke, Manfred Eikelmann and Burkhard Hasebrink, Trends in Medieval Philology, 10 (Berlin: de Gruyter, 2006), pp. 287–307

— *Höfische Kompromisse: Acht Kapitel zur höfischen Epik* (Tübingen: Niemeyer, 2007)

— 'Blinding Sight: Some Observations on German Epics of the Thirteenth Century', in *Rethinking the Medieval Senses: Heritage/ Fascinations/ Frames*, ed. by Stephen G. Nichols, Andreas Kablitz and Alison Calhoun (Baltimore: Johns Hopkins University Press, 2008), pp. 206–17

Müller, Wolfgang G., *Topik des Stilbegriffs: Zur Geschichte des Stilverständnisses von Antike bis zur Gegenwart* (Darmstadt: Wissenschaftliche Buchgesellschaft, 1981)

Mumprecht, Vroni, 'Adler', in *Thesaurus proverbiorum medii aevi: Lexikon der Sprichwörter des romanisch-germanischen Mittelalters*, ed. by Kuratorium Singer, 12 vols (Berlin: de Gruyter, 1995–2002), I (1995), pp. 40–43

— 'Regenbogen', in *Thesaurus proverbiorum medii aevi: Lexikon der Sprichwörter des romanisch-germanischen Mittelalters*, ed. by Kuratorium Singer, 12 vols (Berlin: de Gruyter, 1995–2002), IX (1999), pp. 237–39

Neumann, Birgit, and Ansgar Nünning, 'Metanarration and Metafiction', in *Handbook of Narratology: 2nd edition, fully revised and expanded*, ed. by Peter Hühn and others, 2 vols (Berlin: de Gruyter, 2014), I, pp. 344–52

Neumann, Hans, *Die Schiffsallegorie im Ezzoliede* (Göttingen: Vandenhoeck & Ruprecht, 1960)

Obermaier, Sabine, *Von Nachtigallen und Handwerkern: 'Dichtung über Dichtung' in Minnesang und Sangspruchdichtung*, Hermea, 75 (Tübingen: Niemeyer, 1995)

— 'Möglichkeiten und Grenzen der Interpretation', in *Mittelalterliche Lyrik: Probleme der Poetik*, ed. by Thomas Cramer and Ingrid Kasten (Berlin: Erich Schmidt, 1999), pp. 11–32

Obst, Wolfgang, 'Der Partonopier-Roman Konrads von Würzburg und seine französische Vorlage' (unpublished doctoral thesis, University of Würzburg, 1976)

Ohly, Friedrich, *Die Perle des Wortes: Zur Geschichte eines Bildes für Dichtung* (Frankfurt a.M.: Insel, 2002)

Öhmann, Emil, 'Der französische Einfluss auf die deutsche Sprache im Mittelalter', *Neuphilologische Mitteilungen*, 6/8 (1931), 195–220

— 'Die Bedeutungsentwicklung von dt. *Preis*, frz. *prix*', *Zeitschrift für Mundartforschung*, 26 (1958), 72–75

Okken, Lambertus, *Kommentar zum Tristan-Roman Gottfrieds von Strassburg*, 3 vols, Amsterdamer Publikationen zur Sprache und Literatur, 57, 58, 81 (Amsterdam: Rodopi, 1984–88)

Pastré, Jean-Marc, 'Typologie und Ästhetik: Das Porträt der Helena im *Trojanerkrieg* Konrads von Würzburg', *Jahrbuch der Oswald von Wolkenstein-Gesellschaft*, 5 (1988/1989), 397–408

Peil, Dietmar, 'Allegorie', in *Metzler Lexikon Literatur- und Kulturtheorie: Ansätze - Personen - Grundbegriffe*, ed. by Ansgar Nünning (Stuttgart: Metzler, 2001), p. 8

Peters, Jochen-Ulrich, 'Artefakt', in *Reallexikon der deutschen Literaturwissenschaft*, ed. by Harald Fricke, 3 vols (Berlin: de Gruyter, 1997), I, pp. 143–44

Peters, Ursula, *Literatur in der Stadt: Studien zu den sozialen Voraussetzungen und kulturellen Organisationsformen städtischer Literatur im 13. und 14. Jahrhundert*, Studien und Texte zur Sozialgeschichte der Literatur, 7 (Tübingen: Niemeyer, 1983)

— 'From Social History to the Poetics of the Visual: Philology of the Middle Ages as Cultural History', *Journal of English and Germanic Philology*, 105 (2006), 185–206

— '"Texte vor der Literatur"? Zur Problematik neuerer Alteritätsparadigmen der Mittelalter-Philologie', *Poetica*, 39 (2007), 59–88

Pfennig, Martin, *'erniuwen': zur Erzähltechnik im Trojaroman Konrads von Würzburg*, Europäische Hochschulschriften I, Deutsche Sprache und Literatur, 1537 (Frankfurt a.M.: Lang, 1995)

Ranke, Friedrich, 'Die Allegorie der Minnegrotte in Gottfrieds *Tristan*', in Friedrich Ranke, *Kleinere Schriften*, ed. by Heinz Rupp and Eduard Studer (Bern: Francke, 1971), pp. 13–30

Reinitzer, Heimo, 'Vom Vogel Phoenix: Über Naturbetrachtung und Naturdeutung', in *Natura loquax: Naturkunde und allegorische Deutung vom Mittelalter bis zur frühen Neuzeit*, ed. by Wolfgang Harms and Heimo Reinitzer, Mikrokosmos: Beiträge zur Literaturwissenschaft und Bedeutungsforschung, 7 (Frankfurt a.M.: Lang, 1981), pp. 17–72

Riegler, Richard, 'Fledermaus', in *Handwörterbuch des deutschen Aberglaubens*, ed. by Hanns Bächtold-Stäubli, 10 vols (Berlin: de Gruyter, 1927–42), II (1929–30), cols 1579–98

Röckelein, Hedwig, 'Vom webenden Hagiographen zum hagiographischen Text', in *'Textus' im Mittelalter: Komponenten und Situationen des Wortgebrauchs im schriftsemantischen Feld*, ed. by Ludolf Kuchenbuch and Uta Kleine, Veröffentlichungen des Max-Planck-Instituts für Geschichte, 216 (Göttingen: Vandenhoek & Ruprecht, 2006), pp. 77–110

Ruberg, Uwe, '"Wörtlich verstandene" und "realisierte" Metaphern in der deutschen Dichtung von Veldeke bis Wickram', in *'Sagen mit Sinne': Festschrift für Marie-Luise Dittrich zum 65. Geburtstag*, Göppinger Arbeiten zur Germanistik, 180 (Göppingen: Kümmerle, 1976), pp. 205–20

Ruh, Kurt, *Höfische Epik des deutschen Mittelalters*, 2 vols, Grundlagen der Germanistik, 7, 25 (Berlin: Schmidt, 1967–80), II (1980): *'Reinhard Fuchs', 'Lanzelet', Wolfram von Eschenbach, Gottfried von Straßburg*

Rupp, Heinz, 'Rudolf von Ems und Konrad von Würzburg. Das Problem des Epigonentums', *Der Deutschunterricht*, 17 (1965), 5–17

Sayili, Ayden M., 'The Aristotelian Explanation of the Rainbow', *Isis*, 30 (1939), 65–83

Scheidweiler, Felix, '*kunst* und *list*', *Zeitschrift für deutsches Altertum und deutsche Literatur*, 78 (1941), 62–87

Scherer, Wilhelm, *Geschichte der deutschen Litteratur* (Berlin: Weidmann, 1883)

Scheuer, Hans Jürgen, 'Die Wahrnehmung innerer Bilder im "Carmen Buranum" 62: Überlegungen zur Vermittlung zwischen mediävistischer Medientheorie und mittelalterlicher Poetik', *Das Mittelalter*, 8 (2003), 121–36

— 'Bildintensität: Eine imaginationstheoretische Lektüre des Strickerschen Artusromans "Daniel von dem blühenden Tal"', *Zeitschrift für deutsche Philologie*, 124 (2005), 23–46

— '*Numquam sine phantasmate*: Antike in mittelalterlicher Imagination', in *Germanistik in und für Europa: Faszination – Wissen: Texte des Münchener Germanistentages 2004*, ed. by Konrad Ehlich (Bielefeld: Aisthesis: 2006), pp. 381–90

— 'Wahrnehmen – Blasonieren – Dichten: Das Heraldisch-Imaginäre als poetische Denkform in der Literatur des Mittelalters', in *Wappen als Zeichen: Mittelalterliche Heraldik aus kommunikations- und zeichentheoretischer Perspektive*, ed. by Wolfgang Achnitz (= *Das Mittelalter*, 11 (2006)), pp. 53–70

— '*wîsheit*: Grabungen in einem Wortfeld zwischen Poesie und Wissen', in *Im Wortfeld des Textes: Worthistorische Beiträge zur Bezeichnung von Rede und Schrift im Mittelalter*, ed. by Gerd Dicke, Manfred Eikelmann and Burkhard Hasebrink, Trends in Medieval Philology, 10 (Berlin: de Gruyter, 2006), pp. 83–106

— 'Sichtbarkeit und Evidenz: Strategien des Vor-Augen-Stellens im Mauritius von Craûn und in der Poetria Nova Galfreds von Vinsauf', in *Sehen und Sichtbarkeit in der Literatur des deutschen Mittelalters: XXI. Anglo-German Colloquium London 2009*, ed. by Ricarda Bauschke, Sebastian Coxon and Martin H. Jones (Berlin: Akademie, 2011), pp. 192–210

Scheuer, Hans Jürgen, and Björn Reich, 'Die Realität der inneren Bilder: Candacis Palast und das Bildprogramm auf Burg Runkelstein als Modelle mittelalterlicher Imagination', in *Innenräume in der Literatur des deutschen Mittelalters: XIX. Anglo-German Colloquium Oxford 2005*, ed. by Burkhard Hasebrink, Hans-Jochen Schiewer, Almut Suerbaum and Annette Volfing (Tübingen: Niemeyer, 2008), pp. 101–24

Schleusener-Eichholz, Gudrun, *Das Auge im Mittelalter*, 2 vols, Münstersche Mittelalter-Schriften, 35 (Munich: Fink, 1985)

Schmid, Wolf, *Elemente der Narratologie*, 2nd rev. edn (Berlin: de Gruyter, 2008)

Schmidt, Hans-Joachim, 'Was sind Farben? Fragen und Antworten in der Enzyklopädie von Vinzenz von Beauvais', in *Farbe im Mittelalter: Materialität – Medialität – Semantik*, ed. by Ingrid Bennewitz and Andrea Schindler, 2 vols (Berlin: Akademie, 2011), II, pp. 1035–43

Schmidtke, Dietrich, 'Fledermaus', in *Enzyklopädie des Märchens: Handwörterbuch zur historischen und vergleichenden Erzählforschung*, ed. by Kurt Ranke and others, 13 vols (de Gruyter: Berlin, 1977–2009), IV (1984), cols 1248–56

Schmitt, Stefanie, 'Autorisierung des Erzählens in Romanen mit historischen Stoffen? Überlegungen zu Rudolfs von Ems *Alexander* und Konrads von Würzburg *Trojanerkrieg*', in *Geltung der Literatur: Formen ihrer Autorisierung und Legitimierung im Mittelalter*, ed. by Beate Kellner, Peter

Strohschneider and Franziska Wenzel, Philologische Studien und Quellen, 190 (Berlin: Schmidt, 2005), pp. 187–201

Schneider, Almut, 'Licht-Bilder: Zur Metaphorik poetischer Sprechweisen in frühmittelhochdeutschen Texten', in *Im Wortfeld des Textes: Worthistorische Beiträge zur Bezeichnung von Rede und Schrift im Mittelalter*, ed. by Gerd Dicke, Manfred Eikelmann and Burkhard Hasebrink, Trends in Medieval Philology, 10 (Berlin: de Gruyter, 2006), pp. 189–209

Schneider, Artur, 'Der Gedanke der Erkenntnis des Gleichen durch Gleiches in antiker und patristischer Zeit', in *Abhandlungen zur Geschichte der Philosophie des Mittelalters: Festgabe Clemens Baeumker zum 70. Geburtstag*, ed. by Franz Ehrle and others, Beiträge zur Geschichte der Philosophie des Mittelalters, 2 (Münster: Aschendorff, 1923), pp. 65–77

Schnell, Rüdiger, *Causa Amoris: Liebeskonzeption und Liebesdarstellung in der mittelalterlichen Literatur*, Bibliotheca Germanica, 27 (Bern: Francke, 1985)

Schröder, Edward, 'Studien zu Konrad von Würzburg IV', *Nachrichten von der königlichen Gesellschaft der Wissenschaft zu Göttingen* (1917), 96–116

Schröder, Werner, *Text und Interpretation III: Zur Kunstanschauung Gottfrieds von Straßburg und Konrads von Würzburg nach dem Zeugnis ihrer Prologe*, Sitzungsberichte der Wissenschaftlichen Gesellschaft an der Johann-Wolfgang-Goethe-Universität Frankfurt am Main, 26,5 (Stuttgart: Steiner, 1990)

— *Über die Scheu vor der Tragik in mittelalterlicher Dichtung: Jason und Medea im 'Trojanerkrieg' Konrads von Würzburg*, Abhandlungen der Marburger gelehrten Gesellschaft, 22 (Munich: Fink, 1992)

Schulz, Armin, 'Notwendige Unterscheidungen: Zur Epistemik der Sinne bei Konrad von Würzburg', in *www.germanistik2001.de: Vorträge des Erlanger Germanistentags 2001*, ed. by Hartmut Kugler, 2 vols (Bielefeld: Aisthesis, 2002), I, pp. 129–42

— *Schwieriges Erkennen: Personenidentifizierung in der mittelhochdeutschen Epik*, Münchener Texte und Untersuchungen zur deutschen Literatur des Mittelalters, 135 (Tübingen: Niemeyer, 2008)

— *Erzähltheorie in mediävistischer Perspektive*, ed. by Manuel Braun, Alexandra Dunkel and Jan-Dirk Müller (Berlin: de Gruyter, 2012)

Schulze, Ursula, 'Stationen der *ars poetica* auf dem Weg zu ihrer relativen Autonomie', in *Interartifizialität: Die Diskussion der Künste in der mittelalterlichen Literatur*, ed. by Susanne Bürkle and Ursula Peters (= *Zeitschrift für deutsche Philologie*, 128 (2009)), pp. 93–111

Schumacher, Meinolf, '... *der kann den texst und och die gloß*: Zum Wortgebrauch von "Text" und "Glosse" in deutschen Dichtungen des Spätmittelalters', in *'Textus' im Mittelalter: Komponenten und Situationen des Wortgebrauchs im schriftsemantischen Feld*, ed. by Ludolf Kuchenbuch and Uta Kleine, Veröffentlichungen des Max-Planck-Instituts für Geschichte, 216 (Göttingen: Vandenhoek & Ruprecht, 2006), pp. 207–27

Searle, John R., *Speech Acts: An Essay in the Philosophy of Language* (Cambridge: Cambridge University Press, 1969)

Seifert, Hans-Ulrich, 'Fledermaus', in *Thesaurus proverbiorum medii aevi: Lexikon der Sprichwörter des romanisch-germanischen Mittelalters*, ed. by Kuratorium Singer, 12 vols (Berlin: de Gruyter, 1995–2002), III (1996), pp. 282–83

Seitz, Dieter, 'Konrad von Würzburg', in *Einführung in die deutsche Literatur des 12. bis 16. Jahrhunderts*, ed. by Winfried Frey, Walter Raitz and Dieter Seitz (Opladen: Westdeutscher Verlag, 1982), II: *Patriziat und Landesherrschaft, 13. bis 15. Jahrhundert*, pp. 135–54

Seus, Olga, *Heilsgeschichten vor dem Heil? Studien zu mittelhochdeutschen Trojaverserzählungen* (Stuttgart: Hirzel, 2011)

Sieber, Andrea, '*daz frouwen cleit nie baz gestuont*: Achills Crossdressing im *Trojanerkrieg* Konrads von Würzburg und in der *Weltchronik* des Jans Enikel', in *Genderdiskurse und Körperbilder im Mittelalter: Eine Bilanzierung nach Butler und Laqueur*, ed. by Ingrid Bennewitz and Ingrid Kasten, Bamberger Studien zum Mittelalter, 1 (Münster: Lit, 2002), pp. 49–76

— 'Konfusion der Geschlechter? Zur Sozialisation Achills im *Trojanerkrieg* Konrads von Würzburg', *Der Deutschunterricht*, 55 (2003), 76–89

Speer, Andreas, 'Vom Verstehen mittelalterlicher Kunst', in *Mittelalterliches Kunsterleben nach Quellen des 11. bis 13. Jahrhunderts*, ed. by Günther Binding and Andreas Speer (Stuttgart: Frommann, 1994), pp. 13–52

Spitz, Hans-Jörg, *Die Metaphorik des geistigen Schriftsinns: Ein Beitrag zur allegorischen Bibelauslegung des ersten christlichen Jahrtausends*, Münstersche Mittelalter-Schriften, 12 (Munich: Fink, 1972)

Stackmann, Karl, 'Ovid im deutschen Mittelalter', *Arcadia*, 1 (1966), 231–54

Stegemann, Victor, 'Regenbogen', *Handwörterbuch des deutschen Aberglaubens*, ed. by Hanns Bächtold-Stäubli, 10 vols (Berlin: de Gruyter, 1927–42), VII (1935–36), cols 586–97

Stierle, Karlheinz, 'Säkularisierung und Ästhetisierung im Mittelalter und in der frühen Neuzeit', in *Ästhetik – Religion – Säkularisierung*, ed. by Silvio Vietta and Herbert Uerlings, 2 vols (Munich: Fink, 2008), I: *Von der Renaissance zur Romantik*, pp. 55–74

Stolz, Michael, '*Tum*'-*Studien: Zur dichterischen Gestaltung im Marienpreis Heinrichs von Mügeln*, Bibliotheca Germanica, 36 (Tübingen: Francke, 1996)

Strittmatter, Ellen, *Poetik des Phantasmas: Eine imaginationstheoretische Lektüre der Werke Hartmanns von Aue*, Studien zur historischen Poetik, 15 (Heidelberg: Winter, 2013)

Strohschneider, Peter, 'Kemenate: Geheimnisse höfischer Frauenräume bei Ulrich von dem Türlin und Konrad von Würzburg', in *Das Frauenzimmer: Die Frau bei Hofe in Spätmittelalter und früher Neuzeit: 6. Symposium der Residenz-Kommisssion der Akademie der Wissenschaften in Göttingen*, Residenzforschungen, 11 (Stuttgart: Thorbecke, 2000), pp. 29–45

— 'Sternenschrift: Textkonzepte höfischen Erzählens', in *Text und Text in lateinischer und volkssprachiger Überlieferung des Mittelalters: Freiburger Kolloquium 2004*, ed. by Eckart Conrad Lutz (= *Wolfram Studien*, 19), pp. 33–58

— (ed.), *Literarische und religiöse Kommunikation in Mittelalter und Früher Neuzeit: DFG-Symposion 2006* (Berlin: de Gruyter, 2009)

— 'Weltabschied, Christusnachfolge und die Kraft der Legende', *Germanisch-Romanische Monatsschrift*, 60 (2010), 143–63

— *Höfische Textgeschichten: Über Selbstentwürfe vormoderner Literatur* (Heidelberg: Winter, 2014)

Stuckmann, Manfred, *Wappenschilderungen und historisch-heraldische Anspielungen in Konrads von Würzburg 'Trojanerkrieg'* (doctoral thesis, Bergische Universität Wuppertal, 2003; published online)

Todorov, Tzvetan, 'Les catégories du récit littéraire', *Communications*, 8 (1966), 125–51

Toepfer, Regina, *Höfische Tragik: Motivierungsformen des Unglücks in mittelalterlichen Erzählungen*, Untersuchungen zur deutschen Literaturgeschichte, 144 (Berlin: de Gruyter, 2013)

Trier, Jost, *Der deutsche Wortschatz im Sinnbezirk des Verstandes: Die Geschichte eines sprachlichen Feldes: Von den Anfängen bis zum Beginn des 13. Jahrhunderts* (Heidelberg: Winter, 1931)

Tschižewskij, Dmitrij, 'Wiedergeburt des Formalismus? In welcher Art?', in *Immanente Ästhetik – ästhetische Reflexion. Lyrik als Paradigma der Moderne*, ed. by Wolfgang Iser (Munich: Fink, 1966), pp. 297–305

Ullrich, Wolfgang, 'Kunst/ Künste/ System der Künste', in *Ästhetische Grundbegriffe: Historisches Wörterbuch*, ed. by Karlheinz Barck, Martin Fontius and Dieter Schlenstedt, 7 vols (Stuttgart: Metzler, 2000–05), III (2001), pp. 556–616

Viëtor, Karl, 'Die Kunstanschauung der höfischen Epigonen', *Beiträge zur Geschichte der deutschen Sprache und Literatur*, 46 (1922), 85–124

Wachinger, Burghart, 'Einleitung', in *Geistliches in weltlicher und Weltliches in geistlicher Literatur*, ed. by Christoph Huber, Burghart Wachinger and Hans-Joachim Ziegeler (Tübingen: Niemeyer, 2000), pp. 1–15

Wagner-Hasel, Beate, '*Textus* und texere, *hýphos* und *hyphaínein*: Zur metaphorischen Bedeutung des Webens in der griechisch-römischen Antike', in *'Textus' im Mittelalter: Komponenten und Situationen des Wortgebrauchs im schriftsemantischen Feld*, ed. by Ludolf Kuchenbuch and Uta Kleine, Veröffentlichungen des Max-Planck-Instituts für Geschichte, 216 (Göttingen: Vandenhoek & Ruprecht, 2006), pp. 15–42

Wandhoff, Haiko, '*Âventiure* als Nachricht für Augen und Ohren: Zu Hartmanns von Aue *Erec* und *Iwein*', *Zeitschrift für deutsche Philologie*, 113 (1994), 1–22

— *Der epische Blick: eine mediengeschichtliche Studie zur höfischen Literatur*, Philologische Studien und Quellen, 141 (Berlin: Schmidt, 1996)

— 'Zur Poetik der Sichtbarkeit in den höfischen Epen des Mittelalters', *Zeitschrift für Germanistik*, N.F., 3 (1999), 586–97

— 'Iweins guter Name: Zur medialen Konstruktion von adliger Ehre und Identität in den Artusromanen Hartmanns von Aue', in *Mittelalter: Neue Wege durch einen alten Kontinent*, ed. by Jan-Dirk Müller and Horst Wenzel (Stuttgart: Hirzel, 1999), pp. 111–26

— *Ekphrasis: Kunstbeschreibungen und virtuelle Räume in der Literatur des Mittelalters*, Trends in Medieval Philology, 3 (Berlin: de Gruyter, 2003)

— 'Zur Bildlichkeit mittelalterlicher Texte', in *Zur Bildlichkeit mittelalterlicher Texte*, ed. by Haiko Wandhoff (= *Das Mittelalter*, 13 (2008)), pp. 3–23

— 'Imaginäre Kopfreisen in die Wunderwelt der *âventiure*, oder: Wenn das Sehen zur Allegorie des Lesens wird: Neue Überlegungen zu Hartmanns *Erec* und *Iwein*', in *Sehen und Sichtbarkeit in der Literatur des Mittelalters: XXI. Anglo-German Coloquium London 2009*, ed. by Ricarda Bauschke, Sebastian Coxon and Martin H. Jones (Berlin: Akademie, 2011), pp. 141–59

Warning, Rainer, 'Lyrisches Ich und Öffentlichkeit bei den Trobadors', in *Deutsche Literatur im Mittelalter: Kontakte und Perspektiven: Hugo Kuhn zum Gedenken*, ed. by Christoph Cormeau (Stuttgart: Metzler, 1979), pp. 120–59

— 'Imitatio und Intertextualität: Zur Geschichte lyrischer Dekonstruktion der Amortheologie: Dante, Petrarca, Baudelaire', in Ästhetischer Schein, ed. by Willi Oelmüller, Kolloquium Kunst und Philosophie, 2 (Paderborn: Schöningh, 1982), pp. 168–207

Weber, Alfred, 'Kann die Harfe durch ihre Propeller schießen? Poetologische Lyrik in Amerika', in *Amerikanische Literatur im 20. Jahrhundert*, ed. by Alfred Weber and Dietmar Haack (Göttingen: Vandenhoeck & Ruprecht, 1971), pp. 175–91

Wehrli, Max, 'Roman und Legende im deutschen Hochmittelalter', in Max Wehrli, *Formen mittelalterlicher Erzählung* (Atlantis: Zürich, 1969), pp. 155–76

Weinrich, Harald, 'Semantik der kühnen Metapher', in *Theorie der Metapher*, ed. by Anselm Haverkamp (Darmstadt: Wissenschaftliche Buchgesellschaft, 1982), pp. 316–39 (first publ. *Deutsche Vierteljahrsschrift für Literaturwissenschaft und Geistesgeschichte*, 37 (1963), 325–44)

Wenzel, Horst, 'Fernliebe und hohe Minne: Zur räumlichen und sozialen Distanz in der Minnethematik', in *Liebe als Literatur: Aufsätze zur erotischen Dichtung in Deutschland: Festschrift für Peter Wapnewski*, ed. by Rüdiger Krohn (Munich: Beck, 1983), pp. 187–208

— 'Szene und Gebärde: Zur visuellen Imagination im Nibelungenlied', *Zeitschrift für deutsche Philologie*, 111 (1992), 321–43

— 'Hören und Sehen: Zur Lesbarkeit von Körperzeichen in der höfischen Literatur', in *Personenbeziehungen in der mittelalterlichen Literatur*, ed. by Helmut Brall, Barbara Haupt and Urban Küsters, Studia humaniora, 25 (Düsseldorf: Droste, 1994), pp. 191–218

— *Hören und Sehen - Schrift und Bild: Kultur und Gedächtnis im Mittelalter* (Munich: Beck, 1995)

— 'Visualität: Zur Vorgeschichte der kinästhetischen Wahrnehmung', *Zeitschrift für Germanistik*, N.F., 3 (1999), 549–56

— *Höfische Repräsentation: Symbolische Kommunikation und Literatur im Mittelalter* (Darmstadt: Wissenschaftliche Buchgesellschaft, 2005)

Wessel, Franziska, *Probleme der Metaphorik und die Minnemetaphorik in Gottfrieds von Strassburg 'Tristan und Isolde'*, Münstersche Mittelalter-Schriften, 54 (Munich: Fink, 1984)

Winko, Simone, 'Auf der Suche nach der Weltformel: Literarizität und Poetizität in der neueren literaturtheoretischen Diskussion', in *Grenzen der Literatur: Zu Begriff und Phänomen des Literarischen*, ed. by Simone Winko, Fotis Jannidis and Gerhard Lauer, Revisionen: Grundbegriffe der Literaturtheorie, 2 (Berlin: de Gruyter, 2009), pp. 374–96

Wolf, Werner, 'Metafiktion', in *Grundbegriffe der Literaturtheorie*, ed. by Ansgar Nünning, Sammlung Metzler, 347 (Stuttgart: Metzler, 2004), pp. 172–74

— 'Metatext und Metatextualität', in *Metzler Lexikon Literatur- und Kulturtheorie: Ansätze - Personen - Grundbegriffe*, ed. by Ansgar Nünning, 5th rev. edn (Stuttgart: Metzler, 2013), pp. 520–21

Worstbrock, Franz Josef, '*Dilatatio materiae*: Zur Poetik des *Erec* Hartmanns von Aue', *Frühmittelalterliche Studien*, 19 (1985), 1–30

— 'Der Tod des Hercules: Eine Problemskizze zur Poetik des Zerfalls in Konrads von Würzburg *Trojanerkrieg*', in *Erzählungen in Erzählungen: Phänomene der Narration in Mittelalter und früher Neuzeit*, ed. by Harald

Haferland and Michael Mecklenburg, Forschungen zur Geschichte der älteren deutschen Literatur, 19 (Munich: Fink, 1996), pp. 273–84
— 'Wiedererzählen und Übersetzen', in *Mittelalter und Frühe Neuzeit: Übergänge, Umbrüche und Neuansätze*, ed. by Walter Haug (Tübingen: Niemeyer, 1999), pp. 128–42
— 'Die Erfindung der wahren Geschichte: Über Ziel und Regie der Wiedererzählung im *Trojanerkrieg* Konrads von Würzburg', in *Fiktion und Fiktionalität in den Literaturen des Mittelalters: Jan-Dirk Müller zum 65. Geburtstag*, ed. by Ursula Peters and Rainer Warning (Munich: Fink, 2009), pp. 152–74
— 'Fernliebe: Allgemeines und Besonderes zur Geschichte einer literarischen Konstante', in *Projektion - Reflexion - Ferne: Räumliche Vorstellungen und Denkfiguren im Mittelalter*, ed. by Sonja Glauch, Susanne Köbele and Uta Störmer-Caysa (Berlin: de Gruyter, 2011), pp. 137–59
Wunderlich, Werner, '"Der Wesen flüchtigstes, die schnellste aller Plagen": Fama in antiker und mittelalterlicher Sprache und Literatur: Stimme - Gerücht - Ruhm', *Mittellateinisches Jahrbuch*, 39 (2004), 329–70
Ziegeler, Hans-Joachim, Karl-Ernst Geith and Elke Ukena-Best, 'Der Stricker', in *Die deutsche Literatur des Mittelalters: Verfasserlexikon*, 2nd rev. edn, 14 vols (Berlin: de Gruyter, 1978–2008), v (1995), cols 417–49

INDEX

Since the study deals with the *Trojanerkrieg* throughout references to this text do not appear in this index. Passages dealing with the central subject of metapoetics as well as with the ubiquitous stylistic devices of metaphor, simile and description are only listed if they engage with these issues in a theoretical manner. In addition to names and places, ancient and medieval authors and texts, this index also lists religious, rhetorical and poetic terminology and concepts as well as MHG key terms and source domains for metapoetic imagery in the *Trojanerkrieg*.

www.ingramcontent.com/pod-product-compliance
Lightning Source LLC
LaVergne TN
LVHW022052300826
846742LV00002B/4